The Economics of an Aging Workforce:

Challenges, Opportunities, and Policy Perspectives

Oytun Meçik
https://orcid.org/0000-0002-7409-6266
Eskişehir Osmangazi University, Turkey

IGI Global
Scientific Publishing
Publishing Tomorrow's Research Today

Vice President of Editorial Melissa Wagner
Director of Acquisitions Mikaela Felty
Director of Book Development Jocelynn Hessler
Production Manager Mike Brehm
Cover Design Jose Rosado

Published in the United States of America by
IGI Global Scientific Publishing
701 East Chocolate Avenue
Hershey, PA, 17033, USA
Tel: 717-533-8845 | Fax: 717-533-7115
Website: https://www.igi-global.com E-mail: cust@igi-global.com

Library of Congress Cataloging-in-Publication Data

LCCN: 2026003242 (CIP Data Pending)
ISBN13: 9798337374833
Isbn13Softcover: 9798337374840
EISBN13: 9798337374857
British Cataloguing in Publication Data
A Cataloguing in Publication record for this book is available from the British Library.

Editorial Advisory Board

Table of Contents

Detailed Table of Contents

This paper analyses how wealth annuitization schemes have been routinely introduced in OLG- CGE models to cope with life-length uncertainty, and shows the impact of different annuitization schemes on calibration and simulation results in the context of realistic demographic changes. Imposing full (100%) wealth annuitization leads to deeper capital accumulation (relative to a zero annuitization scheme) and, eventually, overestimates the positive economic impacts of demographic dividends in younger countries where the annuity market is thin. The analysis is reversed for countries more advanced in the ageing process. In this case, the negative impact of ageing will be overestimated (i.e., it will appear worse than it really is) relative to a more realistic assumption of little wealth annuitization.

The present chapter investigates long-term population aging within the BRICS economies using the Old-Age Dependency Ratio (OADR) from 1975 to 2024, with projections up to 2050. The findings show strong heterogeneity in the aging trajectories. Brazil's OADR more than doubles from 16.6 percent in 2025 to above 33 percent by 2050, while Russia stays ahead as the oldest economy, overtaking 31 percent at mid-century. India and South Africa remain relatively young; for instance, India's OADR rises gradually from 10.8 percent to around 17 percent. The forecast evaluation metrics results indicate that ARIMA models perform better than the machine learning approaches in nearly all the BRICS economies. The machine learning models tend to yield flat projections across horizons; thus, they have limited ability to capture the long-run dynamics of demographic change. These findings highlight the importance of reliable demographic forecasting for supporting effective labor market policies, pension planning, and long-term economic decision-making in ageing societies.

This chapter examines the challenges and opportunities of achieving intergenerational equity in the context of aging societies. As populations age, the distribution of income, wealth, and opportunities across generations becomes increasingly strained, affecting labor markets, pension systems, fiscal sustainability, and social welfare. The chapter explores theoretical frameworks, including life-cycle and overlapping generations models, alongside practical mechanisms such as pensions, public transfers, labor market policies, and technological adaptation. Comparative case studies from developed and emerging economies highlight strategies for balancing fairness, efficiency, and sustainability. Emphasizing integrated policy design, lifelong learning, digital inclusion, and participatory governance, the chapter argues that intergenerational equity is attainable through coordinated interventions that ensure all generations share in economic opportunities, social protection, and long-term growth.

Tunisia faces accelerating demographic aging — from 4.2% aged 65+ in 1990 to 9.5% in 2024 — threatening to close its demographic dividend window before structural weaknesses are resolved. Using 1990–2024 time-series data, this chapter combines OLS regressions, VAR dynamic modeling, and scenario-based projections to 2035. Findings show that aging is statistically associated with slower growth and declining labor force participation, with variance decomposition indicating that demographic shocks account for over a quarter of growth fluctuations at longer horizons. These effects are amplified by Tunisia's structural vulnerabilities — 43.9% informality, persistent unemployment, and post-2011 institutional rigidities

— unlike more adaptable economies that mitigate aging pressures through flexible labor markets and productivity gains. Without reforms enabling senior workforce integration and productivity upgrading, Tunisia risks sustained stagnation before 2035, underscoring the urgency of transformative action while the demographic window remains partially open.

This study aims to analyze the long-term relationship among ageing population, elderly workforce and women's employment in Türkiye for the period 1988-2022. In order to reveal this relationship, the ARDL Bound Test were used. Based on the analysis, the findings indicate that that the workforce participation rate of the population aged 55-64 and the urban population growth rate has a positive effect on the employment rate of women aged 15-64, while the workforce participation rate of the population aged 65 and over, life expectancy at age 65 for men, life expectancy at age 65 for women, and the rate of growth in the service sector have a negative effect. Furthermore, a negative but statistically insignificant relationship was found between the employment rate of women aged 15-64 and exclusion index by gender.

Assessing workforce dynamics based solely on chronological age remains a complex endeavor, particularly amidst international debates questioning age as the exclusive determinant of retirement eligibility. Contrary to conventional assumptions that older individuals are both unwilling and unable to continue working post-retirement, recent studies underscore a growing willingness among many seniors to extend their careers beyond statutory retirement ages. This study aims to delve into the multifaceted influences shaping retirement decisions, focusing on factors beyond age alone, including mental and physical health and employee competencies. The study finds compelling evidence that mental and physical health significantly influence retirement choices. Furthermore, insights from respondents' open-ended responses suggest a nuanced subjective perspective, with age often perceived as a predominant factor despite statistical insignificance.

This chapter examines the interdependence between health system sustainability and labor market participation in the context of global population aging. Using an integrated framework based on health capital, human capital, lifecycle labor supply, and systems theories, it analyzes how health, productivity, and fiscal dynamics interact across individual, institutional, and macroeconomic levels. While aging raises dependency ratios, healthcare costs, and pension burdens, it can drive growth through preventive health, lifelong learning, and inclusive labor markets. Drawing on OECD and emerging economy cases, including Japan's productive aging model, Nordic health–labor integration, and China's pension reforms, the chapter proposes an Integrated Health–Labor–Fiscal (IHLF) Framework. It emphasizes cross-sectoral governance, preventive care, flexible employment, and fiscal adaptability, arguing that health must be treated as productive capital to turn longevity into a source of sustainable prosperity.

The main objective of this study is to conduct a comprehensive review of the various studies related to population ageing and its impact on health with a specific focus on the social determinants that influence the same. The present study aims to not only shed light on the evolution and advancement in this research domain but also help to identify key areas for future research exploration. The study used the scientometrics review methodology, which relies on the bibliometric analysis. he R-based bibliometric and visualization of similarities (VOS) viewer open-source software were used to conduct the analysis. The study has found that the most relevant themes identified by the authors in population ageing and social determinants of health are education, affordable healthcare, elderly health, social support and physical activity. The finding of the chosen studies offers a distinctive and valuable contribution to the field of

Preface

INTRODUCTION

The global economy is undergoing a profound demographic transformation. Population aging—once considered a phenomenon confined to advanced economies—has now become a universal structural shift shaping labor markets, fiscal systems, and social institutions across both developed and emerging contexts. As longevity increases and fertility rates decline, the age composition of societies is changing in ways that challenge traditional economic assumptions while opening new avenues for innovation and growth. This volume, The Economics of an Aging Workforce: Challenges, Opportunities, and Policy Perspectives, brings together a diverse set of scholarly contributions to critically examine these evolving dynamics.

The motivation for this edited volume stems from the recognition that aging is not merely a demographic trend but a multidimensional economic force. It intersects with technological change, labor market restructuring, fiscal sustainability, and social equity. Rather than framing aging solely as a burden, the contributors to this book adopt a nuanced perspective that acknowledges both the risks and the transformative opportunities associated with an older workforce. From theoretical modeling to empirical analysis and policy design, the chapters collectively highlight the importance of institutional adaptability and forward-looking strategies.

This book is intended for researchers, policymakers, practitioners, and students seeking to understand the complex interplay between demographic change and economic systems. By integrating insights from economics, public policy, labor studies, and health systems, the volume offers a comprehensive and interdisciplinary perspective. It aims not only to diagnose the challenges posed by population aging but also to illuminate pathways toward inclusive, sustainable, and resilient economic futures.

CHAPTER OVERVIEW

This volume is organized into nine chapters, each addressing a critical dimension of the economics of an aging workforce.

Chapter 1 by Patrick Georges and Aylin Seckin Georges examines the role of life annuities within overlapping generations (OLG) general equilibrium models. The chapter demonstrates how varying assumptions about wealth annuitization significantly affect model calibration and the perceived economic impacts of demographic change, offering important implications for macroeconomic forecasting.

Chapter 2 by Mohd Adil and Saba Ismail compares machine learning and econometric approaches to forecasting population aging in BRICS economies. The chapter underscores the importance of robust demographic projections for policy planning.

Chapter 3 by Md. Adnan Rahman and co-authors addresses intergenerational equity and income distribution. Through theoretical and empirical analysis, it highlights policy mechanisms that balance fairness and efficiency across age groups in aging societies.

Chapter 4 by Zyed Achour examines demographic aging and labor market dynamics in Tunisia. Using time-series and scenario-based modeling, it highlights the risks of stagnation without structural reforms and workforce integration strategies.

Chapter 5 by Sevilay Sarica analyzes the relationship between population aging and women's employment in Türkiye using econometric methods. The findings reveal complex interactions between demographic factors and labor market participation.

Chapter 6 by Wasantha Rajapakshe and H. G. S. M. Hapurugala explores the determinants of retirement decisions beyond chronological age. The study emphasizes the roles of health, competencies, and subjective perceptions in shaping retirement behavior.

Chapter 7 by Lawal Abdulwahab investigates the link between health system sustainability and labor market participation. It introduces the Integrated Health–Labor–Fiscal framework, positioning health as productive capital in aging economies.

Chapter 8 by Amiya Khadar and Pooja Kansra provides a bibliometric review of the social determinants of health in aging populations. The chapter identifies key research themes and future directions in the field.

CONCLUSION

The chapters in this volume collectively underscore that population aging is not a uniform or deterministic process; rather, its economic consequences are shaped by policy choices, institutional frameworks, and societal attitudes. Across diverse contexts, the evidence presented highlights that aging can either constrain or enhance economic performance depending on how effectively systems adapt to demographic realities. In particular, investments in health, education, and inclusive labor markets emerge as central pillars in transforming longevity into an asset.

A recurring theme throughout the book is the importance of integration—across policy domains, generations, and disciplines. Whether addressing fiscal sustainability, technological change, or labor market participation, the contributions emphasize that fragmented approaches are insufficient. Instead, coordinated strategies that align economic, social, and institutional objectives are necessary to ensure both efficiency and equity in aging societies.

As editors, we hope this volume stimulates further research and informed policy dialogue on one of the defining challenges of our time. The economics of an aging workforce is not solely about managing decline; it is about reimagining growth, productivity, and social cohesion in an era of longevity. By advancing a balanced and evidence-based perspective, this book aspires to contribute to the development of sustainable and inclusive economic systems for present and future generations.

Chapter 1

Economic Impacts of Demographic Changes:

Do Life Annuities Matter? An OLG General Equilibrium Investigation

Patrick Georges
http://orcid.org/0000-0003-1944-1300
University of Ottawa, Canada

Aylin Seckin Georges
http://orcid.org/0009-0009-2608-3629
BSL Business School of Lausanne, Switzerland

ABSTRACT

This paper analyses how wealth annuitization schemes have been routinely introduced in OLG- CGE models to cope with life-length uncertainty, and shows the impact of different annuitization schemes on calibration and simulation results in the context of realistic demographic changes. Imposing full (100%) wealth annuitization leads to deeper capital accumulation (relative to a zero annuitization scheme) and, eventually, overestimates the positive economic impacts of demographic dividends in younger countries where the annuity market is thin. The analysis is reversed for countries more advanced in the ageing process. In this case, the negative impact of ageing will be overestimated (i.e., it will appear worse than it really is) relative to a more realistic assumption of little wealth annuitization.

DOI: 10.4018/979-8-3373-7483-3.ch001

1. INTRODUCTION

Wealth accumulation – how much to save and how to invest those savings – is often viewed as the most important aspect of financial planning for retirement. Many specific research topics related to this issue have been explored, including the relative merits of pay-as-you go and fully funded pensions, the issue of early retirement, and the threat of aging on the financial viability of pensions systems. However, according to Brown (2007), an issue that is often underappreciated in financial planning for retirement is the question of how one's assets will be converted into a stream of consumption in retirement. It is only relatively recently that some economists have started to be concerned by the forgotten half of retirement security: the 'decumulation phase'. In a world of life length certainty, an individual could simply spread their wealth over a fixed time horizon until precisely running out of wealth on the last day of life. Converting wealth into consumption is made difficult, however, when faced with the uncertainty about how long the individual will live. Financial contracts exist, life annuities, designed to insure against the risk created by length of life uncertainty and allowing an individual to exchange a lump-sum of wealth for an income stream that is guaranteed to last for the rest of the annuitant's life. However, the demand for life annuities that can be bought on a personal basis is paradoxically small, which amplifies the challenges associated with the decumulation phase. Besides the thinness of the annuity market, Cremer and Pestieau (2010) mention other challenges that explain the recent surge in interests in the decumulation phase, in particular 1) the increase in average longevity, length of retirement, and length of decumulation phase in a context where uncertainty of survival after 60 has not decreased, and 2) a continuing shift from defined benefits to defined contribution pensions (both in the public and private sector) that offer at time of retirement a lump sum capital without the obligation or the incentives of converting it into a flow of annuities.

Until the 1990s, large scale OLG computable general equilibrium (OLG-CGE) models that followed the seminal work of Auerbach and Kotlikoff (1987) assumed away life-length uncertainty so that wealth annuitization was of no specific interest in this strand of literature.[1] However, by the end of the 1990s and early 2000s a series of papers started examining life-length uncertainty in large-scale OLG models (e.g., Rios-Rull, 1996, 2001; Broer and Westerhout, 1997; Chauveau and Loufir, 1997; Imrohoroglu, 1998; Docquier et al., 2002; Chateau, 2003; Börsch-Supan et al. 2006; Krueger and Ludwig, 2007, among others). In these models, uncertainty about life-length implies that individuals may die 'early', and in this case their truncated life cycle implies non-zero net wealth at death that must be distributed.[2] This is referred to as unintended or accidental bequests and two specific methods have been introduced to deal with this outcome. Many of the papers cited above assume that the individual's wealth in case of death is transferred to an insurance company in exchange of an annuity during their lifetime.[3] These papers exploit Yaari's (1965) argument that life annuities substantially increase individual welfare by providing a higher level of lifetime consumption through the elimination of the financial risks associated with uncertain lifetimes, and that, in the absence of voluntary bequest motives, risk-averse individuals would find it optimal to annuitize 100 percent of their wealth. The second method to deal with accidental bequests does not retain Yaari's assumption (and therefore does not assume the existence of an annuity market) because it seems rather unrealistic for many countries with regards to the actual volume of such annuity contracts, as is illustrated by the well-known 'annuity paradox'.[4] Hence, in some papers (e.g., Imrohoroglu, 1998; Docquier et al., 2002; Chateau, 2003; and more recently, Fehr et al., 2017), authors do not assume annuity markets but introduce an assumption on how the assets of those who die early are distributed to the rest of the population. For example, Imrohoroglu (1998) assumes that all accidental bequests across all ages are taxed at 100% by the government and rebated lump-sum among all survivors across all ages. Docquier et al. (2002) assume that accidental bequests among a specific age class are redistributed to agents belonging to a younger age class (i.e., the accidental bequest of agents dying at 80 would be redistributed to the surviving population that is 60 years old).

Hansen and Imrohoroglu (2007) have introduced a model that nests both methods (annuity markets and redistributed accidental bequests) to analyse and compare several wealth annuitization schemes. In this paper, we use the insight of Hansen and Imrohoroglu (2007) by introducing partial annuitization schemes in an OLG model. Specific to our paper, however, we show the impact of this assumption on wealth distribution across agents and the projected pattern of life annuities resulting from this model. Furthermore, in the context of realistic demographic projections based on UN medium variant scenarios, we analyse how different annuitization schemes impact simulation results. We show that a full annuitization assumption tends to lead to deeper capital accumulation (relative to zero annuitization) and, therefore, overestimate the positive economic impacts of demographic dividends for younger countries. The analysis would be reversed for countries more advanced in the ageing process. In this case, the negative impact of ageing will be overestimated (i.e., it will appear worse than it really is) relative to a more realistic assumption of zero or little wealth annuitization. In this regard, assuming zero or little annuitization, which broadly reflects the situation of most countries, would provide a better assessment of the economic impact of the demographic changes, and our OLG model can be used to gauge the empirical significance or magnitude of this effect.

Another contribution of this paper is to model the purchase of an annuity as a decision that is typically postponed, that is, a 'now or later' instead of a 'now or never' decision. According to several papers, it may indeed be optimal to delay annuitisation if annuities purchased later in life are priced more favorably (i.e. at fair prices), as the general population still alive at an older age is more likely to express an interest in annuities.[5] This may result from the fact that the purchase of an annuity is (often) an irreversible investment decision under life length uncertainty, and in this context a decision to postpone purchase may be a better decision as people become more informed about, say, their health type and length of their retirement. We mention this, here, as an analogy to the literature on irreversible investment and the option value of waiting (Dixit and Pyndick, 1994). However, at this stage, we model this idea in a rather simple manner, through a delayed annuitization scheme where the individual starts its active life with a zero annuitization scheme and decide on a positive level much later in life. Hence the annuitization parameter is not constant over the entire life cycle as in Hansen and Imrohoroglu (2007) but can vary as the household ages and revaluates its conditional survival rate.

The financial literature on annuity (see Rusconi, 2008) typically classifies annuities into 'immediate' and 'deferred' annuities where these two terms indicate when the distribution or payout phase of the annuity begins. Immediate annuities are funded with a single lump-sum of cash which is converted into an income stream which begins immediately (or typically within 12 months). With a deferred annuity, the individual typically makes a series of premium payments over an accumulation period during which he builds up a capital of annuitized wealth, while the annuity payout (income stream) is deferred until some time in the future. Immediate annuities are strongly dominating their deferred annuity counterparts in the United Kingdom, Canada, the United States and South Africa. Alternatively, in Germany, Denmark, The Netherlands and Belgium deferred annuities dominate. Our paper shows that the OLG-CGE literature has introduced an implicit annuity mechanism that shares features of both immediate and deferred annuities by having overlapping periods of accumulation and distribution. By postponing the decision to purchase an annuity until much later in life, the delayed (or age dependent) annuitisation scheme introduced in this paper models something that is conceptually closer to the principle of an immediate annuity where the individual makes, later in life, the decision to convert a lump sum of cash into an immediate income stream.

We will illustrate several simulation results with respect to Turkey. In the case of OLG models applied to Turkey, early large-scale OLG CGE models such as those of Kenc and Sayan (2001) and Voyvoda and Yeldan (2005) assumed away mortality risk so that the issue of accidental bequest was irrelevant. Georges and Seçkin (2016) include life-length uncertainty with full annuitization of assets. However, the insurance market in Turkey is underdeveloped. For example, according to a position paper from the Insurance Association of Turkey (2018), the ratio of life insurance premium to GDP was 3.5% globally in 2015, 4.2% in continental Europe, but only 0.2% in Turkey, while the annuity market *per se* is virtually inexistent in Turkey.

In this perspective, assuming full annuitization of assets as in Georges and Seckin (2016) is not realistic. Therefore, this new paper builds an OLG model of the Turkish economy with life-length uncertainty and nested life-annuity schemes including zero, partial, complete, and delayed (age-dependent) assets annuitization schemes. The final objective is to assess whether life annuities scenarios matter when gauging the economic impacts of demographic dividends and whether introducing an annuity market in Turkey would be valuable for the economy as a whole.

2. AN OLG MODEL WITH NESTED ALTERNATIVE LIFE-ANNUITY SCHEMES

The OLG-CGE model used here is a variant of the model used in Georges and Seçkin (2016, 2017), which introduces age-specific mortality with a perfect annuity market and endogenous labour supply. As the annuity market in Turkey is very thin, our objective is to relax this assumption by allowing different wealth annuity schemes (from 0% to 100%) including a delayed annuity scheme. On the other hand, the model simplifies Georges and Seçkin (2016) by assuming exogenous labour supply so as to focus most of the analysis on the economic impact of the annuitization schemes.

2.1. Production Sector

The production sector is characterized by a representative firm which produces a single good using a Cobb–Douglas technology. $Y_{j,\tau}$ represents the (aggregate) output (GDP) of each period τ for country j (Turkey and sometimes Canada in some simulation experiments). A is total factor productivity. In this model, it is kept constant across time. This means that the model does not attempt to capture a realistic growth process but focuses exclusively on the impact of demographic pressures on the economy and how annuitization schemes could affect these results. K and L represent capital stock and effective labor force, respectively. Parameter α_j is the share of physical capital in GDP (Y). The main parameters in the model are given in Table 1. There is no intermediary good. The following is the Cobb–Douglas production function:

$$Y_{j,\tau} = A_{j,\tau} K_{j,\tau}^{\alpha_j} L_{j,\tau}^{1-\alpha_j} 0 < \alpha_j < 1, \tag{1}$$

Table 1. Model variables and parameters

Indices	*Description*
j	Region j (Turkey; Canada)
τ $\tau = t+k$	τ is the period index. Each period represents 5 years Time t is the specific period at which an individual reaches adult/economic life (20-24 years) k is the increment in time (and age) over adult life (20-24 to 100-104), $\tau = t+k$; k=0,..16
γ $\gamma = g+k$	γ is the age index. Each age period represents 5 years Age period g is first period of adult life (20-24 years of age) $g+k$ represents age groups from 20-24 years of age to 100-104 years of age. k is the increment in age (and time) over adult life (20-24 to 100-104), $\gamma= g+k$; k=0,…16
kr	kr is increment in age over retired life: $\gamma= g+8+kr$; kr =1,..,8
kw	kw is increment in age over working life: $\gamma= g+kw$; kw =0,...,8
ka	ka is increment in age over entire lifetime, including childhood: $\gamma= g+ka$; ka= -4,…0, …,16 where ka= -4 to -1 correspond to age groups (0-4) to (15-19); ka = 0,…,8 correspond to age groups (20-25) to (60-65); ka=9…16 correspond to age groups (65-70) to (100-104)
Variables	***Description***
$Y_{j,\tau}$	Representative firm production (Country-j output or GDP)
$P_{j,\tau}$	Output price (Numéraire)
$K_{j,\tau}$	Demand of physical capital by representative firm
$L_{j,\tau}$	Demand of effective units of labour by representative firm
$re_{j,\tau}$	Rental price of capital
$w_{j,\tau}$	Wage rate
$Con_{j,\tau,\gamma}$	Consumption demand of household of generation γ at time τ
$Inv_{j,\tau}$	Investment demand in region-j at time τ
$Gov_{j,\tau}$	Age-independent public expenditures
$GovH_{j,\tau}$	Age-dependent government spending on Health
$GovE_{j,\tau}$	Age-dependent government spending on Education
$HA_{j,\tau,\gamma}$	Stock of wealth of household of generation γ at the start of period τ
$UnBeq_{j,\tau}$	Inheritance at start of period τ ensuing from involuntary bequest of agents deceased at end of period τ-1
$Kstock_{j,\tau}$	Capital stock accumulated at the start of period τ
$Bond_{j,\tau}$	Public debt accumulated at the start of period τ
$ri_{j,\tau}$	Rate of return on assets (public debt and physical capital)
$Pens_{j,\tau,\gamma}$	Pension benefits to retired generations γ
$Y^L_{j,\tau,\gamma}$	Labour income of household of generation γ at time τ
$LS_{j,\gamma}$	Supply of skill-unadjusted units of labour of household of generation γ
$Pop_{j,\tau,\gamma}$	Population size of cohorts of age/generation γ

continued on following page

Table 1. Continued

Indices	*Description*
Parameters	***Description***
$A_{j,\tau}$	Scaling factor of Cobb-Douglas production function (TFP)
α_j	Share of physical capital in Cobb-Douglas production function
ρ_j	Constant rate of time preference
$\lambda_{j,\tau,\gamma}$	Age-dependent annuitization parameter
$\theta_j = 1/sig_j$	Inverse of the constant inter-temporal elasticity of substitution
$EP_{j,\gamma}$	Household age-dependent productivity (earnings) profile
$PART_{j,\gamma}$	Age-dependent labour participation rate
$\tau x^{L}_{j,\tau}$ $(=WTxR)$	Effective tax rate on labour income (endogenous)
$\tau x^{K}_{j,\tau}$	Effective tax rate on capital income
$\tau x^{C}_{j,\tau}$	Effective consumption tax rate
$Ctr_{j,\tau}$	Contribution to the public pension system (endogenous)
$PensR_j$	Pension replacement rate (exogenous)
δ_j	Depreciation rate of capital
$BR_{j,\tau}$	Time dependent birth rate
$SR_{j,\tau,\gamma}$; $MR_{j,\tau,\gamma}$	Age and time dependent survival rate; Age and time dependent migration rate
$HEAC_{j,\gamma}$	Age-specific health expenditure per capita
$EDUC_{j,\gamma}$	Age-specific education expenditure per capita
$GEPC_j$	Age-invariant "other government expenditure" per capita

First order conditions to maximize profit provide the rental rate of capital ($re_{j,\tau}$) and the wage rate per unit of effective labor ($w_{j,\tau}$):

$$re_{j,\tau}/P_{j,\tau} = \alpha_j A_{j,\tau}\left(K_{j,\tau}/L_{j,\tau}\right)^{\alpha_j-1}; P_{j,\tau} = 1\ (Num\acute{e}raire) \quad (2)$$

$$w_{j,\tau}/P_{j,\tau} = (1-\alpha_j)A_{j,\tau}\left(K_{j,\tau}/L_{j,\tau}\right)^{\alpha_j} \quad (3)$$

2.2. Household Behavior

In our setting, the time separable household's utility is of CES type and the intertemporal utility of an individual economically born at time t at age g (i.e., when the individual reaches 20 years of age) is given by the expression:

$$E_t(U_j) = \frac{1}{1-\theta_j}\sum_{i=1}^{i=17}\left\{\frac{1}{(1+\rho_j)^{i-1}}\left(\prod_{k=0}^{k=i-1} SR_{j,t+k-1,g+k-1}\right)\left(Con_{j,t+i-1,g+i-1}\right)^{1-\theta_j}\right\} \quad (4)$$

where E_t is the mathematical expectations operator conditional on information at time t and j is the index of the country, here j=Turkey or Canada, depending on our analysis in Section 4. $\theta = 1/\sigma$ is the inverse of the intertemporal elasticity of substitution. The parameter ρ is the pure rate of time preference, and $SR_{j,t+k,g+k}$ is the conditional probability of surviving period $t+k$ (when the individual is of age $g+k$) and therefore the probability of reaching the start of period $t+k+1$ (when the individual reaches age $g+k+1$). The index k is a period/age increment. Each period of life represents 5 years, and the maximum economic life-length (once the individual starts its economic life at 20 years of age) is 17 periods, from 20-24 until 100-104 years of age. For i=1to 17, $Con_{j,t+i-1,g+i-1}$ is the periodic consumption of this individual over the lifecycle from age group g (20-24 years old) in period t to age group $g+i$-1 = g+16 (100-104 years) in period $t+i$-1 = t+16 in which he completes his maximum life length (104 years). In Eq (4), $SR_{j,t-1,g-1}$pre-multiplies$\left(Con_{j,t,g}\right)^{1-\theta_j}$, $SR_{j,t-1,g-1} \times SR_{j,t,g}$pre-multiplies $\left(Con_{j,t+1,g+1}\right)^{1-\theta_j}$ etc., so that for each successive period t, t+1, etc., of the life-cycle, these terms represent an expected (as of time t) periodic consumption. The term$\prod_{k=0}^{k=i-1} SR_{j,t+k-1,g+k-1} = SR_{j,t-1,g-1} \times SR_{j,t,g} \times SR_{j,t+1,g+1} \times \ldots \times SR_{j,t+i-2,g+i-2}$ is the unconditional probability as of age 20 of surviving age group $g+i$-2 and thus reaching the age group $g+i$-1. As of time t, the last possible term, when i = 17, in$\prod_{k=0}^{k=i-1} SR_{j,t+k-1,g+k-1}isSR_{j,t+15,g+15}$, which gives the conditional probability to survive period t+15 (during which an individual was of age g+15, i.e., 95-99 years old) and hence to reach period t+16 (when an individual reaches age g+16, i.e., the age group 100-104) during which period he will consume$Con_{j,t+16,g+16}$.[6] The model imposes that$SR_{j,t+16,g+16} = 0$, which indicates that any individual that reaches age g+16 (100 years of age) will die with probability 1 at the end of their 104th year. Younger generations (age groups 0-4, to 15-19) are fully dependent on their parents and play no active role in the model, but they influence the age dependent components of public expenditure (health and education) and the population structure.[7]

The household budget constraint can be written as follows:

$$\underbrace{(1-\lambda_{j,\tau,\gamma}(1-SR_{j,\tau,\gamma}))HA_{j,\tau+1,\gamma+1} - (HA_{j,\tau,\gamma} + UnBe_{j,\tau,\gamma})}_{\text{Saving}} =$$

$$\underbrace{\left(1-\tau x^{L}_{j,\tau} - Ctr_{j,\tau}\right)Y^{L}_{j,\tau,\gamma}}_{\text{Labour Income}} + \underbrace{\left[\left(1-\tau x^{K}_{j,\tau}\right)ri_{j,\tau}\right](HA_{j,\tau,\gamma} + UnBe_{j,\tau,\gamma})}_{\text{Asset Income}} + Pens_{j,\tau,\gamma} - \underbrace{\left(1+\tau x^{C}_{j,\tau}\right)Con_{j,\tau,\gamma}}_{\text{Consumption spending}} \quad (5)$$

$$\lambda \in [0,1]\,; \quad \tau = t+k; \quad \gamma = g+k; \quad k = 0,\ldots 16.$$

where$HA_{j,\tau,\gamma}$is asset holding (wealth) of an individual of age group γ at the start of period τ and $HA_{j,\tau+1,\gamma+1}$ is asset holding of the same individual one period later, i.e., of age group γ+1 at the end of period τ, or equivalently, at the start of period τ+1. $Y^{L}_{j,\gamma}$is gross labour income, $Pens_{j,\tau,\gamma}$is pension benefits accruing to retired individuals,

τx^L is the effective tax rate on labour income, Ctr is the worker contribution to the PAYG pension system, τx^K is the effective tax rate on asset income where ri is the rate of return on assets (defined later on in Eq. (18) with respect to the rental price of capital re and the depreciation rate of capital) and τx^C is the effective tax rate on consumption spending. Parameter$\lambda_{j,\tau,\gamma}$, with $0 \leq \lambda \leq 1$, gives the age-dependent wealth annuitization scheme. If $\lambda_{j,\tau,\gamma}$=1, for τ=t, t+1, etc., then the representative individual annuitizes all of his wealth over its life-cycle. If $\lambda_{j,\tau,\gamma}$=0, the representative individual does not annuitize his wealth. All other values, $0 < \lambda_{j,\tau,\gamma} < 1$, represent partial wealth annuitization schemes. For example, $\lambda_{j,\tau,\gamma}= 0.75$ would imply that the individual annuitize 75% of its actual wealth and keeps 25% of its wealth invested in a normal interest-bearing asset. The OLG-CGE literature has typically introduced an annuitization parameter that is most often 1 or 0, over the entire lifecycle of the individual. In reality however, as discussed in the Introduction, most individuals who eventually decide to annuitize their wealth do it quite late in life, once they better know their health type. The model here permits the individual to choose $\lambda_{j,\tau,\gamma}= 0$ as long as he has not reached a specific age, say, 75, and then set it equal to a positive value $\lambda_{j,\tau,\gamma} > 0$ once the individual re-evaluates his health-type through his conditional survival rate.

The left hand side of Eq. (5) is saving during period τ as obvious from the right hand side of this equation giving the difference between net labour income, net asset income, pension benefits in case the individual is entitled to it, and consumption spending inclusive of taxes. The term $\lambda_{j,\tau,\gamma}(1 - SR_{j,\tau,\gamma})HA_{j,\tau+1,\gamma+1}$ in the left hand side of Eq. (5) is the annuity payout expected by the household on that share of its wealth that is annuitized. This term is explained further in Section 3. If there is no annuity purchase then$\lambda_{j,\tau,\gamma} = 0$and the expected annuity payout is of course equal to zero.

It is assumed that people are not altruistic. They do not plan to leave voluntary bequests but, as they can die 'early', there could be unplanned bequests. If they fully annuitize their wealth ($\lambda_{j,\tau,\gamma}$=1), they will leave all their wealth to the insurance company at the time of their death. If, however, they do not fully annuitize their wealth, then we need to compute the amount that will be bequeathed to other agents in the model. If we assume that this amount is equally spread among all survivors of all ages, then we show in Section 3 that this amount can be computed as:

$$UnBeq_{j,\tau,\gamma} = UnBeq_{j,\tau} = \frac{\sum_\gamma (1 - SR_{j,\tau-1,\gamma-1}) Pop_{j,\tau-1,\gamma-1}(1 - \lambda_j) HA_{j,\tau,\gamma}}{\sum_\gamma Pop_{j,\tau,\gamma}} \tag{6}$$

Gross labor income per capita (i.e., per representative household of generation γ) given by given by $Y^L_{j,\gamma}$in (5), is defined in Eq. (7) as the standardized wage rate $w_{j,\gamma}$, (the wage rate of a newly active adult) multiplied by $EP_{j,\gamma}$, an age-dependent productivity (earnings) profile reflecting the individual's change in earning capacity over time, and defined as a quadratic function of age (Eq. 8). *LS* is the individual exogenous supply of potential non-effective units of labour. *PART* is an age-dependent, time-invariant labour participation rate.

$$Y^L_{j,\tau,\gamma} = w_{j,\tau} EP_{j,\gamma} LS_{j,\gamma} PART_{j,\gamma}, \tau = t + k; \gamma = g + k; k = 0...16. \tag{7}$$

$$EP_{j,kw+1} = c + (\pi)(kw + 1) - (\psi)(kw + 1)^2, c,\ \pi,\ \psi \geq 0 kw = 0, \ldots 8 \tag{8}$$

Based on equation (5), the household's lifetime budget constraint can be computed as:[8]

$$\sum_{i=1}^{17} \left\{ \begin{matrix} \dfrac{\prod_{k=0}^{k=i-1} (1 - \lambda_{j,t+k-1,g+k-1}(1 - SR_{j,t+k-1,g+k-1}))}{\prod_{i=1}^{17} \left(1 + \left[\left(1 - \tau x^K_{j,t+i-1}\right) ri_{j,t+i-1}\right]\right)} \\ \left[\begin{matrix} \left(1 - \tau x^L_{j,t+i-1} - Ctr_{j,t+i-1}\right) Y^L_{j,t+i-1,g+i-1} + Pens_{j,t+i-1,g+i-1} \\ + UnBe_{j,t+i-1,g+i-1} - \left(1 + \tau x^C_{j,t+i-1}\right) Con_{j,t+i-1,g+i-1} \end{matrix} \right] \end{matrix} \right\} + UnBe_{j,t,g} = 0 \tag{9}$$

Therefore, the household solves the following Lagrangian maximisation problem where the intertemporal budget constraint is multiplied by the Lagrange parameter $\tilde{\lambda}$:

$$\ell = \frac{1}{1-\theta_j} \sum_{i=1}^{i=17} \left\{ \frac{1}{(1+\rho_j)^{i-1}} \left(\prod_{k=0}^{k=i-1} SR_{j,t+k-1,g+k-1} \right) \left(Con_{j,t+i-1,g+i-1} \right)^{1-\theta_j} \right\}$$
$$+ \tilde{\lambda} \left[\sum_{i=1}^{17} \left\{ \frac{\prod_{k=0}^{k=i-1} (1 - \lambda_{j,t+k-1,g+k-1}(1 - SR_{j,t+k-1,g+k-1}))}{\prod_{i=1}^{17} \left(1 + \left[\left(1 - \tau x^K_{j,t+i-1}\right) ri_{j,t+i-1}\right]\right)} \left[\begin{matrix} \left(1 - \tau x^L_{j,t+i-1} - Ctr_{j,t+i-1}\right) Y^L_{j,t+i-1,g+i-1} + Pens_{j,t+i-1,g+i-1} \\ + UnBe_{j,t+i-1,g+i-1} - \left(1 + \tau x^C_{j,t+i-1}\right) Con_{j,t+i-1,g+i-1} \end{matrix} \right] \right\} + UnBe_{j,t,g} \right]$$

The following Euler condition provides the consumption path of the household from period τ at age γ to the next period/age as:

$$\frac{Con_{j,\tau+1,\gamma+1}}{Con_{j,\tau,\gamma}} = \left(\frac{SR_{j,\tau,\gamma}}{(1 - \lambda_{j,\tau,\gamma}(1 - SR_{j,\tau,\gamma}))} \frac{\left(1 + \left[\left(1 - \tau x^K_{j,\tau+1}\right) ri_{j,\tau+1}\right]\right)}{(1 + \rho_j)} \frac{\left(1 + \tau x^C_{j,\tau}\right)}{\left(1 + \tau x^C_{j,\tau+1}\right)} \right)^{\frac{1}{\theta_j}} \tag{10}$$

Let us first assume a context of life-length certainty ($SR_{j,\tau,\gamma}$=1 for all age group) so that people know that they will only die in the very last period of the model (at the end of their104th year of age), and assume no annuitization scheme ($\lambda_{j,\tau,\gamma}$=0) as it is irrelevant in a life-length certainty context. If we also set $\rho < ri$ in (10) (i.e., the individual is more patient than the market), then the consumer optimally starts out with a relatively low consumption in order to save and take advantage of the high interest rates. Thus, its periodic consumption increases over the lifecycle and this generates an upward–sloping consumption path. The introduction of life-length uncertainty ($SR_{j,\tau,\gamma}$< 1) does not change this result as long as $\lambda_{j,\tau,\gamma}$=1 because in this case $SR_{j,\tau,\gamma}$ in both the numerator and denominator cancels out. Indeed, it is one key result of Yaari (1965) to demonstrate that under the case of full annuitization of wealth (and no voluntary bequests) the Euler consumption equation does not depend on the survival rate (or the probability of dying) in a period. Yet, partial ($\lambda_{j,\tau,\gamma}$<1) or no ($\lambda_{j,\tau,\gamma}$=0) wealth annuitization schemes affect this result because $SR_{j,\tau,\gamma}$ in numerator and denominator does not cancel out. In this case, even if $\rho < ri$ (the agent is patient) an hump-shaped consumption path will arise. When the individual is relatively young (so that the survival rate is high and close to 1), consumption will increase from period to period as before. However, as the individual ages, $SR_{j,\tau,\gamma}$ starts to decline more significantly period after period, and this effect may eventually dominate the effect of having $\rho < ri$ on consumption dynamics so that a fully rational consumer will, at some stage, spend less as they progress through retirement and the end of life. Intuitively the individual deals with longevity risk by planning to reduce future consumption in proportion to the survival probability, linked to their risk aversion. It is as if the rate of time preference (weighted by the survival rate) made the individual more impatient to consume now, instead of in the future when the survival rate will be much lower. This provides a rigorous foundation to Irving Fisher (1930) statements in his book 'The Theory of Interest', that "[e]veryone at some time in his life doubtless changes his degree of impatience for income. When he gets a little older, he expects to die and he thinks: instead of piling up for the remote future, why shouldn't I enjoy myself during the few years that remain?" Hence, "[t]he shortness of life thus tends powerfully to increase the degree of impatience or rate of time preference beyond what it would otherwise be".

One interesting aspect of moving away from the full annuitization scheme in an applied OLG model, besides reflecting market reality (the annuity paradox), is therefore the hump-shaped consumption profiles over lifetime. For example, in our calibration procedure (Section 3), household consumption paths are generated across several annuitization schemes (100%, 75%, 50%, 25%, 0%, and a delayed but full (100%) annuitization scheme starting at age 75 instead of age 20). See Figure 1. This figure is based on the Euler equation describing the dynamic of household consumption over lifetime.[9]

Figure 1. Household consumption profile over life time: diverse wealth annuitization schemes

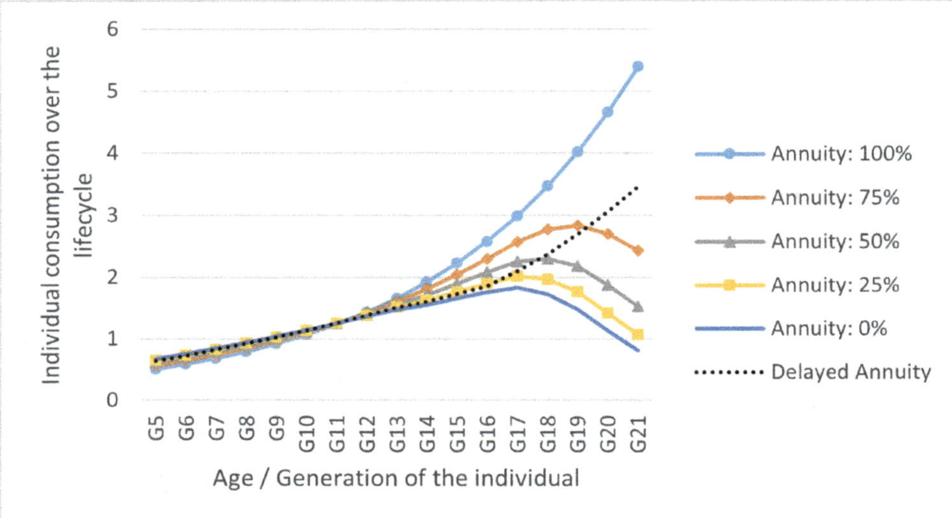

Note: *Generations are labeled in all figures from G5 to G21, i.e. (20-24 to 100-104 years of age)*

2.3. Government Sector and Pension Plans

Public expenditure on health and education (Eqs. 11-12) are age-dependent (i.e., fixed per person of a specific age). Other types of public expenditures (Eq. 13) are assumed to be age invariant, that is, they are fixed per capita, so that other total expenditure depends only on the size of the total population, not on its age structure.

$$GovH_{j,\tau} = \sum_{\gamma=g-4}^{g+ka} Pop_{j,\tau,\gamma} HEAC_{j,\gamma}; ka = -4, \ldots 16 \tag{11}$$

$$GovE_{j,\tau} = \sum_{\gamma=g-4}^{g+ka} Pop_{j,\tau,\gamma} EDUC_{j,\gamma}; ka = -4, \ldots 16 \tag{12}$$

$$Gov_{j,\tau} = TPop_{j,\tau} GEPC_{j} \tag{13}$$

In this version of the model, public debt is assumed to remain constant per capita while the government must respect its budget constraint (Eq.14). Total government spending, including interest on the public debt, must be financed each period by tax revenues from capital and labour, and consumption taxes. Note that $UnBeq_{j,\tau,\gamma}$ as defined in (6), is the bequest inherited from those who died during τ-1 and this amount must be added to the assets of the surviving households at the start of τ. They will generate interest revenues on which the government will also collect taxes. We assume in the model that the tax rate on labour income $\tau x^L_{j,\tau}$, is the endogenous variable that fulfils the government budget constraint. In simulation results the path for this tax rate will therefore be indicative of the fiscal pressure of ageing in the country.

$$\begin{aligned} Bond_{j,\tau+1} - Bond_{j,\tau} &= Gov_{j,\tau} + GovE_{j,\tau} + GovH_{j,\tau} + ri_{j,\tau} Bond_{j,\tau} \\ &- \sum_{\gamma=g}^{g+k} Pop_{j,\tau,\gamma} \left\{ \tau x^C_{j,\tau}(Con_{j,\tau,\gamma}) + \tau x^L_{j,\tau}(w_{j,\tau} EP_{j,\gamma} LS_{j,\gamma} PART_{j,\gamma}) + \tau x^K_{j,\tau}(ri_{j,\tau}(HA_{j,\tau,\gamma} + UnBeq_{j,\tau,\gamma})) \right\} \end{aligned} \tag{14}$$

We assume a PAYG pension plan separated from the government budget constraint so as to gauge the impact of the pension pressure due to ageing independently from the rest of the budget. Retirement age is at 65 years of age. Pension benefits depend on life-time labor income and the pension replacement rate (or pension benefit rate) as follows:

$$Pens_{j,\tau,g+8+kr} = PensR_j \times \frac{1}{9} \sum_{kw=8}^{0} w_{j,\tau-kr-kw,g+8-kw} \times EP_{j,g+8-kw} LS_{j,g+8-kw} PART_{j,g+8-kw} \tag{15}$$

where $kr = 1,\ldots,8$, represents the age increment (over the maximum number of retirement periods) once an individual retires at the end of the last period of work (g+8), and kw=8,...,0, is here an age 'decrement' that allows to unfold 'back' the entire work period of a specific retiree.

The contribution rate, Ctr, applied on gross labour income, is determined endogenously so as to permit, each period, the financing of total pension benefits (Eq. 16). Hence, endogenous increases in the contribution rate will be indicative of future pension plan tensions due to population ageing (separately from other fiscal pressures)

$$\sum_{kr=1}^{kr=8} Pop_{j,\tau,g+8+kr} Pens_{j,\tau,g+8+kr} = Ctr_{j,\tau} \sum_{kw=0}^{8} Pop_{j,\tau,g+kw} Y^L_{j,,\tau,g+kw} \tag{16}$$

2.4 Investment and Asset Returns

The accumulation of capital stock ($Kstock$) is subject to depreciation (Eq 17), where Inv represents investment and δ the depreciation rate of capital. Physical capital ($Kstock$) and government bonds ($Bond$) are assumed to be perfectly substitutable. Hence the expected rate of return on bonds ri is equal to the rate of return on physical assets defined as the rental price of capital minus the depreciation rate (Eq 18).

$$Kstock_{j,\tau+1} = Inv_{j,\tau} + (1 - \delta_j) Kstock_{j,\tau} \tag{17}$$

$$ri_{j,\tau} = re_{j,\tau} - \delta_j \tag{18}$$

2.5 Market and Aggregation Conditions

We assume a closed economy. The equilibrium in the good market and in the factor markets are given as follows:

$$Y_{j,\tau} = \sum_{\gamma=g}^{g+k} Pop_{j,\tau,\gamma} Con_{j,\tau,\gamma} + Inv_{j,\tau} + Gov_{j,\tau} + GovH_{j,\tau} + GovE_{j,\tau} \tag{19}$$

$$L_{j,\tau} = \sum_{\gamma=g}^{g+k} Pop_{j,\tau,\gamma} LS_{j,\gamma} EP_{j,\gamma} PART_{j,\gamma} \tag{20}$$

$$K_{j,\tau} = Kstock_{j,\tau} \tag{21}$$

From an asset point of view, all wealth (including wealth received as part of the involuntary bequest motive) is hold under the form of bonds or capital stock.

$$\sum_{\gamma=g}^{g+k} Pop_{j,\tau,\gamma}(HA_{j,\tau,\gamma} + UnBeq_{j,\tau,\gamma}) = Kstock_{j,\tau} + Bond_{j,\tau} \tag{22}$$

or, in a flow dimension, we have that national saving is equal to domestic investment:

$$\underbrace{\left(\sum_{\gamma=g}^{g+k} Pop_{j,\tau+1,\gamma}(HA_{j,\tau+1,\gamma} + UnBeq_{j,\tau+1,\gamma}) - \sum_{\gamma=g}^{g+k} Pop_{j,\tau,\gamma}(HA_{j,\tau,\gamma} + UnBeq_{j,\tau,\gamma})\right)}_{\text{Private Saving}}$$

$$-\underbrace{\left(Bond_{j,\tau+1} - Bond_{\tau,t}\right)}_{\text{Public Dissaving}} = \underbrace{\left(Kstock_{j,\tau+1} - Kstock_{j,\tau}\right)}_{\text{Domestic Investment}}.$$

2.6 Demographic Process

Following Georges and Seckin (2016), a demographic process (Eq. 23) superimposed on the OLG model provides the exogenous shock behind the simulations results. The first law of motion simply implies that the number of children (age group $g+ka$ for ka=-4, i.e. age group 0-4) born at time τ is equal to the size of the preceding generation multiplied by the birth rate, *BR*, in period τ-1. The second law of motion gives the size of any age group $g+ka$ beyond the first generation, as the size of this age group a period ago, multiplied by the age and time specific conditional survival rate *SR* and migration rate, *MR*. For the final generation (ka=16), the age group 100-104, the conditional survival rate is zero. This means that for the oldest age group, everyone dies with certainty at the end of the period.

$$Pop_{j,\tau,g+ka} = \begin{cases} Pop_{j,\tau-1,g+ka} BR_{j,\tau-1} & \text{for } ka = \text{-4} \\ Pop_{j,\tau-1,g+ka-1}\left(SR0_{j,\tau-1,g+ka-1} + MR_{j,\tau-1,g+ka-1}\right) & \text{for } ka \in [-3, ..., 16]. \end{cases} \quad (23)$$

3. MODEL CALIBRATION, ASSETS HOLDING AND NESTED LIFE-ANNUITY SCHEMES

3.1 Social Accounting Matrix and Population

For model calibration purposes, we initially assume a stationary population at the start of 2015 and total population is normalised at 1. Based on the 2015's UN population (medium variant) data per age groups, we compute birth rates and survival rates so that the population structure per age group would replicate itself periods after periods as shown in Table 2a. This is the population structure that is assumed in the benchmark and which is used together with the model of Section 2 to replicate the Social Accounting Matrix of Tables 3a/b. Then, from 2020 onwards, we use the UN medium variant population projections per age group up to 2100 and extract data-consistent birth rates and survival rates as shown in Table 2b.[10] This procedure allows precise modelling of the population size and structure within the model and replicates the UN demographic projections given in next section from 2020 onwards.

*Table 2. Computing "birth" and "survival" rates from UN projections for Turkey**

Years/Generations	G1 (0-4)	G2 (5-9)	...	G21 (100+)	Total Pop
a) UN population structure per age group in 2015 and stationary population assumption from 2015 onwards					
2015	6821	6670		0.8	78666
2020	6821	6670		0,8	78666
...					
2100	6821	6670		0.8	78666
b) Constructing implied birth rates and survival rates from UN population data from 2015 onwards					
2015	6821	6670		0.8	78666
2020	6252	6708		1.0	82256
...					
2100	4032	4114		310	87983

* Numbers in cells correspond to historical (2015) and projected (UN medium variant) population sizes (in thousands) by years and generations (relabeled here G1 to G21). The "birth rates" are computed "vertically" for

consecutive time periods on the basis of G1 population sizes (e.g., *BR*=6252/6821 = 0.92). "Survival rates" are computed "diagonally" across consecutive age groups and time periods (e.g., *SR*=6708/6821= 0.98). *Source: Compiled by the authors using UN Population Division data – World Population Prospects, the 2015 Revision (esa.un.org/unpd/wpp/unpp/panel_indicators.htm)*

As just mentioned, the model of Section 2 is calibrated so as to replicate, in the benchmark, the Social Accounting Matrix (SAM) given in Tables 3a/b, which is based on National Accounts for Turkey.[11] GDP (and total population) is normalised to 1 in 2015 and Table 3b shows all values with respect to a GDP of 1 (or, equivalently, in terms of GDP). Labour share of the output, 1-α in Eqs. (1) to (3), is set to 0.65.[12] Age-earning profile (*EP*) are estimated with Mincer age-earnings regressions (Mincer, 1958). The resulting wage profile peaks at 50 years of age, and wages at that age are 45% higher than at 20 year old (see Table 4). Turkish age-specific labour force participation rates (PART) are obtained from OECD statistics data.[13] Given the parametrisation of Eq. (7) and (8), pre-multiplying the age-dependent profile for the per capita labour revenue $Y^L_{j,\tau,\gamma}$ by the population size of the relevant generation γ, and summing over all generations gives that $\sum_\gamma Pop_{j,\tau,\gamma} Y^L_{j,\tau,\gamma} = (1-\alpha) Y_{j,t}$ = TL 1519.39 billion as given in the SAM in Table 3a.

*Table 3a. Social Accounting Matrix (2015) in Billions (Turkish Lira)**

	FIRM	CAPITAL	LABOUR	CON	GOV	GOVH	GOVE	INV	PENSION	TOTAL
FIRM				1648.52	274.66	13.08	31.35	369.92		2337.53
CAPITAL	818.14									818.14
LABOUR	1519.39									1519.39
HOUSEHOLD		403.40	1242.21		107.24				93.50	1846.35
TAX		44.82	183.68	197.82	11.92					438.24
SAVING		369.92								369.92
CONTRIBUTION			93.50							93.50
TOTAL	2337.53	818.14	1519.39	1846.35	393.81	13.08	31.35	369.92	93.50	
Tax Rates (%)		10.0	12.9	12.0	10.0					
Ctr Rate (%)			6.6							
Tax Rev/GDP		1.9	7.9	8.5	0.5					

* The SAM assumes a stationary state, and is replicated by the OLG model of Section 2 in the baseline.

*Table 3b. Social Accounting Matrix (2015) in proportion of 2015 GDP**

	FIRM	CAPITAL	LABOUR	CON	GOV	GOVH	GOVE	INV	PENSION	TOTAL
FIRM				0.71	0.12	0.01	0.01	0.16		1.00
CAPITAL	0.35									0.35
LABOUR	0.65									0.65
HOUSEHOLD		0.17	0.53		0.05				0.04	0.79
TAX		0.02	0.08	0.08	0.01					0.19
SAVING		0.16								0.16
CONTRIBUTION			0.04							0.04
TOTAL	1.00	0.35	0.65	0.79	0.17	0.01	0.01	0.16	0.04	

* The SAM assumes a stationary state, and is replicated by the OLG model of Section 2 in the baseline.

Table 4. Some parameter values

Parameters	*Values*
α_j	35%
ρ_j	1.6%
$\theta_j = 1/sig_j$	1/0.25 (inverse of intertemporal elasticity of subst.)
$EP_{j,\gamma}$	$.857+.242\gamma - .018\gamma^2$
$PART_{j,\gamma}$	See Figure 6, Georges and Seçkin (2016)
$\tau x^L_{j,\tau}$ $(=WTxR)$	12.9% (benchmark) (endogenous)
$\tau x^K_{j,\tau}$	10%
$\tau x^C_{j,\tau}$	12%
$Ctr_{j,\tau}$	6.2% (benchmark) (endogenous)
$PensR_j$	66.7%
δ_j	12%
$BR_{j,\tau}$	Based on UN demographic projections: see Table 1
$SR_{j,\tau,\gamma}$	Based on UN demographic projections: see Table 1
$HEAC_{j,\gamma}$	Age-dependent: See Figure 7, Georges and Seçkin (2016)
$EDUC_{j,\gamma}$	Age-dependent: See Figure 7, Georges and Seçkin (2016)

Other parameters of the model, including effective tax rates on consumption, labour, asset incomes, and pension contribution rates are reported in Tables 3a and 4. We set the consumption tax rate at 12% so that it represents roughly 40% of total tax revenue collection.[14] Pension benefit rates and contribution rates were calculated in the benchmark, according to Eq. (15) and (16), so as to generate total pension benefits of 4% of GDP. This generates an equilibrium contribution rate of *Ctr*= 6.2% and a pension benefit rate of 66.7%. The benefit rate is in line with other OECD countries, while the contribution rate is lower in the base year, which reflects a currently low old age dependency ratio (12.9%) in Turkey. The pure rate of time preference is set at 1.6%. The intertemporal elasticity of substitution is set at $sig = 1/\theta = 0.3$. These values are similar in magnitudes to the ones reported in Auerbach and Kotlikoff (1987). Also used in the calibration are the age profiles for per capita government spending on health (*HEAC*) and education (*EDUC*) (Eq.11 and Eq.12) as estimated for Turkey by Seçkin et al. (2014) using the National Transfer Accounts methodology (Lee and Mason, 2011), and reproduced in Figure 7 of Georges and Seçkin (2016). The calibration procedure ensures that aggregate health and education spending by the government in the benchmark are just equal to the data obtained from the Ministry of Finance.

3.2 Assets Holdings and Nested Life-Annuity Schemes

Total private assets must be consistent with total stock of government bonds (*Bond*) and physical capital (*Kstock*) in the economy, while the household and government budget constraints (Eq. 5 and 14) and the Euler equation (Eq. 10) are used to distribute initial private assets ownership across all generations (i.e., to generate the asset structure$HA_{j,\tau,\gamma}$ for each adult age group γ). This is complicated by the fact that we must account for very specific assumptions relative to diverse annuitization schemes. 1) First, we need to distinguish between annuitized wealth and non-annuitized wealth. 2) Second, we need to take into account the expected (periodic) annuity paid by the insurance company to the annuitant. 3) Third, at the end of life of the annuitant the accumulated annuitized wealth is transferred to the insurance company. 4) Fourth, at the end of their life, non-annuitized wealth of individuals becomes an unintentional bequest which must be distributed to surviving agents who, therefore, receive an inheritance.

To shed light on this, we start by observing that the first term on the left hand side of Eq. (5) can be decomposed into two different ways that illustrate two sides of the issues involved. The first decomposition is:

$$\underbrace{(1-\lambda_{j,\tau,\gamma}(1-SR_{j,\tau,\gamma}))HA_{j,\tau+1,\gamma+1}}_{\text{Expected net wealth}} \equiv \underbrace{HA_{j,\tau+1,\gamma+1}}_{\text{Expected wealth}} - \underbrace{\lambda_{j,\tau,\gamma}(1-SR_{j,\tau,\gamma})HA_{j,\tau+1,\gamma+1}}_{\text{Expected annuity payout}} \tag{24}$$

or equivalently,

$$\underbrace{(1-\lambda_{j,\tau,\gamma}(1-SR_{j,\tau,\gamma}))HA_{j,\tau+1,\gamma+1}}_{\text{Expected net wealth}} + \underbrace{\lambda_{j,\tau,\gamma}(1-SR_{j,\tau,\gamma})HA_{j,\tau+1,\gamma+1}}_{\text{Expected annuity payout}} \equiv \underbrace{HA_{j,\tau+1,\gamma+1}}_{\text{Expected wealth}}$$

Let us now show that the last term in Eq. (24), $\lambda_{j,\tau,\gamma}(1 - SR_{j,\tau,\gamma})HA_{j,\tau+1,\gamma+1}$, is the expected (as of time-τ) annuity payout to be received at start of period τ +1, by the annuitant household. Given that an individual is alive at the start of period τ, $SR_{j,\tau,\gamma}$ gives the probability to survive period τ and thus to be alive at the start of period τ+1 while (1-$SR_{j,\tau,\gamma}$) gives the conditional probability to die during period τ. These probabilities can also be viewed as a share or proportion of the overall population of age γ because we assume no aggregate uncertainty for the insurance company.[15] Hence these probabilities are not stochastic but represent proportions known from population mortality tables. Therefore, the number of people of age γ that will not survive period τ is $Pop_{j,\tau,\gamma}(1 - SR_{j,\tau,\gamma})$. And on each of these non-surviving annuitants of age group γ, the insurance company expects to collect at the end of period τ (or start of τ+1) the annuitized wealth $\lambda_{j,\tau,\gamma}HA_{j,\tau+1,\gamma+1}$ where $\lambda_{j,\tau,\gamma} \in [0,1]$ is the share of wealth that is annuitized, so that in total the company collects for this age group γ the amount $Pop_{j,\tau,\gamma}(1 - SR_{j,\tau,\gamma})\lambda_{j,\tau,\gamma}HA_{j,\tau+1,\gamma+1}$.[16] We assume that the insurance industry is in perfect competition and, given free entry, makes zero profit. The insurance company just balances its books: it is receiving payments from those who die (their annuitized wealth) and, with this proceed, can make annuity payouts at the start of period τ+1 to surviving annuitants of the same age class and of cohort size now given by $Pop_{j,\tau+1,\gamma+1} = SR_{j,\tau,\gamma}Pop_{j,\tau,\gamma}$, so that each of them effectively receives:

$$A_{j,\tau+1,\gamma+1} = \frac{Pop_{j,\tau,\gamma}(1 - SR_{j,\tau,\gamma})\lambda_{j,\tau,\gamma}HA_{j,\tau+1,\gamma+1}}{Pop_{j,\tau+1,\gamma+1}} = \frac{(1 - SR_{j,\tau,\gamma})\lambda_{j,\tau,\gamma}HA_{j,\tau+1,\gamma+1}}{SR_{j,\tau,\gamma}} \tag{25}$$

However, during period τ the *expected* annuity payout at the start of τ+1 depends on the probability to survive or not, and is given by $SR_{j,\tau,\gamma}A_{j,\tau+1,\gamma+1} + (1 - SR_{j,\tau,\gamma}) \times 0 = SR_{j,\tau,\gamma}A_{j,\tau+1,\gamma+1}$.

This means that if the annuitant does not survive period τ, which happens with probability $(1 - SR_{j,\tau,\gamma})$, then at start of τ+1 the insurance company will not credit his annuity account (i.e., $A_{j,\tau+1,\gamma+1} = 0$ in this event). Based on this and Eq. 25 the time-τ expected annuity payout is therefore $SR_{j,\tau,\gamma}A_{j,\tau+1,\gamma+1} = \lambda_{j,\tau,\gamma}(1 - SR_{j,\tau,\gamma})HA_{j,\tau+1,\gamma+1}$ as was identified above in Eq. (24).

This has two implications. First, in order to have an amount of assets $HA_{j,\tau+1,\gamma+1}$ at the start of τ +1, the annuitant needs to target a level of asset at the end of τ that is *less* than $HA_{j,\tau+1,\gamma+1}$, and given by the amount $(1 - \lambda_{j,\tau,\gamma}(1 - SR_{j,\tau,\gamma}))HA_{j,\tau+1,\gamma+1}$ in Eq. (24) or Eq (5). We call this amount expected *net* wealth to illustrate that, on top of this amount the annuitant expects to receive additional assets in the form of a life-annuity payout, $\lambda_{j,\tau,\gamma}(1 - SR_{j,\tau,\gamma})HA_{j,\tau+1,\gamma+1}$, so that wealth at start of τ +1 is eventually $HA_{j,\tau+1,\gamma+1}$. Based on the left hand side of Eq. (5) this also means that an annuitant, all else the same, can save 'a bit less' during time τ, and yet reach $HA_{j,\tau+1,\gamma+1}$ at the start of τ +1 when the insurance company credits the annuitant account with the annuity payout.[17] The second implication is that the annuity payout deposit is not a money transfer (unlike, say, the pension benefit in Eq. 5), but an asset that is added (into the annuity account) and that must be sold (through dissaving) if, in the future, the individual wants to spend part of it on consumption goods.

A second useful decomposition of the first term on the left of Eq. 5 is:

$$\underbrace{(1-\lambda_{j,\tau,\gamma}(1-SR_{j,\tau,\gamma}))HA_{j,\tau+1,\gamma+1}}_{\text{Expected net wealth}} \equiv \underbrace{SR_{j,\tau,\gamma}\lambda_{j,\tau,\gamma}HA_{j,\tau+1,\gamma+1}}_{\text{Expected annuitized net wealth}} + \underbrace{(1-\lambda_{j,\tau,\gamma})HA_{j,\tau+1,\gamma+1}}_{\text{Non-annuitized wealth}} \quad (26)$$

This shows how the net wealth (i.e., net of annuity payout) expected as of time τ for the start of $\tau+1$, is split between expected annuitized wealth and non-annuitized wealth. Death has two very distinct effects in this context. With respect to expected annuitized wealth, we can rewrite the first term on the right hand side of Eq. 26 based on the two possible events (surviving or dying) as: $SR_{j,\tau,\gamma}\lambda_{j,\tau,\gamma}HA_{j,\tau+1,\gamma+1} + (1-SR_{j,\tau,\gamma})\times 0$. This means that in the event of an annuitant death during period τ (with probability$(1-SR_{j,\tau,\gamma})$), the amount $\lambda_{j,\tau,\gamma}HA_{j,\tau+1,\gamma+1}$ of wealth accumulated on the annuity account is entirely withdrawn by the insurance company at the start of $\tau+1$, setting the account to zero (i.e., closing the annuity account). With respect to non-annuitized wealth$(1-\lambda_{j,\tau,\gamma})HA_{j,\tau+1,\gamma+1}$, death has a different effect. The whole amount remains in the estate of the individual whether they survive or not, which explains why this term is not weighted by the survival rate in Eq. 26. Yet, the event of not surviving period τ implies that the individual leaves an unintentional bequest as long as $\lambda_{j,\tau,\gamma}\neq 1$. 'Unintentional' means that the deceased did not leave specific orders with respect to his estate at his death. This, of course, reflects the assumption that agents are not altruistic in this model (they do not value leaving a voluntary bequest to a specific heir). This has consequences for other individuals in the model because the accidental bequest must be distributed, and the distribution is arbitrary due to a lack of specific legal orders from the deceased. In the model we have assumed that the government taxes the non-annuitized wealth at death$(1-\lambda_{j,\tau,\gamma})HA_{j,\tau+1,\gamma+1}$, by 100%, and redistributes it equally to the surviving population of all age groups, $\sum_\gamma Pop_{j,\tau+1,\gamma}$. The variable $UnBeq_{j,\tau+1}$ represents the inheritance to be received at the start of period $\tau+1$ and is given by:[18]

$$UnBeq_{j,\tau+1} = \frac{\sum_\gamma (1-SR_{j,\tau,\gamma})Pop_{j,\tau,\gamma}(1-\lambda_{j,\tau,\gamma})HA_{j,\tau+1,\gamma+1}}{\sum_\gamma Pop_{j,\tau+1,\gamma}} \quad (27)$$

Recall that $(1-SR_{j,\tau,\gamma})Pop_{j,\tau,\gamma}$ represents the number of people of a specific age group that will not survive period τ. Hence, the numerator in (27) represents the aggregate non-annuitized wealth of all those, from all age groups, who did not survive period τ (i.e., will not be alive at the start of period $\tau+1$). And these assets are assumed to be equally distributed to all individuals alive at the start of period $\tau+1$(denominator).[19]

We can go from expected to actual/realised wealth by setting $SR_{j,\tau,\gamma} = 1$ in Eq. (26) if the individual indeed survives period τ, so as to obtain his actual wealth at start of period $\tau+1$:

$$\underbrace{HA_{j,\tau+1,\gamma+1}}_{\substack{\text{Actual wealth}\\\text{(inclusive of annuity payout)}}} = \underbrace{\lambda_{j,\tau,\gamma} HA_{j,\tau+1,\gamma+1}}_{\substack{\text{Actual annuitized wealth}\\\text{(inclusive of annuity payout)}}} + \underbrace{(1-\lambda_{j,\tau,\gamma}) HA_{j,\tau+1,\gamma+1}}_{\text{Non-annuitized wealth}} \tag{28}$$

Note that the first term on the right hand side of Eq. (29) necessarily includes the insurance payout. This can also be seen by substituting Eq. (26) into Eq. (24) to obtain that:

$$\underbrace{HA_{j,\tau+1,\gamma+1}}_{\substack{\text{Actual wealth}\\\text{(inclusive of annuity payout)}}} = \underbrace{\lambda_{j,\tau,\gamma}(SR_{j,\tau,\gamma}) HA_{j,\tau+1,\gamma+1}}_{\text{Expected annuitized net wealth}} + \underbrace{\lambda_{j,\tau,\gamma}(1 - SR_{j,\tau,\gamma}) HA_{j,\tau+1,\gamma+1}}_{\text{Expected insurance payout}} + \underbrace{(1-\lambda_{j,\tau,\gamma}) HA_{j,\tau+1,\gamma+1}}_{\text{Non-annuitized wealth}} \tag{29}$$

where the summation of the first two terms on the right hand side gives the first term on the right hand side of Eq.(28),$\lambda_{j,\tau,\gamma} HA_{j,\tau+1,\gamma+1}$. Finally, total actual wealth at start of $\tau+1$ (inclusive of distributed inheritance at start of $\tau+1$), is given by:

$$\underbrace{HA_{j,\tau+1,\gamma+1} + UnBeq_{j,\tau+1}}_{\substack{\text{Total actual wealth}\\\text{(inclusive of insurance pauout and inheritance)}}}$$

$$= \underbrace{\lambda_{j,\tau,\gamma} HA_{j,\tau+1,\gamma+1}}_{\substack{\text{Actual annutized wealth}\\\text{(inclusive of insurance pauout)}}} + \underbrace{(1-\lambda_{j,\tau,\gamma}) HA_{j,\tau+1,\gamma+1}}_{\text{Non-annuitized wealth}} + \underbrace{UnBeq_{j,\tau+1}}_{\text{Inheritance}} \tag{30}$$

All these concepts are represented graphically in Figures 2–6, for our calibrated OLG model under several annuitization schemes. Note that Figure 6b that represents the age profile of actual total wealth inclusive of inheritance is equivalent to Eq. (30) and, as such, these age profiles are the summation of age profiles in Figure 2 (expected/targeted annuitized wealth), Figure (3) (non-annuitized wealth), Figure 4 (expected annuity payout), and Figure 5 (inheritance). When observing these figures, compare the delayed annuity scheme with both the 100% and 0% annuitisation scenarios. Here, the delayed annuity scheme represents an individual who postpones his decision to annuitize until age 75 after which he annuitizes 100% of his wealth. Hence his non-annuitized wealth in Figure3 becomes zero when reaching age group G16 (75-79 years of age) in Figure 3 while his expected annuitized wealth (Figure

2) and annuity payout (Figure4) becomes positive. As discussed in the introduction, when people decide to annuitize their wealth, they generally do it later in life, and not when they start their economic life (here at G5 = 20 years). Of course, this is not a rational decision according to Yaari's (1965) framework whereby, if there is perfect annuity market and no voluntary bequest then individuals should annuitize 100% of their wealth. Yet the loss aversion concept of prospect theory and the desire to avoid regret suggest that individuals do not evaluate annuities as part of an overall optimization exercise but use a narrower framing such as whether the individual will live long enough to make back his initial investment. Annuities do not look attractive in this narrow framing because the losses from the annuity (if one dies young) loom larger than do the potential gains from living a long time (Hu and Scott, 2007). Furthermore, it may be optimal to delay annuitisation because the purchase of an annuity is (often) an irreversible investment decision under life length uncertainty, and in this context a decision to postpone purchase may be a better decision as people become more informed about, say, their health type and length of their retirement.

Figure 2. Expected annuitized net wealth at each age (targeted for next age/period) — First term, r.h.s. of Eq.26

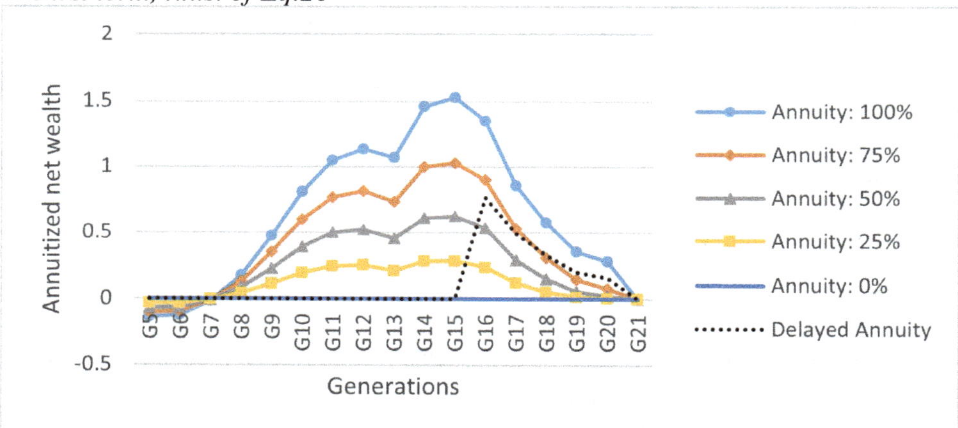

Figure 3. Non-annuitized wealth at each age (expected for start of next age/period) — Second term, r.h.s. of Eq.26

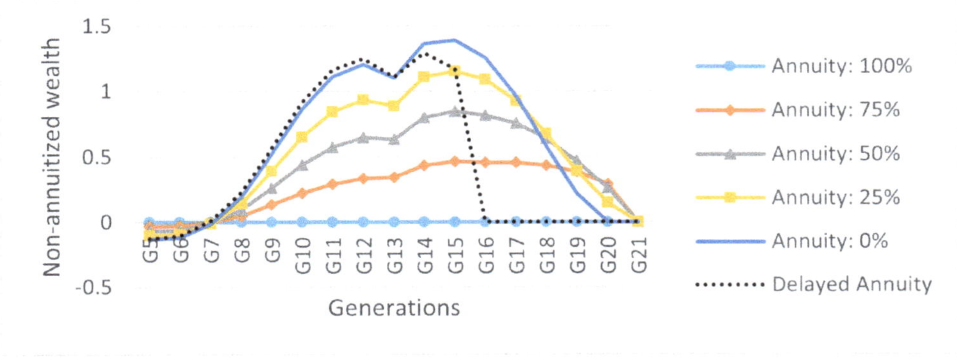

Figure 4. Expected age-dependent annuity payout (expected for start of next age/ period) — Second term, r.h.s. of Eq.24

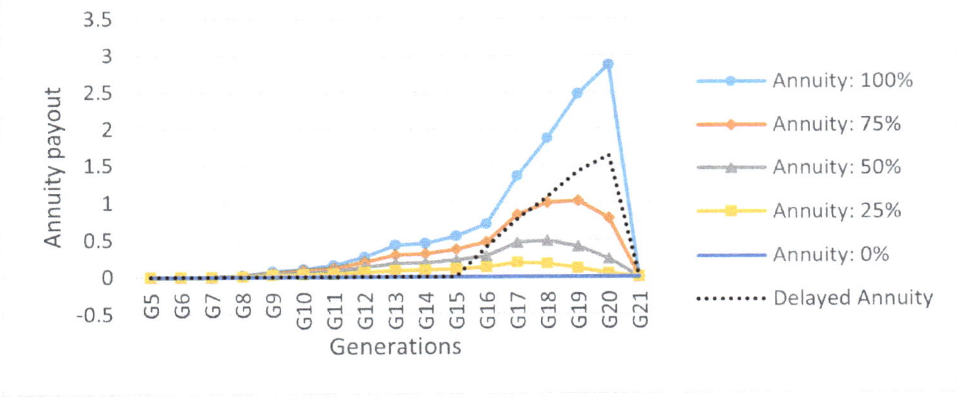

Figure 5. Inheritance from unintended bequests ($UnBeq_{j,\tau,\gamma}$) (start of period/age) —Eq.27

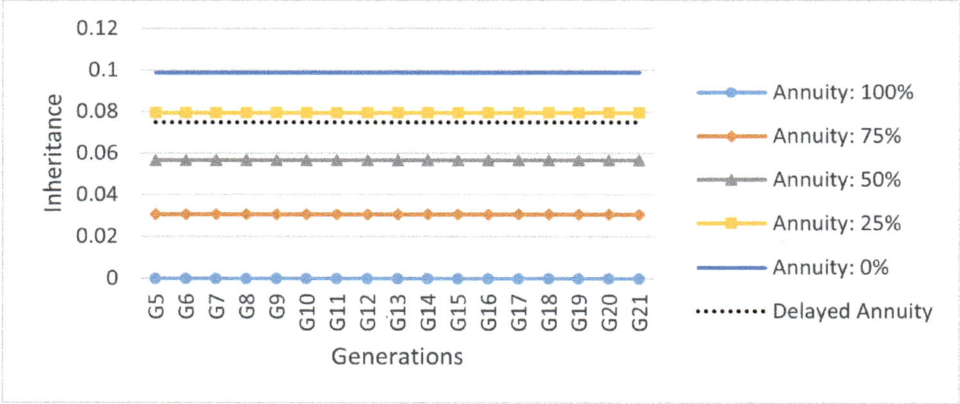

Figure 6a. Actual wealth (HA) at each age (start of period)—Eq.28

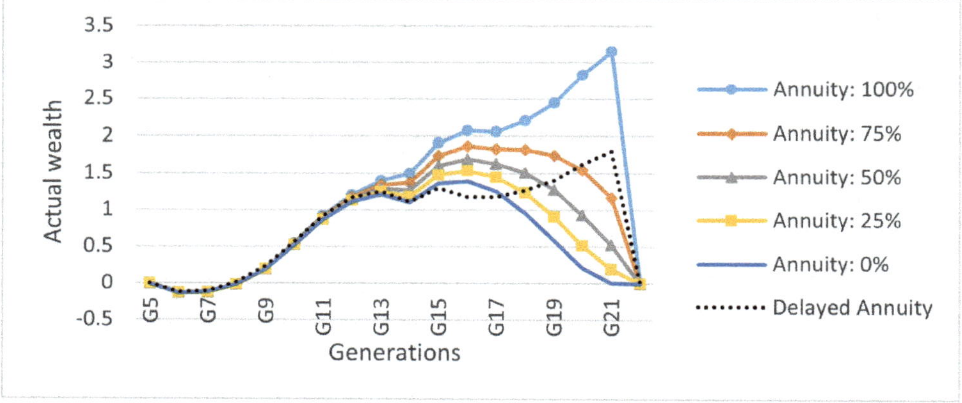

Figure 6b. Actual wealth including inheritance (HA+UnBeq) at each age (start of period) —Eq.30

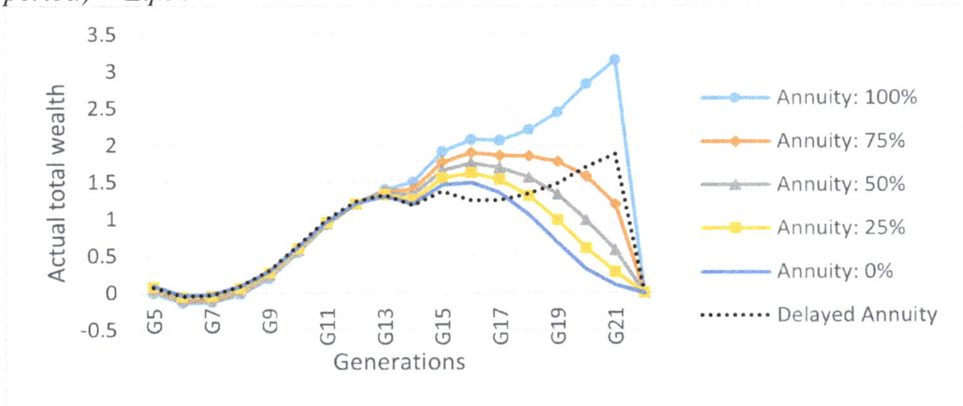

As mentioned in the introduction, the financial literature on annuity (see Rusconi, 2008) typically classifies annuities into 'immediate' and 'deferred' annuities where these two terms indicate when the distribution or payout phase of the annuity begins. Immediate annuities are funded with a single lump-sum of cash which is converted into an income stream which begins immediately. With a deferred annuity, the individual typically makes a series of premium payments over an accumulation period during which he builds up an annuitized wealth but the payout is deferred until some time in the future. In the model of section 2, the household has an annuity account that is made up of two parts, the expected annuitized net wealth and the expected insurance payout as can be seen in the first two terms in the l.h.s of Eq. 29. We can think of the first term as constitutive of the annuitant accumulated premium payments and the second term as the periodic insurance payout (annuitant income stream). Therefore the model of Section 2 does not clearly distinguishes between existing financial instruments of immediate and deferred annuities. There is an accumulation period (here a life-time accumulation period) during which the annuitant saves part of his wealth into an annuity account (the premium payments), which is one characteristic of a deferred annuity and which does not exist for immediate annuities (for which there is no accumulation period towards a specific annuity product). However, there is also a feature associated to an immediate annuity product in the sense that the flow of insurance payment starts immediately (as the insurance company redistributes as income flow the annuitized wealth of individuals who die, to agents of the same age class). Hence, the modeled annuity scheme has overlapping periods of accumulation and distribution which, in some sense, generates a mix of features of both immediate and deferred annuities. When modeling a delayed or age dependent annuity scheme (instead of, say, the 100% or

0% schemes), the individual makes the decision to convert a lump sum of cash into an immediate income stream much later in life and this is conceptually closer to the principle of an immediate annuity as is illustrated in Figures 2-4.

Figure 7 shows household saving (defined as the right hand side of Eq. 5). It shows that saving is slightly less in the earlier ages (G5 to G10, i.e., from 20 to 45 years of age) under the full annuitization scenario, while dissaving is more aggressive after retirement.[20] The reason is of course that the surviving annuitants are collecting substantial mortality insurance payouts (Figure 4) as assets that they sell (i.e., dissave) to increase their consumption (Figure 1). The dissaving in the very last period of life under this scenario is just equal to the annuity payout, and their final period consumption is financed by this dissaving plus the amount they receive under the PAYG pension plan (*Pens* in Eq. 5) and the inheritance they receive from involuntary bequest. The escalating (non-constant) annuity payout (Figure 4) in this modeling approach (and in all OLG-CGE models that have routinely introduced annuitization) illustrates that the annuity is age-dependent. The reason why the annuity payout increases with age is that when agents are modeled as relatively patient (rate of time preference lower than market interest rate), agents tend to save for the future. When surviving annuitants receive the annuity payout (from deceased annuitants from the same age class), they dissave part of it to sustain consumption, yet save the rest. When these annuitants in turn die, they leave a larger annuitized wealth (relative to the case when agents are assumed impatient), to surviving annuitants of the same age that are fewer and fewer as survival rates at these older ages dramatically plummet.

Figure 7. Household saving

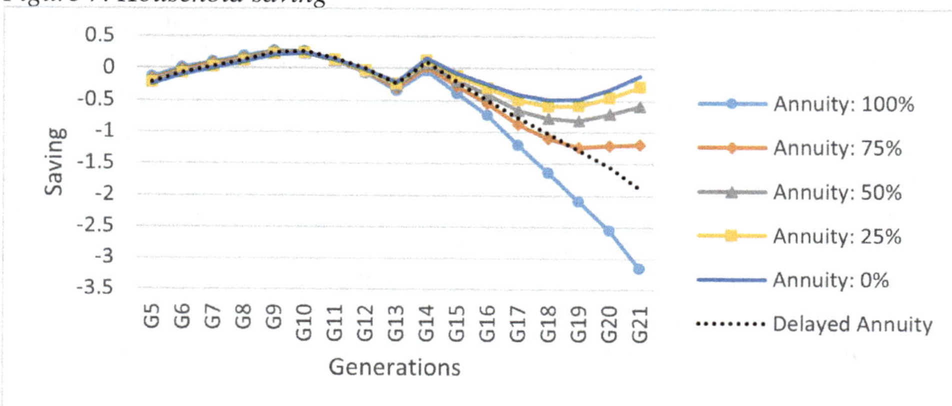

Returning to Figure 7, we see that under the zero annuitization scenario individuals dissave less at all ages relatively to the 100% annuitization scheme. In fact, as was seen in Figure 1, their consumption level starts to decline at some point, which corresponds to a reduced dissaving rate at that same age, reflecting that there remains some positive probability of surviving even longer and that prudence is required in face of wealth depletion (Figure 3). Note that in the zero annuitization case when annuitized wealth is zero across all ages (Figure 2), non-annuitized wealth in the model essentially falls to zero in the period just before the very last one (see Figure 3). This means that dissaving essentially falls to zero (Figure 7) in the very last period of life (G21). The individual's consumption spending is then constrained by the level of social security/pension benefits and inheritance received from unintentional bequests.

4. SOME SIMULATION RESULTS

Turkey's demography as projected by the UN medium variant scenario (UN population division, 2015 revision) and simulated by the model in Section 2, are given in Figure 8 and Figure 9. We see that from a population size of 79 million in 2015, it will reach a maximum of 96 million by 2060, after which it will progressively decline to 88 million by the end of the century. In terms of population structure, Figure 9 shows that the old age dependency ratio (OADR—the ratio of those who are 65 and plus, over the population aged 20-64) will grow from 12.9% in 2015 to 64.3% by end of century. Meanwhile, the young age dependency ratio (YADR—the ratio of those who are less than 20 year old over the population aged 20-64) will progressively decrease from 58.6% to 38.3%. Hence, total age dependency ratio (the summation of the two dependency ratios) will continue falling up to 2035 (from 71.6% to 66.6%) after which it will increase to reach 100% by the end of the century (i.e., one dependent per each adult aged 20-64). Inversely, the support ratio (population of 20-64 age groups over total population) will increase to 60% by 2030 and then very gradually decrease to 50% by the end of the century (i.e., one adult aged 20-64 per 2 consumers of any age).

Figure 8. Population in 1000's: Total (TPop), 0-19, 20-64, and 65 and +

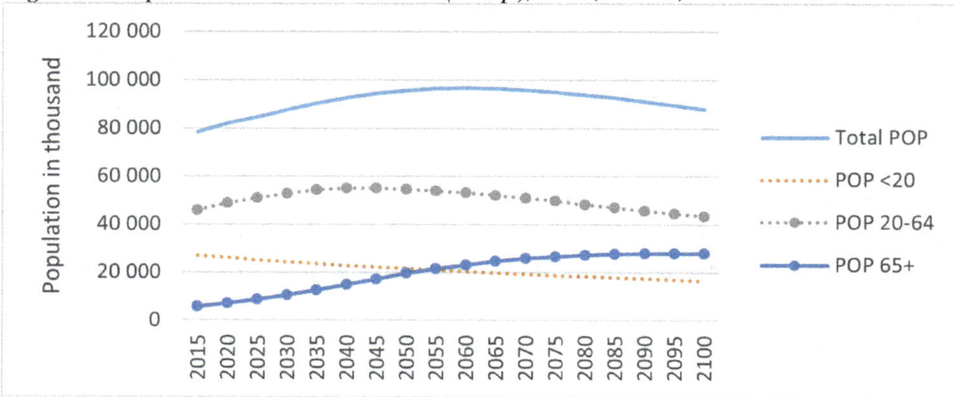

Figure 9. Dependency ratios and support ratio (Pop20-64/TPop) (in proportion)

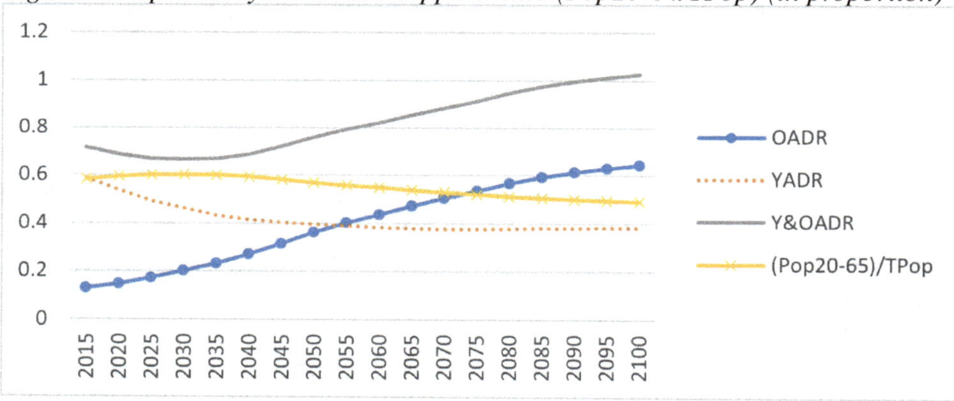

The simulated projections of the model described in Sections 2 and 3 help us to analyse the economic impact of demographic changes in Turkey as a relatively straightforward story.[21] It should be noted at the outset that the purpose of the exercise is not so much that of projecting into the future, but rather to make comparative assessments of alternative assumptions. In our analytical structure, we abstract away from technological progress so as to highlight the impact of wealth annuitization schemes in an environment of demographic changes. Therefore the major source of growth originates in the demographic shock on the labour supply and the endogenous accumulation of physical capital achieved by investment decision resulting itself from the intertemporal saving/consumption decision of households, which itself is affected by alternative annuitization schemes.

Let us first observe the general impacts of demographic changes assuming that the annuitization scheme is 100%, that is, all assets are annuitized. As can be seen in Figure 10, GDP per capita (Y/TPop) tends to increase until 2050 after which the ratio starts falling for demographic reason. To understand the impact on Y/TPop, recall that this ratio can be decomposed into GDP per effective worker (Y/L) times the effective support ratio (L/TPop) while Y/L is itself determined by the capital-labor (K/L) ratio (according to the Cobb-Douglas technology).[22] As can be seen in Figure 11, (and focusing only on the 100% annuitization case), the K/L ratio, and therefore, the Y/L ratio, continues to increase until 2065, while the support ratio L/TPop starts declining much earlier, by 2030. This means that the higher Y/L (or K/L) ratio dominates L/TPop on the evolution of Y/TPop between 2030 and 2050 in Figure 10. Between 2050 and 2065 the decline in the support ratio will dominate the positive effect of a higher K/L on Y/TPop. Finally, after 2065, the decline in the support ratio and K/L contribute to the decline in Y/TPop.

Figure 10. GDP per capita (Y/TPop)

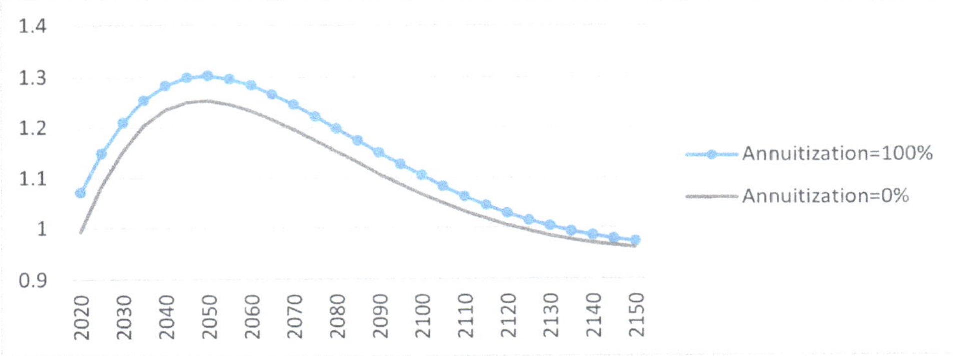

Figure 11. Y/L, K/L, L/Pop

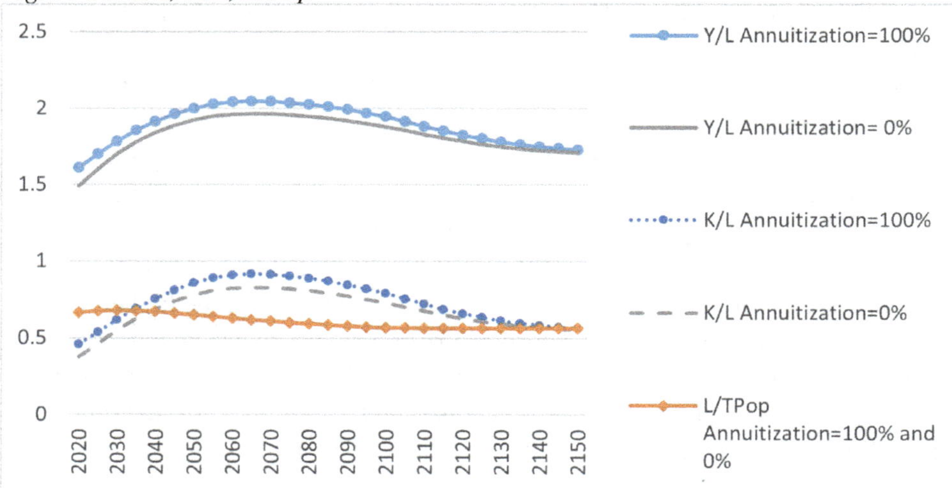

The K/L ratio is of course affected by the demographic trends, the changes in size and age structure of the population and the change in saving behaviour of households over the lifecycle. If the stock of capital remained constant throughout, then only the denominator, the effective labour supply, L, would explain the dynamics of the K/L path. Under this assumption we would expect a U-shaped path for the K/L ratio, mirroring somewhat the inverted-U shaped path of the population aged 20-65 in Figure 8.[23] The stock of capital will not remain constant, however, as shown in Figure 12, where it increases till 2060, triggering a capital deepening (an increase in the K/L ratio). The source of this capital deepening must originate from the saving behaviour of households. As can be seen in Figure 7, as long as the probability mass of the population is centered on middle-aged workers (say, G8-G11, i.e., 35-40 to 50-55 years of age) who reach their saving peaks, then we should expect an increase in capital. This will be progressively reversed once demographic changes push the probability mass of the population towards elder workers and retirees who save less or dis-save (Figure 7). In the case of Turkey, this appears to be in the 2060-2065 horizon, after which both the stock of capital and the K/L ratio decrease.[24] Rental factor prices are directly affected by variations in the K/L ratio (as obvious from Eq.2 and Eq.3) as shown in Figure 13. The wage rate continues to increase until 2065, as long as the K/L ratio increases and then decreases, while the rental price of capital falls first and then increase after 2065.

Figure 12. Kstock

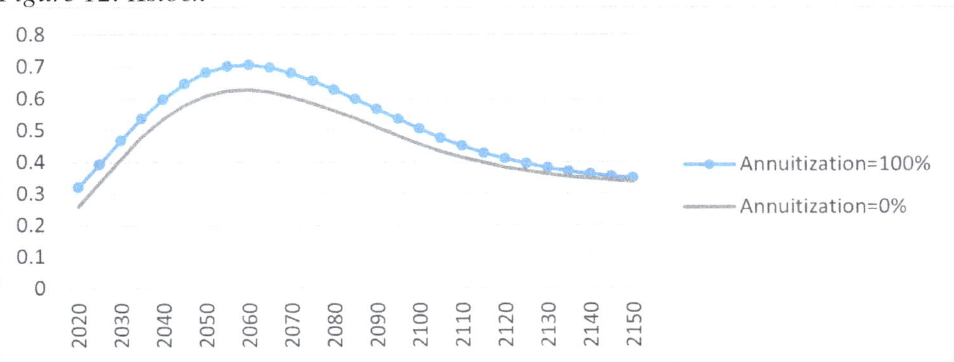

Figure 13. K/L and rental factor prices (wage and rental price of capital)

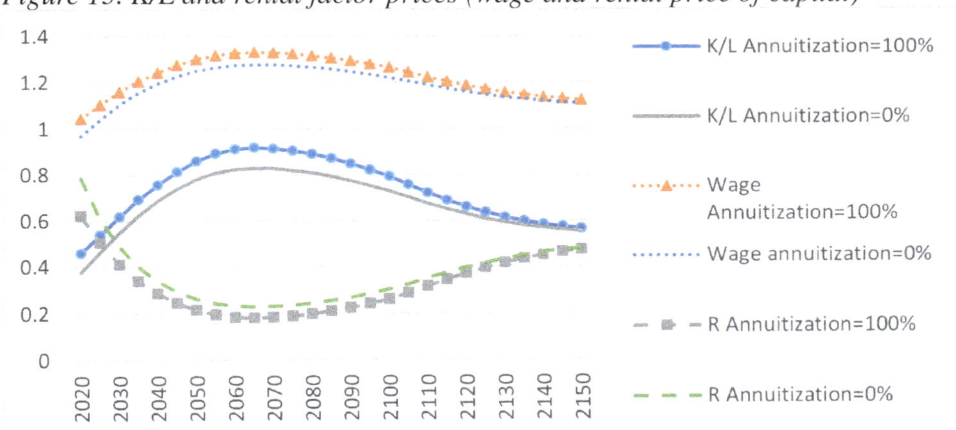

What is the role of annuitization schemes in this analysis? We only represent the two extreme scenarios of 100% and 0% asset annuitization in order to keep figures as clear as possible. All other annuitization scenarios fall graphically between these two extreme scenarios. As long as the country remains 'young', with a population density mass centered on young or middle age individuals (G5 to G11, i.e., 20-25 to 50-55 years of age) as is currently the case for Turkey, we observe in Figure 1 that fully annuitized households tend to consume a bit less (per capita), and thus save a bit more—see Figure 7—at these ages relative to the corresponding rates under a zero annuitization scheme. Consequently, we should expect under these circumstances a higher capital stock and lower interest rates under the 100% annuitization scheme, as can be seen in Figure 12 and Figure 13 in comparison to the 0% annuitization scheme. Concomitantly, the K/L ratio is also higher under the full annuitization scheme (see Figure 13), which props up the levels of Y/L and Y/TPop relative to the levels observed under the zero annuitization scenario (see, respectively, Figure 11 and Figure 10).

Of course, with progressive demographic changes over the time horizon this situation will slowly adjust once the population density mass shifts towards older workers and retirees. By 2055 the old age dependency ratio reaches 40% and the total dependency ratio reaches 80% (see Figure 9). Under the 100% annuitization scenario, as population ages, the high levels of consumption of older surviving annuitants (Figure 1) require large dissaving rates among elderly (Figure 7) which lowers aggregate saving and triggers stronger downward pressures on the stock of capital (Figure12) relative to the zero annuitization scenario where elderly dissaving is moderate. Also we observe stronger upward pressures on the interest rates and stronger downward pressures on the K/L ratio (Figure13) relative to the zero annuity scenario after about 2060. Hence, in Figure 13 we see that the interest rate differential across the two scenarios progressively decrease after 2060, which is also the case for the differentials in the K/L, Y/L and Y/TPop ratios (Figure 10 and Figure 11) that tend to converge across annuitisation scenarios.

One important consequence is therefore that the annuitization assumption imposed in an OLG-CGE model will, over the demographic transition, affect savings, investment, the K/L ratio, the GDP per worker ratio and eventually GDP per capita. In particular, our illustration for Turkey points out that assuming a 100% annuitization scenario might overestimate (be overly optimistic about) the impact of demographic changes in the economy if, *de facto*, people do not annuitize their wealth. Figure 10 shows that the overestimation in the GDP per capita is roughly 5% at the 2050 horizon.

Full annuitization will also typically overestimate the welfare effects of demographic dividends. Here, we use the compensating variation à la Hicks to quantify welfare effects. We compare the expected utility levels resulting from Eq. (4) with demographic changes from 2020 onwards versus a benchmark without the demographic changes. We compute the percentage change in consumption, gc_γ, (constant for each period of the life cycle) that an individual of a specific age group γ would require in the benchmark in order to be as well off as in the demographic change scenario. If an individual can reach an expected utility level of V_1 under the demographic shock and V_0 in absence of the shock, then $gc_\gamma = \left((V1_\gamma / V0_\gamma)^{1/(1-\theta_j)} - 1 \right) \times 100$ for the utility function given in Eq. 4. If gc_γ is positive, then the demographic shock is welfare improving for this age group γ, and vice versa. Figure 14 shows that under full annuitization, the demographic shock will have a positive impact for a few age groups who, in 2020 will be between 0 and 30 years of age, as well as a few age groups yet unborn in 2020. These generations take advantage of the demographic changes through higher wage rates over their entire lifetime while demographic dividends due to changes in the population structure may actually permit to lower the equilibrium wage tax rate (needed to finance the government budget) until 2050 (Figure15). Yet, future generations will bear the cost of the demographic changes through progressively increasing wage tax rates (Figure 15) and eventually very high contribution rates (Figure16) required to finance the social security. Note that the first generation effectively losing from the demographic shock will be born around 2040 according to Figure 14.

Figure 14. Welfare effects (current and future cohorts)

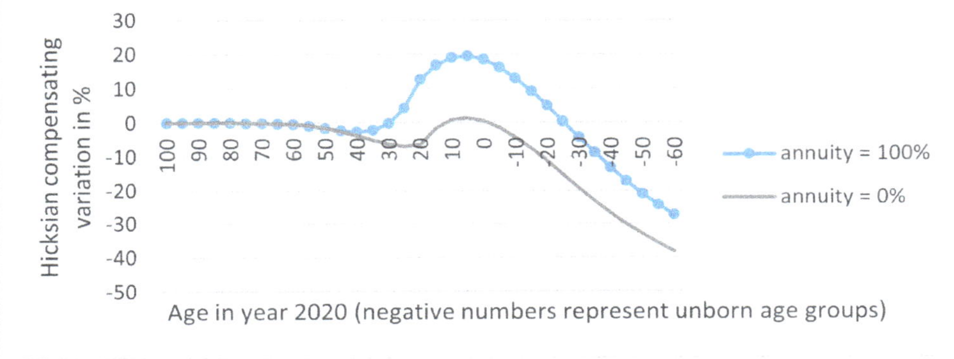

Figure 15. Wage tax rates

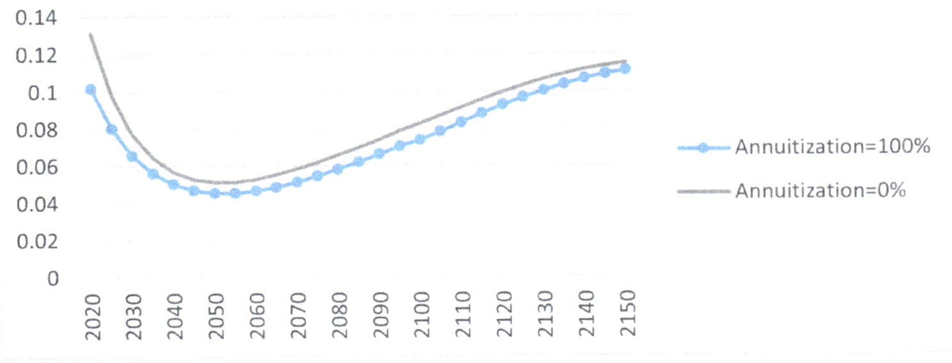

Figure 16. Contribution rates

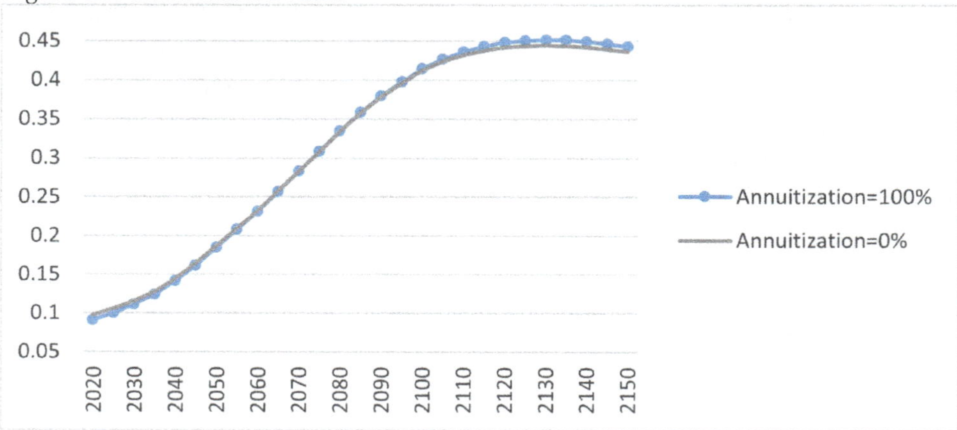

However, the essential point we want to illustrate here is that under a zero annuitization scheme the welfare effects are lower for most age groups. Fewer generations will actually benefit from the demographic changes – those who are 0-10 years old in 2020. Future generations to be born in 2025 and after will lose. The main reason behind this result is that the 100% annuitization scenario overestimates the K/L ratio, and therefore overestimates gross and net wage rates over the demographic transition.[25] Relatively, the 0% annuitization scenario leads to lower wage rates, affecting downwards the welfare of all generations and substantially reducing the number of generations that will effectively gain from the ongoing demographic changes.[26]

CGE studies typically test the robustness of their results by changing a few selected deep parameters such as the elasticity of substitution. More interestingly in our opinion, however, is the issue of whether results would be robust across countries, in particular, countries that are at different demographic stages. We claim that our results for Turkey are conditional on being a relatively young country whose population density mass is centered on young and middle-age population. Had we studied a country with a population density mass centered on an older population, those who tend to save less or dissave, then the economic impact of the counterfactual assumption of full asset annuitization could be reversed. As an illustration we have used the same OLG model but this time calibrated on the Canadian economy and using the UN medium variant demographic projections for Canada.[27] Figure 17 illustrates the K/L ratio for Canada for the two extreme annuitization scenarios. Observe that the Canadian K/L ratio for the 100% annuity case is below the ratio for the zero annuity case, which is the opposite of our results for Turkey (Figure 13). Furthermore, the K/L differential across both annuitisation scenarios *increases* over the simulated time horizon. Indeed, ageing in Canada pushes the population distribution mass from middle-age towards the elderly, generating a stronger dis-saving in the 100% (versus 0%) annuitization scenario and pushing the K/L ratio even further downwards. This will also worsen the negative impact of ageing on Y/L and Y/TPop ratios in Canada relative to a 0% annuity scenario. In other words, when assuming 100% annuitization, the negative impacts of ageing for relatively older countries will be overestimated in simulation results, that is, they will appear worse than they would under a more realistic assumption of no asset annuitization.

Figure 17. Y/L and K/L for Canada

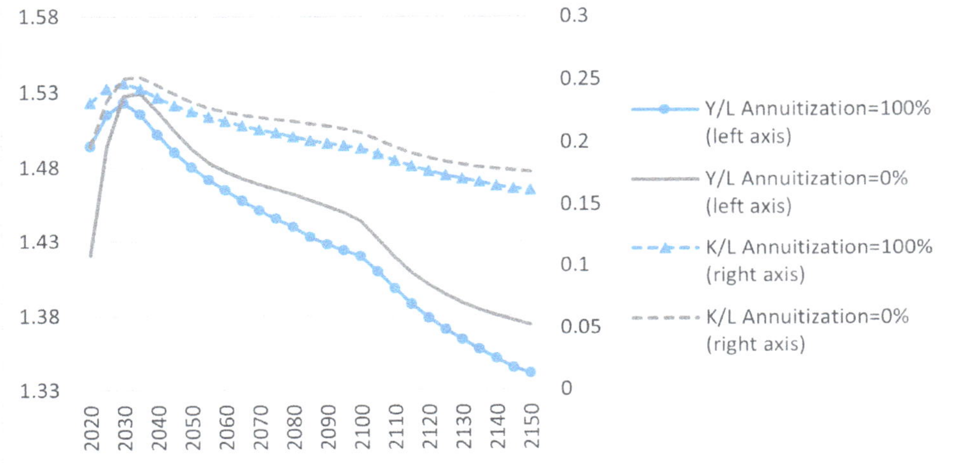

CONCLUSION

This paper analyses how wealth annuitization schemes have been routinely introduced in OLG-CGE models to cope with life-length uncertainty, and shows the impact of different annuitization schemes on calibration and simulation results in the context of realistic demographic changes.

Despite little evidence that agents do annuitize their wealth in the context of life-length uncertainty (i.e., the annuity paradox), over the last fifteen years OLG CGE studies have often introduced life-length uncertainty together with the assumption of fully annuitized assets. This 'counterfactual' assumption, however, is not neutral to the economic assessment of demographic changes.

Imposing full (100%) wealth annuitization leads to deeper capital accumulation (relative to a zero annuitization scheme) and, eventually, overestimates the positive economic impacts of demographic dividends in younger countries where the annuity market is thin. Yet, the analysis also demonstrates that the development of a life annuity market in a relatively young country such as Turkey would help boost the economic impact of the demographic dividends.

The analysis is reversed for countries more advanced in the ageing process. In this case, the negative impact of ageing will be overestimated (i.e., it will appear worse than it really is) relative to an assumption of little or zero wealth annuitization.

REFERENCES

Auerbach, A., & Kotlikoff, L. (1987). *Dynamic fiscal policy*. Cambridge University Press.

Börsch-Supan, A., Ludwig, A., & Winter, J. (2006). Aging, pension reform and capital flows: A multi-country simulation model. *Economica*, *73*, 625–658.

Broer, P., & Westerhout, E. (1997). Pension policies and lifetime uncertainty in an applied general equilibrium model. In Broer, P., & Lassila, J. (Eds.), *Pension policies and public debt in dynamic CGE models* (pp. 110–138). Physica-Verlag.

Brown, J. R. (2007). *Rational and behavioral perspectives on the role of annuities in retirement planning* (NBER Working Paper No. 13537). National Bureau of Economic Research.

Chateau, J. (2003). *Demographic and economic uncertainties in a large scale computable OLG model* (Working Paper No. 187). University of Washington.

Chauveau, T., & Loufir, R. (1997). The future of public pensions in the seven major economies. In Broer, P., & Lassila, J. (Eds.), *Pension policies and public debt in dynamic CGE models* (pp. 16–73). Physica-Verlag.

Cremer, H., & Pestieau, P. (2010). Longevity and annuities: An introduction. *Journal of Public Economic Theory*, *12*(1), 1–5.

Docquier, F., Liégeois, P., Loupias, C., & Crettez, B. (2002). Vieillissement et inégalités intergénérationnelles en France: Une approche par l'équilibre général. *Revue Économique*, *53*(4), 767–786.

Fehr, H., Jokisch, S., Kallweit, M., Kindermann, F., & Kotlikoff, L. (2013). Generational policy in closed and open dynamic general equilibrium models. In Dixon, P., & Jorgenson, D. (Eds.), *Handbook of computable general equilibrium modeling* (Vol. 1, pp. 1719–1800). Elsevier.

Fehr, H., Kallweit, M., & Kindermann, F. (2017). Families and social security. *European Economic Review*, *91*, 30–56.

Finkelstein, A., & Poterba, J. (2002). Selection effects in the United Kingdom individual annuities market. *Economic Journal (London)*, *112*(476), 28–50.

Fisher, I. (1930). *The theory of interest: As determined by impatience to spend income and opportunity to invest it*. The Macmillan Company.

Georges, P., & Seçkin, A. (2016). From pro-natalist rhetoric to population policies in Turkey? An OLG general equilibrium analysis. *Economic Modelling*, *56*, 79–93.

Georges, P., & Seçkin, A. (2017). *The role of life annuities in assessing the economic impact of demographic changes – An OLG general equilibrium investigation* [Manuscript]. University of Ottawa.

Hu, W.-Y., & Scott, J. S. (2007). *Behavioral obstacles to the annuity market* [SSRN Working Paper]. March.

Imrohoroglu, S. (1998). A quantitative analysis of capital income taxation. *International Economic Review*, *39*(2), 307–328.

Insurance Association of Turkey. (2018). *Life insurance review and research committee position paper*. https://www.tsb.org.tr/images/Documents/Teknik/Hayat%20Sigortas%C4%B1%20Pozisyon%20Belgesi%20-%20Ocak%202018-%C4%B0ngilizce.pdf

Kenc, T., & Sayan, S. (2001). Demographic shock transmission from large to small countries: An overlapping generations CGE analysis. *Journal of Policy Modeling*, *23*, 677–702.

Kotlikoff, L. J., Smetters, K. A., & Walliser, J. (2007). Mitigating America's demographic dilemma by pre-funding social security. *Journal of Monetary Economics*, *54*, 247–266.

Krueger, D., & Ludwig, A. (2007). On the consequences of demographic change for rates of return to capital, and the distribution of wealth and welfare. *Journal of Monetary Economics*, *54*(1), 48–87.

Lee, R., & Mason, A. (2011). *Population aging and the generational economy—A global perspective*. Edward Elgar Publishing.

Luo, S. (2017). *Aging, dissaving, and the role of life annuities* [M.A. major paper]. Department of Economics, University of Ottawa.

Rios-Rull, J. (1996). Life-cycle economies and aggregate fluctuations. *The Review of Economic Studies*, *63*, 465–489.

Rios-Rull, J. (2001). Population changes and capital accumulation: The aging of the baby boom. *Advances in Macroeconomics, 1*(1), Article 7.

Rusconi, R. (2008). *National annuity markets: Features and implications* (OECD Working Papers on Insurance and Private Pensions No. 24). OECD Publishing.

Seçkin, A., Georges, P., & Sahanoğulları, N. (2014). *National transfer accounts for Turkey* [Manuscript]. University of Ottawa & Istanbul Bilgi University.

Sinclair, S. H., & Smetters, K. A. (2004). *Health shocks and the demand for annuities* (Technical Paper Series No. 2004-09). Congressional Budget Office.

Turra, C. M., & Mitchell, O. S. (2005). *The impact of health status and out-of-pocket medical expenditures on annuity valuation* (Research Brief No. RB 2005-079). University of Michigan Retirement Research Center.

Voyvoda, E., & Yeldan, E. (2005). Managing Turkish debt: An OLG investigation of the IMF's fiscal programming model for Turkey. *Journal of Policy Modeling*, *27*(6), 743–765.

Yaari, M. E. (1965). Uncertain lifetime, life insurance, and the theory of the consumer. *The Review of Economic Studies*, *32*(2), 137–150.

KEY TERMS AND DEFINITIONS

Aging trap: A situation where rapid population aging slows economic growth and strains public finances before a country becomes sufficiently wealthy.

Annuity: A financial product that provides regular payments to a person, usually after retirement, in exchange for an initial lump-sum payment or series of contributions.

CGE modelling (Computable General Equilibrium modelling): An economic modeling approach that uses mathematical equations to simulate how an economy reacts to policy changes, shocks, or wdemographic shifts, assuming markets clear and agents optimize.

Demographic changes: Shifts in the size, structure, and characteristics of a population over time, including changes in birth rates, death rates, migration, and age distribution.

Demographic window: A period when a country has a high proportion of working-age people relative to dependents (children and elderly), creating potential for accelerated economic growth.

Life annuities: Financial contracts that provide regular payments to an individual for the rest of their life, typically in exchange for an upfront premium.

Life-cycle earnings: The total income an individual earns over their working lifetime, often following a pattern of low income when young, higher in middle age, and lower again near retirement.

OLG model (Overlapping Generations model): A macroeconomic model that analyzes interactions between different generations (young and old) living at the same time, often used to study savings, pensions, and public debt.

Population aging: The increase in the proportion of older individuals (usually 65+) in a population, typically due to lower birth rates and longer life expectancy.

Wealth annuitization: The process of converting accumulated savings or assets into an annuity to generate a steady income stream, usually during retirement.

ENDNOTES

1 Besides the introduction of life length uncertainty, several OLG models have been developed and extended in many other directions over the last 20 years. For a survey of these advances, see Fehr et al. (2013) and references therein.

2 These models typically define a *maximum* life-length (say, 100 years). In case individuals are considered egoistic/not altruistic, they plan their life-time consumption/saving decisions so that their wealth would reach zero in the very last period of their life. 'Early' death (before 100 years) may therefore imply involuntary or unintended bequest. If, on the other hand, individuals are considered altruistic, then a voluntary or intended bequest is specified as an argument of the individual life-time expected utility. It is often assumed that the voluntary bequest is bequeathed conditional on the individual reaching the very last period of his maximum life-length. Early debt would lead to involuntary bequest. We can, however, model a trade-off between consumption and voluntary bequest at each period of the lifecycle and in this case voluntary bequest is effectively transferred in case of early death (see Hansen and Imrohoroglu, 2007). Voluntary bequest is often not modeled, however. In this paper we assume that individuals are not altruistic.

3 The insurance industry is assumed to be in perfect competition and, given free entry, makes zero profit. The insurance company just balances its books: it is receiving payments from those who die (their annuitized wealth) and, with this proceed, can make annuity payouts to surviving annuitants of the same age class. The insurance company faces no uncertainty because, although individuals are uncertain about the length of their life, the population is assumed large enough to ensure aggregate certainty over the population of each cohort.

4 Although much of the economic literature suggests that most individuals would find annuities welfare enhancing, the empirical evidence suggests that individuals do not act as if they value them very highly. Several reasons have been suggested to explain this paradox, such as the existence of a voluntary bequest motive (Yaari, 1965); the existence of public pensions in the form of Pay As You Go defined benefits that already represent a form of annuitization scheme, leading to low demand for additional (private) annuitization (Hu and Scott, 2007); incomplete annuity markets that leaves individuals exposed to

other risks, such as inflation risk (Finkelstein and Poterba, 2002), or annuity contracts that do not generally permit to borrow against the future value of an annuity (as wealth would permit), generating liquidity concerns, for example in the case of unexpected health care expenditures especially when they arise earlier in life (Sinclair and Smetters, 2004; Turra and Mitchell, 2005). Finally, the loss aversion concept of prospect theory and the desire to avoid regret may suggest that individuals do not evaluate annuities as part of an overall optimization exercise but use a narrower framing such as whether the individual will live long enough to make back his initial investment. Annuities do not look attractive in this narrow framing because the losses from the annuity (if one dies young) loom larger than do the potential gains from living a long time (Hu and Scott, 2007).

5 At younger ages, annuity payouts tend to be lower than actually fair levels, or in other terms, the expected net present value of payouts is less that the premium (the wealth transferred to the insurance company in case of death). This may be due to adverse selection in that individuals with poor self-reported health are less likely to express an interest in an annuity scheme so that mortality rates of annuitants is below that of the general population. Of course, unfair prices could also be due to the fact that insurance companies are unable to adequately hedge aggregate mortality risk in the population, and therefore must charge a higher price to compensate for this risk. See Finkelstein and Poterba, 2002, Brown, 2001, Brown, Casey and Mitchell, 2007, Blake and Burrows, 2001, Blake, Cairns and Dowd, 2006, Blake, Burrows and Orszag, 2002, Friedberg and Webb, 2006, Brown and Orszag, 2006, among others.

6 Note also that if an individual dies during a period $t+k$, then death is accounted for at the end of the period $t+k$, so that the individual is assumed to consume $Con_{j,t+k,g+k}$ in its integrality during this last period of his life.

7 Although the individual in Eq. (1) starts its 'economic' adult life at the start of period t, he was previously a dependent child who has survived up to the start of period t. Effectively, these individuals have already been through four 5-years periods, from age groups 0-4 to 15-19. See Eq. (23) for the actual demographic process. Conditional on being alive at the start of period t-1 (when the individual reached age g-1, that is, the age group 15-19), the first term $SR_{j,t-1,g-1}$, in the multiplicative expression $\prod_{k=0}^{k=i-1} SR_{j,t+k-1,g+k-1}$, represents the survival rate or probability to survive period t-1 and thus being alive at the start of period t when they reach age g (the age group 20-24). Ex post, that is, at the start of t this term, $SR_{j,t-1,g-1}$, equals 1.

8 We assume an individual economically born at the start of period $\tau=t$ and whose death will be no later than at end of period $\tau=t+16$. We rewrite Eq. (5) as an intertemporal budget constraint taking into account that, in absence of a voluntary bequest, the individual would plan to save nothing, sell all its remaining assets and consume the proceeds. Hence, at the end of $\tau=t+16, HA_{j,\tau+1,\gamma+1}=HA_{j,t+17,g+17} = 0$ in the first term on the left hand side of Eq. (5). Also, at the start of his first period of adult life the individual has no assets. Hence, at start of $\tau=t, HA_{j,\tau,\gamma}=HA_{j,t,g} = 0$ in the right hand side of Eq. (5).

9 As shown by Hansen and Imrohoroglu (2007), this hump-shaped profile does not necessarily fit the data. There are of course several alternative ways to achieve hump-shaped age consumption profiles. One way to proceed in an OLG model is by introducing endogenous labor supply, as was initially proposed by Auerbach and Kotlikoff (1987). Alternatively, we can introduce explicit household/family formation (instead of having an individual-based household) and allow adults to make explicit consumption decisions on behalf of their children (Attanasio et al. 1999, Kotlikoff et al., 2007, Sánchez-Romero et al., 2012). None of these alternative approaches guarantees that it will fit the hump-shaped age consumption profile observed in data.

10 The procedure in Table 2b is actually applied to two UN projections: the overall medium variant scenario (inclusive of UN migration projections) and a zero migration scenario (net of migration projections). The method in Table 2b permits to compute 1) a 'pure' survival rate *SR*0 (net of the migration rate) –used in Eq. (23)– on the basis of the zero migration scenario and 2) a gross survival rate inclusive of a migration rate, on the basis of the overall medium variant scenario. The difference between these two rates generates an implied age-dependent migration rate, *MR*, which is also used in Eq. (23).

11 Data, when available, are from TUIK, the Turkish Statistical Institute.

12 In general, in developing countries such as Turkey the labor share is around 0.5-0.65 and the capital share, α, is thus around 0.35-0.5. See Altuğ et al. (2008), Ismihan and Metin-Ozcan (2009), and Tiryaki (2011) for discussions on the values of factor income shares in Turkey.

13 *OECD (2015) Labor force participation stats.*

14 Consumption taxes are the most important source of revenues used to finance public spending in Turkey, where the share of taxes on consumption (general consumption taxes plus specific consumption taxes) is more than 40%. Üngör (2014) finds that the average effective tax rate on consumption in Turkey increased from around 10.5% in 1998 to around 15.5-16.5% in 2012.

15 The insurance company faces no uncertainty because, although individuals are uncertain about the length of their life, the population is large enough to ensure aggregate certainty over the population of each cohort.

16 Total wealth collected at the end of period τ by the insurance company on non-surviving individuals across all age groups is: $\sum_{\gamma} Pop_{j,\tau,\gamma}(1 - SR_{j,\tau,\gamma})\lambda_{j,\tau,\gamma} HA_{j,\tau+1,\gamma+1}$.

17 When involuntary bequest is zero, saving 'a bit less' means, here, saving less than the actual difference between assets at end and start of period, $HA_{j,\tau+1,\gamma+1} - HA_{j,\tau,\gamma}$.

18 Given perfect foresight, this is also the inheritance expected as of period τ by any individual in the model and collected at the start of $\tau + 1$.

19 Note that $UnBeq_{j,\tau,\gamma}$ is assumed to be age-independent – each individual receives the same inheritance independent of their age, so that $UnBeq_{j,\tau,\gamma} = UnBeq_{j,\tau}$.

20 Note the saving peak at age 65 (G14) in Figure 7 when the dissaving rate is pushed back into a positive saving rate, which reflects that agents at that age start collecting pension benefits from the PAYG pension system.

21 Technically, the model is simulated from 1940 to 2260. It starts in 1940 for welfare analysis purposes and ends in 2260 to also ensure a stationary sate. The model is simulated using GAMS software.

22 The effective support ratio not only takes into account the working-age over total population ratio (captured in Figure9), but also participation rates of the working age population and the age (i.e., experience) dependent effectiveness of each unit of labour supply.

23 Of course, we would still need to take into account labor participation rates and age-dependent effective labour supply.

24 There is a small lag in the K/L response to the decline in K in 2060 because the decrease in the number of effective workers dominates the decrease in the stock of capital in that period, implying that K/L continues to increase until 2065 even if K starts to decrease in 2060.

25 For the gross wage rate, see Figure 13. For net wage rates, consider the wage tax rates in Figure 15 that is lower under the 100% (vs. 0%) annuitization scenario. One reason is that the 100% annuitization scenario enhances the stock of capital. This leads to larger capital tax revenues, which permits to finance the government budget at lower equilibrium wage tax rates. Note from Figure 16 that the contribution rate is little affected by the annuitization scenario. This results from Eq. (16) where pension benefits of the elderly are directly financed

from labour income of current workers. From Eq. (15), pension benefits under the zero annuity scenario tend to be lower (relative to the full annuity scenario) because labour income over the entire lifetime is lower (Figure13). However, this does not permit to lower the equilibrium contribution rate in Eq. (16) because the labour income of current generations of workers who finance the pension benefits is also lower (the r.h.s. of Eq. 16).

26 Only senior individuals who are 65 years old and over in 2020 (and therefore receiving only interest revenues), are marginally better off in the zero (versus 100%) annuity scenario thanks to a higher interest rate.

27 See Luo (2017) for a description of the Canadian OLG model also used here.

Chapter 2

Forecasting Population Ageing in Emerging Economies:

A Machine Learning and Econometric Comparison of Old-Age Dependency Ratios in BRICS

Mohd Adil
http://orcid.org/0009-0008-7353-0965
Jamia Millia Islamia, New Delhi, India

Saba Ismail
Jamia Millia Islamia, New Delhi, India

ABSTRACT

The present chapter investigates long-term population aging within the BRICS economies using the Old-Age Dependency Ratio (OADR) from 1975 to 2024, with projections up to 2050. The findings show strong heterogeneity in the aging trajectories. Brazil's OADR more than doubles from 16.6 percent in 2025 to above 33 percent by 2050, while Russia stays ahead as the oldest economy, overtaking 31 percent at mid-century. India and South Africa remain relatively young; for instance, India's OADR rises gradually from 10.8 percent to around 17 percent. The forecast evaluation metrics results indicate that ARIMA models perform better than the machine learning approaches in nearly all the BRICS economies. The machine learning models tend to yield flat projections across horizons; thus, they have limited ability to capture the long-run dynamics of demographic change. These findings highlight

DOI: 10.4018/979-8-3373-7483-3.ch002

the importance of reliable demographic forecasting for supporting effective labor market policies, pension planning, and long-term economic decision-making in ageing societies.

1. INTRODUCTION

One of the most significant demographics changes the world has experienced in recent history has been the process of population ageing. This has been caused by the fall in birth rates, the rise in life expectancy, and the natural process of cohort effects over time. This process has been experienced in developed and developing countries alike, with the former traditionally being the focal point of concern. However, the current data indicate that the rising economies are undergoing the process much more rapidly than before, and with much more stringent constraints (Lee & Mason, 2011). The most commonly used measure of the process of population ageing has been the use of the old-age dependency ratio (OADR), which refers to the ratio of the aged population, i.e., those aged 65 and older, to the working age population. An increase in the OADR indicates rising dependency on the working population and, therefore, structural changes in the economy. The BRICS economies, which include Brazil, Russia, India, China, and South Africa, play an important role in the demographic and economic evolution of the world. These five economies account for over 40% of the total population and approximately one-fourth of the total economic output of the world. However, the timing and rate of the process of population ageing vary significantly across the BRICS economies because of significant differences in fertility rates, mortality rates, and levels of development and institutions (Lal, 2023). Thus, the process of population ageing in the BRICS economies assumes significant importance, not only for individual economies but also for the world as a whole.

In all BRICS economies, there are differing rates of population ageing. China and Russia are in a more mature stage of population ageing, with a high dependency ratio attributed to low birth rates and increased longevity (Li et al., 2022; Shcherbakova, 2022). For instance, China's population has been under intense government regulations to control population growth over several decades. This has resulted in a high dependency burden of older persons (Li & Ao, 2026; Mi et al., 2020). In contrast, Russia is also facing a number of challenges in terms of population ageing, health disparities among older persons, and disparities in healthcare services (Ivanova et al., 2023). In Brazil, there is a projected increase in the number of older persons in the coming years. This is a challenge to healthcare services and social protection in Brazil, particularly in terms of the Unified Health System (SUS), which is under pressure from increasing cases of non-communicable diseases among older persons

(Oliveira & Pinheiro, 2023; Souza et al., 2024). Despite a high rate of pension coverage for older persons in Brazil, there are concerns over sustainability of social security in Brazil (Paiva & Ansiliero, 2025).

In contrast to Brazil, India and South Africa are not at a high risk of population ageing at present. However, in both countries, there is a projected increase in population ageing over time. In India, there are several reforms in pension schemes, such as the National Pension System (NPS), which is a significant step towards a sustainable social security system. However, a large number of persons are not covered by pension schemes in India, attributed to high levels of informal labor (Deeti, 2023; Goli et al., 2019). In South Africa, there are socioeconomic challenges attributed to population ageing, such as disparities in healthcare services and labor market inequalities, despite a relatively younger population (Daviaud et al., 2019; MacLennan et al., 2014). While there has been an increasing number of studies on demographic ageing, few have attempted to compare and evaluate the relative merits of traditional econometric modelling and more recent advances in machine learning (ML) algorithms in predicting emerging economic indicators such as the OADR. Most earlier studies relied on traditional econometric modelling techniques, using autoregressive and related techniques to forecast demographic ageing (Chang & Lai, 2019; Hyndman et al., 2021). In more recent times, ML algorithms have gained popularity in economic prediction and modelling due to their ability to identify non-linear patterns and complex data structures (Chen & Guestrin, 2016; Fawagreh et al., 2014). The relative merits of using ML algorithms in long-term prediction, where trends are generally smooth and gradual, are yet to be ascertained.

This chapter aims to fill this gap by presenting a comparative analysis of traditional econometric modelling and ML algorithms in predicting the OADR in BRICS countries. The chapter compares traditional econometric modelling using the Autoregressive Integrated Moving Average (ARIMA) model against more recent advances in ML algorithms, including Random Forest, Extreme Gradient Boosting (XGBoost), and LightGBM. The chapter aims to provide an assessment of which approach is more suitable in predicting demographic ageing in emerging markets. This chapter has two major contributions. The first is to provide a cross-country comparison of ageing trends using traditional econometric modelling and ML algorithms in BRICS economies. The second is to provide an assessment of which approach is more suitable in predicting emerging economic indicators such as the OADR. By combining traditional demographic modelling and prediction, this chapter contributes to both theoretical and practical discussions on the implications of demographic ageing in emerging markets.

The rest of this chapter is organized as follows; Section 2 of this chapter reviews what previous studies had to say about population aging and methods of demographic forecasting; Section 3 of this chapter describes the data sources and methodology;

Section 4 of this chapter presents the results and a comparison of forecasting performance in the BRICS economies; Section 5 of this chapter engages in a broader discussion of demographic forecasting and its implications, especially in terms of labor force ageing; Section 6 concludes the study, And finally, Section 7 complete with a discussion of limitations and future research directions.

2. LITERATURE REVIEW

The issue of population ageing has increasingly been a point of interest for researchers due to its significant effects on labor forces, social protection strategies, and long-term economic sustainability. The OADR is commonly used as a critical parameter to assess the effects of a growing population in relation to ageing. The parameter is used to calculate the number of elderly persons in a population in comparison to the working population. An increasing OADR is a critical parameter indicating growing pressure on the working population, which is a reflection of structural changes in economic and social systems. As a result, the study of OADR is increasingly a point of interest in economic and social studies.

Research into population ageing has been focused on cohort effects and long-term demographic transitions. An age-period-cohort analysis by Rentz & Reynolds (1991) was used to illustrate the effects of ageing in relation to consumption and economic behaviour, which are determined by path-dependent demographic processes. The study of ageing is critical in understanding the effects of ageing in relation to dependency ratios, which are determined by structural factors such as declining birth rates and survival rates (Slaveva, 2023). A number of studies have widely used time series models in forecasting demographic parameters and dependency ratios. The study by Chang & Lai (2019) provided a comprehensive analysis of ARIMA models in forecasting population dependency ratios. The study indicated that ARIMA models are effective in forecasting dependency ratios in relation to trend behaviour and autocorrelation in population data. Similarly, a study by Megeri (2023) focused on forecasting demographic and economic projections in India using ARIMA models. The study confirmed the use of econometric models in forecasting population data. Hyndman et al. (2021) further explored the use of time series models in forecasting OADR in estimating sustainable pensionable ages. Apart from the methods of econometrics, several studies have tried to use other methods of modelling to study demographic ageing. For example, Vahidi Monfared and Moini (2019) applied system dynamics modelling to forecast Iran's ageing population. Although these methods provide interesting results from a theoretical point of view regarding demographic dynamics, they require complex assumptions and procedures that may make it difficult to compare results with other econometric methods of forecasting.

In recent years, researchers have shown interest in using ML methods to forecast demographic and socioeconomic data. ML methods have proven to be very efficient in modelling complex relationships and intricate interactions among data points. For example, Noh et al. (2021) applied an XGBoost-based ML method to forecast fall risks among older adults. ML methods have also proven to be very efficient in analysing health-related outcomes among older adults. For example, Handing et al. (2022) applied ML methods to identify predictors of depression among middle-aged and elderly Europeans. Shen et al. (2023) applied ML methods to forecast life satisfaction among older adults. Despite the mentioned applications of ML methods to forecast health-related outcomes among older adults, few studies have applied ML methods to forecast demographic data. For example, Lu et al. (2021) applied ML estimators to study the relationship between age dependency and energy demand among BRICS economies. ML methods were found to be very efficient in analysing nonlinear relationships among data points. Suresh et al. (n.d.) applied ML methods to study socioeconomic indicators related to demographic dynamics. Although ML methods were found to be very efficient in analysing demographic data, there is no clear evidence of ML methods' superiority over other econometric methods of forecasting.

Recent methodological studies also indicate the limitations in the use of ML models for the forecasting of smooth time series data. Demographic data, like the OADR, tend to change slowly and show strong persistence over time due to more fundamental demographic factors. For these data, the performance of the ML models, particularly tree-based models, might be poor in forecasting long-term trends beyond the data on which the models were trained. This has been supported by the literature on forecasting, which has shown the excellent performance of traditional time series models on variables with strong temporal patterns and gradual changes in trends (Hyndman et al., 2021; Makridakis et al., 2020). Regarding the emerging economies, the BRICS countries represent the most important case for the analysis of demographic ageing. Although demographic ageing affects the BRICS economies, the rate and timing of the process differ substantially. do Nascimento (2020) highlighted the fact that demographic ageing affects the BRICS economies, yet the rate varies over time because of differences in historical demographic and economic development. Johnston (2024) highlighted the potential risks of the emerging economies "getting old before getting rich," particularly in cases when demographic ageing occurs before the start of economic development. The literature on demographic ageing also indicates the economic and social impacts of demographic ageing. Baharin and Saad (2018) highlighted the fact that demographic ageing can lead to increased healthcare costs if the healthcare system fails to adapt to the changing demographic structure. Moreover, Harasty and Ostermeier (2020) highlighted the fact that traditional dependency ratios might underestimate the contribution of older individuals to the labor market, despite the fact that rising dependency ratios pose important problems for the labor market. For the case of India, Vaishnav et al. (2022) highlighted the analysis of the implementation of the National Programme for Health Care of the Elderly and the need for continuous work in adapting to the rising demands of the ageing population.

While there has been an increasing focus on the topic of demographic ageing, there are still some gaps in the literature. There has been little research done on the comparison of conventional econometric approaches and ML methods for predicting emerging economies' OADR. There are still some uncertainties about the interpretability of ML methods and their ability to generate reliable long-term forecasts for smooth demographic time series. There has been little comparative research done on the use of conventional approaches for predicting emerging economies' OADR, focusing particularly on the BRICS economies, despite their significant global influence in shaping the future of demographic trends. This chapter aims to fill this gap by conducting a comparative study of conventional econometric approaches and ML methods for predicting OADR for the BRICS economies. This study combines conventional demographic analysis and forecasting approaches, such as the Autoregressive Integrated Moving Average (ARIMA) method, and ML methods such as the Random Forest, Extreme Gradient Boosting (XGBoost), and Light Gradient Boosting Machine (LightGBM) methods. This study aims to advance the literature on demographic forecasting and provide policy-relevant findings about the economic consequences of demographic ageing in emerging economies.

3. RESEARCH METHODOLOGY

The present study used a comparative and data-driven forecasting approach to examine how OADR performs in BRICS economies. The research methodology combines descriptive analysis, conventional time series econometrics methods, and ML tools to compare their merits in long-term population forecasting. Figure 1 compares the steps involved in the econometric framework with the steps involved in the ML framework. It also highlights the primary distinctions between the conventional econometric model and the ML model for time series forecasting. The conventional econometric model relies on statistical methods, such as stationarity, analysis of residuals, and the extrapolation of past trends. In contrast, the ML model utilizes adaptable algorithms, feature engineering, and iterative learning to capture intricate patterns. In this context, SHAP values illustrate how ML can complement traditional methods by enhancing predictive performance.

Figure 1. Methodological Framework of Econometric and ML Techniques [Source: Authors' Compilation].

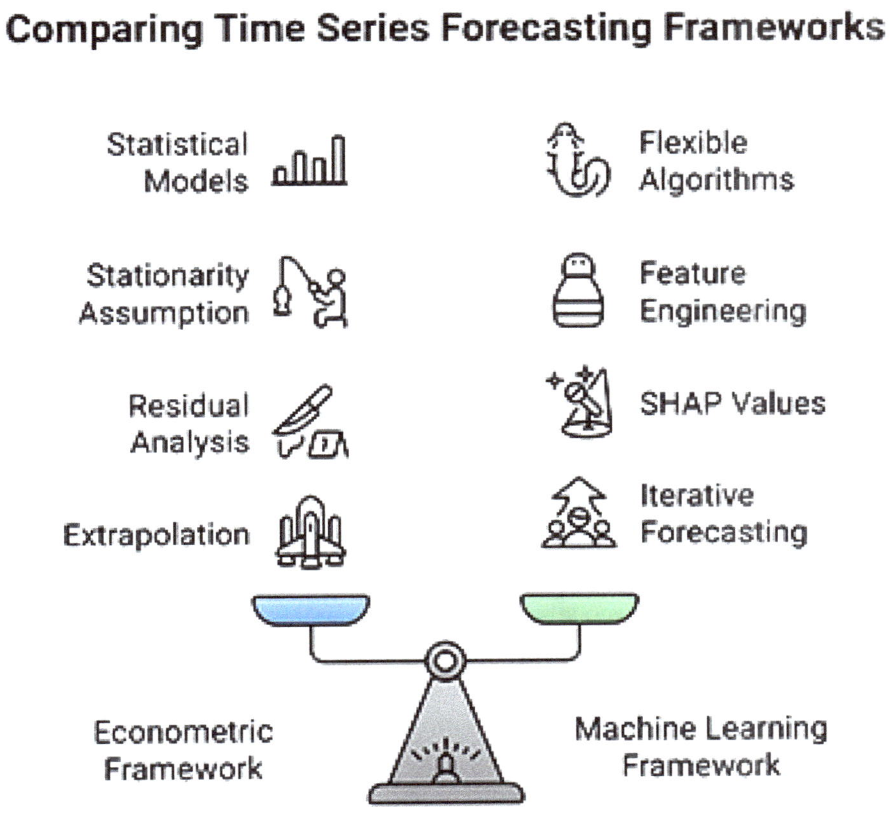

3.1 Data Source and Variable Description

The empirical work uses annual data for the OADR, which refers to the proportion of the population aged 65 years or older to the working-age population (15-64 years). The dataset was collected from the World Bank, World Development Indicators (WDI), and it provides comparative and reliable figures. The empirical work includes all BRICS economies from 1975 to 2024, including Brazil, China, India, Russia, and South Africa. There are no missing values in the dataset, which eliminates the need for interpolation or imputation and enhances the reliability of the subsequent analysis. OADR is defined in equation 1 (Muszyńska & Rau, 2012):

$$\text{OADR}_t = \frac{\text{Population (P) aged } 65+_t}{\text{Population (P) aged } 15-64_t} \times 100 \tag{1}$$

where:

$OADR_t$ represents the old-age dependency ratio at time t,
$P_{65+,t}$ denotes the population aged 65 years and above at time t,
$P_{15-64,t}$ represents the working-age population (15–64 years), and
t refers to the time period of observation.

This is an indicator of the economic burden that working-age citizens carry because of the elderly population. This is commonly used in demographic and fiscal sustainability studies. Annual frequency data is chosen, reflecting that demographic processes are slow-moving. The sample period is held constant across countries to ensure comparability.

3.2 Data Preparation and Preliminary Analysis

Before estimating the models, the data were aggregated into time series per country. Initial data exploration analysis was performed to examine the trends of OADR over time and across various countries. This required the calculation of various descriptive statistics like mean, median, standard deviation (SD), and observed minimum and maximum values during the period of the study. Long-term trends and volatility of the data were also inspected through time series and density distributions to explore the trends of aging across countries. These steps provided important contextual insights and guided model specification choices.

3.3 ARIMA Model Specification

In modelling and forecasting the evolution of OADR for BRICS economies, the study applies the univariate ARIMA framework proposed by Box et al., 2015. As demographic time series often exhibit pertinent features of persistence, trend dynamics, and stochastic shocks, ARIMA models naturally prove to be sound representatives. Autoregressive terms capture demographic persistence, while the moving average terms absorb short-run shocks such as migration fluctuations or cohort-specific effects.

An ARIMA (p, d, q) model is expressed in equation 2:

$$\Phi(L)(1 - L)^d y_t = \Theta(L)\varepsilon_t \quad (2)$$

where,

y_t denotes the OADR at time t,
L is the lag operator,
$(1-L)^d$ the differencing operator, used to transform a non-stationary series into a stationary one,
$\Phi(L)$ the autoregressive (AR) polynomial, defined as: $\Phi(L) = 1 - \phi_1 L - \phi_2 L^2 - \cdots - \phi_p L^p$
$\Theta(L)$ the moving average (MA) polynomial, defined as: $\Theta(L) = 1 + \theta_1 L + \theta_2 L^2 + \cdots + \theta_q L^q$
p is the order of the autoregressive (AR) component,
d is the order of differencing required to achieve stationarity,
q is the order of the moving average (MA) component, and
ε_t is a white-noise error term with zero mean and constant variance.

3.4 Treatment for the Unit Root

For the ARIMA model, there is a need for a stationary series; the first step of the process is the testing of the properties of the OADR series using the augmented dickey-fuller (ADF) test. The ADF regression model is specified in equation (3) (Dickey & Fuller, 1979):

$$\Delta y_t = \alpha + \beta t + \gamma y_{t-1} + \sum_{i=1}^{k} \delta_i \Delta y_{t-i} + \varepsilon_t \quad (3)$$

Δy_t first difference of the time series, defined as $y_t - y_{t-1}$. It represents the change in the variable between two consecutive periods,
y_t denotes the OADR series,
α constant (intercept) term in the regression,
βt is the deterministic time trend, which captures any systematic trend present in the series over time,
γy_{t-1} lagged level of the series, used to test the presence of a unit root. The key hypothesis tested is whether $\gamma = 0$,
Δy_{t-i} is the first-difference operator,
$\sum_{i=1}^{k} \delta_i \Delta y_{t-i}$ are the lagged differences of the dependent variable, included to eliminate serial correlation in the residuals,
t is a deterministic time trend,
k represents the optimal lag length,

δ_i are the coefficients of these lagged differences,

ε_t is the error term, assumed to be white noise with zero mean and constant variance.

A null hypothesis $H_0\!:\!\gamma = 0$ suggests the existence of a unit root and indicates an absence of stationarity. In the case of all BRICS economies, the ADF test does not reject the null hypothesis at level tests and confirms the existence of non-stationarity. First-order differencing (d=1) needs to be used to account for the stochastic trend as represented in equation 4:

$$\Delta y_t = y_t - y_{t-1} \tag{4}$$

Although the ADF p-values in some instances are still moderately high even after differencing, it is known that demographic time series tend to display near-unit root properties, and indeed the validity of the data being stationary can be ascertained by other means and not merely by the p-value test results (Lütkepohl, 2013).

3.5 Model Selection using Akaike Information Criterion (AIC)

The selection of the optimal ARIMA specification is based on the AIC, a widely used information-theoretic measure that explicitly balances model fit with model simplicity. Rather than favouring models that merely fit the historical data well, AIC penalizes excessive parameterization, thereby discouraging overfitting. Formally, AIC is defined as equation 5 (Akaike, 2003):

$$\text{AIC} = -2\ln(L) + 2k \tag{5}$$

where Ldenotes the maximized likelihood function of the estimated model and $k$represents the total number of estimated parameters. The first term rewards goodness of fit, while the second term imposes a penalty for model complexity.

For each of the BRICS economies, different possible specifications of ARIMA (p, d, q) processes can be parameterized given that differencing is used to ensure stationarity. The model with the lowest AIC is selected as the preferred specification, since this is the most parsimonious way to ensure a good explanatory fit. This appears especially fitting for the current situation, where the demographic series are short enough to be measured in terms of years but still quite persistent. Models that are overly parameterized are prone to modelling noise rather than demographic patterns, causing instabilities in the forecasts for the far future. By favouring models that are more parameter-efficient, the AIC selection method improves the credibility of the ageing forecasts.

3.6 Model Estimation and Diagnostic Checking

Following the determination of the most suitable ARIMA model for each of the countries, the parameters of the model are estimated through standard time series estimation techniques available in standard software packages (via Python) for conducting econometric analyses. The estimation of the parameters aims at deriving robust estimates of these parameters that accurately reflect the underlying temporal dynamics of the OADR. To ensure that the chosen ARIMA models fit perfectly well, several diagnostic tests are performed based on residuals of the estimated ARIMA models. An estimated ARIMA model can be defined as equation 6:

$$y_t = \hat{y}_t + \hat{\varepsilon}_t \tag{6}$$

where y_t denotes the observed OADR, $\hat{y}_t$ for the predicted OADR and $\hat{\varepsilon}_t$ represents the model residuals.

Firstly, the residual autocorrelation test using the Ljung-Box Q-test is performed, for which the null hypothesis tested is that the residuals up to a certain lag have joint values of zero, represented in equation 7 (Ljung & Box, 1978):

$$Q(m) = T(T+2)\sum_{k=1}^{m}\frac{\hat{\rho}_k^2}{T-k} \tag{7}$$

In the above equation, Q(m) is the Ljung–Box test statistic, which evaluates whether residual autocorrelations up to lag m are jointly equal to zero, T is the sample size and $\hat{\rho}_k$ represents the sample autocorrelation of residuals at lag k. The failure to reject the null hypothesis means the structure of the temporal dependency in the data has been appropriately modelled by the ARIMA process. Secondly, the distributional characteristics of the residuals are checked using the Jarque-Bera test to see how well they depart from the normal distribution along the dimensions of skewness and kurtosis of the residuals. Although normality is not required for forecasting purposes, this test helps to identify any asymmetry and fat tails of the residuals' distribution. Third, the stability of variance is tested by using heteroskedasticity tests to guarantee that the variance of residuals does not exhibit any systematic pattern over time. A stable variance pattern has particular importance regarding interpreting forecast uncertainty and confidence intervals.

3.7 Methodology for ML models

Though the models like ARIMA are very useful in identifying the linear dependencies and stochastic trends, there can also be nonlinearities in the demographic processes because of the effects of policy interventions, epidemiological transitions, and socio-economic components. To address these nonlinearities, the present study uses econometric models combined with tree-based ML models, which could approximate flexible forms without imposing any parametric assumptions. The study will use three popular forecasting techniques: RF, XGBoost, and LightGBM. These models are preferred in forecasting for their robustness, some degree of interpretability, and strong predictive performance.

3.8 Feature Construction and Data Preparation

Since standard ML models do not work directly with time-indexed stochastic processes, the OADR series is reshaped into a supervised learning format. For every country, we build the following lagged features as represented in equation 8:

$$X_t = \{y_{t-1}, y_{t-2}, \ldots, y_{t-k}\} \tag{8}$$

where y_t denotes the OADR at time t, and k is the number of past observations serving as predictors. The main guidelines for the choice of lag length include:

- Autocorrelation pattern of the OADR series
- Small-sample considerations
- Forecasting performance on validation data

Before model estimation, we check for missing values and standardize variables as required to maintain numerical stability.

3.9 Random Forest (RF) Regression

The RF algorithm is a specific ensemble approach based on bagging. It creates many decision trees from randomly sampled subsets of the training data and then averages their output to reduce variance and prevent overfitting. Put briefly, the RF forecast comes from aggregating all trees' predictions. Formally, the RF forecast is expressed in equation 9 (Fawagreh et al., 2014):

$$\hat{y}_t^{RF} = \frac{1}{B}\sum_{b=1}^{B} f_b(X_t) \tag{9}$$

where $f_b(X_t)$ represents the prediction from the b-th decision tree and B is the number of trees. Key hyperparameters include:

- Number of trees
- Maximum tree depth
- Minimum samples per leaf

RF is most suitable for small datasets because of its stability and resistance to noise.

3.10 Extreme Gradient Boosting (XGBoost)

XGBoost is an ensemble method for boosting, building decision trees one after another. Each new coming tree tries to correct the mistakes made in the previous prediction by the ensemble. XGBoost minimizes the following objective function, which is represented in equation 10 (Chen & Guestrin, 2016):

$$L = \sum_{t=1}^{T} \ell(y_t, \hat{y}_t) + \sum_{m=1}^{M} \Omega(f_m) \tag{10}$$

where:

$\ell(y_t, \hat{y}_t)$ is a differentiable loss function (squared error),
f_m denotes the m-th tree,
$\Omega(f_m)$ is a regularization term penalizing model complexity.

It brings in shrinkage, column subsampling, and regularization; hence, it is very appropriate for modelling nonlinear trends in demographic measures.

3.11 Light Gradient Boosting Machine (LightGBM)

LightGBM is an efficient gradient boosting framework that adopts leaf-wise tree growth and histogram-based splitting to reduce training time and lower memory consumption. On the other hand, despite its computational advantages, LightGBM is sensitive to small sample sizes and may overfit if long time series are not available. This characteristic is particularly relevant in demographic forecasting contexts with limited annual observations.

3.12 Model Training and Validation Strategy

To ensure a fair comparison with the econometric models, the algorithms in ML are trained on identical partitions of training and testing. A rolling-origin evaluation strategy is followed to preserve the temporal ordering of the observations to prevent look-ahead bias. Hyperparameters of individual ML algorithms are selected through cross-validations, which consider the time series nature of the problem; as a result, only past information is used as input in estimating the forecast.

3.13 Explainability via Shapley Additive Explanations (SHAP) Analysis

Despite their strong predictive capabilities, the black-box properties of ML models can sometimes be a hindrance for interpretation, especially within demographic or policy analysis circles. To address these issues, the use of SHAP, a model-agnostic technique based on cooperative game theory, has been employed within the study. SHAP assigns the contribution of each input feature to a model's prediction, providing an equitable and reliable breakdown of the predictions. Specifically, the estimated value at time t, represented as $\hat{y}_t$, can be written as equation 11 (Lundberg & Lee, 2017):

$$\hat{y}_t = \phi_0 + \sum_{i=1}^{k} \phi_i \tag{11}$$

where $\phi_0$is the expected prediction (baseline value) across the training sample, $\phi_i$present the SHAP value for the i^{th}feature, and $k$denotes total number of variables used as an explanatory variable of the model. The SHAP values capture how each feature is moving away from this "baseline", either positively or negatively. Although the forecasting framework is univariate, ML models operate on a multivariate lag structure. Therefore, SHAP analysis is applied to lagged OADR features to interpret how past dependency ratios contribute toward future predictions. Although SHAP does not imply causality, it brings additional transparency and verifies that ML models largely learn demographic persistence.

3.14 Model Evaluation Metrics

There are three of the most popular accuracy measures that have been widely used in assessing and comparing forecasting performances between econometric and ML models, these are mean absolute error (MAE), root mean squared error (RMSE), and mean absolute percentage error (MAPE). Each metric captures a different aspect of forecast accuracy and together provides a comprehensive evaluation of model performance (Hyndman & Koehler, 2006).

3.14.1 Mean Absolute Error (MAE)

The mean absolute error measures the average magnitude of forecast errors without considering their direction. It is defined as equation 12:

$$\text{MAE} = \frac{1}{n}\sum_{t=1}^{n} | y_t - \hat{y}_t | \tag{12}$$

Where, y_t denotes the observed value, $\hat{y}_t$ the forecasted value, and n^{th} number of forecast observations.

MAE is more intuitive because it provides the typical size of forecast errors in the same unit as the original variable, OADR. For instance, an MAE of 0.5 denotes that, on average, the model's forecast deviates from the actual OADR by half a percentage point. Since all errors are given equal weights, MAE exhibits a good balance that is not affected by extreme errors in forecasting.

3.14.2 Root Mean Squared Error (RMSE)

The root mean squared error is defined as equation 13:

$$\text{RMSE} = \sqrt{\frac{1}{n}\sum_{t=1}^{n} (y_t - \hat{y}_t)^2} \tag{13}$$

Contrary to the case where MAE is calculated, RMSE gives more weight to stronger deviations from the forecast by squaring the deviations. Therefore, RMSE is affected by forecast errors, particularly when the errors are significant.

With regard to demographic forecasting, the RMSE measures the extent to which the forecasting model tends to significantly deviate from the actual OADR values, even when its average forecasting accuracy is good. A small RMSE is an indication of both accuracy and forecast stability.

3.14.3 Mean Absolute Percentage Error (MAPE)

The MAPE is defined mathematically as a measure of forecast accuracy in relative (percentage) terms and is expressed as equation 14:

$$\text{MAPE} = \frac{100}{n}\sum_{t=1}^{n} \left| \frac{y_t - \hat{y}_t}{y_t} \right| \tag{14}$$

The MAPE allows comparisons between countries, scaling forecast errors according to the magnitude of the observed series. It is particularly useful for comparing performance in countries that have very different OADR levels because performance can be assessed on a common percentage basis. However, MAPE can be very sensitive in terms of dealing with small values. In the current investigation, OADR values for all countries are large enough so that MAPE can be considered an adequate measure of relative forecasting error.

4. RESULTS AND ANALYSIS

4.1 Temporal Evolution of OADR: Trend Analysis

Figure 2 demonstrates the long-run path of OADR growth performance of all BRICS economies. A pronounced positive trend is apparent in all these economies. However, the nature of the trend differs greatly.

Figure 2. OADR of BRICS economies [Source: Authors' Compilation].

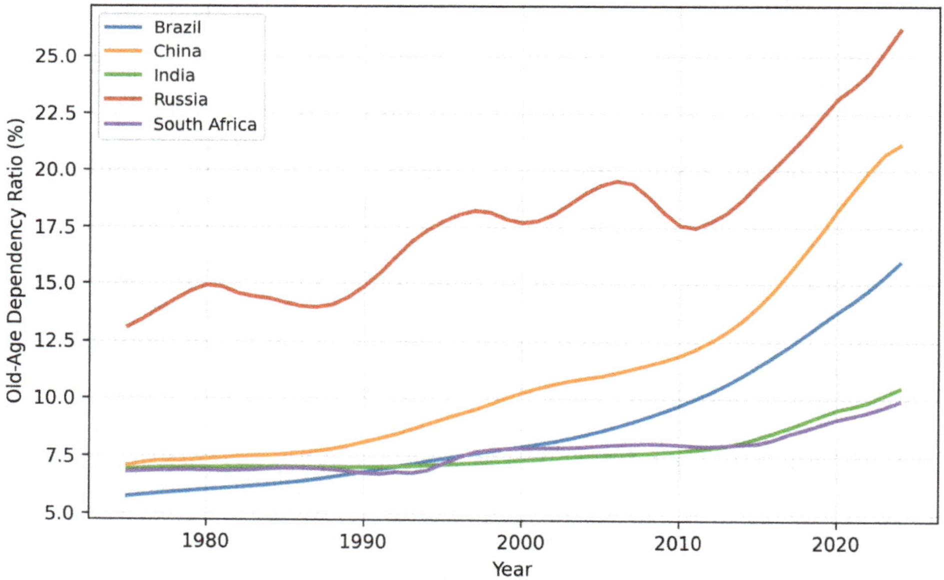

The figure depicts the long-run development of the OADR across the BRICS economies from 1975 to 2024, thus allowing a clear comparison of demographic aging trajectories within the major emerging economies. A common upward trend is evident for all five countries, indicating that population ageing is no longer limited to developed economies and has become a fundamental characteristic of the developing regions as well. Nonetheless, the speed and severity of ageing vary significantly among them. Russia shows the highest OADR throughout the period, reflecting its early fertility decline and persistent mortality dynamics with a pronounced acceleration after 2010. China presents a relatively moderate ageing profile up to 2000 and a steep rise thereafter, consistent with the long-term effects of sustained low fertility and rapid improvements in life expectancy. Brazil also shows a steady but increasingly steep rise, especially after 2010, signalling its transition into a more advanced phase of ageing.

In contrast, India and South Africa show relatively low OADR values throughout, reflecting their younger population structures. However, the steady incline upwards indicates the onset of ageing pressures and how these are likely to increase more dramatically in the decades ahead. Through this, the figure 2 indicates the universality of ageing within BRICS and the heterogeneity of demographic transition, with strong justification for country-specific forecasting and policy analysis in ageing research.

4.2 Descriptive Statistics of OADR (1975–2024)

The descriptive statistics provide an overview of the distribution of OADR across BRICS economies from 1975 to 2024. The statistics reveal that there is a wide variation in OADR across different economies. The highest average OADR is found in Russia, at 17.74, indicating a high percentage of older individuals in its population. The second highest average OADR is found in China, at 11.04. The OADR is found to be low in India, at an average of 7.71, as well as in South Africa, at an average of 7.70. The OADR in Brazil is found to be at an average of 8.79, indicating a wide variation in its OADR across different years. The high and low standard deviation (SD) statistics as shown in table 1 reveal that there is a wide variation in OADR in China as well as in Russia. The OADR in India and South Africa remains low and stable throughout.

The gaps in dependency ratios observed are a result of unique demographic experiences of BRICS nations. The high dependency ratios of Russia over time are a result of earlier experiences of decline in fertility rates and natural ageing processes that started in the later part of the 20th century. The Chinese dependency ratios, which were relatively moderate up to the beginning of the 2000s, started rising sharply due to long-run effects of continuous decline in fertility rates and population control measures taken by the government.

Table 1. Descriptive Statistics of OADR (1975-2024) [Source: Authors' Calculation].

Country	count	mean	SD	min	25%	50%	75%	max
Brazil	50	8.79	2.82	5.76	6.53	7.88	10.22	15.95
China	50	11.04	3.92	7.08	7.75	10.14	12.43	21.15
India	50	7.71	0.94	6.93	7.03	7.33	7.88	10.47
Russia	50	17.74	3.22	13.12	14.72	17.77	19.25	26.21
South Africa	50	7.70	0.85	6.74	6.89	7.85	8.06	9.92

While India has always had the lowest average and median OADR value, reflecting its relatively young population structure, the rising maximum in recent decades suggests that India is now reaching a phase of rapid ageing. Brazil and South Africa take an intermediate position, as indicated by their moderate averages and strongly upward trends in recent decades. These standard deviation values reflect relatively stable patterns of ageing in India and South Africa, while China and Russia have larger values, reflecting sharper changes in specific sub-periods. Overall, the descriptive statistics presented in table 1 summarize the central tendency and dispersion of OADR values for each BRICS economies over the period.

4.3 Distributional Characteristics of Ageing Across BRICS

The present study begins with examining the ageing patterns of each BRICS nation. Figure 3 displays the kernel density estimates of the OADR. The density curves reveal notable variations in both the extent and distribution of ageing among these economies.

Figure 3. BRICS nations' Kernel Density of OADR (1975-2024) [Source: Authors' Compilation].

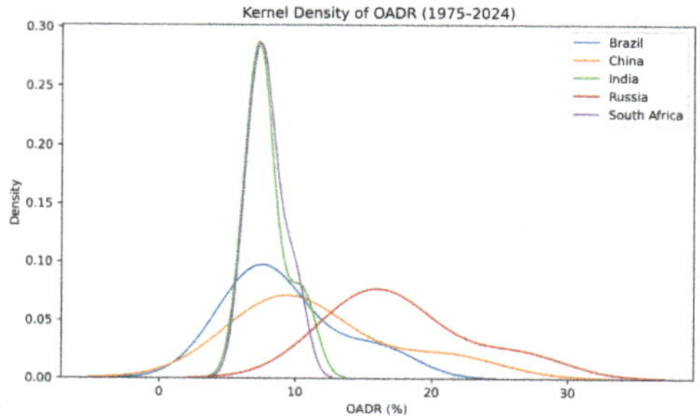

Russia exhibits a distribution that is noticeably skewed to the right, indicating its persistently high dependency ratios throughout the analysed period. In contrast,

China's distribution is more varied, demonstrating its swift transition from relatively low to high OADR over a brief timeframe. Brazil portrays a moderately varied pattern, indicating a gradual ageing process without significant fluctuations. Both India and South Africa present pronounced peaks at lower OADR, highlighting their traditionally youthful populations. However, in India's case, a rightward tail suggests increasing ageing pressures in recent years, pointing towards forthcoming demographic challenges.

Taken together, descriptive statistics and visual analysis lead to three important inferences: firstly, ageing is a shared characteristic of BRICS, though at different country-specific speeds; secondly, the ageing path for India has been behind the rest but is now accelerating; and thirdly, country-specific forecasting models are in order given the diverse historical patterns. These findings provide a sound empirical foundation for the projection exercises described next, in which both conventional econometric and ML methods are applied to forecast OADR through 2050.

4.4 Specification of ARIMA Model

Table 2 presents the results of appropriate ARIMA model of each BRICS economy. Also, incorporated the unit root test results, where time series of demographic data is non-stationary (having unit root problem) at level and at 1st difference as $p > 0.05$.

Table 2. Results of ARIMA model [Source: Authors' Calculation].

Country	ADF p-value (Level)	ADF p-value (1st Difference	Differencing Order (d)	Selected ARIMA Model	Key Significant Parameters ($p < 0.05$)	AIC
Brazil	0.9982	0.9983	1	ARIMA (2,1,1)	AR (1), AR (2)	−291.06
China	1.0000	0.4517	1	ARIMA (1,1,1)	AR (1), MA (1), σ^2	−146.05
India	1.0000	0.9987	1	ARIMA (1,1,2)	AR (1)	−226.77
Russia	0.9956	0.7083	1	ARIMA (1,1,2)	AR (1)	−68.84
South Africa	0.9979	0.2398	1	ARIMA (2,1,1)	AR (1), AR (2)	−145.13

Before turning to time-series modelling, we checked the stochastic properties of the OADR to make sure that ARIMA specifications were appropriate. Given the strong downward or upward trends in demographic indicators, we tested for stationarity using the ADF test for each BRICS economy, both at levels and first differences as shown in table 2. The ADF results presented in table 2 indicate that the null hypothesis of a unit root cannot be rejected for the OADR at levels for any of the countries considered at conventional levels of significance (0.05). Moreover, even when first-order differencing is applied, a few countries produce test statistics that are statistically insignificant. This is consistent with what has often been documented in demographic time-series work: smooth, slowly changing population ratios tend to have near-unit-root behaviour, and unit root tests have low power in small samples and in the presence of deterministic demographic trends. In this respect, the fact that the unit root is not challenged after the first differencing step is not an indicator of misspecification in the model. Difference stationarity is of greater importance to demographic forecasting than covariance stationarity, particularly in applications aiming at forecasting over longer horizons as opposed to shorter cycles. To preclude over-differencing, in this study, the second form of differencing, i.e., d = 2, was avoided, as this can result in the loss of significant demographic information in the long run. The first form of differencing, i.e., d = 1, was retained as the best different form in terms of theoretical and empirical aspects as suggested by demographic studies and the Box and Jenkins (2015) approach to modelling.

We then specified ARIMA (p, 1, q) models for each country after performing differencing. We used autoregressive and moving average structures focused on identifying models that conveyed an understanding of country-based persistence and ageing process inertia as a means of identifying models, as opposed to using significance or unit root tests as the criteria for final model selection. The final selection of models is based on the AIC. In the case of all BRICS economies, the reported ARIMA models have ensured the optimal value of AIC within the search space. Brazil and South Africa have exhibited high values of demographic persistence over multiple periods and have ensured optimal fit using the ARIMA (2, 1, 1) models. China has ensured the optimal modelling of the demographic transition phase using the ARIMA (1,1,1) models. On the other hand, the Indian and Russian economies have ensured optimal modelling using the ARIMA (1, 1, 2) models.

Overall, the combination of differencing diagnostics, AIC, and stable variations for the residuals supports the use of first-order differenced ARIMA models as an appropriate framework for the description and prediction of demographic trends for the BRICS countries. This is especially important for overcoming the drawbacks inherent in the unit root tests on demographic statistics.

4.5 Forecast using ARIMA

Table 3 presents the BRICS' forecasted values of OADR for each of four important horizons, 2025, 2030, 2040, and 2050, along with 95 percent confidence bands. The projection for each country is based on the best model for that country, selected according to accuracy tests. The table puts in perspective the pace at which aging proceeds across these emerging economies.

Table 3. Forecasting OADR using ARIMA for BRICS [Source: Authors' Calculation].

Country	Year	OADR_Forecast	Lower_95_CI	Upper_95_CI
Brazil	2025	16.61	16.59	16.63
China	2025	21.41	21.32	21.51
India	2025	10.77	10.73	10.81
Russia	2025	27.16	26.96	27.36
South Africa	2025	10.16	10.07	10.26
Brazil	2030	20.07	19.5	20.64
China	2030	22.58	21.11	24.05
India	2030	12.17	11.67	12.66
Russia	2030	30.03	26.46	33.61
South Africa	2030	10.93	10.03	11.83
Brazil	2040	26.85	23.81	29.89
China	2040	24.32	18.72	29.92
India	2040	14.71	12.78	16.65
Russia	2040	31.44	21.5	41.38
South Africa	2040	11.49	8.98	14
Brazil	2050	33.29	26.75	39.82
China	2050	25.5	15.27	35.72
India	2050	16.97	13.19	20.74
Russia	2050	31.63	17.16	46.09
South Africa	2050	11.63	7.86	15.4

Brazil exhibits a clear, steady rise in the OADR throughout the projection period. From 16.6 percent in 2025, it climbs to just over 33 percent by 2050, thus more than doubling within 25 years. The confidence intervals stand relatively narrow, signalling strong forecast certainty and reflecting Brazil's long-running ageing trend driven by many decades of falling fertility. China's forecast shows that the OADR will keep increasing after 2030 but at a slower speed. The ratio increases from 21.4 percent in 2025 to 25.5 percent in 2050. In later years, the confidence intervals are wider, reflecting greater uncertainty about long-run outcomes. This is like other countries with structural demographic changes, such as cohort effects, produced by many years of population-control policies. India's projected ratio stays well below its BRICS peers for the whole horizon. Yet, the upward trend is unmistakable, from

10.8 percent in 2025 to about 17 percent by 2050, as shown in table 3. Even with this rise, the ageing path of India still looks more gradual and in tune with a delayed demographic transition and a relatively young population base. The narrower confidence bands suggest more stability and predictability in its ageing process, indicating India to be an ageing society in transition rather than confronting an acute demographic squeeze. Russia is at the top end for OADR within BRICS. The forecast increases from 27.2 percent in 2025 to over 31 percent by 2050. The notably wide confidence intervals, however, especially after 2040, point to greater uncertainty, likely tied to historical demographic volatility, including swings in mortality and population size. South Africa has the lowest ageing rate among BRICS countries. Looking forward, it expects a slight increase in the OADR from 10.2 percent in 2025 to 11.6 percent in 2050, as shown in table 3. The confidence intervals for the later years are relatively broad, implying some degree of uncertainty about ageing trajectories, probably driven by regional variations and health-related factors.

When considering the BRICS nations, the ageing process in the group tends to be quite diverse. Brazil, Russia, and India, as well as South Africa, are growing older faster, while India, still a relatively youthful nation, remains in the early stages of this ageing process. A middle nation in terms of aging would be China, reflecting its unique demographic history. Perhaps the most interesting nation in terms of ageing would be India, as it presents both challenge and opportunity, as it is ageing slowly.

4.6 Graphical Representation of ARIMA Forecast

Figure 4 illustrates the historical trends and projected forecasts for the OADR based on the ARIMA model from 1975 to 2050. Actual values of OADR are represented by the blue lines up to 2024, while the dotted, orange lines indicate the forecast up to 2050. Shaded zones represent 95 percent confidence levels.

Figure 4. Graphical representation of OADR forecast using ARIMA [Source: Authors' Compilation].

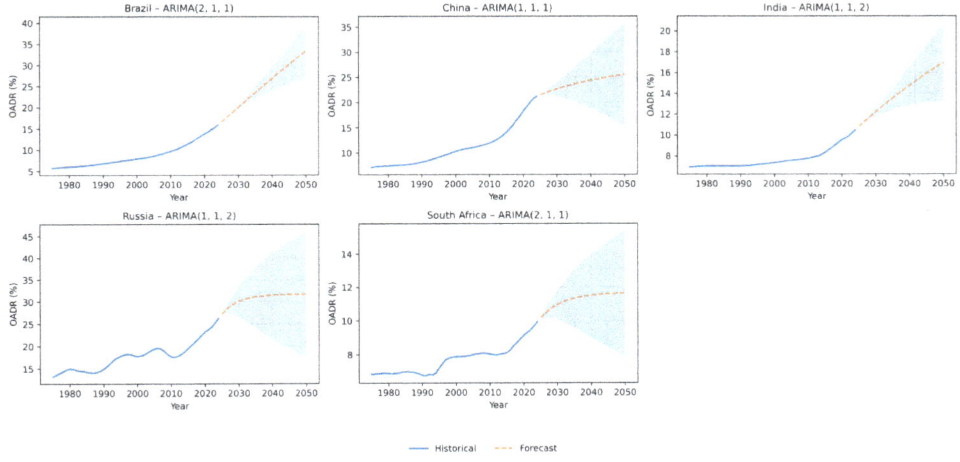

There is a clear, accelerating increase in OADR in the case of Brazil, especially from the mid-2010s. The projection given by ARIMA (2,1,1) suggests a strong aging process, where OADR keeps increasing till 2050. The increasing bands indicate more uncertainty at longer-term horizons. Nonetheless, it is clear that rapid ageing of the population, led by fertility rates declining and life expectancy increasing. In the case of China's forecast, which is based on ARIMA (1,1,1), it projects a very pronounced ageing transition from the early 2020s. The model incorporates the impact of the continuing fertility decline and ageing groups in the aftermath of the 1978 reforms. Despite increasing long-term uncertainty, the pattern remains decidedly positive, implying that working-aged people in China will continue to face pressures.

The OADR curve of India follows a relatively smoother path compared with BRICS countries. The ARIMA (1,1,2) model forecast represents a steadily increasing trend of older people, reflected in a relatively young age structure and delayed transitional pattern of India's population. The narrow confidence intervals up to the mid-2030s indicate high forecast stability, which further emphasizes that time-series econometrics is appropriate for modelling India's elderly dynamics. The ageing process of Russia's elderly dependency ratio series has had more fluctuations, which included phases of stagnation with sudden accelerations. The projection of the ARIMA (1, 1, 2) model illustrates ageing dynamics but at a slower rate compared to China and Brazil. The notably wider confidence intervals represent uncertainties of demographic discontinuities, mortality rates, or structural changes that influenced Russia's series of population trends. South Africa is currently at the tail end of the BRICS countries regarding its OADR value, both for the past as well as the forecasted values. The ARIMA (2, 1, 1) forecast tends towards a small increase in its ageing level that is influenced by fertility as well as health-related factors related to demographics. Despite the increasing uncertainty level with each passage of a year, the projected aging impact is relatively small.

Across all BRICS economies, the ARIMA forecasts indicate a universal upward trend in OADR, confirming ageing as a shared long-term challenge. Heterogeneous ageing speeds, with Brazil and China experiencing the most rapid transitions and India and South Africa ageing more gradually; increasing forecast uncertainty at longer horizons, a common characteristic of demographic projections. For each of the BRICS, the ARIMA forecast indicates a joint positive trend in OADR, reinforcing ageing as a shared long-term issue; a non-homogeneous rate of ageing, with Brazil and China ageing faster, while India and South Africa age at a slower pace. Growing forecast uncertainty as the time horizons increase, as typically observed within population ageing projections. The future projections of OADR show that there is a significant heterogeneity in BRICS economies. Brazil, China, and Russia are expected to face maximum pressure of ageing in the future. This is because they have high dependency ratios and are expected to increase steadily in the future. This is a result of earlier decline in fertility rates and natural ageing processes. India and South Africa maintain lower dependency ratios in the future, indicating that they are at an earlier stage of demographic transition. However, a steady increase in dependency ratios of both nations indicates that they will also face pressure of ageing in the future.

4.7 ML forecasts for the BRICS

The ML models give the same predictions for all future periods because they use lagged inputs in a static supervised learning framework. It is impossible to make these kinds of demographic changes happen in a dynamic way without recursive updates or clear temporal trend factors. Table 4 illustrates the projected OADRs for the BRICS nations in the years 2025, 2030, 2040, and 2050, employing three different ML models named RF, XGBoost, and LightGBM. One interesting observation here was the fact that the stability of predictions regarding future years for each of these countries remains constant for all these BRICS economies for a particular ML model. In other words, for all these economies, the future OADR remains constant from 2025 to 2050 for a particular model of ML. The ML models produce identical forecasts across future horizons because the ML models are estimated in a static supervised-learning framework relying on lagged dependency ratios; their forecasts are identical across future horizons. In the absence of either recursive updating or explicit temporal trend variables, these models do not internally propagate the ageing process forward in time. Given the most recent demographic structure, the models will therefore always produce the same conditional expectation for all future periods. Such a feature explains the remarkable stability observed in the forecasts of all BRICS economies, where the OADR projected for 2025 remains unchanged in 2050 within each model. Plateau-like projections are an intrinsic characteristic of tree-based algorithms, which are designed to learn historical relationships and structural patterns but not to extrapolate long-run demographic trends. While this behaviour captures demographic inertia, this limits the usefulness of ML methods for long-horizon population forecasting. In contrast, the time-series model ARIMA explicitly models the trend and temporal dependence, allowing forecasts to evolve dynamically over time and further reinforcing methodological suitability in demographic applications.

From a comparative point of view, Russia and China consistently show the highest projected dependency ratios across the BRICS economies. In Russia, OADR levels range between approximately 20 and 26 percent depending on the model, reflecting a strongly pronounced ageing burden already quite well-established. China is the next closest, with XGBoost yielding particularly high estimates, reflecting its rapid demographic transition and shrinking working-age population. Brazil would fall into an intermediate position, with dependency ratios around 15-16 percent under RF and XGB, whereas LightGBM yields considerably lower values. This divergence across models suggests that Brazil's ageing trajectory is more sensitive to the underlying modelling approach, possibly due to its transitional demographic structure. India and South Africa consistently record the lowest projected OADR values across all three ML models. For India, forecasts remain close to 10 percent under RF and XGBoost, and even lower under LightGBM. These results reinforce the view that India is still at an earlier stage of population ageing compared with other BRICS economies. While ageing pressures are expected to increase in the long run, the ML projections suggest the magnitude of OADR growth is likely to be more gradual for India. Across BRICS economies, XGBoost consistently tends to return the highest dependency ratios, with LightGBM maintaining itself on the more conservative side and the RF model somewhere in between. The consistent ordering reveals how different ensemble methods are recognizing historical demographic signals and also why comparing models is important in demographic forecasting.

Overall, this suggests that ML models are good at ranking ageing levels across countries, but their limited grasp of the long-term temporal dynamics means that they should be compared to traditional econometric methods such as ARIMA. In practice, these results are best read as complementary benchmarks rather than as a standalone long-term projection.

Table 4. Forecasts of OADR using ML for the BRICS [Source: Authors' Calculation].

Country	Year	Random Forest	XGBoost	LightGBM
Brazil	2025	15.61	15.95	11.33
	2030	15.61	15.95	11.33
	2040	15.61	15.95	11.33
	2050	15.61	15.95	11.33
China	2025	20.83	21.15	14.47
	2030	20.83	21.15	14.47
	2040	20.83	21.15	14.47
	2050	20.83	21.15	14.47
India	2025	10.31	10.47	8.48
	2030	10.31	10.47	8.48
	2040	10.31	10.47	8.48
	2050	10.31	10.47	8.48
Russia	2025	25.67	26.21	20.42
	2030	25.67	26.21	20.42
	2040	25.67	26.21	20.42
	2050	25.67	26.21	20.42
South Africa	2025	9.79	9.92	8.46
	2030	9.79	9.92	8.46
	2040	9.79	9.92	8.46
	2050	9.79	9.92	8.46

4.8 Model Evaluation Metrics

Table 5 presents the evaluation metrics MAE, RMSE, and MAPE for ARIMA and ML models across the BRICS nations. Put together, these metrics can show both the size and the relative accuracy of forecasting errors, therefore providing a sound basis for model comparisons. For Brazil, the ARIMA (2, 1, 1) model clearly outperforms ML models, with the smallest MAE of 0.6170, RMSE of 0.7975, and MAPE of 4.21 percent, as shown in table 5. While XGBoost and RF yield average errors, LightGBM performed substantially worse, with its MAPE above 43 percent. This suggests that OADR in Brazil has a relatively smooth, stable trajectory that can be better captured by a traditional stochastic process than by nonlinear tree-based methods.

A similar pattern emerges for China, for which ARIMA (1, 1, 1) again gives the best forecast with the smallest errors according to all metrics. Although the

XGBoost and RF models can capture some nonlinear patterns, their larger MAE and MAPE indicate that they are not as good at forecasting compared to ARIMA. LightGBM performs particularly poorly, with a MAPE of 47.3 percent, signifying that complex boosting models struggle to generalize China's demographic dynamics over the evaluation period. India thus presents the most straightforward case for an ARIMA-based forecast. This is quite evident from the remarkably low errors of the ARIMA (1, 1, 2) model, with a MAPE of only 0.41 percent, signalling close to perfect short-run predictability. ML models lag noticeably behind them, with LightGBM errors a few orders of magnitude higher. These results suggest that India's OADR changes according to a highly predictable pattern wrought by slow changes in demographic composition that fit linear time-series modelling quite well. For Russia, the ARIMA (1, 1, 2) model again performs distinctly well by having the lowest values of evaluation metrics MAE, RMSE, and MAPE, performing better than all other models. Although XGBoost and RF models perform well, their elevated values of the error metrics indicate a less strong performance on the Russia's demographic dynamics. LightGBM performs relatively poor, as it is of little use in this regard.

On the other hand, the South Africa data slightly suggests an alternative trend. ARIMA (2,1,1) performs well, although XGBoost performs better in MAE and RMSE and has a better MAPE of 5.92 percent compared to the subsequent value of 9.16 percent for the latter. This is an indication that the demographic trends in South Africa may be nonlinear and better handled by gradient boosting models. As usual, LightGBM performs poorly. Few important findings can be derived from the Table 5. Firstly, the models that consistently perform at a top-notch or near-top-notch level for countries such as Brazil, China, India, and Russia are the ARIMA models, emphasizing the long-lasting advantage of the traditional time-series models when the demographic metrics tend to have smooth and steady trends. Secondly, the most reliable form of ML model is the XGBoost algorithm, particularly in the case of South Africa, where it slightly outperforms the ARIMA models. Thirdly, the LightGBM algorithm is the poorest-performing algorithm in each category, indicating overfitting and a lack of generalizability in handling the short-term trends of the demographic indicators.

Table 5. Model evaluation metrics of each model [Source: Authors' Calculation].

Country	Model	MAE	RMSE	MAPE (%)
Brazil	ARIMA (2,1,1)	0.6170	0.7975	4.21
	XGBoost	1.4953	1.6804	9.86
	Random Forest	1.7445	1.9056	11.55
	LightGBM	6.4036	6.4493	43.10

continued on following page

Table 5. Continued

Country	Model	MAE	RMSE	MAPE (%)
China	ARIMA (1,1,1)	1.4980	1.7765	7.86
	XGBoost	2.5309	2.7473	12.51
	Random Forest	2.9685	3.1550	14.72
	LightGBM	9.4072	9.4677	47.30
India	ARIMA (1,1,2)	0.0393	0.0489	0.41
	XGBoost	0.6574	0.7382	6.50
	Random Forest	0.8110	0.8829	8.04
	LightGBM	2.4340	2.4571	24.37
Russia	ARIMA (1,1,2)	1.5168	2.0453	6.20
	XGBoost	2.1114	2.3805	8.44
	Random Forest	2.7058	2.9490	10.86
	LightGBM	7.1169	7.2013	28.92
South Africa	ARIMA (2,1,1)	0.8561	1.0179	9.16
	XGBoost	0.5694	0.6341	5.92
	Random Forest	0.6971	0.7522	7.26
	LightGBM	1.9060	1.9264	20.01

There is one important methodological point to remember when we compare the forecasting models. The indicators we are employing, like the OADR, don't change very quickly and are mostly affected by long-term changes in the structure of the population. Consequently, methodologies that explicitly account for temporal dependency and trend persistence are more dependable in this situation. The fact that ARIMA works well in most BRICS economies is not because of ML approaches; it's just because of the way demographic data works. ML is fantastic at finding nonlinear patterns in complicated data, but it doesn't fare as well at predicting long-term demographic trends that go beyond the training window. Again, this shows how important it is to use the right methodology based on how things really work.

4.9 Model Interpretability and Feature Contribution Analysis

SHAP is employed to interpret how ML models internally explain variations in OADR. In this study, SHAP values are derived from the RF model to uncover the relative contribution of past demographic information (lags, trends, and rolling means) to OADR predictions across BRICS economies. Importantly, SHAP analysis is not used to replace econometric inference but to enhance interpretability and validate whether ML models learn demographically meaningful patterns.

Figure 5. SHAP Summary for BRICS [Source: Authors' Compilation].

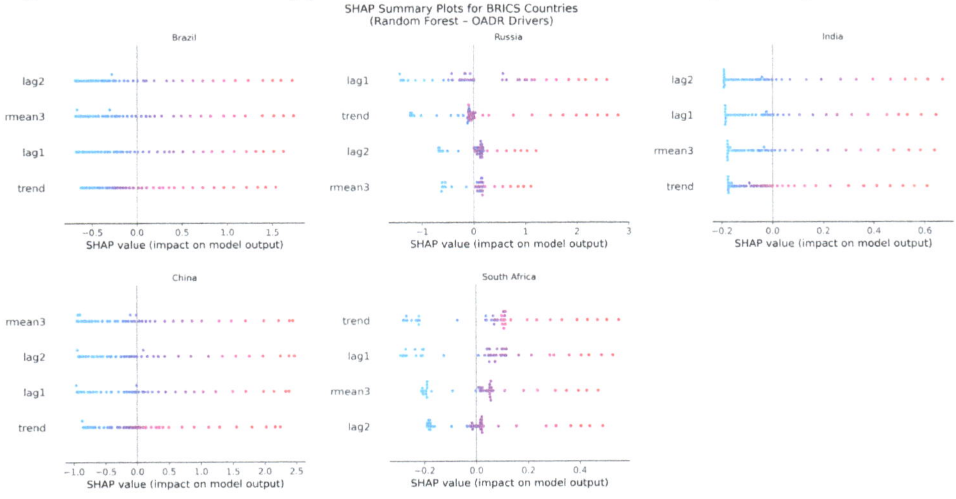

Figure 5 illustrates the SHAP summary plot for the BRICS economies, explaining the effect of the lagged demographic variables on the predicted value of OADR. In the plot, a positive value in SHAP indicates a variable that raises the OADR value, whereas a negative value dampens it. Additionally, the colour bars represent the values of the underlying features. SHAP summary plot of Brazil illustrates that lagged OADR variables, including lag1, lag2, and the trend, are primarily responsible for influencing ageing outcomes. Aspects of previous ageing values push SHAP values positively, which indicates that previous ageing outcomes influence ageing results to some extent. Zero volatility, as indicated by the SHAP plot, may have resulted in ARIMA performing better than ML algorithms.

In the case of China, the three-year rolling mean variable (rmean3) is the most important predictor, with the lagged series and trend second. This reflects the demographic smooth with ties to China's gradual transition with fertility policy changes. The wide range of the SHAP distribution indicates the presence of interactions, hence the models' ability to pick some pattern yet still not perform better than the ARIMA models. India displays a relatively smooth and spread-out SHAP pattern among the BRICS nations. The relatively recent past does contribute to pushing the predictions upward, although this effect is fairly small, representing India's delayed demographic transition and young demographic structure. The SHAP findings do verify that ML approaches are essentially based on inertia rather than strong structural breaks, which explains why their superiority over ARIMA is small. Most importantly, the SHAP analysis does confirm and strengthen the notion that the ageing process in

India occurs in a steady and orderly manner, making it very competitive in terms of predictions through traditional econometrics.

Russia's values are more dispersed in terms of SHAP values, particularly for lag1 and the trend. Though lag dependence is always paramount, the level of variation captured in ML is in line with what Russia experiences in terms of post-transition demographic fluctuation. However, the ARIMA model performs better because it can filter shock effects. South Africa exhibits the strongest nonlinear behaviour among BRICS economies. From the SHAP plot shown in figure 5, it can be derived that short-run lags and rolling averages tend to have greater influence, while long-term trends are relatively less influential. This fits with the observation that XGBoost only slightly outperforms ARIMA, since ML models tend to adapt to the shifts in demographics and varied ageing patterns. This SHAP-based interpretability gives some intuitive cross-country perspectives on what drives demographic ageing across BRICS. Among all five nations, the lagged OADR is always the most important predictor; this means that future ageing largely follows from past demographic structures. Such a strong link with history underlines that population ageing is path-dependent: cohort sizes, survival, and past fertility decisions cascade forward.

Again, the SHAP results in rather strong evidence that trend components are dominating when it comes to long-run dynamics, which further supports the view that demographic change unfolds gradually and predictably rather than through sudden nonlinear jumps. Although ML models can capture complex interactions, the interpretability evidence suggests that their predictive strength here arises mainly from autoregressive and trend-based patterns already in the data, not from uncovering genuinely new nonlinear drivers of ageing. This offers a key methodological takeaway: the apparent sophistication of ML does not automatically yield better explanatory power for demographic forecasts. When we combine all of this information, we can say that while population ageing is a general tendency in all of the BRICS economies, the rate and degree of this shift vary greatly. This emphasizes once more how crucial it is to create country specific national-level economic and demographic policies rather than employing a one-size-fits-all strategy for ageing in emerging markets.

5. COMPARATIVE DISCUSSION AND POLICY IMPLICATIONS

A key insight from this research is that demographic inertia remains the main factor influencing long-term ageing trends in BRICS. The OADR is a slowly changing variable, heavily influenced by structural demographic drivers like declining birth rates, cohort effects, and increasing life expectancy. As all of these factors evolve at a very gradual pace, there is a significant level of time-based persistence and autocorrelation present in the data. This is exactly why an ARIMA model outperforms ML models in forecasting long-term demographic paths. The reason is that ARIMA models are based on understanding how a variable is changing over time and in which direction. In this manner, ARIMA models are able to sense the slow drift of demographic change and are able to forecast future paths in a stable manner. This is in line with previous studies in demographic forecasting, which have found that time series models perform better for variables that have smooth long-term trends and high temporal continuity (Hyndman et al., 2021; Makridakis et al., 2020). On the other hand, ML models like Random Forest, XGBoost, and LightGBM are powerful tools for forecasting nonlinear relationships. However, they are heavily dependent on lagged variables. This is exactly why ML models are not suitable for forecasting long-term demographic paths.

In addition to population growth, rising dependency ratios are expected to influence labor markets and long-term productivity. As the ratio of the ageing population increases relative to those in the workforce, there may be a gradual reduction in labor supply over time, unless productivity improves or there is an increase in migration or labor participants. Countries experiencing significant demographic changes include China, Brazil, and Russia, which may need to implement policies that boost labor supply by promoting longer working lives, enhancing female workforce participation, and developing human capital. The effects of technological progress on productivity could also help counterbalance the challenges posed by a growing share of ageing population compared to the working-age population. Prior research also emphasizes that productivity and technological advancements are key to sustaining growth in an ageing population (Bloom et al., 2010). For developing economies like India and South Africa, investments in education and skills are likely to create a window of opportunity to reap a demographic dividend before moving into an aging population.

The anticipated increase in OADR is also important in assessing long-term pension schemes and health-care spending. Many economies operate a pay-as-you-go pension scheme, where retirement benefits are paid from contributions made by those of working age. With increasing dependency ratios, many economies are likely to experience increasing pressure on their budgets. Developing economies that are rapidly experiencing demographic shifts include China, Brazil, and Russia. Such economies are likely to require policies that increase labor supply by encouraging workers to work longer, increasing female labor force participation, and improving human capital. Developing economies like India and South Africa are still relatively young in terms of demographic composition and are likely to require policies that increase labor supply and sustain long-term growth. In short, demographic forecasting, including OADR, is important in assessing long-term labor markets and designing labor policies to meet future challenges.

6. CONCLUSION OF THE STUDY

Population ageing is a critical demographic and economic phenomenon that is becoming a significant concern in the context of emerging economies, particularly in the context of BRICS economies. In this context, the present chapter has sought to explore and forecast the future trends in the OADR in Brazil, Russia, India, China, and South Africa using conventional econometric techniques and state-of-the-art ML algorithms. Using historical data, it has been demonstrated that ML algorithms are not as effective as conventional ARIMA models in forecasting demographic indicators that experience gradual structural changes and high temporal persistence. Furthermore, it has been demonstrated that demographic ageing is a critical phenomenon that is likely to be experienced in all these countries, though at varying rates. In other words, Brazil, China, and Russia are likely to experience a rapid change in their dependency ratios, while India and South Africa have a relatively younger demographic structure and are also likely to experience gradual changes in their demographic structure. In addition to these theoretical and analytical implications, it is also critical to note that accurate demographic forecasting is a critical tool that can be used to support policy planning. In addition to its analytical and theoretical implications, it is also critical to note that the present chapter has also demonstrated its applied implications in terms of its potential to be used as a tool to understand and address the challenges posed by demographic ageing.

7. LIMITATIONS OF THE STUDY

The present study has some limitations that are worth bearing in mind. Firstly, it is based on annual time series data, which are very useful for observing long-term trends of demography. They reduce the number of samples that can be used for ML algorithms and the observation of more complex dynamics of the system when it comes to ageing demographics. Secondly, the forecasting model that will be employed here is a simple one that measures the changes that have taken place over time in the senior citizen ratio alone.

Third, while we include ML models for comparison, we are careful in our modelling to only utilize these models in a very comparable way to that of ARIMA. This conservative approach may underestimate the potential for ML in more complex models. Fourth, demographic forecasts are prone to breaks that may result from events that are impossible to forecast from past data alone, such as pandemics or policy changes. Fifth, because we focus on BRICS, while these results are useful for comparison across countries, they may not generalize directly to smaller or demographically deviant economies. These limitations suggest that these results should be carefully interpreted considering future research.

REFERENCES

Akaike, H. (2003). A new look at the statistical model identification. *IEEE Transactions on Automatic Control, 19*(6), 716–723. DOI: 10.1109/TAC.1974.1100705

Baharin, R., & Saad, S. (2018). Ageing population and health care expenditure: Evidence using time series analysis. *Geografia, 14*(4).

Bloom, D. E., Canning, D., & Fink, G. (2010). Implications of population ageing for economic growth. *Oxford Review of Economic Policy, 26*(4), 583–612. DOI: 10.1093/oxrep/grq038

Box, G. E. P., Jenkins, G. M., Reinsel, G. C., & Ljung, G. M. (2015). *Time series analysis: Forecasting and control* (5th ed.). Wiley.

Chang, D. F., & Lai, K. L. (2019). Trajectory of the population dependency index by using ARIMA models. *ICIC Express Letters. Part B, Applications, 10*(3), 195–202.

Chen, T., & Guestrin, C. (2016). XGBoost: A scalable tree boosting system. In *Proceedings of the 22nd ACM SIGKDD International Conference on Knowledge Discovery and Data Mining* (pp. 785–794).

Daviaud, E., Kelly, G., Cornell, J., Geffen, L., & Solanki, G. (2019). Population ageing in South Africa: Trends, impact, and challenges for the health sector. *South African Health Review, 2019*(1), 175–182. PMID: 34671174

Deeti, A. (2023). *The conundrum of the pension system in India: A comprehensive study in the context of India's growth story.*

Dickey, D. A., & Fuller, W. A. (1979). Distribution of the estimators for autoregressive time series with a unit root. *Journal of the American Statistical Association, 74*(366), 427–431. DOI: 10.2307/2286348

do Nascimento, L. G. (2020). Population trends in BRICS: Developments and projections. *BRICS Journal of Economics, 1*(4), 82–94. DOI: 10.38050/2712-7508-2020-1-4-8

Fawagreh, K., Gaber, M. M., & Elyan, E. (2014). Random forests: From early developments to recent advancements. *Systems Science & Control Engineering, 2*(1), 602–609. DOI: 10.1080/21642583.2014.956265

Goli, S., Reddy, A. B., James, K. S., & Srinivasan, V. (2019). Economic independence and social security among India's elderly. *Economic and Political Weekly, 54*(39), 32–41.

Handing, E. P., Strobl, C., Jiao, Y., Feliciano, L., & Aichele, S. (2022). Predictors of depression among middle-aged and older men and women in Europe: A machine learning approach. *The Lancet Regional Health. Europe*, *18*, 18. DOI: 10.1016/j.lanepe.2022.100391 PMID: 35519235

Harasty, C., & Ostermeier, M. (2020). *Population ageing: Alternative measures of dependency and implications for the future of work.*

Hyndman, R. J., & Koehler, A. B. (2006). Another look at measures of forecast accuracy. *International Journal of Forecasting*, *22*(4), 679–688. DOI: 10.1016/j.ijforecast.2006.03.001

Hyndman, R. J., Zeng, Y., & Shang, H. L. (2021). Forecasting the old-age dependency ratio to determine a sustainable pension age. *Australian & New Zealand Journal of Statistics*, *63*(2), 241–256. DOI: 10.1111/anzs.12330

Ivanova, A., Zemlyanova, E., Sabgayda, T., Semyonova, V., Zubko, A., & Kryukova, I. (2023). Demographic ageing, health status and life quality of the elderly in Russia. *China Population and Development Studies*, *7*(2), 130–159. DOI: 10.1007/s42379-023-00133-4

Johnston, L. A. (2024). The BRICS are "getting old before getting rich": Trends and prospects. In *Complexity thinking and China's demography within and beyond mainland China: A geopolitical overview* (pp. 215–248). Springer. DOI: 10.1007/978-981-97-0172-8_9

Lal, B. (2023). The BRICS countries: Trends of demographic and economic development. *International Journal of Scientific Research*, *12*(4), 702–708.

Lee, R., & Mason, A. (2011). *Population aging and the generational economy: A global perspective.* Edward Elgar Publishing. DOI: 10.4337/9780857930583

Li, H., Zeng, Y., Gan, L., Tuersun, Y., Yang, J., Liu, J., & Chen, J. (2022). Urban–rural disparities in the healthy ageing trajectory in China: A population-based study. *BMC Public Health*, *22*(1), 1406. DOI: 10.1186/s12889-022-13757-x PMID: 35870914

Li, M., & Ao, Y. (2026). Equity in public decision-making: A dynamic comparative study of urban–rural elderly care institution resource allocation in China. In *Institutional elderly care in China: Resource allocation and spatial optimization* (pp. 81–112). Springer. DOI: 10.1007/978-981-95-5092-0_4

Ljung, G. M., & Box, G. E. P. (1978). On a measure of lack of fit in time series models. *Biometrika*, *65*(2), 297–303. DOI: 10.1093/biomet/65.2.297

Lu, Z., Mahalik, M. K., Padhan, H., Gupta, M., & Gozgor, G. (2021). Effects of age dependency and urbanization on energy demand in BRICS: Evidence from the machine learning estimator. *Frontiers in Energy Research, 9*, 749065. DOI: 10.3389/fenrg.2021.749065

Lundberg, S. M., & Lee, S. I. (2017). A unified approach to interpreting model predictions. In *Advances in Neural Information Processing Systems* (Vol. 30).

Lütkepohl, H. (2013). *Introduction to multiple time series analysis*. Springer.

MacLennan, M., Osório, R. G., & de Arruda, P. L. (2014). *Youth and employment among the BRICS* (Issue 28).

Megeri, M. N., & Bheemanna, B. (2023). Forecasting population and economic characteristics with ARIMA models in India. *International Journal of Agricultural and Statistics Sciences, 19*(2), 513-526. DOI: 10.59467/IJASS.2023.19.513

Mi, H., Fan, X., Lu, B., Cai, L., & Piggott, J. (2020). Preparing for population ageing: Estimating the cost of formal aged care in China. *The Journal of the Economics of Ageing, 17*, 100183. DOI: 10.1016/j.jeoa.2018.12.002

Muszyńska, M. M., & Rau, R. (2012). The old-age healthy dependency ratio in Europe. *Journal of Population Ageing, 5*(3), 151–162. DOI: 10.1007/s12062-012-9068-6 PMID: 22924086

Noh, B., Youm, C., Goh, E., Lee, M., Park, H., Jeon, H., & Kim, O. Y. (2021). XGBoost-based machine learning approach to predict the risk of falls in older adults using gait outcomes. *Scientific Reports, 11*(1), 12183. DOI: 10.1038/s41598-021-91797-w PMID: 34108595

Oliveira, B. L. C. A., & Pinheiro, A. K. B. (2023). Changes in health behaviors in elderly Brazilians: Data from the 2013 and 2019 National Health Surveys. *Ciencia & Saude Coletiva, 28*, 3111–3122. DOI: 10.1590/1413-812320232811.16702022 PMID: 37970996

Paiva, L. H., & Ansiliero, G. (2025). The Brazilian Old-Age Social Protection System. In *Handbook of Aging, Health and Public Policy: Perspectives from Asia* (pp. 1471–1485). Springer Nature Singapore. DOI: 10.1007/978-981-99-7842-7_18

Rentz, J. O., & Reynolds, F. D. (1991). Forecasting the effects of an aging population on product consumption: An age–period–cohort framework. *JMR, Journal of Marketing Research, 28*(3), 355–360. DOI: 10.1177/002224379102800310

Shcherbakova, E. M. (2022). Population dynamics in Russia in the context of global trends. *Studies on Russian Economic Development*, *33*(4), 409–421. DOI: 10.1134/S1075700722040098 PMID: 35911060

Shen, X., Yin, F., & Jiao, C. (2023). Predictive models of life satisfaction in older people: A machine learning approach. *International Journal of Environmental Research and Public Health*, *20*(3), 2445. DOI: 10.3390/ijerph20032445 PMID: 36767810

Slaveva, K. (2023). Study on the changes in the age dependency ratio and their effects on the economy. *Population (Naselenie)*, *41*(2), 83–105.

Souza, J. S., Reis, E. A., Godman, B., Campbell, S. M., Meyer, J. C., Sena, L. W., & Godói, I. P. (2024). Users' perceptions of access to and quality of Unified Health System services in Brazil: Implications for healthcare management. *International Journal of Environmental Research and Public Health*, *21*(6), 721. DOI: 10.3390/ijerph21060721 PMID: 38928967

Suresh, K. G., Thomas, J., Menon, V. A., & TK, S. K. (n.d.). Exploring the socioeconomic determinants of population and economic indicators using machine learning and time series analysis.

Vahidi Monfared, H., & Moini, A. (2019). A system dynamics model to forecast population ageing in Iran. *Kybernetes*, *48*(6), 1216–1241. DOI: 10.1108/K-04-2018-0166

Vaishnav, L. M., Joshi, S. H., Joshi, A. U., & Mehendale, A. M. (2022). The National Programme for Health Care of the Elderly: Achievements and challenges in India. *Annals of Geriatric Medicine and Research*, *26*(3), 183–189. DOI: 10.4235/agmr.22.0062 PMID: 36039665

Xie, Z., Chen, S., He, C., Cao, Y., Du, Y., Yi, L., & Wang, P. (2024). Trends and age–period–cohort effects on the incidence of falls from 1990 to 2019 in BRICS countries. *Heliyon*, *10*(5), e26771. DOI: 10.1016/j.heliyon.2024.e26771

KEY TERMS AND DEFINITIONS

Autoregressive Integrated Moving Average (ARIMA): One of the most frequently used econometric methods in time series forecasting, which incorporates trends, seasonality, and one-off correlations. ARIMA is best suited to predict demographic data with a low rate of change over time.

Demographic Forecasting: Demographic forecasting is the process through which future population characteristics, such as population growth, dependency ratios, fertility rates, and mortality rates, can be predicted.

Demographic Inertia: The inertia of the population structure, arising from the impact of past fertility, mortality, and migration rates, continues to affect the population even if the underlying factors have changed.

Light Gradient Boosting Machine (LightGBM): A ML framework optimized to work on large data sets, which uses gradient-boosted trees to speed up the training process. It is the most frequently used ML method because it is faster compared to other ML methods.

Machine Learning (ML): A group of computational methods through which algorithms can find hidden patterns in data without explicit programming. ML methods can manage complicated data sets and uncover hidden links between data points.

Old Age Dependency Ratio (OADR): The proportion of persons aged 65+ years relative to the number of persons at working ages (15-64 years). This is one of the most used measures of the impact of the ageing population on the working population.

Population Ageing: The gradual process through which the proportion of the population represented by the elderly increases over time, owing to declining birth rates and rising longevity.

Random Forest: A supervised ML method based on a combination of decision trees. It is generally more accurate in predicting the outcome of complicated data sets.

Time-Series Forecasting: A statistical technique used to forecast future values by analyzing past time-series data to identify patterns, trends, and relationships.

XGBoost (Extreme Gradient Boosting): A sophisticated ML method through which algorithms can find hidden patterns in data. XGBoost is the most frequently used ML method because it is faster compared to other ML methods.

Chapter 3
Balancing the Scales:
Intergenerational Equity and the Dynamics of Income Distribution in an Aging Economy

Md. Adnan Rahman
http://orcid.org/0000-0003-3378-0958
Uttara University, Bangladesh

Md Mahdi Hasan Ahid
http://orcid.org/0009-0008-2304-5283
American International University-Bangladesh, Bangladesh

Soeb Md Shoayeb Noman
http://orcid.org/0000-0003-0834-111X
Uttara University, Bangladesh

Sharmin Jahan
http://orcid.org/0009-0005-8489-2636
Daffodil International University, Bangladesh

Zerin Tasnim
http://orcid.org/0000-0002-5705-1648
North South University, Bangladesh

Javed Mahmud
http://orcid.org/0009-0007-8428-6382
Uttara University, Bangladesh

ABSTRACT

This chapter examines the challenges and opportunities of achieving intergenerational equity in the context of aging societies. As populations age, the distribution of income, wealth, and opportunities across generations becomes increasingly strained, affecting labor markets, pension systems, fiscal sustainability, and social welfare. The chapter explores theoretical frameworks, including life-cycle and overlapping generations models, alongside practical mechanisms such as pensions, public transfers, labor market policies, and technological adaptation. Comparative case studies from developed and emerging economies highlight strategies for balancing fairness, efficiency, and sustainability. Emphasizing integrated policy design, lifelong learning, digital inclusion, and participatory governance, the chapter argues

DOI: 10.4018/979-8-3373-7483-3.ch003

that intergenerational equity is attainable through coordinated interventions that ensure all generations share in economic opportunities, social protection, and long-term growth.

INTRODUCTION

The aging of the population is currently becoming one of the most important demographic facts, which affect the contemporary economy and social organization at its very principles. The declining fertility and rising life expectancy of both the developed and the developing nations has changed the composition of the population in terms of age at an unprecedented rate. The percentage of the population aged 65 and above-65 years is rising in virtually all regions, but certain regions in Asia and Latin America will transform rapidly (Woodman, 2022). The impacts of this shift are much bigger than the demand in the healthcare or the pension cost. It wholly alters the generation, allocation and re-allocation of income in life cycle at different stages of life. The most basic section of such changes is a normative and an economic issue of how can nations employ intergenerational equity and, at the same time, counteract demographic reality? The paradigm used in this discourse is intergenerational equity. It generally implies the idea that the price of the current policies and the existing economic systems should not be too high to the generations to come and they also are not supposed to favor the current ones (Hantrais et al., 2020). An increasing equilibrium is becoming complex to achieve in the ancient cultures. The rising cost of ageing population is putting the populace budget at its threshold as the work age group which is the largest tax payer is increasingly less productive or is even more declining. This presents a social security among the aged and economic prospects of the young dilemma. These differences in this are particularly noticeable in the field of income distribution. The aging is also influential regarding the level of the output in general and the distribution of the income among the various age groups. The old people tend to rely on the incomes of pension and savings and assets, on the other hand, the younger generation relies primarily on the payment (Emon et al., 2026). Unstable labor markets, untimely access to the labor market, and higher housing prices in the labor markets may make it difficult to accumulate wealth by the young generation at a pace similar to their counterparts (Chichilnisky et al., 2020). In the meantime, older generations also tend to have a substantial share of financial and real goods that increases intergenerational disparities in wealth even in the cases when there is no increase or decrease in the income inequality in the generation.

These dynamics are also decided by the fiscal policy. Decisions of the tax, government debt and social expenditure determine the allocation of resources of the various age groups and even over a period of time. To take the example, the manner in which the existing consumption is funded through borrowings can introduce some adjustment cost to the future taxpayers in such a way that they are facing more concerns about long-term equity (Corak, 2020). The formulation of pension and healthcare systems also dictates how risks and rewards of cohorts will be allocated. Therefore, the interplay between the institutional framework and the demographic change can be a buffer effect or escalate the level of the generational inequalities. These challenges, in the context of the model of the holistic analysis, are explained in this chapter as the combination of the demographic transition and income distribution and the public policy. It uses the theory of life-cycle, life-cycle transfer models and comparative research to look at how economic sustainability and distributive equity can be attained by the aging societies. Alternatives to aging as a financial burden are institutional adaptation, social investing and inclusive growth. Highlighting the interaction between the labor markets, fiscal change, technological change and demographic change is the theme of this chapter with the intention of explaining the decisions on how to have a more even and robust intergenerational accord.

BACKGROUND

The issue of the intergenerational justice is not fresh, though, it has become more topical because of the high population growth rate. The regimes of development during the years after the World War II were the creation of the post-World War II welfare states, where the high working age people would sustain the comparatively low numbers of the retirees. The social insurance schemes (particularly, the pay-as-you-go schemes of pension) have presupposed the presence of the constant growth of population and the constant pattern of employment. These are the demographic and economic reasons, which cannot be omitted in most countries in the modern world. The developed nations are lowering their fertility rate to a below replacement rate, yet the lifespan is raising to further the retirement age (Woodman, 2022). One of the useful ways is an economic theory which explains the implication of such changes. The life-cycle models assume that people receive the benefit of time by saving during the time they are working and decrease the resources during their late years of retirement. This generates predictable generations transfers of the markets and the state institutions. With the changing population structures, there is a disbalance between these fluxes. The number of working age groups will be called upon to sustain the rising number of persons of retirement that will burden the contribution rates, the level of benefits and it will also be a strain to the sustainability of the transfer systems (Emon, 2025g; Tang et al., 2021).

The models of overlapping generations subsequently become a better expression of this model since they are interested in firsthand examination of the effects of cohort-cohort allocation of resources with regards to policy choices. The national debt can be considered as transferring the future generation of taxpayers to the current victims. On the same note, the unfunded pension liabilities are implicit claims to the earnings of the future generation. The ideas of these models refer to the fact that the budgetary sustainability and the intergenerational equity are rather similar as the activities that seem to be easy to reach within the short-term are rather heavy in the long-term outlook (Emon & Ahmed, 2025; Olmsted, 2024). These hypothetical conclusions are backed by facts. In most countries, the expenditure on pensions and health care has also been rising at a faster rate as compared to expenditure on education or family support (O'Loughlin et al., 2021). These tendencies can not only affect the distribution of income, but also the opportunities system where the decreased investment in the human capital may be restraining the productivity and level of income of the young generations. Simultaneously, the transformations of the labor market caused by the globalization process, technological innovation, and the new patterns of the employment relationships resulted in the fact that the initial phases of the career have become more uncertain with the long-term impact on the lifetime pattern of incomes (H. Zhang et al., 2021). It is a meeting point that the contextual environment is set by the demographic, economical and institutional considerations. Aging population is bound to increase the ratio of dependency and the existing welfare systems would be overstretched and redistribution of income and wealth will occur. These trends though vary according to the national establishments, according to the institutional capacity and the labor market systems but also on the policy decisions. This complexity will also be realized in the design of its activities that will be sustainable and at the same time be acceptable to finance and social responsibility. The subsequent sections expand on this premise and explain the ways in which these elements of policies, such as fiscal systems, pensions, labor market, and coping with technological advances can play a part in the potential of intergenerational justice in the ageing economy.

UNDERSTANDING INTERGENERATIONAL EQUITY THROUGH ECONOMIC THEORY

The elucidation of intergenerational equity depends on a massive bulk of literature economic and philosophical to contend with the manner in which to share the resources, chances, and duties between two or more generations. The term has acquired a meaning more recently in policy discussions, especially as the aging of the older generations, escalating national debt, and climate change represent a serious threat, yet the theoretical basis of intergenerational thought is very deep in standard economic theory. Coming up with a paradigm of unifying concepts of life-cycle behavior, overlapping generations models, public finance, and ethical theories of justice has turned intergenerational equity into a question of economic efficiency and moral duty (Chichilnisky et al., 2020; Emon, 2025d). The life-cycle theory that studies how individuals spend income and consumption in their lives is one of the primary aspects of this paradigm. According to the life-cycle concept, individuals attempt to stabilize the consumption even when their incomes are likely to fluctuate. The income during early adulthood is usually low and as such may be compelled to go into borrowing or rely on family. The peak income and favorable savings are closely linked to the middle age, but retirement suggests the stage of dissaving when people live on the accumulated investment, pensions, and transfers (Woodman, 2022). The outcomes of these individual trends are age-to-age systematic flows of resources at the aggregate level. It is not only the working-age population who finances their future consumption while taxing and contributing to the social funds used by the older generations. These flows can be time-balanced in non-demographic cultures. But as fertility decreases and lifespan increases, the ratios of contributors and recipients change exerting strain on those systems that depend on intergenerational transfers. Population aging changes the saving and dissaving macroeconomic equilibrium in terms of life-cycle, and potentially affects capital accumulation, interest rates and long-term growth patterns (Jafino et al., 2021). These transformations have important questions of how the burden of adjustment can be fairly shared between cohorts.

The presence and co-existence of two or more cohorts of people in an economy at a point make the overlap generations (OLG) models an extension of the life-cycle analysis models. OLG frameworks can then be applied by economists to study dissimilar impact of policy changes on various generations as opposed to the representative-agent frameworks. The public debt is viewed as redistribution of resources between the new generators of future taxpayers and the present benefactors. By the government financing its expenditure using borrowings instead of taxation, it simply establishes debts on the future income of the yet to be adequately represented in the political decision-making processes (Spear & Young, 2023). Debt can be useful in productive activities such as infrastructure or education that can assist future workers but may lead to intergenerational inequality in the event that an individual primarily utilizes it in consumption. On the same note, social insurance schemes are the OLG key. Pay as you go pension plans are founded on the input of the current workers to fund the pensions of the retired workers. They are hence attached to their sustainability basing on the demographic composition and the workforce efficiency (Ahmed & Ahmed, 2026; Hasan et al., 2026). The dwindling labor force in the ageing societies must support more retirees, which means higher contribution rate, less benefits or more state subsidies. All these alterations have the generational distribution implications. On the contrary, funded pension systems are more dependent on the capital markets, transferring the risks to the individuals and potentially creating the inequalities because of the life-time income and returns on investments (Wicaksono & Mansury, 2020). OLG models are a good model to comprehend the contribution of institutional design to intergenerational transfers (Ahmed et al., 2026; Hasan et al., 2026). Theory of public finance supplements this research by looking at the impacts of the taxation and expenditure policies in the resource redistribution among the age groups. The society possesses aims and unwritten social agreements to manifest the age-related expenditure on education, health, pensions, and family benefits. As the proportion of the state budget allocated to the expenditure within the age sphere is constantly increasing, one might start worrying about the adequacy of investment in the young generations, more so, the human capital formation sphere. Generational accounting is an idea that aims to quantify these imbalances by the net lifetime fiscal position of different generations hence turning implicit transfers explicit (Campiglio & Lorenzetti, 2022).

In addition to the favorable models of the economy, ethical aspect of justice is highly crucial in the process of establishing justice intergenerationally. Rawls views underscore the necessity of equality in institutional formulation by advancing the view that just regimes must not discriminate on specific classes of people including the future generations. The principle of just savings states that each generation has a responsibility of ensuring that there are enough resources and institutional capabilities to cater to the future generations (Das et al., 2024). This moral perspective is particularly applicable to the topic of sustainability of the public debt, pension reform and the environmental policy. Sustainability is based on economic decisions and medium- and long-term ecological and social effects. The argument on sustainable development is based on the notion that the current generation must not intrude into the capacity of the generations to come to meet their needs. This entails ensuring that there is sufficient level of human, physical and ecological capital in the long-term. The aging societies must balance the present welfare requirements and future investments, which will boost future productivity and resilience (X. Wang & Squires, 2024). All these theoretical methods combined assist in putting a focus on the notion that intergenerational justice does not conclude with demographic or fiscal naivety. It is a type of structural aspect in the resource allocation of economies over time and a normative premise, which is appealed on in order to establish equity among generations.

Figure 1. Theoretical Foundations of Intergenerational Equity

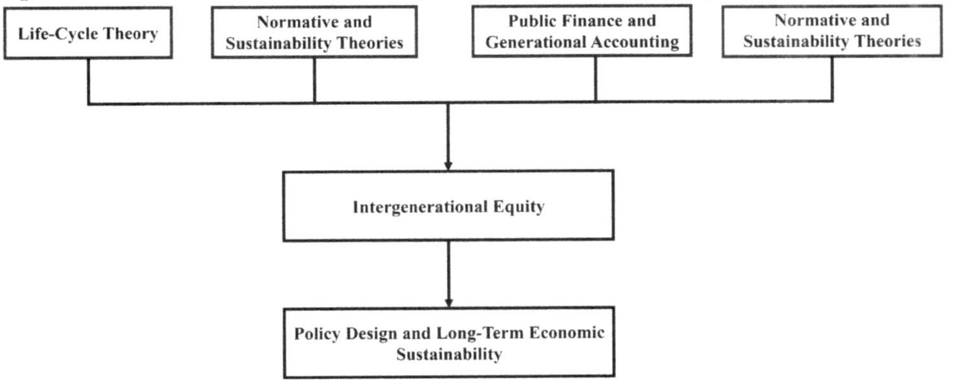

The life-cycle and overlapping generations models have been used to account the dynamics of intertemporal transfer, however, studies of the public finance show policy instruments that may influence such transfers. Normative theories also give assessment standards of the degree of justice and sustainability of such systems. All these perspectives, put in the context of the demographic aging, all contribute to the essence of establishing a protectionist institution to verify that the elderly individuals residing in the institution are well-insured, and the younger and future generations have an opportunity and are secure.

INCOME DISTRIBUTION IN AGING SOCIETIES AND EMERGING GLOBAL PATTERNS

The effecting factors on the labor markets, on the capital ownership and the funding of the public are so many and interrelated that the aging population changes the distribution of income. They are not machines, the way they are functioning is varying according to the institutional structures, stage of development and rate of population growth. However, one of the similarities between modern literature is the maturity of the already existing changes in the distribution of income between labor and capital and the distribution of resources among the age cohorts (Gölçek, 2024). One of the short-term channels is the one that can be functioning with the assistance of the labor market. It can be considered a demerit to the availability of the labor force since birth rate is low and the population of those entering the labor market is on the decline. Decline in the labor force will be in a place to increase salaries particularly in the areas with skills deficiency. It is also evident that the wage pressure has been rising in some of the occupations found in other existing markets due to the retiring of the older workforce and the lack of the younger ones to take their place (Wang, 2020). This is not always the case. It may also paralyze the aggregate economic growth by aging population because it will not only reduce the rate of growth in the labor force but also the aggregate demand in the case an imbalance in consumption behavior exists between the aged families and the young families (Hasan Emon et al., 2026). It can only be tamed by a lower growth to lower the increase in wages and formation of new employment opportunities and more in volume among the new entrants into the labor market. Furthermore, the technological substitution will have a negative impact on the reduction of unemployed individuals that will undermine the bargaining power of the job holder in the clerical position. Because of this, the demographic aging has two effects on the technological development, and the labor market that may result in the decline or rise in the income inequality.

The second distinction that is required is associated with the difference in the ownerships of the assets by different groups of age. The wealth on the other hand is enjoying much more disparity than a source of income and it is concentrated in older families that have had time to save more, purchase property and then cash in to it as the price of assets increases (Emon, 2023). The largest component of household wealth in most nations is housing, and the long-term growth in the prices of housing has been excessively generous to the older generations, whose access to the housing market has been relatively cheap at the point when it was relatively cheap relative to household income (Grinin et al., 2023). It is also backed by financial resources and occupational pensions. In turn, the intergenerational wealth gap can become even significantly greater even in the situation when the labor wage gap will be rather inelastic. Another economic situation has been meted out to the youth. All this is disadvantageous to them concerning acquiring property and saving in the long-term as academic research, the rise of the cases of precarious employment, and the emergence of rising costs of housing are all working against them (Tibber et al., 2022). Nevertheless, in some countries the problem of untimely accrual of wealth is even more difficult due to the debts of the student loans. These effects may be in the form of cohort inequality in that the next generation is poorer than the parents respectively. The interpretation of such time lapses is that, the trends of life time income are not the only ones but the intergenerational mobility is influenced by the wealth, which becomes the determinant of education and entrepreneurship in addition to housing. The third important experience on aging on incomes distribution is a policy. Another source of stress to the government is the elderly population as it stretches the limits of expenditure on pensions, medical as well as long term care. The programs are much impactful in causing poverty among the old age and have been able to reduce the income disparities in the old age in the few cases (Ngcamu, 2023).

However, further expenditure on the age-related problems could lessen the ability to generate investments in the sector that will have significant impact on the younger generations such as education, aggressive labor market policies and family support policies. In such a case, the likelihood of getting more in the long-term and the growth of the productivity can be reduced and the income distributions in the future is affected indirectly. The case of elderly population is also made up of taxation trends. It will be preconditioned by the increasing expense of funding the aging that will be in turn demanding the increase in the shares of payroll or consumption tax that will be overburdening the working age cohort. As labor incomes are high taxed and little tax on wealth and property, the comparative position of the upscale older households can be improved in comparison with the younger employees. Rather, capital income and progressive tax suggestions based on inheritance will add to the issue of intergenerational inequality but it is not the popular politics choice (Elgar et al., 2020). Most importantly they are more local processes. The poverty risk of the aged has been cushioned by the social security that has been experienced in other Europe welfare states but there is the fear that the financial feasibility of the younger generation who are able to afford the high costs of houses and the volatile labor markets may be limited in the future. In some regions of East Asia, demographic ageing processes are incredibly high due to saving large sums of money by families and family support systems are high in those regions that have created a disequilibrium between the social and personal transfer. A number of other nations with an equivalent population comprising of a middle-income citizenry are a greying population too, and they do not have the higher levels of per capita income or it is resulting in the stresses in their budgets that, on the other hand, do not have the benefits of mass social security (Patterson & Balderas, 2020). These trends are augmented by gender and migration. The money and life prospects of the women who do not have them are destroyed and as such, they tend to grow old with little to live on thus, becoming more and more reliant on social welfare. In the meantime, the migration will mitigate the shortage of labor and reshape the demographics related to age and, thus, to the remuneration patterns and economic sustainability (Keyes & Platt, 2024). The above attributes imply that the aging process is a game to a certain extent in which income distribution is established through the macro social and economic structures (Khan & Emon, 2025b).

FISCAL POLICY AND REDISTRIBUTION IN THE CONTEXT OF DEMOGRAPHIC CHANGE

Intergenerational justice has the fiscal policy as its key component, as it regulates the way resources could be mobilized and allocated by different groups of different ages and different time periods. The governments influence the nature of redistributing the economic risks and opportunities between the present and the future generation through taxation, government expenditure and borrowing. The economic policies have more long-term effects that are controversial in the aging civilizations whose population structure is undergoing a rapid change. The key challenge is the creation of the fiscally sustainable systems that do not hamper the equilibrium between the generations (Emon & Khan, 2025a; Petmesidou & Guillén, 2022). One of the most important instruments of resource distribution across and within generations is the taxation. The progressive taxation with income taxation would assist in cutting down the gaps in the age brackets, but its generation model is based on the structure of the tax base. The systems that are based on heavy use of payroll contribution impose the greatest burden on working-age categories of individuals with poor labor market participation or income. The increase in the dependence of the property, inheritance and growth of capital income tax, on the other hand, can transfer part of the fiscal burden to the richest household of average, older age. The system of taxation also influences the temporal unequal contribution and distribution of the contributions during a life span of a person (Luo, 2023). It is also significant to make conclusions about government spending. Education, child development and infrastructure investment are widely regarded as expenditure which increases the productivity and wage potential of the future workers. This expenditure will be in a position to sustain the expansion in the long term, and relieve strain on the budget as a result of the aging population because of increasing the future tax base (Hasan Emon et al., 2026; Mounsey et al., 2020). Conversely, as the age-related spending continues to eat up the budgetary space especially the pensions and health care, governments are at times unable to sustain the sufficient investment to the young generations. This trade off does not mean that the expenditure of the older generation is inefficient but what the tradeoff implies is that a balance should be created such that the future success is not ruined by the demands that must be fulfilled by current retirees (Emon & Khan, 2025c).

Public debt has a new intertemporal dimension of fiscal policy. Borrowing assists governments to stabilize their expenditure in the long run, countercyclical efforts during recessions as well as the investments in the long run. Nevertheless, the structural deficits might be left uncovered in the long run and the responsibility to pay may be placed on the future taxpayers, creating intergenerational equity concerns. In the definition of the transfer of debt being an unfair transaction, the usage of the borrowed funds is a condition. Debt that is spent productively such as digital infrastructure or climate conditions can improve the prosperity of future generation and hence payback costs can be eradicated. Conversely, since the debt consumed is mostly used to spend on present without generating future returns, the situation between generations might be inequitable (Walker et al., 2021). The aging population exacerbates these fiscal problems. The problem that is confronting pay-as-you-go pension system and healthcare system is the increasing financial burden with the ratio of the retiree to the worker increasing. There is less growth in the contribution receipts and there is an increase in benefits obligations. And unless it changes, the governments will be subject to growing deficits and debt, and they will have to make hard decisions among tax increase, reduction of benefits, or reduction of other areas of expenditure. Both alternatives are distributional. An increase in payroll taxes will lower the incentives to work and will favor the younger workers, and benefit reforms will increase the risks of poverty by the aged without proper savings (Malla & Pathranarakul, 2022). Progressive and open change is needed in order to have just distribution of changes. Most nations have implemented parametrical reforms, including linking the retirement age to life expectancy, altering the ways of indexing benefits and expanding the contribution bases. These programs put in place in a systematic and equal manner can redistribute the budgetary burden on many cohorts but not merely place it on a single generation. Complementary measures will help to reduce adverse social outcomes and secure low-income pensioners, as well as motivate older workers to employ (Wietzke, 2020). The significant supportive role is played by fiscal regulations and automatic stabilizers. Well established stabilizers, such as unemployment insurance and progressive taxation, cushion the economy against economic shocks without necessitating the haphazard reforms in the policies, thereby cushioning present and future taxpayers against the surprise developments in the fiscal environment. The expectations are stabilizable, particularly those related to sustainability and long-term fiscal systems and debt regulations, which must be adaptable and sensitive to demographic changes and investments resulting in the growth (Bazzana, 2020; Emon & Khan, 2024b). The emergence of the generational accounting as a measure of the intergenerational effect of fiscal policy has risen. This method is used to explain implicit transfers through measurement of net present value of payment of taxes and benefits that the various cohorts receive. The methodological issues can be overcome with the help of generational accounting to explain social discourse concerning the division of fiscal adjustment expenditures and the sustainability of existing policies in the long run (Dax & Copus, 2022; Emon & Khan, 2026).

PENSION SYSTEMS AND INTERGENERATIONAL TRANSFERS

Intergenerational equity debate requires the existence of the pension systems since it requires high amounts of transfers among the working-age population and the pensioners. In old age, the principal source of income is the public pensions which strongly influence the risk of poverty and the spending patterns and overall distribution of income among the aged in different countries. The funding of these systems is founded on the contribution of the sitting employees and, over time, on general tax revenues. With the growing pace of population aging, the world has to face one of the most significant sectors where equity, sustainability, and social cohesion collide, which is the topic of pension systems (Wang & Squires, 2024). Two primary institutional structures are applied in the design of pension namely: pay-as-you-go (PAYG) and funded systems. Contributions of current workers towards Pay-as-you-go (PAYG) schemes continue to be popular in most areas and as such continue to pay the benefits of current retirees. Demographic ratios and the efficiency of the labor market are thus closely related to their sustainability. This is due to the shrinking rate of fertility and the rising life expectancy; this will reduce the percentage of people that contributed to the number of beneficiaries and this would necessitate an increase in contribution rate or a general funds transfer. Such conditions may make the young generations believe that they are foregoing more benefits, which they may not even enjoy in the next several years, which will destroy intergenerational trust (Khan & Hasan Emon, 2025; Lee, 2020). Rather, funded systems rely on individual or collective savings that are made in working years and invested in the financial market. Basically, these systems cut down the first order demographic growth because the returns on the capital turn more contingent than the scale of the next generation. Nevertheless, they transfer the risks within the society to individuals. The retirement income can have vast differences due to the volatility of the market, low interests, and other lifetime earnings. In addition, the shift to the funded systems frequently results in introducing the necessity to contribute twice because one generation will have to support the existing Passionists and future savings on their own (Lundberg, 2024). In the real world, there are mixed or multi-pillar systems in most of the nations which are government, occupational and private. This diversification helps in the removal of risks and enhancing the resilience but it adds complexity and uneven coverage. The workers in the informal sector and those who lack an employment record especially women are more likely to access less contributory pensions which puts them at a higher dependency on minimum guarantees or non-contributory benefits, or funded by taxes in general (Valls Martínez et al., 2021).

The recent years have witnessed the enhancement of the reforms which are to guarantee the long-term sustainability. Raising the age of mandatory retirement is a rather general strategy, and it implies the enhancement of life expectancy and the necessity to lengthen the working time (Emon et al., 2025). On the financial aspect the impact of delayed retirement is reducing the period of benefit accession and the contribution date. The issues of equity, however, are extremely high in this process. The rise in the life expectancy is not uniformly spread throughout the social economic strata. The former is that individuals with a physically demanding occupation or reduced lifetime earnings tend to experience a reduced healthy life expectancy, and this implies that regardless of the retirement age increasing regularly, the age might be counterproductive (van Bilsen et al., 2022). The most common method of reform is the moderation of the benefit formula and regulations of indexation. Financial equilibrium may be obtained by a shift to wage to price indexation, alteration of the rate of accrual, or through the improved coat of rewards with lifetime service. However, the changes can reduce the replacement rates especially of the workers with low and middle income as their income and limited history of contributions. This is usually accompanied by the suggestion of tax incentives or compulsory funded pillars to promote saving in the private sector, though, the saving powers of the various income groups differ widely. Absence of redistribution is also likely to intensify inequality among the retirees because they will be more dependent on the provision of the private sector (Klos et al., 2022). Intergenerational equity also cuts across formalities of the pension schemes. Families are still significant in the sense of solid support structure particularly in those countries whereby the government pension plans are minimal. Older parents and adults can make such gifts, including financial ones, housing benefits, and unpaid childcare, which would allow the younger generation to raise funds and enter the labor markets more actively. On the other hand, when the care and social security systems are immature, adult children are able to assist frail parents financially or physically (D. Zhang et al., 2022). The degree to which the privatization process is mitigating or contributing to the inequities that are inherent in the public systems is determined by the distribution of the wealth and income among the households. The issues of inheritance and legacies also influence intergenerational distribution. Most countries are experiencing an increase in the rate of wealth transfer across generations as the population is ageing and the prices of assets are increasing. Even though the inheritances could assist the economy to foster intergenerational mobility among some of the family members, they may as well result in wealth concentration and lead to differences in the equality of opportunity through high disparity in assets access (Hantrais et al., 2020). The taxation of inter vivo transfers and the estates is involved in the general policy framework that aims at minimizing the intergenerational inequalities.

The interaction of the relations between the public pensions and the private transfers demonstrates that the intergenerational redistribution works in many various and intricate ways. It implies that the synergetic impacts of formal institutions and family support systems should be considered in terms of sensible policy. Enhancement of the pension system by increasing minimum pension protection, coverage of non-standard workers and gender equity in lifetime incomes can make the fairness of the pension system. Meanwhile, complementary policies, as to services available in the long term care, and housing services can alleviate the stress on the family in respect of attending to the risks that otherwise would threaten the intergenerational parity.

Figure 2. Intergenerational transfers via pensions and private support

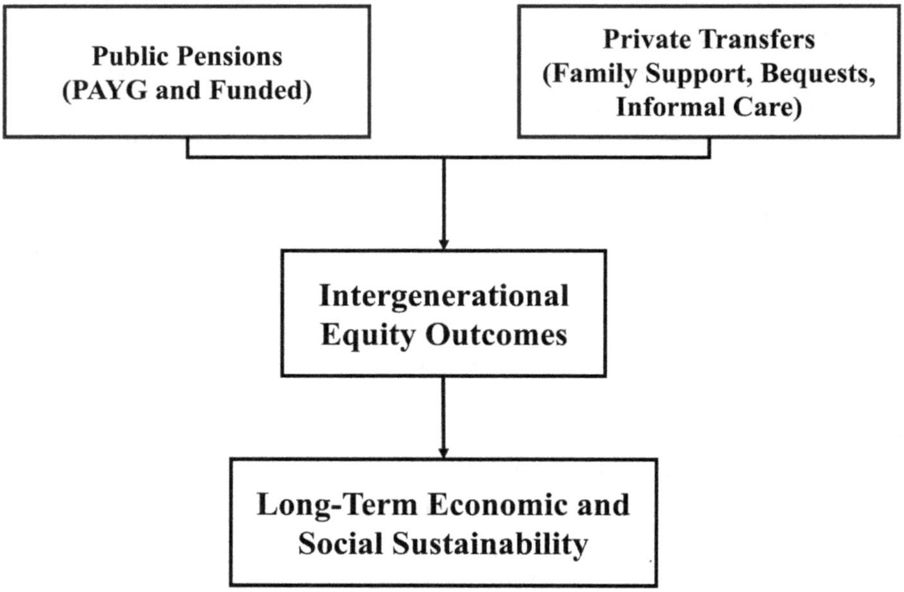

Pension schemes are never technical financial processes per se, but they are components of the social contract between generations. In their design, they identify the ways in which the societies distribute the economic effects of the longevity effects and demographic changes. This is a sustainable change requirement of the balance between prudent fiscal policy and sufficient protection and the consciousness of the variations in life expectancy, working life experience and exposure to personal resources. The retirement schemes must strike a reasonable balance that would mean that they would receive security during their later years without straining the current and future generations.

LABOR MARKET SHIFTS IN AGING ECONOMIES

Demographic aging has been transforming labor markets beyond labor supply and demand. It alters the structure of labor supply, the skill structure of demand and the organization of labor institutions that regulate the employment at various levels of life. Having a higher proportion of the population of adult individuals of advanced age and a reduced proportion of young participants, labor markets ought to be adjusted in such a way that it can sustain productivity, financial viability and integration into the society. The implications of such changes on the intergenerational equity are severe since the employment opportunities and income patterns at an age influence the lifetime income distribution (Perez-Arce & Prados, 2021). The push in legislation into longer working life has been a brilliant response to the aging process. The increasing life span and the later years of being healthy has given most governments a second thought on the classic way of retiring. The reforms include increasing statutory retirement age, restricting the options on early retirement and decreasing the disincentives on working after pension age. Macroeconomically, the rise in the number of older people in the labor force leads to a decrease in the contraction of the working-age population, to the increase of the impetus to economic growth, and to the contribution base to the social safety systems (Donovan & Schoellman, 2023). Other very critical issues that define the viability of extended careers include working conditions, applicability skills, and health condition. These reforms without some accompanying actions may make inequalities between those doing less physically demanding work and those doing manual or insecure work. Age friendly work places should therefore be established. One of them is workplace flexibility, part-time work, ergonomic accommodations, and anti-discrimination practices which could facilitate the productivity of the elderly employees and address the evolving capabilities. Lifelong learning is also an important issue. This is the reason why the skills learnt at a very young age are rendered obsolete before the retiring age due to such a speedy rush in technology. They need constant training programs that include not only the employees of the middle age but also the employees of the late generations to avoid the loss of skills and the exclusion of the older generations in the labor market (Andabayeva et al., 2024). In this regard, the schemes that may assist older employees not only to the fact that they are not triggered to retire but also to work until the last day of their lives.

Youth employment takes some of the key attributes of intergenerational equilibrium that is reflected by extending working life. The young people of the present-day generation who are forced to join the labor force usually experience long education-to-long term employment periods. In most economies, especially after the economic downturns and changes associated with digitization and globalization, younger populations tend to be in some form of temporary contracts, informal jobs, and joblessness (Klasen et al., 2021). Alternatively, a chaotic period in the first years of professional activity might be accompanied by the irreversible consequences, decreased lifetime income, and a shortage of wealth-generating opportunities. The consequences of such scarring increase the gap between generations since older groups were in a better position to be accommodated by the state of the labor market in their early working age.

Intergenerational fairness means that there must be policies to facilitate easy transition between education and working. The linking of both education and work is possible through apprenticeships, vocational training and active labor market programs. There is also need to invest in high quality education that is in line with the emerging skills. Otherwise, with the delayed entry to the labor market and unsustainable employment, the economic opportunities of the future generations are in danger although the general employment rate is expected to be safe. There is a close interaction between gender relationships and age issues. The rise in women entry into the labor force has also significantly contributed to the economic growth and also to a certain degree alleviated the decline in population in certain regions. The issue of the responsibility of care frequently brings the career patterns of females to the table, and results in interrupted career, part-time employment and low lifetime earnings. Nurture of children and the elderly is a growing need in the aged societies and may contribute even more to the inequality of gender through the absence of friendly policies. Accessible childcare, policies to give maternity leaves to promote shared duties, and long-term care facilities can ensure greater sustained labor market rates among women (Geza et al., 2022; Jackson & Tomlinson, 2020). The accomplishment of equal outcomes throughout the lifelong period is also contributed by reductions in gender pay gaps and pension credits on the periods of caregiving.

Migration and inclusion of the marginalized groups also affect adaptation of the labor market to demographic aging. Migrants will be in a position to reduce the shortage of labor, especially in such sectors as the healthcare sector, construction, and services. Good policies regarding integration, qualification recognition and anti-discrimination schemes are highly essential in enabling the migrant workers to work effectively and under equitable working conditions (Cristea et al., 2020). This will enhance the efficient labor force and social integration as more opportunities to work are given to the disabled and to the other marginalized groups. Technological change is abundant in all these dynamic. Automation and digitalization could drive away labor in one region and develop new working positions in other regions. The junior employees will be quick to adjust to new technology and the senior workers can offer a lot of expertise and knowledge of the organization. These resources can be united by the policies towards the intergenerational collaboration in the workplaces, instead of undermining the age groups. Lastly, the restructuring of the labor market of the aging nations is also a life-course problem. It demands policies that will facilitate the employability among young and old age, structural barriers that women and other migrants may face as well as competency that is aligned to the economic requirements. The consideration of such policies in an inclusive way not only may be used to improve productivity, but it also may lead to fairer distribution of opportunities and risks of the generations.

TECHNOLOGY, AUTOMATION, AND OPPORTUNITY DISTRIBUTION BETWEEN GENERATIONS

The technological introduction has never stopped to revolutionize the labor market as well as the economic opportunities; however, the interplay between the technological factor and the aging of the demography also leads to the new distributional forces that are just starting to be fully achieved. A productive solution is automation, artificial intelligence, and digitalization so that even with a shortage of employees (in the aging population), in particular, one can stay productive (Emon, 2025c). At the same time the new technologies are able to change the needs of particular skills, change the occupations and redistribute the economic advantages between the generations. What has been created is a complex world in which technological advances can make or break the intergenerational gap, based on the reaction of the institutions and policies to them (Emon & Khan, 2024a; Mourtzis et al., 2022).

Figure 3. Technology and Intergenerational Opportunity

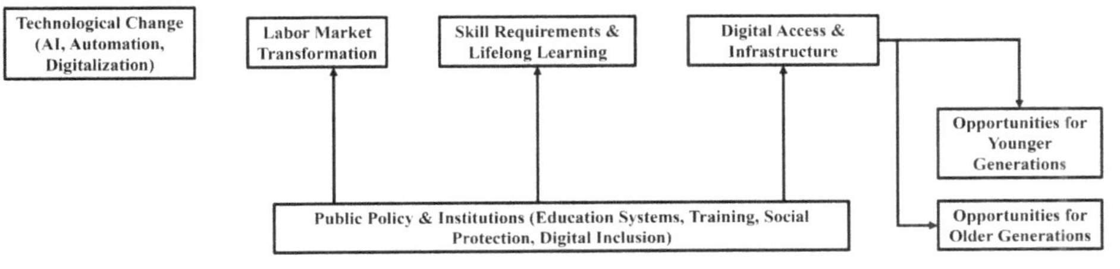

One of the ways, through which technology is transforming the opportunity across generations, is the changed nature of the labor demand. These automations typically replace the boredom and repetitiveness of the tasks, the analysis, imagination and interpersonal abilities are also increased. By implication, the consequence of this trend can be polarization of the labor markets between the high-skilled and highly paid jobs on one side and conversely, the middle-skilled jobs that are conventionally associated to the long-term jobs on the other hand. The positions in the technology-driven industries may not be as problematic with creative education and reinforced digital abilities of the junior workers who are generally new to the field. Conversely, highly skilled employees face high risks of losing their jobs since it is likely that their skills will be associated with the processes that are automated (Ayub Khan et al., 2023). However, the role of the generational differences cannot be over-rated with regard to the issue of adjusting to technology. Even in the event of the possible high level of formal digital literacy among younger generations, the employees of an older age could have much of tacit knowledge, professional networks and skills of solving problems, which remain critical in the complex working conditions. The important issue of concern does not lie in age but acquiring an opportunity to improve skills. In the absence of a coordinated tool of reskilling, technological change may force a segment of mid- and late-career workers into long-term unemployment or prematurely retire the labor force with such effects not only being long-term in terms of income security but also pension sufficiency (Sharma et al., 2020). The lifelong learning systems are the answer to the question on the fair sharing of the fruits of the technological progress. The traditional education practices where the focus lies in education at the initial stages of life are very much misadjusting to an age of rapid and continuous technological change. The workers must receive the possibility to advance their skills at all times in the professional life. Advancement in technology allows people to shift to new jobs and positions that the publicly funded training programs, employer-sponsored reskilling and flexible certification systems are able to attend. Better said, the systems should be designed in a way that will attract people into working in the small businesses, informal jobs, or nonstandard employment, which would otherwise not have access to training (Ayerbe et al., 2022). It is these digital infrastructures and access that constitute the intergenerational allocation of the technological privilege. The rapid internet, low prices of devices, the presence of online services are the requirements of the interaction of the majority of the spheres of the economic and social life. This disparity in the access to these resources (regional, income or age) can be applied in order to supplement other enduring inequities brought about by technology. The cost, competency, or belief in the use of digital technologies might be the possible barriers, particularly, of older adults. The digital policies should be made universally accessible, preventing the further growth of the digital divide with age, and certain digital literacy programs targeted at older people (Lee, 2020).

Technology is also transforming the delivery of other basic services like healthcare, banking and education besides the labor market. Web-based banking, web-based learning and telehealth services would be effective in increasing efficiency and access to underserved populations. The digital health technologies (remote monitoring devices and AI-assisted diagnostics, etc.) will allow the adult population to become self-reliant and reduce the burden of the healthcare system in the aging societies. These advantages are not easily available though. The old are likely to be dis-enfranchised as the services overtime start to be online and they are unable to master the digital interface or have no confidence in the digital platform. There should be age sensitive design, communication and hybrid models of service that will be used to combine digital and real services (Swanepoel, 2023). The effects of technological change in terms of generation can also be seen in wealth creation and entrepreneurship. Youth demographics are more permissive towards digital entrepreneurship, platform-based working and innovation-based businesses. The wealth accruals of a considerable scale may be created through venture finance, digital markets and international market. However, the opportunities are not equally distributed and their enjoyment is usually enjoyed by those individuals, who are well educated, living in cities and have already access to the financial resources. The advantages of the technical industries without the introduction of innovation policies can be restricted to a few regions of the younger and high trained population instead of being spread over whole generations. The macroeconomic level can resolve the labor shortage issue in the ageing population by automation to enhance better production per worker. Such effect can help in productivity in high wages, high public incomes, and stable systems of social protection. Nonetheless, these general benefits have no equitable deliverables. The productivity gains are determined using the vehicle of wage-setting, taxation and social policies. The inter-generational inequality and within-generational inequality can also rise in the event that the technology gains advantage among the capitalists or the most skilled workforce (Challoumis, 2025; Ferreira et al., 2026).

COMPARATIVE CASE STUDIES FROM DIVERSE ECONOMIC CONTEXTS

The issue of population and the generation equality do not also manifest in nations in the same manner. The response to population transition in the society is a matter that varies according to the institutional backgrounds, economic growth rates, labor market systems and social conventions in the society. Comparative research would offer invaluable information regarding combinations of policies that will create fiscal sustainability and equity between age groups. Common and context-specific problems are manifested by experiences of developed welfare states, the rapidly aging middle-income economies, and other developing nations that continue to be at the initial stages of demographic transition (Rovsca et al., 2020).

Table 1. Comparative Approaches to Population Aging and Intergenerational Equity Across Economic Contexts

Country / Region Type	Demographic Situation	Key Institutional Features	Main Intergenerational Challenges	Policy Responses for Equity	Key Lesson for Intergenerational Balance
Nordic Welfare States (e.g., Sweden, Denmark)	Advanced aging, high life expectancy, stable institutions	Universal welfare systems, strong tax base, automatic pension stabilizers, active labor market policies	Rising pension and healthcare costs while maintaining youth investment	Life-expectancy-linked pensions, lifelong learning, subsidized childcare, high female employment	Equity works best when policies support both young and old across the life course
Emerging Economies (Latin America, South Asia)	Rapid aging at lower income levels, large informal sectors	Limited contributory coverage, reliance on informal support networks	Narrow tax base, old-age poverty vs. need for youth investment	Non-contributory social pensions, targeted transfers, community-based elderly care	Informal and formal systems must complement each other where fiscal space is limited
Japan	One of the world's oldest populations, shrinking workforce	Mature pension system, high public debt, strong technology adoption	Heavy fiscal burden on working-age population, labor shortages	Gradual retirement age increases, pension formula adjustments, robotics and automation, female & elderly employment promotion	Technology and labor inclusion can offset demographic pressure
South Korea	Rapid aging, late pension system maturation	Expanding but uneven pension coverage, strong education system	High elderly poverty, generational inequality in pension access	Basic pension expansion, gradual system maturation, youth human capital investment	Delayed welfare expansion creates reverse intergenerational inequality (elderly at risk)

continued on following page

Table 1. Continued

Country / Region Type	Demographic Situation	Key Institutional Features	Main Intergenerational Challenges	Policy Responses for Equity	Key Lesson for Intergenerational Balance
China (Transitional East Asia)	Fast aging following one-child policy	Fragmented pension system, urban–rural disparities	Shrinking workforce, regional and generational inequality	Pension consolidation efforts, digital economy investment, gradual retirement reforms	Institutional reform must keep pace with demographic speed
Small Open European Economies (e.g., Netherlands, Estonia)	Moderate-to-advanced aging, open economies	Multi-pillar pensions, digital governance, strong labor participation	Balancing funded pension risks with housing and wealth inequality	Funded + public pension mix, digital public services, later retirement incentives	Institutional flexibility and digital governance improve sustainability

The Nordic countries tend to be the examples of how large welfare states could adapt to the ageing population without sacrificing the intergenerational equity. They also rely on their policy that is grounded on the combination of universalizing social insurance, high labor force participation, and intensive government investment in human capital. In other countries, e.g. in Sweden and Denmark the automatic adjustment schemes have been part of the public pension system, which links the benefits to life expectancy and economic success by directly making the costs of being a demographic change visible to the various generations. In the meantime, the policy of active labor market and lifelong learning will allow keeping the older population more active and employed, and reducing the burden on the younger generation of taxpayers (Arnberg et al., 2022; Comolli et al., 2021). Notably, the value of investing in their early life is also attached in such systems. The timely parental leave, childcare benefits, and quality education can contribute to the acquisition of skills and the high level of activity in the labor market of the representatives of younger generations, which is an advantage to the tax base needed to finance the social protection. This form of life-course intervention whose funding is provided both at the beginning and at the end of life illustrates how intergenerational justice could be factored into the institution design, as opposed to it being viewed as a zero-sum trade-off. To the contrary, in fact, most of the emergent economies are aging and with much less incomes and low fiscal capacities. The demographic trends of the South American and Latin America countries, including the one in the example, are extremely high, and the informal sectors are numerous and disrupt contributory social insurance systems. In this instance, the antique pay-as-you-go pension plans cannot afford to support a massive demographic and the youth of the workforce usually makes contribution to the pension plans without any guarantee of what they will receive in the future (Khan & Emon, 2025a). Governments have responded to this by expanding non-contributory or means-tested social pensions financed by general revenues, which will not only impoverish old age, but will also prevent governments from putting an even greater strain on the small labor force through heavy contributions to a formal labor force (Islam & Hossen, 2025). However, these efforts lead to the inter-generational financial problems, where the population reserves are forced to choose between meeting the spending of the already retired already old population and investing in the education and infrastructure and new employment of the young generations. Complementary to formal programs, community-based long term care and family-based support systems have been trialed in a few countries to supplement the continued usefulness of informal institutions where care is any but minimally state based (Zhuang et al., 2025).

This is seen in a very different perspective by the East Asian economies due to the ageing population and a strong culture of investing in human capital and culture of industrial growth. Japan, the Republic of Korea and more lately China have experienced monumental shifts in the field of pension and labor market and have promoted the technological change in a bid to keep up with productivity. The case of Japan is very instructive. It has increased the age of retirement, altered benefit and promotion formulae of benefits and encouraged late retirement, and made colossal investments in robotics and automation to offset labor shortages, and one of the highest levels of old-age dependency in the world (F. Ahmed et al., 2022). These plans explain how the flexibility of technology can be used to benefit the social policy in alleviating the demographic strains. At the same time, we have also seen the development of intergenerational struggles especially when it comes to the escalating national debts and the weight that the older employees put on the younger employees. In turn, efforts to accommodate women and the aged in the labor force, on a more systematic scale, have been in the limelight of reinstating the balance between the producers and consumers. Korea has a unique trend. The fast economic growth and development in education has benefited the young generations but the introduction of the pension system is late leaving many people who are already aging with minimal benefits. There is a high level of industrial poverty in Korea although it is a high-income economy. The current policy has been pursuing an increase in basic pensions and social assistance which has been increase slowly and progressively on contributory schemes in the younger generations. The given situation shows that the problem of intergenerational fairness might be a two-way problem since the younger generations might have too high demands, and older ones might be under-insured in case social systems are not developing fast enough in terms of alterations in the population (Shahjahan et al., 2022).

The significance of the institutional flexibility is attested in small open economies such as Estonia and the Netherlands. These countries have been enjoying the presence of multi-pillar pension system and electronic governance and enhanced engagement of the labor market (Khan et al., 2025). The online public services reduce the administration cost and improve the access to services by different age brackets and either funded pension is reducing the risks. The problem of affordability of houses to younger families and the accumulation of wealth to older groups are still debated, and they demonstrate the fact that no distributive free system can exist (Betancourt Morales & Zartha Sossa, 2020; Saleem et al., 2020). Amongst such different situations, we are able to see several lessons that are universal. First, there is the investment in education and skills that should be provided on a periodic basis and a high number so that it could still have a labor force that would be capable of addressing the ageing populations. The pensions reforms as well as the fiscal policy will become timelier and more sustainable both politically and socially when they become progressive and accessible to various cohorts. Third, women, old workers and migrants should be included in the labor market which is pressurizing problematic in terms of alleviating demographic pressures. Finally, technological and institutional innovation can be upgraded as part of the re-distributable resources pool yet they are coupled with policies that enable a significant number of people to take advantage of the new opportunities. Comparative evidence that intergenerational parity is not achieved through the application of a single policy instrument, but through a complex of life-course based, cohering policies, and social safety and labor market, policies that interact to bring about social safety, labor market policy, and human capital development has been provided. Irrespective of the global concern of the population trends, the reaction of the countries indicates that with the measures adopted in the policy the balance of the burdens and the benefits of the aging process are established between the generations.

POLICY INNOVATION FOR INTERGENERATIONAL FAIRNESS

This involves an active and multi-faceted policy framework, comprising of; the social protection, budget sustainability, labor market processes and human capital development, as opposed to peace-meal changes, to see that intergenerational parity in any given aging country is realized. The overall principle of the innovation is that the opportunities and responsibilities of the generations must be fairly shared by the public policy and the effectiveness of economics and social solidarity must be ensured. As the recent research claims, this type of balance is achievable only through the means of a coordinated effort that can be used to tackle the demographic, economic, and environmental issues at the same time (Olmsted, 2024; Yeh, 2022).

The fourth main component of the intergenerational policy innovation is the alignment of the policies of retirement and labor market with the demographic facts. Taking into account the fact that the life expectancy has grown, the predetermined age that was set as the retirement a few decades ago may not be the best anymore. By gradually increasing statutory retirement age and making property of work more flexible, older persons are able to keep working will reduce the financial burden on pension provision, and equalize the balance between years of contribution and years of benefit between generations (O'Loughlin et al., 2021). Moreover, the multi-pillar pension schemes such as the pay-as-you-go, fully funded, and the voluntary private ones can decrease the risk and distribute the burden of a few generations and encourage the intergenerational fairness. Calculated indexation procedures and readjustment algorithms will make sure that the benefits will be sustainable and adjusting to the changes in the population (Chichilnisky et al., 2020). Healthcare financing is one of the important policy areas. The growth in the number of older adults increases the demand of the long-term care, chronic diseases, and prophylaxis. Risk pooling and co-contributions and insurance schemes are just some of the many examples of sustainable finance interventions that can safeguard older adults without overwhelming the young taxpayers. Meanwhile, the investment in the preventative care, digital health infrastructure, and community-based services of the population may decrease long-run cost-related concerns and make the aging healthier, thereby safeguarding productive potential among the populations (Nelischer & Loukaitou-Sideris, 2023). The process of the formation of human capital is quite relevant to ensure that there is intergenerational equity. The policies of early childhood development, policies of egalitarian education, vocation training, and lifelong learning supplement the productivity of future generations and decrease the inequalities in the results of the labor market. The benefits of early interventions, like universal pre-primary education, nutrition and specialized support of less fortunate children, have long-term impacts on their entire lifespan, which produce stronger and better qualified groups of children capable of supporting welfare systems and generating economic development (Khan & Emon, 2024; Meinhold et al., 2025). Simultaneously, active labor markets policies (with youth in the focus) (apprenticeships, job placement programs, and skill certification programs) will enhance the ease of education-to-employment transitions and eliminate early-career scars which can disadvantage young generations (Gerhardinger et al., 2020).

Intergenerational impact assessment is a new step in the process of policy-making. The policymakers will detect the unforeseen expenses to the young and the aging group by conducting systematic assessment of the impacts the policies have on the various age groups over time. These evaluations are especially applicable to the fiscal policy, tax modifications, and decisions concerning the government investment, and they increase the openness and evidence-based nature of the changes. The lack of representation by several generations brings legitimacy, social cohesion and accountability to governance through the application of participatory governance processes. Citizen assemblies, intergenerational advisory councils, and organized public deliberations can be used to empower the younger and older representatives of the population to have a voice in the process of making decisions that would directly impact them (Atta & Sharifi, 2024) Sustainable development and environmental policy have grave inter-generational implications. Climate change, depletion and degradation of resources and the environment has a disproportionate impact on subsequent generations. Investments in the green infrastructure, renewable energy, and the circular economy, as well as the development of climate-resilient urban planning, reduce the risks because they provide working opportunities and technological innovation benefiting the present and future generations (Ullman & Kittner, 2024). The fact that the environmental factors were incorporated in the fiscal and the social policy means that the burdens of the developments are not put on the younger generation or the future generation in an unjust manner. Lastly, technology and innovation policies are needed in intergenerational equity. Inequality in access to opportunities can be addressed by the social acceptance of digital infrastructure, equal access to emerging technology, and continuous digital literacy programs. Proactive management and skill investment must be undertaken to ensure that change of technology, such as automation and artificial intelligence, among others, can contribute to more manpower other than the vulnerable population (Emon et al., 2025; Ly & Cope, 2023). Specifically, the policies that promote the sharing of knowledge between the generations, guidance, and intergenerational cooperation at the work place utilize the resources of all age groups and reduce possible disparities (Khan et al., 2024).

DISCUSSION ON PATHWAYS TOWARD INCLUSIVE AND SUSTAINABLE GROWTH

In order to achieve the inclusive and sustainable growth in aging societies, a complicated understanding about the connection of demographic changes, economic systems and policy interventions over the years exists. In its deeper meaning, the intergenerational needs meeting approach is not a zero-sum game, policies that enhance production, opportunity, and resilience can be beneficial to all ages, instead of disadvantaging one group of people at the expense of the other. The results of the previous chapters in the field of labor markets, pensions, technology, and policy innovations will be integrated in this section as one of the methods of explaining coherent patterns towards sustainable intergenerational development (Emon, 2025h; Ferraz et al., 2021). The first one is the integration of the human capital investments and the changes in the technological and labor markets. The constantly developing digital skills and professional training make the employees of all ages willing to work in the active labor markets. The young people are also advantaged by exposure to the modifications in the technologies at a younger age and the older workers have the reskilling chances, long-term commitment and assured increased income. The collaboration between the business world and the government to provide opportunities to flexible and lifelong learning leads to intergenerational equity because of the higher productivity and reduced dependency rates (Kamran et al., 2023). These policies that entail mentoring programs and generational-to-generational knowledge transfer will lead to teamwork and learning other to hence reduction of the potential generation gap. Intergenerational equity goes hand in hand with fiscal sustainability (Emon, 2025a). This is because open and lifelong budgeting can help avoid the policy trade-offs, and its impact will have a greater effect on some communities than others. The aid of the generational accounting tools such as the long-term fiscal policies and intergenerational effects analysis makes the predictability of the distributional effects of the pension, healthcare and tax reforms possible. Education and infrastructure short term costs and preventive health investments are beneficial in increasing economic capacity of the future generation and reducing the social costs in the long run (Schoneveld, 2020). These measures together with multi-pillar pension schemes, and flexible retirement schemes would constitute a system where all age groups will enjoy the fruits and liabilities of economic growth.

One more challenge and opportunity related to the use of technology is connected with inclusive growth. The labor shortage, increased productivity, and new promising economic opportunities may be handled with the help of automation and digitalization and artificial intelligence (Khan & Hasan Emon, 2024). However, it is important to note that unless equal access to digital infrastructure and capacity build is made, these benefits can be biased towards younger and more urbanized and more affluent citizens. Technology will facilitate the opportunities rather than bringing a wider gap between various groups of the population in the field of inclusive policies, specific digital-literacy campaigns, affordable internet access, and work-related environment accommodating the aged (Emon, 2025e; Werners et al., 2021). The older generation as well as the younger generation can also be enhanced with generational synergistic benefits by incorporating the technological innovation in delivery of services within the healthcare sector, education sector and the finance sector. The policy efficacy facilitators are social cohesion and trust (Khan et al., 2024). The basis of the public support of fiscal and social programs including pension schemes, healthcare investment, tax policy, etc. is the intergenerational solidarity. An articulate conveying of the demographic trends, resource constraint and policy trade-offs promotes the collective responsibility, reduces the opposition towards the required reforms and improves long-term stability. The society that is embracing aging as an opportunity, instead of a financial loss, is more likely to invent new solutions in the labor markets, technological integration, and social services (Danladi et al., 2023). The legitimacy can be increased by improving civic participation by having participatory governments as well as multigenerational advisory committees wherein the policies to be made would be designed in such a way that every demographic would be able to identify with it and also see it as an extension of their goals and objectives. Sustainable development is a considerable degree of integrative development to equitable development (Emon & Chowdhury, 2025a). In its turn, intergenerational is associated with the environmental policy and the sustainable investments as well as the climate adaptation. The quality of the future generations is also secured by providing the safety of the environment, reducing climate and investing in renewable sources power plants, also giving the present generation an immediate source of job and innovations. Through the relation of economic growth and sustainability, nations will have an opportunity to avoid the trade-offs countering the present prosperity and safe future (Ahmad et al., 2023). Finally, equity will suggest not only a certain degree of economic indicators but the social inclusion. Such factors as gender parity, inclusion of migrants and access to high quality healthcare and education by all people are elements of inclusive growth. The policies strengthen the benefits of demographic transition as it means that the barriers to entry into the participation of the marginalized groups will be eliminated, and a larger tax base will be established, the work force will become stronger, and income distribution will become more equal. In addition to the intervention in support of vulnerable populations, i.e. older adults, informal workers, and younger people with lower incomes, these efforts can help to achieve social and economic sustainability (Khan & Emon, 2025c).

FUTURE RESEARCH DIRECTIONS

Despite the fact that the relationship between demographic aging, income distribution, and intergenerational equity has been considerably clarified, there are certain gaps in the knowledge, which should be addressed by other scholars. The impact of the emerging technology on the generational opportunity and inequality can be considered one of the most important areas that should be explored in future. The nature of the labor markets, prerequisite and wealth distribution is altering due to robots, AI and e-commerce, but it is not entirely clear what the long-term implications of these factors will have on the relationship between generations. Future studies should look into how technological adoption and the public policy have interacted with the institution of labor market and the educational systems and how they could either lessen or add to the disparities between the age cohorts

(Ferraz et al., 2021). Migration as well as mobility patterns of ageing populations is one of the areas of concern. International migration can bring about changes in the labor supply, dependence ratios, and the skill distribution and internal migration can influence the access to education, healthcare and employment opportunities in the regions (Emon, 2025i). The combination of demographic, economic, and social data in surveys at the regional and generational level helps to form a better picture of the impact of migration on the intergenerational equity and further specific policy reaction (Awan et al., 2021; Emon, 2025f). In the same manner, an analysis of the relationship between urbanization and housing market and intergenerational wealth accumulation could indicate systemic inhibition of the equal distribution of income.

The systems of family and informal support groups are evolving and this is also having a tremendous impact on the intergenerational transfers. Reducing birth rate, later marriage and longer lifespan changes nature and level of inter-generational transfer of financial and care. Longitudinal and household data can be used to explain these dynamics as they associate transfers on privacy, inheritance and government assistance with the economic performance of various cohorts and can be used to draw inform informational policies of social protection, which improves family support, without raising inequality (Emon & Mazid-Ul-Haque, 2025; Munim et al., 2020). The analysis is especially applicable when it comes to emerging economies as informal transfer may very well end up being a considerable part of the social security (Emon, 2025b). The comparative institutional study is quite a crucial path to theory and practice enhancement. Cross-country assessment can be used to identify the most appropriate policy tools (such as pension reform, lifelong learning, and environmental policy) that will facilitate the solution to the intergenerational equity-budgetary sustainability dilemmas (Emon & Khan, 2025b). Through the study of various welfare, labor markets, and technology adoption patterns, researchers can determine contextual issues that facilitate or inhibit the effectiveness of a policy, which policy-makers can apply to facilitate the aging process (Goyal & Kumar, 2021). Lastly, the methodological refinements can be used to enhance future research on the topic of intergenerational equity. Using the longitudinal panel data in conjunction with the computational model, simulation as well as scenario analysis, the researchers will be able to foresee the outcomes of demographic transitions and policy making in the long run (Emon & Chowdhury, 2025b). These methods can reveal the latent trade-offs, can be used to see whether policies are synergistic, and can assess the robustness of social and economic institutions among varied courses of demographics and technology.

CONCLUSION

Intergenerational justice of aging countries demands a detailed insight of interaction between demographic, economic, social and technical factors over the years. The aging population puts the conventional allocation of resources and opportunities among the generations and strains the labor markets, pension plans, state budgets, and social welfare agencies. As has been proved in this chapter, equity between the age groups is not simply about redistribution of income or taking alteration in fiscal policies, but is a complex process that involves policy, innovation and social foresight. The economic process of engagement is affected in a significant way by the aging process. In the meantime, the older generations rely on pensions, medical institutions and wealth and savings and the youth rely on labor and taxation which has not always been guaranteed in a reward after retirement. It is due to these dynamics that systems should be developed without straining some generation. They must be adequate pension reforms, sustainable healthcare financing, and progressive fiscal measures, but they must be complemented by investments into human capital, lifelong learning, and digital inclusion so that all the generations could be meaningfully involved in the economic life. Technology is a challenge in this case and an opportunity. The automation and digitalization can assist in solving labor issues by assisting to boost productivity, offer novel entrepreneurial and innovative prospects. Simultaneously, such improvements are a menace to the escalation of the inequalities should the access to digital skills, infrastructure, and finance be distributed unevenly. The technology adaptation is to be carried out in an inclusive approach to the extent that, the specialized reskilling schemes, flexible work schedules, and age-sensitive digital schemes should be established in such a way that the benefits of innovation become even-handed among the generations.

As per practice on various economic environments, intergenerational equity has proved to be impossible to achieve based on a universal model. An example of policies that are life-course oriented, labor market flexibility, and high levels of social protection supporting equity and high production is seen in high-welfare states. Evidence of the significance of new approaches is found in developing and developing countries in terms of the integration of institutional and informal systems of support, provided with specific social assistance, and with specific intention of investing in the human capital. Whichever it may be, intergenerational solidarity, open government, and policy involvement are tenets that guarantee trust, as well as cooperation among the generations. Lastly, accomplishment of intergenerational equity is linked directly to inclusive and sustainable development sets of goals. The policies must also be able to respond to the population concerns, the budget sustainability, the economic growth and societal inclusiveness as well as anticipate the needs of the future generations. Old age can elicit institutional innovation, the introduction of new technology and solidarity when it is not just perceived as a blemish but also as an opportunity. In the societies that are preoccupied with education, health, labor market involvement and environmentally sustainable, the framework is designed in a manner that intergenerational equity is built into the economic framework.

REFERENCES

Ahmad, M., Peng, T., Awan, A., & Ahmed, Z. (2023). Policy framework considering resource curse, renewable energy transition, and institutional issues: Fostering sustainable development and sustainable natural resource consumption practices. *Resources Policy*, *86*, 104173. DOI: 10.1016/j.resourpol.2023.104173

Ahmed, F., Kousar, S., Pervaiz, A., Trinidad-Segovia, J. E., del Pilar Casado-Belmonte, M., & Ahmed, W. (2022). Role of green innovation, trade and energy to promote green economic growth: A case of South Asian Nations. *Environmental Science and Pollution Research International*, *29*(5), 6871–6885. DOI: 10.1007/s11356-021-15881-4 PMID: 34462851

Ahmed, M., & Ahmed, M. J. (2026). Sustainable Industrial Operations Through IoT-Generated Big Data Insights. In *Sustainable Operations in the Age of AI and Big Data* (pp. 37–82). DOI: 10.4018/979-8-2600-0216-2.ch002

Ahmed, M., Al Amareen, O. S., & Arafat, Y. (2026). Harnessing Big Data for Reverse Logistics and Waste Management: Pathways to Sustainable Supply Chains. In *Enhancing Sustainability in Global Supply Chains With Big Data Analytics* (pp. 175–210). IGI Global Scientific Publishing. DOI: 10.4018/979-8-3373-6896-2.ch006

Andabayeva, G., Movchun, V., Dubovik, M., Kurpebayeva, G., & Cai, X. (2024). Labor market dynamics in developing countries: Analysis of employment transformation at the macro-level. *Journal of Innovation and Entrepreneurship*, *13*(1), 65. DOI: 10.1186/s13731-024-00417-0

Arnberg, K., Larsen, E., & Östman, A.-C. (2022). Gender and economic history in the Nordic countries. *The Scandinavian Economic History Review*, *70*(2), 113–122. DOI: 10.1080/03585522.2022.2078403

Atta, N., & Sharifi, A. (2024). A systematic literature review of the relationship between the rule of law and environmental sustainability. *Sustainable Development (Bradford)*, *32*(6), 7051–7068. DOI: 10.1002/sd.3087

Awan, U., Sroufe, R., & Shahbaz, M. (2021). Industry 4.0 and the circular economy: A literature review and recommendations for future research. *Business Strategy and the Environment*, *30*(4), 2038–2060. DOI: 10.1002/bse.2731

Ayerbe, E., Berecibar, M., Clark, S., Franco, A. A., & Ruhland, J. (2022). Digitalization of Battery Manufacturing: Current Status, Challenges, and Opportunities. *Advanced Energy Materials*, *12*(17), 2102696. Advance online publication. DOI: 10.1002/aenm.202102696

Ayub Khan, A., Ali Laghari, A., Rashid, M., Li, H., Rehman Javed, A., & Reddy Gadekallu, T. (2023). Artificial intelligence and blockchain technology for secure smart grid and power distribution Automation: A State-of-the-Art Review. *Sustainable Energy Technologies and Assessments*, *57*, 103282. DOI: 10.1016/j.seta.2023.103282

Bazzana, D. (2020). Ageing population and pension system sustainability: Reforms and redistributive implications. *Economia Politica (Bologna)*, *37*(3), 971–992. DOI: 10.1007/s40888-020-00183-8

Betancourt Morales, C. M., & Zartha Sossa, J. W. (2020). Circular economy in Latin America: A systematic literature review. *Business Strategy and the Environment*, *29*(6), 2479–2497. DOI: 10.1002/bse.2515

Campiglio, L., & Lorenzetti, L. A. (2022). *Generational Economics.*, DOI: 10.1007/978-3-031-14541-4_8

Challoumis, C. (2025). Economocracy: Global Economic Governance. *Economies*, *13*(8), 230. DOI: 10.3390/economies13080230

Chichilnisky, G., Hammond, P. J., & Stern, N. (2020). Fundamental utilitarianism and intergenerational equity with extinction discounting. *Social Choice and Welfare*, *54*(2–3), 397–427. DOI: 10.1007/s00355-019-01236-z

Comolli, C. L., Neyer, G., Andersson, G., Dommermuth, L., Fallesen, P., Jalovaara, M., Jónsson, A. K., Kolk, M., & Lappegård, T. (2021). Beyond the Economic Gaze: Childbearing During and After Recessions in the Nordic Countries. *European Journal of Population = Revue Européenne de Démographie*, *37*(2), 473–520. DOI: 10.1007/s10680-020-09570-0 PMID: 33230356

Corak, M. (2020). Intergenerational Mobility: What Do We Care About? What Should We Care About? *The Australian Economic Review*, *53*(2), 230–240. DOI: 10.1111/1467-8462.12372

Corlet Walker, C., Druckman, A., & Jackson, T. (2021). Welfare systems without economic growth: A review of the challenges and next steps for the field. *Ecological Economics*, *186*, 107066. DOI: 10.1016/j.ecolecon.2021.107066

Cristea, M., Noja, G. G., Stefea, P., & Sala, A. L. (2020). The Impact of Population Aging and Public Health Support on EU Labor Markets. *International Journal of Environmental Research and Public Health*, *17*(4), 1439. DOI: 10.3390/ijerph17041439 PMID: 32102277

Danladi, S., Prasad, M. S. V., Modibbo, U. M., Ahmadi, S. A., & Ghasemi, P. (2023). Attaining Sustainable Development Goals through Financial Inclusion: Exploring Collaborative Approaches to Fintech Adoption in Developing Economies. *Sustainability (Basel), 15*(17), 13039. DOI: 10.3390/su151713039

Das, S., Mourmouras, A., & Rangazas, P. (2024). *Overlapping-Generations Model of Economic Growth.*, DOI: 10.1007/978-3-031-59728-2_2

Dax, T., & Copus, A. (2022). European Rural Demographic Strategies: Foreshadowing Post-Lisbon Rural Development Policy? *WORLD (Oakland, Calif.), 3*(4), 938–956. DOI: 10.3390/world3040053

Donovan, K., & Schoellman, T. (2023). The role of labor market frictions in structural transformation*. *Oxford Development Studies, 51*(4), 362–374. DOI: 10.1080/13600818.2023.2276702

Elgar, F. J., Stefaniak, A., & Wohl, M. J. A. (2020). The trouble with trust: Time-series analysis of social capital, income inequality, and COVID-19 deaths in 84 countries. *Social Science & Medicine, 263*, 113365. DOI: 10.1016/j.socscimed.2020.113365 PMID: 32981770

Emon, M. M. H. (2023). A Systematic Review of the Causes and Consequences of Price Hikes in Bangladesh. *Review of Business and Economics Studies, 11*(2), 49–58. DOI: 10.26794/2308-944X-2023-11-2-49-58

Emon, M. M. H. (2025a). Circularity Meets AI: Revolutionizing Consumer Engagement Through Green Marketing. In *Transforming Business Practices With AI-Powered Green Marketing* (pp. 169–208). IGI Global Scientific Publishing. DOI: 10.4018/979-8-3373-3017-4.ch007

Emon, M. M. H. (2025b). Cybersecurity in the Smart City Era: Overcoming Challenges With Modern Cryptographic Solutions. In *Securing Smart Cities Through Modern Cryptography Technologies* (pp. 43–74). IGI Global Scientific Publishing. DOI: 10.4018/979-8-3373-3326-7.ch002

Emon, M. M. H. (2025c). Digital transformation in emerging markets: Adoption dynamics of AI image generation in marketing practices. *Telematics and Informatics Reports, 20*, 100267. DOI: 10.1016/j.teler.2025.100267

Emon, M. M. H. (2025d). Ethical Intelligence in Motion: Leveraging AI for Responsible Sourcing in Supply Chain and Logistics. In *Navigating Responsible Business Practices Through Ethical AI* (pp. 207–240). DOI: 10.4018/979-8-3373-3104-1.ch008

Emon, M. M. H. (2025e). Leveraging AI on Social Media & Digital Platforms to Enhance English Language Teaching and Learning. In *AI-Powered English Teaching* (pp. 211–238). IGI Global Scientific Publishing., DOI: 10.4018/979-8-3373-1952-0.ch007

Emon, M. M. H. (2025f). Navigating the Digital Labyrinth: Personal Data Privacy and Security at Individual and Organizational Levels. In *User-Centric Cybersecurity Implications for Sustainable Digital Transformation* (pp. 257–288). IGI Global Scientific Publishing. DOI: 10.4018/979-8-3373-3171-3.ch008

Emon, M. M. H. (2025g). Overcoming Hurdles: Navigating Challenges in the Adoption of Smart Logistics. In *Emerging Trends in Smart Logistics Technologies* (A. Hlali, pp. 197–228). IGI Global Scientific Publishing. DOI: 10.4018/979-8-3373-2434-0.ch007

Emon, M. M. H. (2025h). Purpose-Driven Intelligence in Green Marketing: Leveraging AI for CSR-Centric and Sustainable Brand Positioning. In *Transforming Business Practices With AI-Powered Green Marketing* (pp. 89–122). IGI Global Scientific Publishing. DOI: 10.4018/979-8-3373-3017-4.ch004

Emon, M. M. H. (2025i). The Mediating Role of Supply Chain Responsiveness in the Relationship Between Key Supply Chain Drivers and Performance: Evidence from the FMCG Industry. *Brazilian Journal of Operations & Production Management, 22*(1), 2580. DOI: 10.14488/BJOPM.2580.2025

Emon, M. M. H., & Ahmed, M. (2025). Technological adoption in green practices as a mediator between green supply chain practices and operational performance: Evidence from the agro-processing and food industry. *Brazilian Journal of Operations & Production Management, 22*(4), 2695. DOI: 10.14488/BJOPM.2695.2025

Emon, M. M. H., & Chowdhury, M. S. A. (2025a). AI and IoT-Powered Smart Logistics: Transforming Supply Chains for Efficiency and Sustainability. In *Emerging Trends in Smart Logistics Technologies* (A. Hlali, pp. 45–72). IGI Global Scientific Publishing. DOI: 10.4018/979-8-3373-2434-0.ch002

Emon, M. M. H., & Chowdhury, M. S. A. (2025b). Safeguarding Student Data: Privacy and Security Challenges in AI-Powered Education Tools. In *Enhancing Student Support and Learning Through Conversational AI* (pp. 191–228). IGI Global Scientific Publishing. DOI: 10.4018/979-8-3373-3316-8.ch008

Emon, M. M. H., Chowdhury, M. S. A., Islam, M. S., & Nath, A. (2026). Value Perception, Digital Ownership, and Scarcity in Consumer-Brand Interactions Within Digital Payment Ecosystems. In *Impacts of Digital Payment Systems on Marketing* (pp. 231–270). IGI Global Scientific Publishing., DOI: 10.4018/979-8-3373-4526-0.ch008

Emon, M. M. H., & Khan, T. (2024a). A Systematic Literature Review on Sustainability Integration and Marketing Intelligence in the Era of Artificial Intelligence. *Review of Business and Economics Studies*, *12*(4), 6–28. DOI: 10.26794/2308-944X-2024-12-4-6-28

Emon, M. M. H., & Khan, T. (2024b). Unlocking Sustainability through Supply Chain Visibility: Insights from the Manufacturing Sector of Bangladesh. *Brazilian Journal of Operations & Production Management*, *21*(4), 2194. DOI: 10.14488/BJOPM.2194.2024

Emon, M. M. H., & Khan, T. (2025a). Corporate Social Responsibility for Sustainable Development: A Systematic Review of Business Contributions to Address Global Challenges. *Review of Business and Economics Studies*, *13*(2), 6–39. DOI: 10.26794/2308-944X-2025-13-2-6-39

Emon, M. M. H., & Khan, T. (2025b). The Rise of Circular Supply Chains: Recycling and Closed-Loop Systems Could Mitigate Inflationary Pressures. In *Supply Chain Disruptions and Impact on Global Inflation* (pp. 195–226). IGI Global., DOI: 10.4018/979-8-3373-1982-7.ch008

Emon, M. M. H., & Khan, T. (2025c). The Role of Traditional Media in Crisis Amplification: How Mainstream Media Magnifies Fake News and Ethical Dilemmas in Supply Chain Crises. In *Mass Media and Impact of Fake News on Supply Chains* (pp. 59–90). IGI Global., DOI: 10.4018/979-8-3373-2175-2.ch003

Emon, M. M. H., & Khan, T. (2026). Decoding Visual Brand Identity Through Computer Vision: AI-Driven Insights for Modern Branding. In *AI, Machine Learning, and Image Processing in Market Research and Branding* (pp. 33–66). IGI Global Scientific Publishing. DOI: 10.4018/979-8-3373-4506-2.ch002

Emon, M. M. H., & Mazid-Ul-Haque, M. (2025). Balancing Usability and Security: Enhancing User Experience Without Compromising Privacy. In *User-Centric Cybersecurity Implications for Sustainable Digital Transformation* (pp. 309–342). IGI Global Scientific Publishing. DOI: 10.4018/979-8-3373-3171-3.ch010

Emon, M. M. H., Nath, A., & Nipa, M. N. (2025). *AI for a Greener Tomorrow: Harnessing Artificial Intelligence for Environmental Sustainability*. IGI Global Scientific Publishing., DOI: 10.4018/979-8-3373-2387-9.ch010

Emon, M. M. H., Rahman, K. M., Nath, A., Mahsin-Ul-Islam, M., Rifat, H. H., & Kutub, J. (2025). Exploring Drivers of Sustainable E-Commerce Adoption among SMEs in Bangladesh: A TOE Framework Approach for Industry 5.0 Transformation. *2025 IEEE 7th International Conference on Sustainable Technologies For Industry 5.0 (STI)*, 1–6. DOI: 10.1109/STI69347.2025.11367600

Ferraz, D., Falguera, F. P. S., Mariano, E. B., & Hartmann, D. (2021). Linking Economic Complexity, Diversification, and Industrial Policy with Sustainable Development: A Structured Literature Review. *Sustainability (Basel)*, *13*(3), 1265. DOI: 10.3390/su13031265

Ferreira, F. H. G., Moramarco, D., & Peragine, V. (2026). Economic development and inequality of opportunity: Kuznets meets the Great Gatsby? *Structural Change and Economic Dynamics*, *76*, 94–114. DOI: 10.1016/j.strueco.2025.11.006

Gerhardinger, L. C., de Andrade, M. M., Corrêa, M. R., & Turra, A. (2020). Crafting a sustainability transition experiment for the brazilian blue economy. *Marine Policy*, *120*, 104157. DOI: 10.1016/j.marpol.2020.104157

Geza, W., Ngidi, M. S. C., Slotow, R., & Mabhaudhi, T. (2022). The Dynamics of Youth Employment and Empowerment in Agriculture and Rural Development in South Africa: A Scoping Review. *Sustainability*, *14*(9), 5041. DOI: 10.3390/su14095041 PMID: 37691717

Gölçek, A. G. (2024). The Economics of Aging: Global Trends and Perspectives. In *Perspectives on the Economics of Aging* (pp. 1–20). IGI Global Scientific Publishing., DOI: 10.4018/979-8-3693-7753-6.ch001

Goyal, K., & Kumar, S. (2021). Financial literacy: A systematic review and bibliometric analysis. *International Journal of Consumer Studies*, *45*(1), 80–105. DOI: 10.1111/ijcs.12605

Grinin, L., Grinin, A., & Korotayev, A. (2023). Global Aging and our Futures. *World Futures*, •••, 1–21. DOI: 10.1080/02604027.2023.2204791

Hantrais, L., Brannen, J., & Bennett, F. (2020). Family change, intergenerational relations and policy implications. *Contemporary Social Science*, *15*(3), 275–290. DOI: 10.1080/21582041.2018.1519195

Hasan, M. K., Emon, M. M. H., Hlali, A., & Khan, T. (2026). *Sustainable Operations in the Age of AI and Big Data* (Hasan, M. K., Emon, M. M. H., Hlali, A., & Khan, T., Eds.). IGI Global Scientific Publishing., DOI: 10.4018/979-8-2600-0216-2

Hasan, M. K., Khan, T., Hlali, A., & Emon, M. M. H. (2026). *Enhancing Sustainability in Global Supply Chains With Big Data Analytics* (Hasan, M. K., Khan, T., Hlali, A., & Emon, M. M. H., Eds.). IGI Global Scientific Publishing., DOI: 10.4018/979-8-3373-6896-2

Hasan Emon, M. M., Mustafizur Rahman, K., Ahmed, M., Ara Chowdhury, M. S., Ferdous Emee, A., & Kutub, J. (2026). AI Enabled Industry 4.0 Practices for Enhancing Sustainability Performance: Evidence from Manufacturing Firms in an Emerging Economy. *2026 5th International Conference on Electrical, Computer & Telecommunication Engineering (ICECTE)*, 1–6. DOI: 10.1109/ICECTE69292.2026.11429215

Hasan Emon, M. M., Rahman, K. M., Ahmed, M., Islam, M. R., Kabir, S. M. I., & Emee, A. F. (2026). Understanding Employees' Behavioral Intentions Toward Cybersecurity Adoption in Banks: Evidence from an Emerging Economy. *2026 5th International Conference on Electrical, Computer & Telecommunication Engineering (ICECTE)*, 1–6. DOI: 10.1109/ICECTE69292.2026.11429312

Islam, M. T., & Hossen, M. B. (2025). *Latin American Countries (LAC): An Economic Overview* (pp. 45–73). DOI: 10.1007/978-3-031-81362-7_3

Jackson, D., & Tomlinson, M. (2020). Investigating the relationship between career planning, proactivity and employability perceptions among higher education students in uncertain labour market conditions. *Higher Education*, *80*(3), 435–455. DOI: 10.1007/s10734-019-00490-5

Jafino, B. A., Kwakkel, J. H., & Taebi, B. (2021). Enabling assessment of distributive justice through models for climate change planning: A review of recent advances and a research agenda. *Wiley Interdisciplinary Reviews: Climate Change*, *12*(4), e721. Advance online publication. DOI: 10.1002/wcc.721

Kamran, M., Rafique, M. Z., Nadeem, A. M., & Anwar, S. (2023). Does Inclusive Growth Contribute Towards Sustainable Development? Evidence from Selected Developing Countries. *Social Indicators Research*, *165*(2), 409–429. DOI: 10.1007/s11205-022-03020-6

Keyes, K. M., & Platt, J. M. (2024). Annual Research Review: Sex, gender, and internalizing conditions among adolescents in the 21st century – trends, causes, consequences. *Journal of Child Psychology and Psychiatry, and Allied Disciplines*, *65*(4), 384–407. DOI: 10.1111/jcpp.13864 PMID: 37458091

Khan, T., & Emon, M. M. H. (2024). Exploring the Potential of the Blue Economy: A Systematic Review of Strategies for Enhancing International Business in Bangladesh in the context of Indo-Pacific Region. *Review of Business and Economics Studies*, *12*(2), 55–73. DOI: 10.26794/2308-944X-2024-12-2-55-73

Khan, T., & Emon, M. M. H. (2025a). Preparing for the Next Disruption: Lessons Learned From Past Crises and Building a Playbook for Future Supply Chain Shocks. In *Supply Chain Disruptions and Impact on Global Inflation* (pp. 253–286). IGI Global Scientific Publishing. DOI: 10.4018/979-8-3373-1982-7.ch010

Khan, T., & Emon, M. M. H. (2025b). Resilient Supply Chains: Lessons From Past Crisis Strategies Companies Can Adopt to Create More Resilient Supply Chains. In *Mass Media and Impact of Fake News on Supply Chains* (pp. 285–318). IGI Global. DOI: 10.4018/979-8-3373-2175-2.ch011

Khan, T., & Emon, M. M. H. (2025c). The role of digital supply chain practices in enhancing firm performance: Insights from the manufacturing sector of Bangladesh. *Brazilian Journal of Operations & Production Management*, *22*(2), 2493. DOI: 10.14488/BJOPM.2493.2025

Khan, T., Emon, M. M. H., & Nath, A. (2024). Quantifying the Effects of AI-Driven Inventory Management on Operational Efficiency in Online Retail. *2024 27th International Conference on Computer and Information Technology (ICCIT)*, 2092–2097. DOI: 10.1109/ICCIT64611.2024.11021996

Khan, T., Emon, M. M. H., Rahman, K. M., Nipa, M. N., & Fuad, M. N. (2025). The Role of AI in Driving Customer Engagement Through Technological, Organizational and Environmental Enablers in E-Commerce. *2025 International Conference on Quantum Photonics, Artificial Intelligence, and Networking (QPAIN)*, 1–6. DOI: 10.1109/QPAIN66474.2025.11171949

Khan, T., Emon, M. M. H., & Rahman, S. (2024). Marketing Strategy Innovation via AI Adoption: A Study on Bangladeshi SMEs in the Context of Industry 5.0. *2024 6th International Conference on Sustainable Technologies for Industry 5.0 (STI)*, 1–6. DOI: 10.1109/STI64222.2024.10951050

Khan, T., & Hasan Emon, M. M. (2024). Determinants of AI Image Generator Adoption Among Marketing Agencies: The Mediating Effects of Perceived Usefulness. *2024 IEEE 3rd International Conference on Robotics, Automation, Artificial-Intelligence and Internet-of-Things (RAAICON)*, 177–182. DOI: 10.1109/RAAICON64172.2024.10928548

Khan, T., & Hasan Emon, M. M. (2025). AI-Generated Content and Its Influence on Consumer Trust and Purchase Behaviour: Evidence from Bangladesh's E-Commerce Industry. *2025 IEEE 2nd International Conference on Computing, Applications and Systems (COMPAS)*, 1–6. DOI: 10.1109/COMPAS67506.2025.11381790

Klasen, S., Le, T. T. N., Pieters, J., & Santos Silva, M. (2021). What Drives Female Labour Force Participation? Comparable Micro-level Evidence from Eight Developing and Emerging Economies. *The Journal of Development Studies*, *57*(3), 417–442. DOI: 10.1080/00220388.2020.1790533

Klos, J., Krieger, T., & Stöwhase, S. (2022). Measuring intra-generational redistribution in PAYG pension schemes. *Public Choice*, *190*(1–2), 53–73. DOI: 10.1007/s11127-021-00914-w

Lee, R. (2020). Population aging and the historical development of intergenerational transfer systems. *Genus*, *76*(1), 31. DOI: 10.1186/s41118-020-00100-8

Lundberg, J. (2024). Intergenerational redistribution in a pay-as-you-go pension system. *The Journal of the Economics of Ageing*, *29*, 100534. DOI: 10.1016/j.jeoa.2024.100534

Luo, W. (2023). *Inequality, Demography and Fiscal Policy*. Springer Nature Singapore., DOI: 10.1007/978-981-99-0518-8

Ly, A. M., & Cope, M. R. (2023). New Conceptual Model of Social Sustainability: Review from Past Concepts and Ideas. *International Journal of Environmental Research and Public Health*, *20*(7), 5350. DOI: 10.3390/ijerph20075350 PMID: 37047965

Malla, M. H., & Pathranarakul, P. (2022). Fiscal Policy and Income Inequality: The Critical Role of Institutional Capacity. *Economies*, *10*(5), 115. DOI: 10.3390/economies10050115

Meinhold, R., Wagner, C., & Dhar, B. K. (2025). Digital sustainability and eco-environmental sustainability: A review of emerging technologies, resource challenges, and policy implications. *Sustainable Development (Bradford)*, *33*(2), 2323–2338. DOI: 10.1002/sd.3240

Mounsey, S., Veerman, L., Jan, S., & Thow, A. M. (2020). The macroeconomic impacts of diet-related fiscal policy for NCD prevention: A systematic review. *Economics and Human Biology*, *37*, 100854. DOI: 10.1016/j.ehb.2020.100854 PMID: 32062400

Mourtzis, D., Angelopoulos, J., & Panopoulos, N. (2022). A Literature Review of the Challenges and Opportunities of the Transition from Industry 4.0 to Society 5.0. *Energies*, *15*(17), 6276. DOI: 10.3390/en15176276

Munim, Z. H., Dushenko, M., Jimenez, V. J., Shakil, M. H., & Imset, M. (2020). Big data and artificial intelligence in the maritime industry: A bibliometric review and future research directions. *Maritime Policy & Management*, *47*(5), 577–597. DOI: 10.1080/03088839.2020.1788731

Nelischer, C., & Loukaitou-Sideris, A. (2023). Intergenerational Public Space Design and Policy: A Review of the Literature. *Journal of Planning Literature*, *38*(1), 19–32. DOI: 10.1177/08854122221092175

Ngcamu, B. S. (2023). Climate change effects on vulnerable populations in the Global South: A systematic review. *Natural Hazards*, *118*(2), 977–991. DOI: 10.1007/s11069-023-06070-2

O'Loughlin, K., Hussain, R., & Kendig, H. (2021). Attitudes towards Australia's baby boomers and intergenerational equity. *The Sociological Review*, *69*(4), 792–811. DOI: 10.1177/0038026120963367

Olmsted, J. C. (2024). Care labor, intergenerational equity, and (social) sustainability. *Review of Social Economy*, *82*(1), 51–75. DOI: 10.1080/00346764.2021.1964586

Patterson, I., & Balderas, A. (2020). Continuing and Emerging Trends of Senior Tourism: A Review of the Literature. *Journal of Population Ageing*, *13*(3), 385–399. DOI: 10.1007/s12062-018-9228-4

Perez-Arce, F., & Prados, M. J. (2021). THE DECLINE IN THE U.S. LABOR FORCE PARTICIPATION RATE: A LITERATURE REVIEW. *Journal of Economic Surveys*, *35*(2), 615–652. DOI: 10.1111/joes.12402

Petmesidou, M., & Guillén, A. M. (2022). Europe's green, digital and demographic transition: A social policy research perspective. *Transfer: European Review of Labour and Research*, *28*(3), 317–332. DOI: 10.1177/10242589221107498

Saleem, H., Shabbir, M. S., & Bilal khan, M. (2020). The short-run and long-run dynamics among FDI, trade openness and economic growth: Using a bootstrap ARDL test for co-integration in selected South Asian countries. *South Asian Journal of Business Studies*, *9*(2), 279–295. DOI: 10.1108/SAJBS-07-2019-0124

Schoneveld, G. C. (2020). Sustainable business models for inclusive growth: Towards a conceptual foundation of inclusive business. *Journal of Cleaner Production*, *277*, 124062. DOI: 10.1016/j.jclepro.2020.124062

Shahjahan, R. A., Estera, A. L., Surla, K. L., & Edwards, K. T. (2022). "Decolonizing" Curriculum and Pedagogy: A Comparative Review Across Disciplines and Global Higher Education Contexts. *Review of Educational Research*, *92*(1), 73–113. DOI: 10.3102/00346543211042423

Sharma, H. B., Vanapalli, K. R., Cheela, V. S., Ranjan, V. P., Jaglan, A. K., Dubey, B., Goel, S., & Bhattacharya, J. (2020). Challenges, opportunities, and innovations for effective solid waste management during and post COVID-19 pandemic. *Resources, Conservation and Recycling*, *162*, 105052. DOI: 10.1016/j.resconrec.2020.105052 PMID: 32834486

Spear, S. E., & Young, W. (2023). OLG – The Next Generations, 1960–1970. In *Overlapping Generations: Methods, Models and Morphology* (pp. 19–41). Emerald Publishing Limited. DOI: 10.1108/S1571-038620230000032006

Swanepoel, D. (2023). An Intergenerational Justice Approach to Technological Unemployment. *Asian Journal of Business Ethics*, *12*(2), 239–256. DOI: 10.1007/s13520-023-00172-7

Tang, L., Sun, S., & Yang, W. (2021). Does government education expenditure boost intergenerational mobility? Evidence from China. *International Review of Economics & Finance*, *74*, 13–22. DOI: 10.1016/j.iref.2021.02.001

Tibber, M. S., Walji, F., Kirkbride, J. B., & Huddy, V. (2022). The association between income inequality and adult mental health at the subnational level—A systematic review. *Social Psychiatry and Psychiatric Epidemiology*, *57*(1), 1–24. DOI: 10.1007/s00127-021-02159-w PMID: 34386869

Ullman, A. N., & Kittner, N. (2024). Are global efforts coordinated for a Just Transition? A review of civil society, financial, government, and academic Just Transition frameworks. *Energy Research & Social Science*, *108*, 103371. DOI: 10.1016/j.erss.2023.103371

Valls Martínez, M., Santos-Jaén, J. M., Amin, F., & Martín-Cervantes, P. A. (2021). Pensions, Ageing and Social Security Research: Literature Review and Global Trends. *Mathematics*, *9*(24), 3258. DOI: 10.3390/math9243258

van Bilsen, S., Mehlkopf, R. J., & van Stalborch, S. (2022). Intergenerational Transfers in the New Dutch Pension Contract. *De Economist*, *170*(1), 37–67. DOI: 10.1007/s10645-022-09399-4

Wang, S. (2020). Spatial patterns and social-economic influential factors of population aging: A global assessment from 1990 to 2010. *Social Science & Medicine*, *253*, 112963. DOI: 10.1016/j.socscimed.2020.112963 PMID: 32289647

Wang, X., & Squires, G. (2024). Intergenerational transfer, parental support and housing: A literature review. *Property Management*, *42*(2), 192–234. DOI: 10.1108/PM-04-2023-0037

Werners, S. E., Wise, R. M., Butler, J. R. A., Totin, E., & Vincent, K. (2021). Adaptation pathways: A review of approaches and a learning framework. *Environmental Science & Policy*, *116*, 266–275. DOI: 10.1016/j.envsci.2020.11.003

Wicaksono, G., & Mansury, Y. (2020). An Agent-Based Model of Wealth Inequality with Overlapping Generations, Local Interactions, and Intergenerational Transfers. In *Innovations in Urban and Regional Systems* (pp. 213–239). Springer International Publishing., DOI: 10.1007/978-3-030-43694-0_10

Wietzke, F. (2020). Poverty, Inequality, and Fertility: The Contribution of Demographic Change to Global Poverty Reduction. *Population and Development Review*, *46*(1), 65–99. DOI: 10.1111/padr.12317

Woodman, D. (2022). Generational change and intergenerational relationships in the context of the asset economy. *Distinktion : Scandinavian Journal of Social Theory*, *23*(1), 55–69. DOI: 10.1080/1600910X.2020.1752275

Yeh, M.-J. (2022). Intergenerational contract in Ageing Democracies: Sustainable Welfare Systems and the interests of future generations. *Medicine, Health Care, and Philosophy*, *25*(3), 531–539. DOI: 10.1007/s11019-022-10098-9 PMID: 35697971

Zhang, D., Wang, Y., & Jiao, Y. (2022). The Impact of Social Pension Schemes on the Mental Health of the Chinese Elderly: A Mediating Effect Perspective of Two-Way Intergenerational Support. *International Journal of Environmental Research and Public Health*, *19*(14), 8721. DOI: 10.3390/ijerph19148721 PMID: 35886572

Zhang, H., Ke, L., & Ding, D. (2021). The Effect of Chinese Population Aging on Income Inequality: Based on a Micro-Macro Multiregional Dynamic CGE Modelling Analysis. *Emerging Markets Finance & Trade*, *57*(5), 1399–1419. DOI: 10.1080/1540496X.2019.1623781

Zhuang, J., Khaskheli, M. B., Shen, C., Jafri, M. A. H., & Shamsi, I. H. (2025). A comparative study of economic activity and sustainable development in China and Three South Asian Countries. *Discover Sustainability*, *6*(1), 170. DOI: 10.1007/s43621-025-00885-8

KEY TERMS AND DEFINITIONS

Aging Economy: The term Aging Economy is used to refer to an economic system where the ratio of old to the working population is increasing and this affects the labor supply, labor productivity, consumption, and social welfare system.

Digital Inclusion: Digital inclusion ought to refer to the availability of digital technologies, skills and opportunities to participate in the digital economy by all people, irrespective of their age, income or geographic location.

Fiscal Sustainability: This refers to whether the government can maintain the government spending, social support programs and government debts in the long-term without placing undue strain on the future generation.

Income Distribution: The allocation of income to individuals or groups within a society consisting of earnings, in form of transfers and wealth and which influences economic disparity within or between generations.

Intergenerational Equity: The concept that there should be equal distribution of economic resources and opportunities, social benefits across different ages without a generation having to shoulder unequal burdens or to have disproportionately greater benefits in comparison with another generation.

Labor Market Transformation: The change in workforce in the labor market with respect to structure, composition and functioning due to demographic change, technology application and new working trends.

Life-Cycle Economics: Theoretical approach founded upon the observation of changes in income, consumption, saving, and resource demands experienced by people throughout their life, and upon which intergenerational transfer mechanisms, as well as policy formulation are conditioned.

Pension Systems: These are institutional arrangements designed to provide financial support to individuals who are retired and tend to be funded by the contributions of the existing employees, savings of the employees or government fund.

Chapter 4
Demographic Aging and Labor Market Dynamics in Tunisia:
Trajectories and Perspectives

Zyed Achour
http://orcid.org/0000-0002-1578-9062
National Institute of Labor and Social Studies, University of Carthage, Tunisia

ABSTRACT

Tunisia faces accelerating demographic aging — from 4.2% aged 65+ in 1990 to 9.5% in 2024 — threatening to close its demographic dividend window before structural weaknesses are resolved. Using 1990–2024 time-series data, this chapter combines OLS regressions, VAR dynamic modeling, and scenario-based projections to 2035. Findings show that aging is statistically associated with slower growth and declining labor force participation, with variance decomposition indicating that demographic shocks account for over a quarter of growth fluctuations at longer horizons. These effects are amplified by Tunisia's structural vulnerabilities — 43.9% informality, persistent unemployment, and post-2011 institutional rigidities — unlike more adaptable economies that mitigate aging pressures through flexible labor markets and productivity gains. Without reforms enabling senior workforce integration and productivity upgrading, Tunisia risks sustained stagnation before 2035, underscoring the urgency of transformative action while the demographic window remains partially open.

DOI: 10.4018/979-8-3373-7483-3.ch004

INTRODUCTION

Over the past three decades, Tunisia has undergone a rapid and profound demographic transition. The share of the population aged 65 and above has more than doubled, rising from around 4.2% in 1990 to about 9.5% (World Bank, 2024; Institut National de la Statistique [INS], 2025). This shift reflects sustained declines in fertility rates—now well below replacement level—alongside steady gains in life expectancy, signaling Tunisia's move from a young society to one entering the advanced stage of its demographic transition. While these changes reflect real progress in health and living standards, they also point to a narrowing window of demographic opportunity that is reshaping the country's growth outlook.

Demographic aging alters the foundations of economic performance through multiple channels. As the working-age population grows more slowly relative to the total population, pressures on labor supply intensify, potentially slowing growth and placing increasing strain on public finances and social protection systems. Yet Tunisia's situation is more complex than a simple narrative of inevitable decline. Tunisia is approaching the peak of its demographic dividend, with the window narrowing by the mid-2030s with the demographic peak captured by this study's horizon (up to 2035). The central question is therefore not whether Tunisia has already exhausted its demographic dividend, but whether it can still leverage what remains of it before institutional rigidities and unresolved structural weaknesses transform demographic maturation into economic stagnation.

These demographic dynamics unfold in a context already characterized by persistent structural weaknesses: unemployment rates averaging around 15–16% in recent years, relatively low labor force participation by international comparison, widespread informality affecting a substantial share of employment, and modest productivity growth. The convergence of advancing demographic transition and unresolved labor-market dysfunctions raises critical questions about Tunisia's capacity to navigate this closing window effectively. Unlike advanced economies that aged after achieving high income levels, Tunisia faces the prospect of growing old before growing rich—a predicament shared by many middle-income countries but rendered particularly acute by the country's post-2011 institutional fragility.

Despite the urgency of these issues, empirical research on the macroeconomic consequences of aging in Tunisia remains limited. While a substantial body of literature documents aging-related growth slowdowns in advanced economies and large emerging markets, middle-income countries undergoing late-stage demographic transitions under constrained institutional and fiscal capacity remain comparatively understudied. This gap is especially consequential, as the economic effects of aging are likely to vary systematically across development levels, labor-market structures, and social-protection regimes. Tunisia's experience—marked by a prolonged demographic transition, persistent informality, and labor-market rigidities that limit the integration of older workers—offers a timely and relevant case for examining how demographic aging interacts with labor-market dynamics and economic growth in a resource-constrained setting that still retains, at least in principle, a few years to adjust its trajectory.

Tunisia is furthermore a particularly compelling case in the Maghreb context: it is experiencing the fastest demographic aging in the region, compounded by post-2011 institutional fragility and the classic middle-income risk of growing old before growing rich — a combination that makes its experience analytically distinctive and policy-relevant well beyond its borders.

This chapter seeks to contribute to this debate by providing an empirical assessment of the statistical relationships between demographic aging, labor-force participation, and economic growth in Tunisia over the period 1990–2024. By combining descriptive evidence with econometric analysis and dynamic modeling, the chapter documents how Tunisia's demographic and economic patterns have evolved together, situating these observed associations within broader international discussions while highlighting the specific institutional and structural features shaping their co-movement. Beyond retrospective analysis, the chapter also explores plausible medium-term trajectories, offering insights into how demographic pressures may evolve under alternative policy scenarios—ranging from continued institutional inertia to coordinated reform efforts.

The primary objective of this chapter is to characterize the joint evolution of demographic aging, labor-market outcomes, and economic performance in Tunisia during its late-stage demographic transition. More specifically, the analysis pursues four interrelated objectives.

First, the chapter documents the statistical associations between population aging and economic growth, conditional on labor-force participation, longevity, and income levels. Given the strong interdependence among these variables during demographic transitions, the analysis explicitly recognizes that isolating independent causal effects is inherently challenging—and arguably inappropriate—in time-series data spanning just over three decades and shaped by multiple major shocks, including the 2011 revolution, the European debt crisis, and the COVID-19 pandemic. The objective is therefore to characterize conditional correlations and joint evolution rather than to attribute growth variation to isolated factors.

Second, the study examines the relationship between demographic aging and labor-force participation, exploring whether gains in life expectancy and rising income levels are associated positively or negatively with participation rates. While these patterns cannot establish causal mechanisms, they can reveal whether Tunisia's experience aligns with or diverges from lifecycle labor-supply theories that predict extended working lives in response to longer lifespans and economic development.

Given the scale of informality and the rigidity of labor-market institutions, Tunisia may be expected to depart from patterns observed in more flexible and formalized economies.

Third, the chapter characterizes temporal co-movements and feedback patterns between demographic change, labor-market participation, and economic performance using vector autoregression techniques. This framework allows the data to reveal empirical regularities in how these variables evolve together over time, without imposing strong assumptions regarding causal ordering or structural relationships.

Finally, drawing on observed historical patterns, the chapter develops conditional projections through 2035 to illustrate how demographic and labor-market trends might unfold under alternative assumptions about institutional adaptation and policy responses. These projections are explicitly scenario-based rather than predictive, designed to inform policy discussion by highlighting divergent trajectories depending on whether Tunisia succeeds in using its remaining demographic window up to the demographic peak in 2035, or risks entering the closure phase thereafter without meaningful structural adjustment. They should be interpreted as stylized reference paths rather than forecasts, intended to clarify the choices facing the country rather than predict its future.

LITERATURE REVIEW

Demographic aging has gradually become a central analytical framework in macroeconomic research, particularly in relation to long-term growth prospects, labor supply dynamics, and the sustainability of economic systems. A growing body of literature converges on the idea that demographic structure constitutes a fundamental determinant of economic performance, operating through labor input, productivity, savings behavior, and public finance channels (Bloom et al., 2003; Lee & Mason, 2011; OECD, 2025).

From a theoretical perspective, the economic implications of demographic change are most commonly analyzed through demographic transition theory and the life-cycle hypothesis. Demographic transition theory highlights the temporary growth-enhancing effects associated with declining fertility and mortality, which increase the relative size of the working-age population and generate what is commonly referred to as the demographic dividend (Notestein, 1945; Bloom & Williamson, 1998). This framework suggests that countries experience a window of opportunity during which favorable age structures can accelerate growth—but this window eventually closes as populations age and dependency ratios rise again. Empirical studies show that this dividend has played a significant role in accelerating economic growth in many countries during periods of structural transformation (Bloom et al.,

2003). However, once favorable demographics begin to fade, economies face the challenge of sustaining growth with a shrinking or stagnant workforce and rising old-age dependency—a challenge that becomes particularly acute when the transition occurs before countries have fully developed the institutions and productivity levels needed to support aging populations (Imrohoroglu, 2025).

Complementing this framework, the life-cycle hypothesis (Modigliani & Brumberg, 2013) provides insights into how population aging affects macroeconomic dynamics through changes in individual behavior over the life course. As populations age, aggregate savings and investment patterns tend to shift, reflecting declining labor income and increased dissaving among older cohorts. These mechanisms can reduce capital accumulation and weaken growth dynamics, particularly in economies where pension systems and financial markets are insufficiently developed (Lee & Mason, 2011). Such effects are especially relevant in middle-income countries, where demographic aging often occurs before income convergence is fully achieved—a pattern that distinguishes these economies from the historical experience of advanced countries that aged after becoming rich.

Demographic Aging in Advanced vs. Middle-Income Economies

Empirical evidence from advanced economies largely supports the existence of a negative association between population aging and economic growth. Studies focusing on OECD countries generally find that increases in the old-age dependency ratio are associated with lower GDP growth, mainly through reductions in labor input and total factor productivity (Feyrer, 2007; Acemoglu & Restrepo, 2017). At the same time, the literature emphasizes that these effects are not uniform across countries. Institutional factors, technological adaptation, human capital accumulation, and delayed retirement can partly offset the growth-reducing impact of aging, suggesting that policy responses play a critical role (Bloom et al., 2010; OECD, 2025). Recent evidence from the IMF suggests that healthier aging populations in high-income countries could potentially add 0.4 percentage points to annual GDP growth if older workers remain productively engaged—but this benefit depends critically on flexible labor markets and adaptive institutions (Gruss & Noureldin, 2025).

In emerging and middle-income economies, empirical findings remain more heterogeneous and context-dependent. While cross-country analyses report growth slowdowns associated with rapid population aging (Maestas et al., 2014; Thanh Trong et al., 2024; Mihajlović & Miladinov, 2024), other studies highlight that the economic consequences of aging depend strongly on labor market structure, informality, institutional quality, and participation patterns (Prskawetz et al., 2007). A critical distinction emerges between countries with flexible labor markets capable of absorbing older workers and those with rigid institutions that push workers out prematurely. In contexts characterized by persistent unemployment and weak labor absorption capacity, demographic aging may therefore reinforce existing structural constraints rather than act as an independent macroeconomic shock.

The challenge facing middle-income countries differs fundamentally from that of advanced economies. Unlike Japan or Western Europe, which aged gradually after achieving high income levels, many middle-income countries—particularly in Latin America, North Africa, and parts of Asia—are experiencing compressed demographic transitions (Caldwell & Caldwell, 1997). These "compressed transitions" create a timing problem: countries must adapt institutions, labor markets, and social protection systems to aging populations on accelerated schedules and with fewer fiscal resources than their high-income predecessors had available (Imrohoroglu, 2025). This sequencing issue—aging before wealth—creates vulnerabilities that are absent in the historical experience of today's developed economies.

Labor Market Institutions, Informality, and the MENA Context

Labor force participation occupies a central position in this debate. Standard labor supply models predict that aging reduces aggregate participation through cohort replacement effects. However, empirical evidence shows that participation outcomes are shaped by income levels, health improvements, education, and institutional incentives such as retirement rules and labor market flexibility (Bloom et al., 2010). Increases in life expectancy may thus coexist with declining participation rates when labor markets fail to integrate older workers or when structural unemployment persists among younger cohorts.

For MENA countries, and Tunisia in particular, these dynamics are further complicated by pervasive labor market informality and institutional rigidities that distinguish the region from other middle-income contexts. World Bank research documents that Tunisia's 43.9% informal employment rate, while lower than Egypt's 62.5% or Morocco's 77.3%, represents a massive departure from formal social protection systems and reflects institutional failures rather than economic necessity. The same comprehensive analysis emphasizes that informality is not inevitable but results largely from legal, regulatory, and institutional deficiencies—including inadequate social protection, rigid labor regulations, weak enforcement, and unfair competition that incentivizes firms to remain informal (Lopez-Acevedo et al., 2023).

Recent research on Tunisia's persistently high unemployment provides critical insights into how institutional degradation compounds demographic pressures. Belgacem and Vacher (2023) find that the deterioration of institutional factors—including business environment quality, product market rigidity, and financial constraints—explains approximately one-quarter of Tunisia's unemployment rate increase in the post-2011 period. Their analysis reveals that Tunisia's labor market exhibits excess sensitivity to output fluctuations compared to other middle-income countries, driven not just by high unemployment but by institutional rigidities that prevent adjustment. The study documents that while Tunisia's labor market laws barely changed during the last decade, employers perceive regulations as becoming more rigid due to centralized bargaining and deteriorating business climate, creating a gap between de jure flexibility and de facto rigidity.

This institutional context fundamentally shapes how demographic aging translates into economic outcomes. In economies with flexible labor markets, aging populations might extend working careers, increase part-time employment among older workers, or reallocate labor toward less physically demanding sectors. In Tunisia's context, however, rigid employment protection for permanent contracts, weak enforcement of labor standards in the informal sector, and limited opportunities for gradual retirement mean that workers often exit the labor force entirely rather than transitioning to less intensive employment (Adair et al., 2024). The interaction between informality and aging creates a vicious cycle: older workers in informal employment lack pension security and thus must continue working, but formal sector opportunities shrink with age, trapping many in precarious informal jobs or pushing them out of the labor force entirely.

Methodological Approaches and the Challenge of Causal Inference

A methodological gap separates much of the international literature from the analytical possibilities available for single-country time-series studies like the present analysis. The influential studies documenting aging's growth effects—including Feyrer (2007), Maestas et al. (2014), and Acemoglu and Restrepo (2017)—rely on panel data covering dozens of countries and exploit cross-sectional variation to identify relationships while controlling for country-specific factors. These approaches provide statistical power and enable causal identification strategies that are simply unavailable in single-country time series with fewer than 40 observations.

For national case studies, the analytical task shifts from causal identification toward descriptive characterization of joint evolution and conditional associations. This does not render such studies uninformative—indeed, detailed national analyses can reveal institutional specificities and temporal dynamics that cross-country averages obscure—but it does require transparency about inferential limits. Time-series analyses of demographic-economic relationships within single countries are better understood as exercises in pattern documentation and scenario exploration rather than causal attribution (Imrohoroglu, 2025).

This distinction is particularly important when multiple shocks—such as Tunisia's 2011 revolution, the European debt crisis, and the COVID-19 pandemic—compress into a short observation window, making it nearly impossible to isolate demographic effects from political, institutional, and economic disruptions. The appropriate interpretive frame for such analyses recognizes that observed correlations reflect the joint outcome of demographic change, institutional evolution, and policy choices rather than cleanly separable causal mechanisms.

Tunisia's Positioning in the Literature

In the Tunisian context, empirical research on demographic aging remains limited and fragmented. Existing studies tend to focus on unemployment, labor market segmentation, or fiscal sustainability, often treating demographic variables as background trends rather than core explanatory factors (Belgacem & Vacher, 2023; World Bank, 2014). Consequently, the interaction between population aging, labor force participation, and economic growth has not been systematically examined using macroeconomic time-series data. This gap is particularly important given Tunisia's rapid demographic transition and persistent labor market challenges, including high unemployment, low participation rates, widespread informality, and rigid institutions that prevent the integration of older workers into productive employment.

Tunisia's experience offers a valuable counterpoint to the East Asian model of rapid transition combined with institutional adaptation. While countries like South Korea and Thailand experienced similarly compressed demographic transitions, they coupled aging with productivity growth, export-led industrialization, and gradually improving labor market institutions (Caldwell & Caldwell, 1997). Tunisia, by contrast, faces aging within a context of post-2011 institutional deterioration, stagnant productivity, and labor market structures that have become more rather than less rigid over time (Belgacem & Vacher, 2023). This divergence from the successful East Asian pattern places Tunisia closer to Latin American experiences, where favorable demographics often failed to translate into sustained growth due to institutional deficiencies and persistent informality.

Building on demographic transition theory and the life-cycle hypothesis, and drawing on recent empirical contributions, this chapter addresses this gap through a focused national analysis. The methodological choices — combining OLS regressions with a VAR approach and conditional projections — are directly motivated by the limitations identified in the existing literature, particularly the absence of dynamic time-series evidence for Tunisia. It documents systematic statistical relationships between demographic aging, labor market participation, and growth dynamics in Tunisia, a middle-income economy in the late stages of its demographic transition that has yet to fully resolve its structural employment constraints. While the time-series approach precludes strong causal inference, the analysis provides valuable descriptive evidence on whether Tunisia's experience aligns with theoretical expectations and international empirical patterns—or whether institutional rigidities and informality create divergent dynamics that distinguish Tunisia from both advanced economies and more successful middle-income transitions.

DATA AND METHODOLOGY

Empirical Approach

This study relies on annual time-series data covering the period 1990–2024. The choice of this timeframe reflects both data availability and the acceleration of Tunisia's demographic transition during the post-1990 period.

The empirical approach adopted in this chapter unfolds across three complementary stages.

First, a descriptive analysis traces the major trends in demographic structure, labor force participation, and economic growth. This step provides the necessary context for understanding the pace of population aging and how it coincides with evolving labor market conditions.

Next, multivariate regression models are employed to highlight the statistical associations between demographic aging, labor force participation, and economic growth. Ordinary least squares estimations are used to adjust these relationships while accounting for income levels and longevity. Given the relatively small sample size (fewer than 35 observations) and the strong correlations among demographic variables (see correlation matrix, Table 3), the results should be interpreted as partial correlations rather than independent effects. Robustness checks—such as tests for multicollinearity and model stability—are systematically conducted and discussed to clarify the scope of the findings.

Then, to capture temporal co-movements and dynamic correlations, the chapter turns to a vector autoregression (VAR) model. This framework treats all variables as endogenous, allowing each to depend on both its own past values and those of the other variables. The VAR approach is particularly well suited to documenting empirical regularities in the joint evolution of demographic and economic variables, without imposing strong assumptions about causal ordering.

Finally, based on the VAR(2) estimates, conditional scenario projections are developed through 2035. These projections illustrate how demographic and economic variables might evolve if the observed correlations persist and no major structural breaks occur. They are not intended as forecasts, but rather as stylized trajectories designed to inform discussion about the demographic pressures that lie ahead.

These projections are explicitly scenario-based rather than forecasts, and several distinctions are worth emphasizing. They rest on the continuation of statistical relationships observed between 1990 and 2024, even though such patterns may not necessarily hold in different institutional contexts. They also incorporate parameter uncertainty through Monte Carlo simulations—1,000 draws from the estimated coefficient distributions—yet they cannot account for model uncertainty or the possibility of structural breaks. The eleven-year horizon represents the upper limit of what can reasonably be projected given a thirty-four-year estimation period, which means that results should be interpreted with increasing caution beyond five to seven years.

Before presenting the projections, the chapter conducts an out-of-sample validation. The VAR model is re-estimated on data from 1990 to 2019 and then used to "predict" the period 2020–2024, with projected values compared against actual outcomes to assess performance. This validation is stress-tested by the COVID-19 shock, which lies outside demographic dynamics. It therefore serves as a robustness check rather than a strict accuracy test. The baseline projections are subsequently complemented by alternative policy scenarios that adjust key parameters, such as labor force participation trends or productivity growth, in order to illustrate how sensitive the results are to different assumptions.

Definition of Variables and Data Sources

An overview of the variables used in the analysis, including their definitions, measurement units, and data sources, is provided in Table 1.

Table 1. Variables and Data Sources

Variable	Code	Definition	Unit / Measure	Source (year)
Population aged 65+	Pop65	Percentage of the population aged 65 and above	%	World Bank (2024) [[1]]
Life expectancy at birth	LifeExp	Life expectancy at birth (both sexes)	Years	World Bank (2024) [[2]]
GDP per capita	GDPpc	GDP per capita (current US$)	USD	World Bank (2024) [[3]]

continued on following page

Table 1. Continued

Variable	Code	Definition	Unit / Measure	Source (year)
GDP growth rate	GDPg	Annual real GDP growth rate	%	World Bank (2024) [4]
Labor force participation rate (15–64)	LFP15-64	Labor force participation rate for population aged 15–64 (both sexes)	%	World Bank (2024) [5]

Note: All data are sourced from the World Bank Open Data database, which compiles indicators based on International Labour Organization (ILO) modeled estimates for labor market statistics.

[1] World Bank. (2024). Population ages 65 and above (% of total population) [Data set]. World Bank Open Data. https://data.worldbank.org/indicator/SP.POP.65UP.TO.ZS?locations=TN

[2] World Bank. (2024). Life expectancy at birth, total (years) [Data set]. World Bank Open Data. https://data.worldbank.org/indicator/SP.DYN.LE00.IN?locations=TN

[3] World Bank. (2024). GDP per capita (current US$) [Data set]. World Bank Open Data. https://data.worldbank.org/indicator/NY.GDP.PCAP.CD?locations=TN

[4] World Bank. (2024). GDP growth (annual %) [Data set]. World Bank Open Data. https://data.worldbank.org/indicator/NY.GDP.MKTP.KD.ZG?locations=TN

[5] World Bank. (2024). Labor force participation rate, total (% of total population ages 15-64) (modeled ILO estimate) [Data set]. World Bank Open Data. https://data.worldbank.org/indicator/SL.TLF.CACT.ZS?locations=TN

Model Specification

Baseline Model: Economic Growth and Demographic Aging

Relationships between demographic aging and economic growth are estimated using ordinary least squares (OLS) linear regression. Model 1 adopts a parsimonious specification to minimize multicollinearity while retaining theoretically central variables:

$$GDPg_t = \alpha_0 + \beta\ Pop65_t + \beta\ LFP15-64_t + u_t \qquad (1)$$

Where,

GDPg denotes the annual real GDP growth rate,
Pop65 represents the share of the population aged 65 and above,
LFP15-64 captures the labor force participation rate of the working-age population (15–64 years).

The error term u absorbs unobserved factors, including institutional arrangements, technological change, and policy shocks.

This specification estimates the conditional association between demographic aging (β_1) and economic growth while adjusting for labor supply dynamics. The theoretical foundation rests on growth accounting frameworks wherein aging populations may constrain economic dynamism through reduced labor supply and compositional effects on aggregate productivity (Bloom et al., 2011; Lee & Mason, 2011).

Diagnostic tests accompany the estimates to ensure specification adequacy: heteroskedasticity (Breusch-Pagan test), multicollinearity (variance inflation factors), normality of residuals (Jarque-Bera test), and serial correlation (Durbin-Watson statistic). Standard errors are computed using heteroskedasticity-robust methods (White) to account for potential non-constant variance. Parameter stability is further assessed through a Chow test at 2011 — the most salient potential break point given Tunisia's political transition — which fails to reject the null of stable coefficients ($F = 0.733$, $p = 0.546$).

Workforce Integration Model: Labor Market Dynamics

To explicitly integrate the workforce dimension, we extend the analysis with a complementary model examining labor force participation:

$$LFP15-64_t \;=\; \gamma_0 + \gamma\; Pop65_t \;+\; \gamma\; GDPpc_t \;+\; v_t \tag{2}$$

Where LFP15-64 represents the labor force participation rate of the working-age population (15–64 years), Pop65 captures demographic aging, and GDPpc measures GDP per capita.

Model 2 examines whether demographic aging reduces labor supply through compositional effects associated with a shrinking working-age population ($\gamma_1 < 0$), and whether income levels support labor force participation by expanding economic opportunities and formal employment ($\gamma_2 > 0$).

Dynamic Analysis and Projections

To characterize temporal co-movements and dynamic correlations, a vector autoregressive model (Model 3) is estimated, treating all variables as jointly endogenous:

$$Y_t \;=\; A\; Y_{t-1} + A\; Y_{t-2} \;+\; \varepsilon_t \tag{3}$$

Where Y is a vector comprising the share of the population aged 65 and above (Pop65), the labor force participation rate of the working-age population (LFP15-64), the annual real GDP growth rate (GDPg), and GDP per capita (GDPpc). The matrices A_1 and A_2 capture dynamic interdependencies among variables, while the error term ε represents vector innovations.

Before estimating the system, the time-series properties of each variable are examined using Augmented Dickey-Fuller (ADF) tests, and the optimal lag structure is determined through standard information criteria. Both steps are prerequisites for a well-specified VAR and their results are reported in Table 2

As shown in Panel A of Table 2, GDPg and GDPpc are stationary at conventional significance levels ($p < 0.01$ and $p < 0.05$, respectively), supporting their direct inclusion in the system. LFP15-64 and Pop65, by contrast, do not reject the unit root null in these tests. This outcome is not unexpected: ADF tests are known to have low power in short samples, and both variables exhibit the kind of smooth, persistent movement — driven by structural labor market dynamics and demographic inertia — that makes formal rejection of non-stationarity difficult even when the series are bounded and mean-reverting over longer horizons. VAR(2) stability is confirmed through eigenvalue analysis, with all roots lying strictly inside the unit circle, which supports the validity of the estimated system.

Panel B reports the lag selection results. Both AIC and SBC reach their minimum at $p = 2$, pointing unambiguously to a VAR(2) specification. This two-lag structure offers a reasonable balance between capturing short-run dynamics and preserving degrees of freedom given the sample size of 34 observations.

Table 2. Unit Root Tests (ADF) and VAR Lag Selection Criteria

Panel A: Augmented Dickey-Fuller Tests						
Variable	**ADF Statistic**	**Lags**	**p-value**	**CV 5%**	**CV 1%**	**Conclusion**
GDPg	−4.413	0	**< 0.01**	−3.00	−3.75	Stationary I(0)
GDPpc	−3.060	4	**< 0.05**	−3.00	−3.75	Stationary I(0)
LFP15-64	−1.511	0	> 0.10	−3.00	−3.75	Near-stationary*
Pop65	+1.889	1	> 0.10	−3.00	−3.75	Near-stationary*
Panel B: VAR Lag Selection Criteria						
Lag (p)	**AIC**	**SBC**				
1	0.947	1.934				
2	**−0.873**	**0.912**				
3	−2.175	0.411				

Notes: ADF tests include an intercept; lag length selected by AIC. Critical values (MacKinnon, 1996) for n ≈ 24: −3.75 (1%) and −3.00 (5%). ✓ denotes the selected lag order. * Pop65 and LFP15-64 exhibit high persistence consistent with slow-moving demographic and structural variables; ADF tests have well-documented low power in short samples.

Eigenvalue analysis of the companion matrix confirms that the system is dynamically bounded, with seven of the eight roots lying strictly inside the unit circle. The dominant root (modulus = 1.078) sits marginally above unity, reflecting the well-documented high persistence of demographic variables in short samples rather than explosive dynamics — a pattern consistent with the descriptive and conditional nature of the analysis throughout this chapter.

To explore dynamic relationships, the forecast error variance decomposition (FEVD) applies a Cholesky ordering: [Pop65, LFP15-64, GDPpc, GDPg]. This ordering assumes that demographic variables adjust slowly and are largely predetermined. Labor force participation responds at intermediate horizons, while growth reacts more quickly. The choice is consistent with demographic inertia and evidence on adjustment speeds, though alternative orderings remain valid under different structural interpretations.

Projections for 2025–2035 are then built using the VAR estimates. Monte Carlo simulations, based on 1,000 draws from the estimated coefficients, capture parameter uncertainty and provide 95% confidence intervals around the baseline results. These projections assume that historical statistical relationships continue into the future. Baseline assumptions include annual growth in the share of the population aged 65 and above of 0.3 percentage points (in line with World Bank projections), GDP per capita growth of 1.2% (consistent with IMF medium-term forecasts), and annual gains in life expectancy of 0.03 years (extrapolating post-pandemic trends).

Before presenting these projections, the model is validated out-of-sample. The VAR is re-estimated on data from 1990–2019 and used to predict the years 2020–2024. The comparison between predicted and actual values provides a reality check on model performance, even when accounting for the COVID-19 shock. Finally, the baseline projections are complemented by alternative policy scenarios. These scenarios adjust key parameters, such as labor force participation or productivity growth, to test the sensitivity of the results to different assumptions.

Methodological Limitations and Inferential Caveats

Before turning to the empirical results, it is important to recognize the main limitations of this analysis and to interpret the findings with caution. The data are purely observational time series, which raises familiar challenges of endogeneity: growth can shape demographic behavior just as demographics influence growth. This simultaneity, along with unmeasured institutional or social factors, means that correlations may not reflect clean causal effects.

The sample itself is modest—about 34 annual observations—leaving limited statistical power and sensitivity to shocks such as the 2011 revolution or the COVID-19 crisis. Multicollinearity also complicates interpretation: aging and income are highly correlated, so coefficients should be read as partial associations rather than independent effects.

Finally, the choice of models (OLS and VAR with two lags) reflects pragmatic decisions rather than definitive specifications. Alternative forms, structural breaks, or measurement errors—especially in labor force participation given widespread informality—remain possible.

Taken together, these caveats mean that the results should be viewed as conditional associations consistent with theory and international evidence, not as proof of causality. The analysis documents how Tunisia's demographic and economic patterns align with broader expectations, offering insights for policy while acknowledging uncertainty.

RESULTS

Descriptive Statistics

Table 3 presents descriptive statistics for the period 1990–2024, serving as a reference for the interpretation of subsequent econometric results.

Table 3. Descriptive Statistics (1990–2024)

Variable	n	Mean	Std. Dev.	CV (%)	Minimum	Maximum
GDP growth rate (%) (GDPg)	35	3.10	2.60	83.9	-8.98	7.95
Population aged 65+ (% total) (Pop65)	35	6.64	1.60	24.1	4.19	9.53
Life expectancy at birth (years) (LifeExp)	35	73.78	2.33	3.2	69.09	76.51
GDP per capita (PPP constant 2021 $) (GDPpc)	35	10,516	2,145	20.4	6,743	13,244
Labor force participation rate (% 15-64) (LFP15-64)	35	51.23	1.23	2.4	49.22	54.54

Note: CV = Coefficient of variation (Std. Dev. / Mean × 100). All monetary values are expressed in purchasing power parity (PPP) constant 2021 international dollars.

These statistics reveal contrasting patterns of variability across demographic, economic, and labor market indicators. GDP growth exhibits exceptionally high volatility (CV ≈ 83.9%), reflecting Tunisia's exposure to major structural shocks over the period: the political transition following the 2011 revolution, the European debt crisis (2011–2013), repeated security incidents (2015–2016), and the COVID-19 pandemic (2020), which triggered an unprecedented 8.98% contraction. This extreme volatility stands in sharp contrast to the relative stability of labor market indicators, where the labor force participation rate shows a coefficient of variation of only 2.4%, suggesting structural rigidities in labor market dynamics that buffer short-term economic fluctuations.

Demographic aging displays elevated variability (CV ≈ 24.1%), with the share of the population aged 65 and above rising from 4.19% in 1990 to 9.53% in 2024. A 5.34 percentage point increase over 35 years, or approximately 0.15 percentage points annually. This progression signals Tunisia's transition from the early to the advanced stage of demographic aging, as large cohorts born during the high-fertility period of the 1960s and early 1970s approach retirement age. Life expectancy shows also steady improvement with low variability (CV = 3.2%), increasing from 69 years in 1990 to 76.5 years in 2024, reflecting sustained gains in public health despite economic turbulence.

GDP per capita exhibits substantial variability (CV ≈ 20.4%), with values ranging from $6,743 to $13,244 (PPP constant 2021 dollars). The mean of $10,516 masks significant fluctuations driven by both the post-2011 political crisis and the COVID-19 shock. The labor force participation rate of the working-age population (15–64 years) averages 51.23% over the period. These relatively low participation and employment rates, combined with their limited temporal variation, underscore persistent structural challenges in Tunisia's labor market, including high youth unemployment, low female labor force participation, and a substantial informal sector estimated at 30–40% of total employment.

Correlation Matrix

Table 4 highlights a set of strong and economically meaningful correlations that reflect the joint evolution of Tunisia's demographic and economic structures over the period 1990–2024. Most strikingly, the near-perfect association between population aging (Pop65) and life expectancy confirms that aging is inseparable from longevity gains within the broader demographic transition. This pattern reflects both sustained declines in fertility and improvements in survival at older ages, two long-term forces that have reshaped Tunisia's population structure.

Economic development appears closely intertwined with this demographic shift. GDP per capita is strongly correlated with both aging and life expectancy, suggesting that demographic change has unfolded alongside improvements in living standards rather than acting as an external constraint. In this sense, aging in Tunisia should be understood as an endogenous outcome of the development process, consistent with the demographic dividend framework (Bloom et al., 2011).

By contrast, the relationship between demographic variables and short-term economic performance tells a different story. GDP growth is negatively correlated with both aging and longevity, reflecting the temporal sequencing of growth and demographic change. Periods of rapid expansion preceded the acceleration of aging, while the post-2011 slowdown coincided with a sharper demographic shift. This divergence between levels and growth rates suggests that the economic benefits of the demographic transition may have largely run their course.

An apparent paradox emerges in the labor market indicators. Despite conventional expectations, aging is positively correlated with labor force participation and employment. Rather than indicating a causal effect of aging, this pattern likely captures cohort-specific and structural dynamics, including rising female participation, delayed retirement among educated workers, and gradual formalization of employment.

Finally, the weak link between GDP growth and employment points to the persistence of jobless growth, particularly after 2011, highlighting structural rigidities and mismatches that weaken the transmission of growth into labor market outcomes.

Taken together, the strong correlations among Pop65, LifeExp, and GDP per capita underscore the difficulty of disentangling their independent effects within a relatively short time series, an issue that motivates the multivariate specifications developed in the next section.

Table 4. Correlation Matrix (Pearson, 1990–2024)

Variables	Pop65	LifeExp	GDPpc	GDPg	LFP15-64
Pop65	1.000				
LifeExp	0.950***	1.000			
GDPpc	0.890***	0.910***	1.000		
GDPg	-0.420**	-0.390**	-0.310*	1.000	
LFP15-64	0.610***	0.590***	0.520***	-0.280*	1.000

Significance levels: *** $p < 0.01$, ** $p < 0.05$, * $p < 0.10$

OLS Estimates: Determinants of Economic Growth and Labor Force Participation

Table 5 presents OLS estimation results for both Model 1 (economic growth) and Model 2 (labor force participation), estimated over the period 1990–2024 (n=35) for which complete data are available.

Table 5. OLS Regression

Variable	Model 1: GDP Growth Rate (%)				Model 2: Labor Force Participation (% 15-64)			
	Coef.	**Std. Err.**	**t-stat**	**p-value**	**Coef.**	**Std. Err.**	**t-stat**	**p-value**
Population 65+ (%)	-0.587**	0.241	-2.435	0.021	-0.521**	0.208	-2.505	0.018
Labor force participation (% 15-64)	0.315**	0.128	2.461	0.020	—	—	—	—
GDP per capita (PPP $)	—	—	—	—	0.00038**	0.00017	2.235	0.033
Constant	10.234**	4.123	2.482	0.019	38.142***	9.234	4.132	0.000
Model Statistics								
Observations	35				35			
R^2	0.238				0.164			
Adjusted R^2	0.189				0.110			
F-statistic	4.85**				3.03*			

Notes: Significance levels: *** p<0.01, ** p<0.05, * p<0.10. Standard errors are heteroskedasticity-robust (White). Both models estimated over 1990–2024 (n=35).

Economic Growth and Demographic Aging

Model 1 accounts for a meaningful share of variation in GDP growth over the period under study, with an R^2 of 0.238 and an adjusted R^2 of 0.189. While these values may appear modest at first glance, they are broadly in line with expectations for growth regressions applied to a short and volatile time series such as Tunisia's. The overall F-statistic (4.85, $p < 0.05$) indicates that the set of explanatory variables jointly contributes to explaining growth dynamics beyond what would be captured by a constant-only specification. In this context, the explanatory power of the model should be interpreted cautiously, as reflecting both the intrinsic volatility of GDP growth and the deliberate choice of a parsimonious specification.

Demographic aging emerges as a central variable in this first specification. The coefficient associated with the share of the population aged 65 and above is negative and statistically significant ($\beta = -0.587$, $p = 0.021$), suggesting that increases in the elderly population are associated with slower economic growth, conditional on labor force participation. Substantively, a one percentage point increase in Pop65 is associated with an average reduction of approximately 0.6 percentage points in annual GDP growth. This finding aligns with a growing body of literature emphasizing the potential macroeconomic constraints associated with population aging, including pressures on labor supply, shifts in saving and investment behavior, and possible productivity slowdowns as demographic structures change (Bloom et al., 2011; Maestas et al., 2014).

To provide an order-of-magnitude interpretation, the increase in Pop65 observed between 1990 and 2024—roughly 5.3 percentage points—would correspond to a cumulative reduction in growth of about three percentage points over the period. This calculation is illustrative rather than causal. It serves to underscore the economic relevance of demographic change, while recognizing that the estimated relationship captures conditional correlations rather than identified causal effects. Moreover, potential indirect channels operating through capital accumulation, technological change, or sectoral reallocation cannot be fully isolated within the present framework.

Labor force participation also plays a role in shaping growth outcomes. The coefficient on the participation rate of the working-age population (LFP15–64) is positive and statistically significant ($\beta = 0.315$, $p = 0.020$), indicating that higher participation is associated with faster GDP growth, once demographic aging is taken into account. This result is consistent with standard growth accounting logic, in which labor input contributes directly to output dynamics (Lee & Mason, 2011). However, the relatively moderate magnitude of the coefficient points to important limitations. In a labor market characterized by persistently high unemployment, increases in participation do not automatically translate into effective labor utilization, which likely dampens the growth impact of expanded labor supply.

Determinants of Labor Market Participation

Model 2 focuses on the determinants of labor force participation and exhibits lower explanatory power than the growth equation, with an R^2 of 0.164 and an adjusted R^2 of 0.110. The model is only marginally significant overall ($F = 3.03$, $p < 0.10$), a result that reflects the relative stability of labor force participation rates in Tunisia over the period considered. With a coefficient of variation of just 2.4%, participation evolves slowly over time, making it inherently difficult to explain using demographic and macroeconomic variables that themselves change gradually.

Within this specification, demographic aging is again a significant factor. The coefficient on Pop65 is negative and statistically significant ($\beta = -0.521$, $p = 0.018$), indicating that a higher share of elderly individuals is associated with a lower labor force participation rate among the 15–64 age group, conditional on income levels. This result is consistent with basic demographic accounting: as the proportion of older individuals rises, the working-age population contracts relative to the total population, exerting mechanical downward pressure on aggregate participation measures (Bloom & Sousa-Poza, 2013).

Importantly, this conditional relationship contrasts with the positive bivariate correlation observed earlier. The divergence highlights the role of confounding factors. While raw correlations reflect the simultaneous influence of cohort effects and structural transformations—such as rising female participation and delayed retirement—the regression framework reveals the underlying compositional effect of aging once differences in income levels are taken into account.

Income per capita also appears to matter for labor supply decisions. GDP per capita enters the model with a positive and statistically significant coefficient ($\beta = 0.00038$, $p = 0.033$), implying that higher income levels are associated with increased labor force participation. Interpreted in practical terms, a $1,000 increase in GDP per capita (PPP) corresponds to an increase of roughly 0.4 percentage points in participation. This pattern is consistent with processes of labor market formalization and structural change, whereby economic development expands formal employment opportunities and supports greater labor market attachment, particularly among women (Klasen & Pieters, 2015). At Tunisia's current stage of development, these effects appear to dominate potential income-substitution mechanisms that might otherwise reduce labor supply.

Diagnostic Assessment

Table 6 reports the main diagnostic tests for both regression models. Overall, the results suggest that the estimated specifications are statistically sound and suitable for inference, with a few expected limitations related to the time-series nature of the data.

For the growth equation (Model 1), the Durbin–Watson statistic (1.72) falls within the acceptable range, indicating no serious concern regarding serial correlation. In contrast, the lower Durbin–Watson value observed for the labor force participation equation (Model 2) points to positive autocorrelation of residuals, a result that is not unexpected given the strong persistence of participation rates over time. To mitigate potential bias in inference, heteroskedasticity-robust standard errors are therefore used in both models.

Normality of residuals is not an issue in either specification. As shown in Table 6, Jarque–Bera tests fail to reject the null hypothesis of normally distributed residuals, supporting the validity of conventional t- and F-tests.

Multicollinearity diagnostics further confirm the robustness of the chosen specifications. In Model 1, variance inflation factors remain very low, reflecting the parsimonious structure of the growth regression. In Model 2, VIF values are higher but remain within acceptable bounds, consistent with the close relationship between demographic aging and income levels. Importantly, these levels do not threaten coefficient stability and are substantially lower than those obtained under less restrictive specifications.

Table 6. Diagnostic Tests

Diagnostic Test	Model 1 (Growth)	Model 2 (LFP 15-64)	Interpretation
Durbin-Watson	1.72	1.08	Acceptable in Model 1; possible autocorrelation in Model 2
Jarque-Bera	0.31	0.29	Residuals approximately normal (p>0.05) in both models
VIF (Pop65)	1.59	5.28	Excellent in Model 1; acceptable in Model 2
VIF (LFP15-64)	1.59	—	Excellent in Model 1
VIF (GDPpc)	—	5.28	Acceptable in Model 2
Breusch-Pagan (LM)	1.288(p = 0.525)	—	No evidence of heteroskedasticity in Model 1
Chow test (2011)	0.733 (p = 0.546)	—	No structural break detected at 2011

The Aging-Growth-Workforce Nexus

Reading the two model's results reveals a consistent pattern in the way demographic change interacts with economic dynamics in Tunisia.

Population aging is statistically associated with slower growth not only directly, but also through its correlation with labor market participation. While higher participation rates are associated with stronger growth, this positive channel only partially offsets the broader demographic pressures linked to an aging population.

At the same time, income levels matter for labor supply decisions. Higher GDP per capita is associated with greater labor force participation, pointing to a reinforcing relationship between economic development and employment opportunities. Yet the magnitude of this effect remains limited, suggesting that development alone is unlikely to fully counterbalance the structural forces generated by demographic aging.

More broadly, the results highlight a central difficulty inherent to demographic transitions: aging and development evolve jointly, making it challenging to disentangle their individual effects within a short time-series framework. This interdependence implies that policy responses *cannot* be narrowly targeted. Sustaining growth in the face of demographic change will likely require coordinated interventions that simultaneously address labor market participation, productivity, and the broader institutional environment, rather than isolated measures focused on a single margin.

Dynamic Analysis

While the OLS results provide useful evidence on average relationships, they remain ill-suited to capturing the temporal feedbacks that characterize demographic and economic change. For this reason, we complement the static analysis with a vector autoregressive framework designed to trace the dynamic co-movements among population aging (Pop65), labor force participation (LFP15–64), GDP growth, and GDP per capita. Treating these variables as jointly endogenous allows us to examine how shocks propagate over time, rather than imposing a priori causal ordering.

Before estimating the system, we verified that the series are sufficiently well behaved for VAR analysis. Unit root tests, reported in Table 2, confirm that GDPg and GDPpc are stationary in levels, while Pop65 and LFP15-64 exhibit high persistence, as discussed in Section 3.3.3. We then selected a two-lag specification based on standard information criteria, which offered a reasonable compromise between parsimony and the need to capture short-run dynamics. Stability diagnostics confirm that the system is dynamically bounded, with seven of the eight companion matrix roots lying inside the unit circle.

As a prerequisite to the variance decomposition, Table 7 reports pairwise Granger causality tests for all variables in the system. These tests assess whether the past values of one variable carry predictive content for another, beyond what is already captured by the variable's own history.

Table 7. Pairwise Granger Causality Tests (VAR, 2 lags)

Null Hypothesis	F-statistic	p-value
GDPg ⇏ Pop65	1.504	0.259
GDPpc ⇏ Pop65	1.387	0.285
LFP15-64 ⇏ Pop65	0.337	0.720
Pop65 ⇏ GDPg	0.028	0.973
GDPpc ⇏ GDPg	0.118	0.890
LFP15-64 ⇏ GDPg	2.144	0.157
Pop65 ⇏ GDPpc	0.017	0.984
GDPg ⇏ GDPpc	1.456	0.269
LFP15-64 ⇏ GDPpc	2.443	0.126
Pop65 ⇏ LFP15-64	1.042	0.380
GDPg ⇏ LFP15-64	1.494	0.261
GDPpc ⇏ LFP15-64	**3.311**	**0.069***

Notes: ⇏ denotes "does not Granger-cause". F-tests based on VAR(2), T = 22. Significance levels: * $p < 0.10$. All other null hypotheses are not rejected at conventional levels.

The results indicate that predictive relationships among variables are generally weak at the two-lag horizon, which is consistent with the short sample and the high persistence of demographic variables. The single exception is GDP per capita, which marginally Granger-causes labor force participation (p = 0.069), suggesting that income growth carries some predictive content for labor market dynamics — a finding coherent with the OLS results in Model 2. The absence of significant Granger causality from Pop65 to GDPg should not be read as contradicting the OLS and FEVD results. Granger tests capture short-run predictive content at the two-lag horizon, whereas the negative association between aging and growth documented elsewhere operates through slower structural channels — labor supply contraction, generational turnover — that unfold beyond what two annual lags can detect

Within this dynamic setting, we rely on forecast error variance decomposition to assess the relative contribution of demographic, labor market, and income-related shocks to fluctuations in GDP growth. Table 8 reports the variance decomposition of GDP growth over a ten-period horizon and provides a compact summary of how uncertainty in growth is redistributed across the different structural forces as time progresses.

Table 8. Forecast Error Variance Decomposition of GDP Growth (%)

Horizon (Periods)	GDPg	Pop65	LFP15-64	GDPpc
1	100.0	0.0	0.0	0.0
2	78.3	8.4	7.2	6.1
3	64.1	14.8	11.3	9.8
4	55.7	19.2	13.5	11.6
5	50.8	21.9	14.8	12.5
6	48.2	23.5	15.4	12.9
7	46.9	24.6	15.7	13.0
8	46.1	25.3	15.9	12.9
9	45.7	25.8	16.0	12.7
10	45.5	26.1	16.1	12.5

Note: Values indicate the percentage contribution of each structural shock to the forecast error variance of GDP growth.

As the forecast horizon extends, the dynamic role of demographic aging becomes increasingly apparent. In the short run, shocks to the share of the population aged 65 and above account for only a limited portion of GDP growth fluctuations. Over time, however, their contribution rises steadily, reaching more than one quarter of growth variance at the ten-period horizon. This gradual build-up is consistent with the slow-moving nature of demographic change and suggests that aging affects economic performance through persistent channels rather than immediate disruptions.

Labor force participation also plays a meaningful, though comparatively smaller, role in shaping growth dynamics. Its contribution to growth variance increases progressively over the forecast horizon, indicating that labor market adjustments accumulate over time. This pattern reinforces the idea that participation matters for growth not as a short-term shock, but through sustained effects on labor input and productive capacity.

By contrast, shocks to GDP per capita explain a more moderate share of growth variance, with their influence rising in the early periods before stabilizing. This trajectory is consistent with productivity and income effects that operate with some delay but do not dominate longer-term growth dynamics in the same way as demographic forces.

Impulse response analysis provides additional insight into these dynamics. A positive shock to population aging generates a delayed but persistent decline in GDP growth, with the strongest effects emerging several periods after the initial shock and fading only gradually. This timing reinforces the interpretation that aging operates through structural mechanisms — such as labor supply adjustments and generational turnover — rather than through immediate macroeconomic channels. In contrast, positive shocks to labor force participation are associated with a short-lived negative impact on GDP growth before dissipating, a pattern consistent with the absorption constraints of Tunisia's labor market, where expanded labor supply does not automatically translate into productive employment. Feedback effects within the VAR system are notably asymmetric. While demographic shocks have meaningful implications for growth and labor market outcomes, growth shocks exert little influence on the aging process itself, which is largely predetermined by past fertility and mortality trends. Growth does, however, appear to affect labor force participation with a short lag, suggesting that economic expansions may gradually draw additional workers into the labor market. The reverse effect — from participation to aging — remains weak, confirming the largely unidirectional influence of demographic structure on economic outcomes.

Overall, the VAR results do not overturn the conclusions drawn from the static regressions; rather, they deepen them. They confirm the central role of demographic aging in shaping growth dynamics, clarify the relative importance of labor market and income channels, and reveal that these effects unfold gradually over multiple years. Economic adjustment to demographic change in Tunisia thus appears to be a slow process, driven by long-term structural forces rather than abrupt shocks

Prospective Projections (2025–2035)

To explore how the demographic and economic dynamics identified in the VAR analysis may unfold over the coming decade, we construct conditional projections for population aging, labor force participation, and macroeconomic performance through 2035. These projections are derived from the estimated VAR(2) model and are generated using Monte Carlo simulations, which allow us to incorporate parameter uncertainty rather than relying on a single deterministic path.

We emphasize from the outset that these exercises are not forecasts in the strict sense. Instead, they should be read as reference scenarios that illustrate plausible trajectories under the assumption that historical relationships continue to hold. In particular, the projections abstract from major structural breaks, large-scale policy shifts, or exceptional exogenous shocks—such as pandemics, geopolitical disruptions, or sudden migration flows—that could substantially alter outcomes.

The baseline assumptions underlying the projections are summarized in Table 9. They reflect a post–demographic dividend context in which population aging continues to advance, income growth remains moderate, and labor market outcomes adjust endogenously to demographic and economic forces. In line with medium-term demographic projections, the share of the population aged 65 and above is assumed to increase steadily, driven by continued fertility decline and improvements in old-age survival. GDP per capita growth is set at a moderate pace, consistent with recent international projections and a scenario of gradual, incomplete structural reform. Labor force participation, by contrast, is not imposed exogenously but is allowed to evolve within the VAR system, capturing feedback effects from aging and income dynamics.

Taken together, these assumptions imply a gradual contraction of the working-age population and a rising old-age dependency ratio over the projection horizon. This shift provides the demographic backdrop against which the conditional economic trajectories should be interpreted. Under this baseline scenario, Table 10 reports the resulting projections for the main variables of interest, along with 95% confidence intervals derived from the simulation procedure.

Table 9. Baseline Projection Assumptions (2025–2035)

Variable	Assumptions
Population aged 65+ (Pop65)	+0.30 percentage points per year, consistent with the World Bank's medium demographic projections for Tunisia, reflecting continued fertility decline (total fertility rate projected at 2.0–2.1 children per woman) and sustained improvements in old-age mortality.
GDP per capita (GDPpc)	+1.2% annual growth (constant 2021 PPP dollars), consistent with the International Monetary Fund's medium-term growth projections for Tunisia (2024–2029), incorporating ongoing fiscal consolidation, gradual implementation of structural reforms, and moderate regional economic integration.
Labor force participation (LFP15-64)	Endogenously determined by the VAR model, reflecting feedback from aging and income growth. No additional exogenous assumptions imposed.

Note: These assumptions reflect Tunisia's post-demographic-dividend context. The working-age population share (ages 15–64) is projected to decline from approximately 67% in 2024 to about 63% by 2035, reducing potential GDP growth while simultaneously increasing old-age dependency ratios from approximately 14% to 20%.

These baseline assumptions align with recent demographic analyses suggesting that Tunisia will maintain a dependency ratio of approximately 2:1 (two workers per dependent) through 2040 (ISS Africa, 2019), representing a final window during which the country retains moderately favorable demographics. The projections therefore explore how Tunisia might navigate this closing window under different institutional and policy contexts.

Table 10. Projections and 95% Confidence Intervals (2025–2035)

Year	Variable	Central Forecast	95% CI Lower	95% CI Upper
2025	Population 65+ (%)	9.8	9.5	10.1
	Labor force participation (%)	51.3	50.8	51.8
	GDP growth rate (%)	2.6	1.8	3.4
	GDP per capita (PPP $)	12,900	12,550	13,250
2030	Population 65+ (%)	11.3	10.8	11.8
	Labor force participation (%)	51.1	50.3	51.9
	GDP growth rate (%)	2.4	1.4	3.4
	GDP per capita (PPP $)	13,700	12,900	14,500
2035	Population 65+ (%)	12.8	12.2	13.4
	Labor force participation (%)	50.9	49.9	51.9
	GDP growth rate (%)	2.2	1.1	3.3
	GDP per capita (PPP $)	14,600	13,500	15,700

Note: Confidence intervals derived from 1,000 Monte Carlo draws, propagating parameter uncertainty and stochastic shocks forward. Uncertainty widens over the forecast horizon due to cumulative error accumulation. Projections assume no major policy reforms, pandemics, or structural breaks.

The main projections derived from this model can be summarized as follows (Figure 1)

Figure 1. Tunisia's Demographic and Economic Projections (2024-2035)

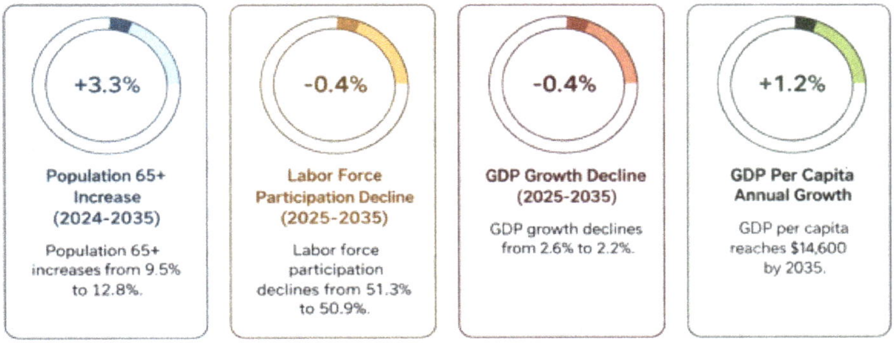

These projections suggest three trajectories corresponding to different policy and institutional responses:

The first corresponds to a *Demographic Inertia Scenario* (upper limit of the confidence interval): If Tunisia maintains its current policies without structural reforms, GDP growth could slow to 1.1% by 2035, while the labor force participation rate would fall to 49.9%. This trajectory reflects the persistent pressures related to the aging population: the rising dependency ratio of the elderly could severely strain pension systems and public finances, while labor market rigidity makes it impossible to retain older workers or integrate young people. GDP per capita growth stagnates at 0.8% per year, a level insufficient to create jobs for new entrants to the labor market and which risks generating social instability. This scenario is highly likely if pension reforms remain incomplete and if productivity growth stagnates.

The second scenario corresponds to an *Adaptive Reform Scenario* (central forecast): Based on baseline assumptions incorporating gradual efficiency gains—continued pension reforms, expansion of active employment programs that promote the retention of older workers, and moderate productivity improvements, particularly through the adoption of new technologies—growth could stabilize at around 2.2%. GDP per capita reaches $14,600, an amount sufficient to maintain living standards and finance increased social spending. This trajectory requires sustained reforms:

parametric adjustments to pensions, targeted subsidies for companies hiring older workers, and strengthened training programs.

Finally, the third scenario would be that of *Inclusive Innovation* (lower bound of the confidence interval): The ambitious implementation of comprehensive active aging policies—substantial pension reforms incentivizing delayed retirement, massive investments in continuing education, flexible working arrangements, and investments in digital infrastructure to improve productivity and encourage senior entrepreneurship—could maintain growth at 3.3% while preserving the labor force participation rate at nearly 51.9%. GDP per capita could reach $15,700, generating fiscal space for social investments and healthcare coverage. This scenario requires coordinated action among several ministries, sustained political commitment, and challenging negotiations with social partners regarding reforms.

These scenarios underscore that Tunisia's economic future is not predetermined by demographics alone. The political choices of the next three to five years will determine whether population aging becomes a major obstacle to growth and living standards or whether Tunisia will succeed in effectively adapting its labor market institutions and productivity dynamics to an aging society. The demographic transition is inevitable; its economic consequences, however, are not.

DISCUSSION

The findings reveal a Tunisia caught between demographic transition and institutional inertia. What stands out is not simply that aging correlates with slower growth—this much aligns with theory—but rather how pronounced the associations appear and through what institutional channels they seem to operate. The empirical evidence points to substantial negative correlations between elderly population shares and economic performance, relationships that become more visible once we account for Tunisia's particular labor market rigidities.

These associations appear stronger than recent international projections might suggest. The 2025 OECD Employment Outlook notes that without policy changes, GDP per capita growth will slow significantly in most OECD countries, but that mobilizing older workers could substantially offset this trend (OECD, 2025). Similarly, recent OECD research demonstrates that extending working lives as longevity rises could mitigate—though not completely offset—the negative employment effects of aging (André et al., 2024). The key finding from this body of work is that healthy aging can translate into productive aging when institutions adapt. Tunisia's experience tells a different story. The country appears unable to capitalize on its healthier aging population—life expectancy has climbed to 76.5 years—because labor markets cannot absorb older workers. Early exits from formal employment, combined with scarce opportunities for productive engagement beyond age 50, mean that longevity gains translate into extended dependency rather than extended productivity. There's an uncomfortable reality here: people are living longer but working less, not by choice but by institutional constraint.

The institutional backdrop matters enormously. Belgacem and Vacher's (2023) careful analysis of Tunisia's unemployment crisis offers crucial context: they find that the deterioration of institutional factors explains about a quarter of the unemployment rate increase in the post-2011 period. This institutional degradation—encompassing weakened business environments, rigid labor regulations, and reduced financial access—compounds demographic pressures rather than mitigating them. Where flexible labor markets might absorb aging through delayed retirement or part-time arrangements, Tunisia's rigidities convert demographic change into a binding constraint. The system lacks shock absorbers.

Recent labor market reforms complicate this picture but have yet to demonstrate transformative effects. Tunisia's Law No. 2025-9 (May 2025) imposed sweeping changes—criminalizing subcontracting, converting most fixed-term contracts to permanent positions, and restricting probation periods—ostensibly to protect workers and reduce informality. Yet early evidence suggests these measures may have stiffened labor market rigidities further. Employers facing higher adjustment costs are less likely to hire at all, particularly for older workers perceived as costly to dismiss. World Bank data show labor force participation stood at just 45.54% in Q3 2024, down from 45.78% the previous year and 1.2 percentage points below pre-COVID levels (World Bank, 2024). Meanwhile, unemployment remained elevated at 16% in Q3 2024, with youth unemployment exceeding 40% (World Bank, 2024). These trends suggest that well-intentioned reforms designed to formalize employment may paradoxically entrench informality and discourage formal hiring, particularly of demographic groups already marginalized.

The informality dimension deepens the puzzle considerably. World Bank (2023) research on MENA labor markets reveals that Tunisia's 43.9% informal employment rate represents a massive departure from formal social protection systems. The report emphasizes that informality does not have to be inevitable: rather it results largely from legal, regulatory, and institutional issues (Lopez-Acevedo et al., 2023). In Tunisia's case, widespread informality means that many workers—particularly those in their 50s and 60s—exit the labor force not because of age per se, but because informal employment offers no retirement security and formal opportunities vanish. They fall through the cracks.

This creates a vicious cycle. Aging reduces measured participation not primarily through biological limitations but through institutional failures that push older workers out prematurely. The observed decline in participation thus reflects less about demographic destiny than about a labor market unable to integrate its aging workforce. Income growth helps, certainly, but only modestly. Even substantial economic development cannot fully offset these structural barriers when the institutions governing work remain fundamentally misaligned with demographic realities.

The contrast with successful aging economies is instructive. OECD research highlights that countries maintaining high employment among older workers—such as Japan, where 50% of 65-69 year-olds were employed in 2020—combine flexible work arrangements, continuous learning opportunities, pension reforms that reward delayed retirement, and active anti-discrimination policies (OECD, 2025). Tunisia has implemented virtually none of these complementary measures. Pension reforms remain incomplete. Training programs for older workers are minimal. The 2024 World Bank initiative to digitalize ANETI's employment services represents a step forward, but deployment remains limited to 42% of local offices as of September 2024 (World Bank, 2024). Without comprehensive institutional adaptation, demographic aging will continue to expose rather than create Tunisia's growth constraints.

The dynamic analysis reinforces these interpretations. The gradual build-up of aging's influence over time—its growing explanatory power for growth variance—suggests that Tunisia faces not a sudden shock but a slow strangulation. Yet this temporal pattern also reveals something critical: the policy window is narrowing, but it has not yet closed. Tunisia retains until approximately 2035 a dependency ratio of roughly 2:1 (two workers per dependent), a final demographic window during which coordinated policy action could still make a meaningful difference (ISS Africa, 2019). Whether it will remains an open question.

Three scenarios emerge from the projections, each corresponding to different institutional responses. Under continued institutional paralysis (the upper confidence bound trajectory), GDP growth could slow to 1.1% by 2035 while labor force participation falls to 49.9%—a recipe for fiscal crisis and social instability. Under gradual reform (the central forecast), growth stabilizes around 2.2% with GDP per capita reaching $14,600—sufficient to maintain living standards but insufficient to rapidly create jobs or reduce unemployment. Under comprehensive adaptation (the lower bound)—combining pension reforms, productivity investments, flexible work arrangements, and aggressive formalization efforts—growth could reach 3.3% with participation near 52%, generating fiscal space for social investments.

These are not forecasts. They are choices. The arithmetic of aging is largely predetermined by past fertility decisions, but the economic consequences of that arithmetic remain contingent on institutional capacity and political will. Tunisia's challenge is not primarily demographic—it is institutional. The country has perhaps 10-15 years to build the labor market flexibility, productivity infrastructure, and social protection systems needed to support an aging population. The clock is ticking, but it has not yet run out.

POLICY IMPLICATIONS AND CONCLUSION

The findings of this chapter should worry Tunisian policymakers, but they should not paralyze them. Demographic aging is not an unavoidable sentence—it is a pressure test that reveals where institutions and labor markets are failing. The evidence here suggests that aging acts less as an isolated demographic shock than as a magnifying glass held up to inefficiencies that accumulated during the demographic dividend phase, when Tunisia had numbers on its side but failed to build the structures needed for the late transition stage it now inhabits.

Start with labor force participation. The empirical patterns show that aging is statistically associated with downward pressure on participation, but this relationship is neither mechanical nor universal. What matters is whether institutions can adapt. International experience offers some guidance: higher participation rates in aging societies typically emerge alongside flexible employment arrangements, lifelong learning systems, and retirement rules that reward continued economic activity (OECD, 2019; André et al., 2024). Tunisia has few of these. Trying to expand labor supply through participation policies—targeting women and older workers especially—makes sense in principle, but only if job creation keeps pace. Otherwise, you risk pushing more people toward a labor market that cannot absorb them. The problem is not just supply; it is the mismatch between supply and demand that has persisted for decades and that recent labor reforms may have inadvertently deepened.

Productivity becomes even more critical when the working-age population stops growing. In aging economies, growth depends less on adding workers and more on making each worker more productive. This means investment in human capital, skill upgrading, and technological adoption—all areas where Tunisia lags. Studies on advanced and emerging economies show that productivity gains can partially offset the growth slowdowns associated with aging, but only when education, innovation, and labor market policies work together rather than at cross purposes (Acemoglu & Restrepo, 2017; OECD, 2025). Tunisia's challenge is that its policy instruments remain fragmented, and coordination across ministries is weak.

Then there is timing. Tunisia's demographic transition has outpaced its structural transformation, which leaves the country facing aging pressures before it has resolved basic labor market dysfunctions. This sequencing problem is not unique—other middle-income countries have experienced similar misalignments—but it is particularly acute when the demographic dividend's final phase has already begun without sufficient institutional modernization. Aging, in this sense, is a catalyst that narrows the window for reform. Tunisia still has roughly 10-15 years before its dependency ratio deteriorates substantially beyond 2:1 (ISS Africa, 2019). The longer Tunisia waits, the harder adjustment becomes.

So where does this leave us? The analysis documents systematic statistical associations between aging and Tunisia's growth constraints, associations that seem to be intensifying as the country advances through its late-stage demographic transition. Demographic trends cannot be reversed quickly, but their economic consequences are not set in stone. Policy responses that enhance labor market inclusion, improve productivity, and adapt institutions to an aging workforce can still make a difference. The projections presented here are not forecasts but scenarios that illustrate divergent futures depending on institutional choices made in the next few years. The question is whether Tunisia has the political will to implement them while the demographic window remains partially open. Without such reforms, demographic pressures will likely reinforce existing growth limitations, turning what could be a manageable transition into a prolonged stagnation. The choice, ultimately, is not whether to act but how soon.

REFERENCES

Acemoglu, D., & Restrepo, P. (2017). Secular stagnation? The effect of aging on economic growth in the age of automation. *The American Economic Review*, *107*(5), 174–179. DOI: 10.1257/aer.p20171101

Adair, P., AlAzzawi, S., & Hlasny, V. (2024). Fostering decent jobs, formalising informal employment and spurring job mobility in MENA countries. *Economic Notes*, *53*(2), e12240. DOI: 10.1111/ecno.12240

André, C., Gal, P., & Schief, M. (2024). Enhancing productivity and growth in an ageing society: Key mechanisms and policy options (OECD Economics Department Working Papers No. 1807). OECD Publishing. DOI: 10.1787/18151973

Belgacem, A., & Vacher, J. (2023). *Why is Tunisia's unemployment so high? Evidence from policy factors* (IMF Working Paper No. 2023/219). International Monetary Fund. DOI: 10.5089/9798400257025.001

Bloom, D., Canning, D., & Sevilla, J. (2003). *The demographic dividend: A new perspective on the economic consequences of population change*. Rand Corporation. DOI: 10.7249/MR1274

Bloom, D. E., Boersch-Supan, A., McGee, P., & Seike, A. (2011). Population aging: facts, challenges, and responses. *Benefits and compensation International, 41*(1), 22.

Bloom, D. E., Canning, D., & Fink, G. (2010). Implications of population ageing for economic growth. *Oxford Review of Economic Policy*, *26*(4), 583–612. DOI: 10.1093/oxrep/grq038

Bloom, D. E., & Sousa-Poza, A. (2013). *Ageing and productivity* (No. 63-2012). FZID Discussion Paper. https://www.econstor.eu/bitstream/10419/68601/1/735218625.pdf

Bloom, D. E., & Williamson, J. G. (1998). Demographic transitions and economic miracles in emerging Asia. *The World Bank Economic Review*, *12*(3), 419–455. DOI: 10.1093/wber/12.3.419

Caldwell, J. C., & Caldwell, B. K. (1997). Asia's demographic transition. *Asian Development Review*, *15*(1), 52–87. DOI: 10.1142/S0116110597000031

Feyrer, J. (2007). Demographics and productivity. *The Review of Economics and Statistics*, *89*(1), 100–109. DOI: 10.1162/rest.89.1.100

Gruss, B., & Noureldin, D. (2025). Sustaining growth in an aging world. *Finance & Development, 62*(2). International Monetary Fund. https://www.imf.org/en/publications/fandd/issues/2025/06/sustaining-growth-in-an-aging-world-bertrand-gruss

Imrohoroglu, S. (2025). Aging, population projections, and public pensions (CIGS Working Paper Series 25-018E). The Canon Institute for Global Studies. https://cigs.canon/en/uploads/2025/07/WP25-018E_250717_selahattin02.pdf

Institut National de la Statistique (INS). (2025). Recensement Général de la Population et de l'Habitat 2024: Bilan Démographique. https://www.ins.tn/sites/default/files-ftp3/files/2025-05/Bilan_D%C3%A9mographique.pdf

International Labour Organization (ILO). (2024). *ILOSTAT database: Labour force participation rate – Tunisia*. https://ilostat.ilo.org/data/

Klasen, S., & Pieters, J. (2015). What explains the stagnation of female labor force participation in urban India? *The World Bank Economic Review*, *29*(3), 449–478. DOI: 10.1093/wber/lhv003

Lee, R. D., & Mason, A. (Eds.). (2011). *Population aging and the generational economy: A global perspective*. Edward Elgar Publishing. DOI: 10.4337/9780857930583

Lopez-Acevedo, G., Ranzani, M., Sinha, N., & Elsheikhi, A. (2023). *Informality and inclusive growth in the Middle East and North Africa*. World Bank Group. DOI: 10.1596/978-1-4648-1988-9

MacKinnon, J. G. (1996). Numerical distribution functions for unit root and cointegration tests. *Journal of Applied Econometrics*, *11*(6), 601–618. DOI: 10.1002/(SICI)1099-1255(199611)11:6<601::AID-JAE417>3.0.CO;2-T

Maestas, N., Mullen, K., & Powell, D. (2014). *The Effect of Population Aging on Economic Growth* (No. 14-012). Stanford Institute for Economic Policy Research.

Mihajlović, V., & Miladinov, G. (2024). Impact of population ageing on economic growth in emerging EU countries. *Ekonomický časopis. Journal of Economics*, *72*(1-2), 50–71.

Mihajlović, V., & Miladinov, G. (2024). Population ageing and economic growth: Evidence from advanced and emerging economies. *Economic Modelling*, *125*, 106286. DOI: 10.1016/j.econmod.2023.106286

Modigliani, F., & Brumberg, R. (2013). Utility Analysis and the Consumption Function: An Interpretation of Cross-Section Data 1. In *Post-keynesian economics* (pp. 388-436). Routledge.

Notestein, F. W. (1945). Population-The long view. *Food for the World.*, 36-57.

OECD. (2019). *Working Better with Age*. OECD Publishing. https://www.oecd.org/content/dam/oecd/en/publications/reports/2019/08/working-better-with-age_e6265636/c4d4f66a-en.pdf

OECD. (2025). *OECD Employment Outlook 2025: Can We Get Through the Demographic Crunch?* OECD Publishing., DOI: 10.1787/194a947b-

OECD. (2025). *OECD Employment Outlook 2025: Can we get through the demographic crunch?* OECD Publishing., DOI: 10.1787/194a947b-

Organisation for Economic Co-operation and Development (OECD). (2023). *Pensions at a Glance: Dependency ratios and population ageing*. OECD Publishing. https://www.oecd.org/en/publications/pensions-at-a-glance-2023_678055dd-en.html

Prskawetz, A., Fent, T., Barthel, W., Crespo-Cuaresma, J., Lindh, T., Malmberg, B., & Halvarsson, M. (2007). The relationship between demographic change and economic growth in the EU. *Report for Tender VT/2005/035*.

Thanh Trong, L., Nguyen, C. V., & Pham, T. H. (2024). Demographic ageing and economic growth: New evidence from emerging economies. *Journal of Asian Economics*, *88*, 101646. DOI: 10.1016/j.asieco.2023.101646

Thanh Trong, N., Thi Dong, N., & Thi Ly, P. (2024). Population aging and economic growth: Evidence from ASEAN countries. *Cogent Business &amp. Cogent Business & Management*, *11*(1), 2298055. Advance online publication. DOI: 10.1080/23311975.2023.2298055

World Bank. (2014). The unfinished revolution: Bringing opportunity, good jobs and greater wealth to all Tunisians. World Bank Group. https://www.worldbank.org/content/dam/Worldbank/document/MNA/tunisia_report/tunisia_report_the_unfinished_revolution_eng_synthesis.pdf

World Bank. (2024). *Fertility rate, total (births per woman) – Tunisia*. World Development Indicators. https://data.worldbank.org/indicator/SP.DYN.TFRT.IN?locations=TN

World Bank. (2024). *Life expectancy at birth, total (years) – Tunisia*. World Development Indicators. https://data.worldbank.org/indicator/SP.DYN.LE00.IN?locations=TN

World Bank. (2024). *Population ages 65 and above (% of total population) – Tunisia*. World Development Indicators. https://data.worldbank.org/indicator/SP.POP.65UP.TO.ZS?locations=TN

World Bank. (2024). Tunisia economic monitor, Fall 2024. World Bank Group. https://www.worldbank.org/en/country/tunisia/overview

World Bank. (2024). *Unemployment, total (% of total labor force) – Tunisia*. World Development Indicators. https://data.worldbank.org/indicator/SL.UEM.TOTL.ZS ?locations=TN

ADDITIONAL READING

Achour, Z., & Abid, I. (Eds.). (2026). *Economic transformations in population aging: Unlocking the silver economy*. IGI Global Scientific Publishing., DOI: 10.4018/979-8-3373-6117-8

Gölçek, A. G. (Ed.). (2025). *Perspectives on the economics of aging*. IGI Global Scientific Publishing., DOI: 10.4018/979-8-3693-7753-6

Gruss, B., Huang, E., Lagerborg, A., Noureldin, D., & Ozhan, G. K. (2025). The rise of the silver economy: Global implications of population aging. In *World Economic Outlook, April 2025*. International Monetary Fund., DOI: 10.5089/9798400289583.081

KEY TERMS AND DEFINITIONS

Compressed Demographic Transition: A pattern observed in many middle-income countries whereby the shift from high to low fertility and mortality rates occurs over a significantly shorter timeframe than in historical Western European experience, leaving governments, labor markets, and social protection systems with insufficient time to adapt.

Demographic Aging: A structural shift in a population's age composition driven by sustained fertility decline and rising life expectancy, resulting in a growing share of older individuals relative to the total population.

Demographic Dividend: The temporary economic growth bonus that arises when falling fertility rates produce a favorable age structure — a large working-age cohort relative to dependents. This window of opportunity can accelerate savings, investment, and output, but only if labor markets and institutions are capable of absorbing the expanded workforce productively.

Informal Employment: Work arrangements that fall outside the scope of formal labor regulation, social protection coverage, and contractual employment standards. Rather than representing a deliberate economic choice, informality usually reflects institutional failures — weak enforcement, rigid formal regulations, and inadequate social protection — that push workers and firms toward unregulated activity.

Jobless Growth: A macroeconomic phenomenon in which periods of positive GDP expansion fail to generate proportional gains in employment or meaningful reductions in unemployment.

Labor Force Participation Rate (LFPR): The proportion of the working-age population (ages 15–64) that is either employed or actively seeking employment.

Life-Cycle Hypothesis: A theory of individual economic behavior positing that people smooth their consumption over their lifetime by saving during their working years and drawing down accumulated assets in retirement.

Old-Age Dependency Ratio: A demographic measure expressing the number of individuals aged 65 and above relative to the working-age population (typically ages 15–64). A rising dependency ratio signals increasing pressure on workers, pension systems, and public finances, as fewer economically active individuals must support a growing elderly population.

Chapter 5

The Impact of Population Aging and an Aging Workforce on Women's Employment in Türkiye: ARDL Bounds Test

Sevilay Sarıca

Çankırı Karatekin Üniversitesi, Turkey

ABSTRACT

This study aims to analyze the long-term relationship among ageing population, elderly workforce and women's employment in Türkiye for the period 1988-2022. In order to reveal this relationship, the ARDL Bound Test were used. Based on the analysis, the findings indicate that that the workforce participation rate of the population aged 55-64 and the urban population growth rate has a positive effect on the employment rate of women aged 15-64, while the workforce participation rate of the population aged 65 and over, life expectancy at age 65 for men, life expectancy at age 65 for women, and the rate of growth in the service sector have a negative effect. Furthermore, a negative but statistically insignificant relationship was found between the employment rate of women aged 15-64 and exclusion index by gender.

1. INTRODUCTION

The issue of population ageing is one of the most important problems that countries face, impacting all aspects of their economic and social transformation. The ageing of the population leads to changes in the structure of a country's population,

DOI: 10.4018/979-8-3373-7483-3.ch005

employment, and workforce market, resulting in significant problems in many areas such as care, social protection, health expenditures, and retirement systems (WAPES, 2023). The population of Türkiye is ageing rapidly, just like the rest of the world. Among the reasons for this are the increase in average life expectancy due to better living conditions, a decrease in mortality rates as a result of advances in medicine, a decrease in crude death rates as a result of increased awareness in societies, and a decline in fertility rates as a result of the preference for one or two children instead of many children, which is a consequence of the deterioration of economic conditions and changes in the family structure as a result of changes in the social structure (Zweifel & Ferrari, 1992, p. 312; Erol, 2012, p. 55; Bloom et al., 2011, p. 1). In many developed and developing countries, birth rates are observed to be declining. Considering this, the decline in birth rates stands out as the most significant factor in the increase in the labor force participation of women (Bloom & Finlay, 2008, pp. 1-31). While the decline in birth rates has increased the labor force participation of women, the proportion of the working-age population has declined. However, the decline in the proportion of the working-age population has a negative impact on economic growth. Therefore, in order to increase the percentage of the working-age population, governments are encouraged to take measures to increase fertility rates. Nevertheless, it is anticipated that the resulting high fertility rates will subsequently limit the labor force participation of women. Consequently, this development will have a negative impact on economic growth (Bloom et al., 2007, pp. 1-43). As such, the issue of ageing populations is a significant concern for both developed and developing countries. To be classified as an ageing country according to international standards, a country must have either 10% of its population aged 60 and over or 7% of its population aged 65 and over (Nordin, Nordin, & Ahmad, 2015, p. 298). In the classification of societies and countries as ageing populations and in the presentation of the phenomenon of population ageing, the retirement age is usually used as a reference point (Öğütoğulları & Kılıç, 2016, p. 87). Within this framework, 65 is generally accepted as the retirement age, and an increase in the proportion of the population over retirement age within the total population means that these societies are confronted with the problem of population ageing (Gavrilov & Heuveline, 2003, pp. 32-37). Looking at this aspect, countries where the population aged 65 and over accounts for more than 10% the proportion of the total population are classified as very old societies, countries where is between 7% and 10% of the share of the total population, are classified as old societies, countries where is between 4% and 7% of the share of the total population, are classified as mature societies, and countries where the share is less than 4% are classified as young societies. (Uyanık & Başyiğit, 2018, p. 278). At the global level, the proportion of population aged 65 and over are growing faster than other age groups. In 2024, when looking at the proportion of the population aged 65 and over within the total population, Japan ranks 1st with 29.8%, Italy 2nd with 24.6%, Finland and Greece 3rd with 23.9%, Germany 4th with 23.2%, and France 5th with 22.1% (World Bank, 2025d). While the proportion of the population aged 65 and over in Türkiye's total population was 8.92% in 2019, this share increased to 9.3% in 2020, 9.82% in 2022, 10.1% in 2023, and 10.4% in 2024 (OECD, 2025a). According to 2024 data, Türkiye currently ranks as a "very old society" with a share of 10.4%. Based on the population projections made by the OECD, it is estimated that the share of the population aged 65 and over in Türkiye will be 10.8% in 2025, 12.7% in 2030, 14.2% in 2035, 16.2% in 2040, 20.1% in 2050, 22.6% in 2060, 24.2% in 2070, and 25.6% in 2080. This data suggests that in the coming years, Türkiye will be classified as a "significantly older society" and that its population is ageing further (OECD, 2025b; TÜİK, 2025). As the total population ages, the share of young people and those of working age in the total population decreases, causing a change in the population structure that impacts the workforce market by changing the workforce profile. As the population ages, percentage of young people and those of working age decrease in the total population, while the percentage of older people increases (Žnidaršič & Dimovski, 2010, p. 83-100). The result is that the number of young (aged 15-24) and mature (aged 25-54) individuals in the total workforce is decreasing, whereas the number of older (aged 55-64) individuals is increasing (Maestas et al., 2016). Furthermore, due to the ageing of the workforce, there is a significant impact on the workforce market, primarily in terms of workforce supply, labor force participation rates, employment and unemployment rates, and productivity of the workforce. Social security policies are influential in the practical definition of older workers or the older workforce. Specifically, the legal retirement age of 65 in many developed countries represents the upper limit of the age range for older workers. Accordingly, "older workers" are defined as those aged 55-64, which is the period prior to normal retirement (Ghosheh et al., 2006). With this in mind, steps are being taken to raise the retirement age in countries with an increasing elderly population, particularly in developed European Union countries, and regulations are being put in place to keep the elderly workforce in the working life for more years (Žnidaršič & Dimovski, 2010, p. 83-100).

In countries that have a younger population and are experiencing rising unemployment rates, the issue of early retirement for older workers is coming to the fore as a means of reducing unemployment. However, if the decline in older employment associated with early retirement causes a decline in youth and women's employment, then this suggests that there is a complementary link between older employment and youth or women's employment (Bingley, 2010). On the other hand, when the decline in employment among older workers causes an increase in youth and women's employment, the situation reveals a substitutive correlation between the employment of older workers and the employment of youth or women. Regarding the dismissal of employees, there are two different views. The first view suggests that productivity declines with age. Consequently, a person whose productivity declines should be dismissed and replaced with a younger and more dynamic worker. The second view claims that older workers are more productive as they are more experienced. This means that when employers lay off workers, they should lay off younger workers rather than older workers (Grimshaw, 2014, p. 1). This preference by employers is also influenced by their unwillingness to cover the cost of training young people for the work.

Meanwhile, it is said that in countries with an ageing population structure (countries whose populations are ageing), both the increase in healthcare spending caused by population ageing and the payments of retirement pensions after retirement will place a burden on the social security system. To this end, many European Union countries with an ageing population structure, where the number of elderly people is increasing day by day, such as Germany, are extending the retirement age, aiming to keep the elderly workforce in working life for longer, in order to alleviate the burden that ageing will create. In these countries with a high rate of population aging, viewing the problem from this perspective, older labor force remaining in the working life for longer periods will cause an increase in the number and participation of older labor within the labor supply. In this case, young and mature workers, as well as women (who are underrepresented in the workforce market and face discrimination in the workplace), who account for a smaller share of the total workforce, will either be excluded from the workforce market (i.e., substitution effect) or integrated into the workforce market in the context of the complementarity effect (Salem et al., 2008). Alternatively, should an increase in older employment result in an increase in youth employment, this indicates a complementary effect between older employment and youth or women's employment. On the other hand, it is clear that if an increase in the employment of older workers leads to a decrease in the employment of younger workers, this indicates a substitution effect between the employment of older workers and the employment of younger or women workers.

Countries in the European Union, which are rapidly ageing, are at the forefront of the problem of population ageing, which is a common issue for many countries. But the way these countries approach this common problem is really different. For example, because of the decline in productivity among older workers, some countries are letting older workers go or encouraging them to retire early. Encouraging early retirement pushes individuals out of the workforce market, creating two fundamental problems for countries that adopt this method. For one, when people are pushed out of the workforce market at an early age, it causes problems in the financing of the social security system. Secondly, once these individuals re-enter the workforce market, primarily for economic reasons, they face age-related discrimination, are unable to find work, and therefore remain unemployed, which in turn affects the rate of unemployment. Subsequently, it causes these individuals to turn to informal employment, leading to an increase in informal employment. It is reflected in an inverted U-shaped parabola between age and labor force participation rate (Faruqee, 2002; Uğur, 2002, p. 139-140). Considering this, most early retirement programs, which cover workers aged 50 and 55 and above, are preferred during periods of economic stagnation. This is why there was a noticeable trend toward dismissing older workers in the 1990s (Baybora, 2010, p. 10).

It is a known fact that women make up more than half of the total population, both globally and nationally (Kinoshita & Kochhar, 2016). It is observed, however, that there is serious discrimination against women in employment in many countries, including developed ones, and that the women's workforce is pushed out of the workforce market. The exclusion of young and women workers, who constitute a significant portion of the total workforce, prevents countries from achieving their full growth potential and results in growth below their potential. But there is an important point here that both at birth and at age 65, life expectancy is longer for women than for men. Given the ageing of the population, these figures suggest that women will account for a significantly higher proportion of the older workforce (aged 55-64 and 65+) than men in the future. Due to longer life spans, older people will remain in the workforce market for longer, thereby changing the workforce supply and impacting employment. Women are expected to play two critical roles in this demographic structure resulting from population ageing. One is to sustain growth by replacing the workforce that will leave the market due to ageing with women. The other is that they will play a role in covering the increase in healthcare spending due to ageing and in compensating for the burden that retirement pension payments will place on the social security system. To put it another way, while women who are not in the workforce will fill the gap in the workforce supply caused by population ageing, thus ensuring sustainable growth, at the same time they will play an important role in compensating for the burden that the passive workforce (retired workers) places on the social security system due to healthcare expenditures and retirement payments (by joining the workforce and paying social security payments).

As of 2024, people aged 65 and over account for 10.4% of Türkiye's total population. In other words, Türkiye is currently classified as a "very old society". Nevertheless, the OECD population projections reveal that this percentage will continue to increase in the coming years, meaning that Türkiye will become an "significantly older society" in the future (OECD, 2025b). Due to population ageing, youth and working-age populations will decrease as a proportion of the total population, while the elderly population will increase. The situation indicates that Türkiye will see a further decline in the number of young (aged 15-24) and mature-aged (aged 25-54) workers in the total workforce supply in the coming years, whereas the number of older workers (aged 55-64 and 65+) will increase. As in many other ageing countries, Türkiye has a higher life expectancy at birth and at age 65 for women than for men (OECD 2024). These trends reveal that the share of women in the total elderly labour force supply in Türkiye will be higher in the years to come. In this context, the labor force participation of women, which constitutes approximately half of the total population of Türkiye but has been pushed out of the workforce, is crucial both for sustaining growth (by replacing the workforce that will leave the market due to ageing with the employment of women) and in compensating for the increase in health expenditures that will result from ageing, as well as the burden that the working elderly workforce will place on the social security system with their post-retirement pension payments (by joining the workforce and paying social security payments).

The share of women in overall employment in Türkiye is not very different from other countries. Roughly half of the women's workforce is excluded from employment and therefore not included in the workforce. In terms of the number of women employed by sector in Türkiye, the services sector ranked first in employment between 2005 and 2022, with the agricultural sector in second place and the manufacturing industry sector, a subcategory of the industrial sector, in third place. Women's employment in the services sector is primarily in the following areas: health and social services, wholesaling and retailing, education, accommodation and food service activities, public administration and defense, administrative and support service activities, professional, scientific, and technical activities, shipping and storage, financial and insurance activities, information and communication, real estate activities, culture, arts, entertainment, recreation, and sports (TURKSTAT, 2023; TURKSTAT 2025). Especially after 1950, as a result of the policies implemented in Türkiye, agriculture's share in the economy declined, while the share of industry and services began to increase. One of the most striking points of this period is the decline in agriculture's share of the economy, which led to migration from rural areas to cities and a further increase in unemployment. This was particularly true for women who had found work in agriculture while living in rural areas but were unable to find appropriate jobs in the industrial sector after migrating to cities. These circumstances contributed to an increase in the share of unemployed women among the unemployed groups in cities (Şahin & Yıldırım, 2015, p. 134; Şen, 2018, p. 96). Moreover, as Türkiye adopted an exports-based industrialization strategy in the 1980s and began to open up to the outside world, unemployment increased even further in those years. When the 2000s arrived, the more prominent emergence of both technological development and globalization caused the demand for workforce to shift towards a more educated and qualified workforce. As a result, the women's workforce, which was already exposed to gender discrimination in the workplace (due to age, education level, and marital status), also became subject to digital gender discrimination in the digitalizing economy that emerged in the wake of advances in technology (Satı & Yılmaz, 2020). It is a fact that the STEM (science, technology, engineering, and mathematics) and ICT (information and communication technologies) sectors, which drive the emergence and development of digital technologies, employ fewer women and offer them lower levels of representation. Such lower representation and employment of women in these fields is considered to be a form of digital gender discrimination against the women's workforce. Looking at the fields where artificial intelligence and robots are replacing the workforce as a result of technological development and digitalization, one can see that these fields require no specific qualifications, such as secretarial work, office work, sales positions, cleaning, restaurants, warehousing, etc. Furthermore, the vast majority of these job sectors are in the service industry, and a large portion of the employees are women. This means that women working in these sectors will be at risk of unemployment in the digital economy (Karakaş, 2020).

Reviewing the studies conducted in this field to date, the majority of them address changes in the demographic structure and explore and analyze the relationship between these demographic changes and economic growth, wages, and inflation. But there are very few studies that look at and analyze the impact of population ageing, the most important demographic change in today's world, on women's employment. As in many countries around the world, primarily the developed European Union countries, Türkiye is confronted with the problem of population ageing. In comparison to developed European Union countries and many OECD countries, the working-age population in Türkiye is still relatively young. Considering the fact that the share of the population aged 0-14 in the total population is gradually decreasing, it can be concluded that the working-age population in Türkiye is also ageing (World Bank, 2025c). Given all these statements, we aim in this study to analyze the impact of population ageing and the elderly workforce on women's employment by examining data from the period 1988-2022 in an ageing Türkiye, thereby determining if this impact is substitutive or complementary, and guiding policymakers to take measures in this respect. To reveal the long-term relationship between the variables in the analysis, the ARDL Model will be applied. This study's first section provides a brief explanation of the phenomenon of population ageing, how it affects the labour force structure, and the relation between population ageing and women's employment. In the second section, demographic changes in Türkiye, as well as changes in the labor force participation rates, employment rates, and unemployment rates among the young, working-age, elderly, and women populations, will be revealed and explained with numbers. In the third section, a summary of the literature, namely empirical studies that examine the relationship between population ageing and employment will be provided. The fourth section describes the methods and model used in the study. In the fifth section, after defining the variables in the study, an empirical analysis will be carried out. The final chapter will set out the findings obtained from the analysis and propose recommendations for policymakers.

2. THE AGEING, WORKFORCE PARTICIPATION, EMPLOYMENT AND UNEMPLOYMENT RATES IN TURKEY

European Union countries being the most prominent, population ageing is one of the most significant socio-demographic issues for many countries around the world. It causes the share of elderly people in the total active population to grow, changing the workforce profile. As the population ages, there is an increase in the proportion of older workers in the total workforce and a decrease in the proportion of young workers (Samorodov, 1999, p. 4). In addition, as the population ages, there are changes in the participation, employment, and unemployment rates of age groups in the workforce market, thus affecting the workforce market and workforce availability. In line with population ageing, there will be a decrease in the share of young people in the total population, as well as in the supply of young workforce. The most striking feature of the young workforce, which is not considered human capital, is that they work in labor-intensive sectors. As a result, with the ageing of the population, the resulting decline in the supply of young workforce will have a significant impact on these sectors (Liu & Zhao, 2024, p. 68). Further, due to the ageing population, working-age people will make up a smaller proportion of the total population, while the supply of working-age workforce will decrease. The economic impact of this development will be a workforce shortage in the workforce market. To address this situation, pressure will increase in the areas of automation and technology use. It will bring to the fore the issue of increasing the employment of information, communication, and technology experts and engineers in order to create and maintain these automation systems. Without sufficient automation and technology use, it will only be possible to close this workforce gap by keeping the elderly workforce in the workforce market for longer and ensuring that they undergo continuous education and learning. However, only if countries invest more in adult education, skills development, and programs that enable adaptation to technological developments, this will be possible (Liu & Zhao, 2024, p. 68). It is also observed that, in line with the ageing of the population, there will be a tendency for industrial demand to move towards sectors targeting the elderly (such as healthcare services, nursing care, nursing homes, rehabilitation, home services for the elderly, services aimed at ensuring the safety of the elderly, etc.). As a result of this trend, pension and healthcare expenditures, which are increasing in proportion to the rising dependency ratio of the elderly population, are expected to exceed the increase in revenue from taxes. In the coming years, with the ageing of the population, this issue brings to the fore the threat of a serious imbalance between public expenditures and tax revenues (Liu & Zhao, 2024, p. 68).

Compared to many European Union countries with ageing populations, Türkiye is currently among the countries with a slightly younger working-age population structure. Nevertheless, a decline in birth rates, largely due to the preference of most families to have only one or at most two children, particularly as living conditions become increasingly difficult on the other hand, medical advances leading to lower mortality rates and the increase in both average life expectancy and life expectancy at age 65 and above on the other show that Turkish population will undergo a very rapid ageing process in the not-too-distant future.

When we look at the birth rate numbers in Türkiye, it is clear that the birth rate (crude (per 1000 people)) has been declining over the years. In 1960, the birth rate was 45%, in 1970 it was 40.5%, in 1980 it was 33.6%, in 1990 it was 25.4%, in 2000 it was 21.4%, in 2010 it was 17.2%, in 2020 it was 13.4%, and in 2023 it was 11.2% (World Bank, 2025a).

There has also been a downward trend in the death rate (crude (per 1000 people)) over the years. In 1960, the the death rate was 17.7%, falling to 13.4% in 1970, 9.6% in 1980, 6.8% in 1990, 5.8% in 2000, 5% in 2010, 6.1% in 2020, and 5.9% in 2022 (World Bank, 2025b).

A significant change has occurred in the proportion of age groups within the total population:

- In 1970, the share of the population aged 0-14 in the total population was 42.7%, while this share decreased to 39.7% in 1980, 35.8% in 1990, 30.2% in 2000, 25.8% in 2010, 22.7% in 2020, and 21.4% in 2024. This shows that there is a steady decline in the number of young people in Türkiye (World Bank, 2025c). Looking at the share of the population aged 0-14 in the total population in terms of population projections, this share, which was 23.5% in 2018 and 22.6% in 2023, is predicted to fall to 19.3% in 2040; 16.9% in 2060, and 15.7% in 2080 (TÜİK, 2025).

- Between 1970 and 2024, the share of the population aged 15-24 in the total population was 18.5% in 1970, rising to 20.2% in 1980, 20% in 1990, 19.5% in 2000, 17.1% in 2010, 15.5% in 2020, and 15% in 2024. This data highlights that the proportion of the population aged 15-24 within the total population in Türkiye has been on a downward trend since 1990 (OECD, 2025c).

- It can be seen that while the share of the working-age population aged 15-64 in the total population was 53.9% in 1970, this share increased to 56.3% in 1980, 60.9% in 1990, 63.8% in 2000, 67.1% in 2010, 67.7% in 2020, and 68.4% in 2024 (OECD, 2025c). Today, compared to many OECD countries, Türkiye has a more advantageous population structure and an ideal population pyramid in terms of the share of the working-age population in the total population, as shown by these figures. Nevertheless, it is expected that this will change in the years to come.

According to population projections, the share of the population aged 15-64 in the total population, which was 67.8% in 2018 and 67.2% in 2023, is expected to fall to 64.4% in 2040, 60.4% in 2060, and 58.7% in 2080 (TÜİK, 2025). It reveals that the working-age population is getting older and that in the coming years, the share of the ageing workforce in the total workforce will be higher.

- In 1970, the share of the population aged 65 and over in the total population was 4.4%, rising to 4.7% in 1980, 4.4% in 1990, 6.7% in 2000, 7.1% in 2010, 9.3% in 2020, and 10.4% in 2024 (OECD, 2025c). Viewed in terms of population projections, it is estimated that the share of the population aged 65 and over in the total population will be 12.7% in 2030, 16.2% in 2040, 20.1% in 2050, 22.6% in 2060, 24.2% in 2070, and 25.6% in 2080 (OECD, 2025b; TÜİK, 2025).

- In 1970, women aged 65 and over made up 4.9% of the total population, rising to 5.2% in 1980, falling to 4.7% in 1985, and dropping to 3.9% in 1990. It rose again after 1990, reaching 6.1% in 1995, 7.6% in 2000, 8% in 2010, 10.4% in 2020, and 11.6% in 2024. This data highlights the fact that the share of women aged 65 and over in the total population has been increasing consistently since 1991 (OECD, 2025c).

- In 1970, the share of men aged 65 and over in the total population was 3.9%, and this figure rose to 4.2% in 1980, 4.9% in 1990, 5.8% in 2000, 6.2% in 2010, 8.2% in 2020, and 9.3% in 2024. This data demonstrates that the share of men aged 65 and over in the total population has increased annually, just as it has for women (OECD, 2025c). When the share of women and men aged 65 and over in the total population is compared, this age group of women is found to be greater than the share of men in the total population. To put another way, in the total population, the share of women aged 65 and over is greater than the share of men in the same age group.

Given the population structure and projections outlined above, it can be said that the share of the 0-14 age group in Türkiye's total population is decreasing, whereas the share of the 65 and over age group (in particular, the share of women compared to men) is increasing. In 2024, the share of the population aged 65 and older in Turkey's total population is 10.4%. This shows that indicates that Türkiye currently falls within the "very old society" classification. On the other hand, it is evident that Turkey's working-age population (those aged 15–64) is aging, and that the share of the aging workforce within the total labor force will increase in the coming years. Ageing populations have resulted in regulations raising the retirement age in many countries. The retirement age in many OECD countries is currently 65 for both women and men. In contrast, Türkiye stands out as one of the countries with the earliest retirement age among OECD countries. Until 1999, Türkiye had an early retirement system, which resulted in most individuals who entered the workforce at a young age retiring early. Examining the period from the 1980s to 1999, a decline in the labor force participation rate of the population aged 55-64, classified as the older workforce, can be seen. Then, in 1999, changes were made to gradually increase the retirement age to 58 for insured women and 60 for insured men. Another amendment was made in 2008, deciding to gradually increase the retirement age until 2036 and raise it to 65 for both women and men by 2048. Since this change, the labor force participation rate of the population aged 55-64, considered the older workforce, has increased (OECD, 2025d; Öğütoğulları & Kılıç, 2016, p. 85-97).

Women's labor force participation in Turkey follows a U-shaped trend. During the period when agriculture accounted for the largest share of the economy, women participated in the labor force as unpaid family workers. Following the decline in agriculture's share of the economy after 1980, rural-to-urban migration began; however, female laborers arriving in cities were pushed out of the labor force due to their low educational levels and lack of skills. Subsequently, as the shares of the industrial (manufacturing) and service sectors in the economy increased and women's educational levels rose, women's labor force participation has grown (Serel ve Özdemir, 2017, p. 133-134).

An analysis of the labor force participation rates by age group reveals significant changes;

- In 1988, the labor force participation rate of the population aged 15-24 was 56%, but this fell to 51.1% in 1994, 46.6% in 1999, and 37.6% in 2007, increased to 38.1% in 2008, reached 40.8% in 2014, 44.4% in 2019, and 47.1% in 2024 (OECD, 2025d).
- In 1988, the labor force participation rate of the population aged 25-54 was 65.1%, but this rate fell to 63.7% in 1994, 61.8% in 1999, 58.1% in 2007, rising to 58.9% in 2008, 64.4% in 2014, reached 68.1% in 2019, and 69.5% in 2024 (OECD, 2025d).
- In 1988, labor force participation rate of the population aged 55-64 was 45.7%, but this rate fell to 41.8% in 1994, 40.1% in 1999, 28.2% in 2007, rising to 28.9% in 2008, 33.4% in 2014, 36.5% in 2019, and 41% in 2024 (OECD, 2025d).
- In 1988, the labor force participation rate of the population aged 65 and over was 21.8%, this rate fell to 18.9% in 1994, rose to 23.5% in 1999, fell to 20.8% in 2000, fell to 11.4% in 2007, increased to 11.6% in 2008, 12.4% in 2012, fell to 11.9% in 2019, 9.9% in 2020 and increased to 13.1% in 2024 (OECD, 2025d).

It can be observed that the labor participation rates of both women and men aged 55-64 declined between 1988 and 2007. In contrast, following population ageing and the 2008 regulation that increased the retirement age to 65 for both women and men through a gradual transition (especially after 2008), the labor force participation rate of the population aged 55-64 has continuously increased for both women and men. It is also noteworthy that the labor force participation rate of the population aged 65 and over, which had fluctuated until 2016, began to increase from 2017 onwards. Retirement pensions or incomes of individuals aged 65 and over falling below the poverty or even hunger line could be considered a contributing factor to this increase (OECD, 2025d). When viewed from this angle, it can be noted that individuals who retire in many developing countries, as well as in Türkiye, suffer a loss of income after retirement and even live below the threshold of poverty. As a result, individuals aged 65 and over are entering the workforce market again after retirement and seeking employment. To put it another way, in cases where the income obtained by elderly individuals after retirement is not sufficient, or where their current income drops to the poverty or starvation level as a result of negative economic developments, the elderly workforce (aged 65 and above) wants to re-enter the workforce market and work after their retirement (Samorodov, 1999, p. 14). It will not be easy for these older individuals who enter the workforce market to find work. Due to their advanced age, they will be subject to age discrimination (especially older women in the workforce). These circumstances will pose the problem of elderly unemployment in the coming years for many developing countries (especially those with low pensions and/or where many people live on the threshold of poverty and hunger) as they face an ageing population.

Significant changes over the years can also be observed when employment rates by age group are examined;

- In 1988, the employment rate for the 15-24 age group was 46.2%, but this rate fell to 43% in 1994, 39.7% in 1999, and 30.2% in 2007, rose to 32.1% in 2011, 35% in 2018, but fell again during the COVID-19 pandemic, rising again to 35.3% in 2022 and 39.5% in 2024 (OECD, 2025d).
- In 1988, the employment rate for the 25-54 age group was 61.9%, but this rate fell to 59.8% in 1994, 58.2% in 1999, 54% in 2003, and 53.5% in 2008. After 2008, it began to increase, reaching 59.1% in 2013, reaching 61% in 2018, but falling again during the COVID-19 pandemic, rising again in 2022 to 62.8%, and reaching 64.1% in 2024 (OECD, 2025d).
- In 1988, the employment rate for the 55-64 age group was 43.9%, but this rate fell to 40.8% in 1994, 39.3% in 1999, 29.5% in 2004; and 27.1% in 2007. It began to increase after 2008, reaching 31.9% in 2012, reaching 35.3% in 2018, falling again during the COVID-19 pandemic, rising again in 2022 to 35.2%, and reaching 38.8% in 2024 (OECD, 2025d).
- In 1988, the employment rate for the 65 and over age group was 21.5%, but this rate fell to 15.9% in 1993. It began to rise after 1995, reaching 20.7% in 1995, 23.4% in 1999, and then began to decline after 2000, falling to 20.7% in 2000, 13.3% in 2005, 11.6% in 2008, rose to 12.1% in 2018, fell again during the COVID-19 pandemic, rose again in 2022 to 11.7%, and rose to 12.7% in 2024 (OECD, 2025d).

It appears that the age group ranked first in terms of the highest women's employment rate in Türkiye is the 25-54 age group, followed by the 15-24 age group in second place, the 55-64 age group in third place, and the 65 and over age group in fourth place. Among men, the age group with the highest employment rate is, likewise the women, the 25-54 age group, followed by the 55-64 age group, and then the 65 and over age group, then the 15-24 age group (OECD, 2025d). Other notable points regarding employment rates are;

- It is observed the employment rate for women increased during the 2005-2024 period and for men increased during the 2004-2024 period in the 25-54 age group, in which the employment rate is highest for both women and men (OECD, 2025d).

- Among the age groups with the highest women's employment rates, the 15-24 age group ranked second showed an increase during the 2008-2024 period. In the same age group, men's employment rates increased during the 2004-2024 period (OECD, 2025d).

- The 55-64 age group, ranked third in terms of the highest women's employment rate, experienced a decline in the women's employment rate during the 2000-2007 period, but it started to increase during the 2008-2024 period. In the same age group, the men's employment rate increased during the 2008-2024 period (OECD, 2025d).

- Among the age groups with the highest employment rates for both women and men, the employment rate for those aged 65 and over, which ranks fourth, appears to have declined among women between 2000 and 2007 but increased between 2008 and 2024. On the other hand, the employment rate for men in the same age group decreased between 2000 and 2015 but increased between 2016 and 2024 (OECD, 2025d).

- When we look at the employment rates of women by age group, another interesting point emerges. Women's employment rates in the 15-19, 45-49, 50-54, 55-59, 60-64 age groups and the 65 and over age group have steadily increased in 2022, 2023, and 2024. From a sectoral perspective, in terms of the number of women employed in Türkiye, from 2005 to 2022, the services sector ranked first in terms of employment, followed by the agriculture sector in second place and the manufacturing industry sector under the industry sector in third place. As for the activities and job areas in the services sector where women are employed, they are human health and social work activities, wholesale and retail trade, education, accommodation and food service activities, public administration and defense, administrative and support service activities, professional, scientific, and technical activities, transportation and storage, financial and insurance activities, information and communication, real estate activities, and culture, arts, entertainment, recreation, and sports, in an orderly way (TURKSTAT, 2023; TURKSTAT 2025).

3. LITERATURE

3.1. The Relation Between Population Ageing and Employment

In their study on the Japanese economy, Oshio and their colleagues point out that there is a positive relationship between the labor force participation of older people and the employment of young people. In addition, their study shows that there is a major difference in terms of productivity between older and younger workers, and that this difference in productivity has no effect on the substitution between older and younger employment (Oshio et al., 2010, p. 217-241). Bingley and their colleagues analyzed the Danish economy and the impact of changes in the employment rate of older people (aged 55-64) on the employment rates and unemployment rates of young people (aged 20-24) and adults (aged 25-54). Their study concluded that there is a correlation between the employment of older individuals and the employment of younger individuals, showing that increases or decreases in older employment are accompanied by parallel trends in younger employment. Moreover, they pointed out that there was a tendency for adult employment to increase in response to a decrease in older employment as a result of retirement incentives. Based on these two key outcomes, it appears that there is a complementary relationship between older and youth employment, as well as a substitutive relationship between older and adult employment. It has been pointed out that the increase in the labor force participation rates of women during the period considered in the study has been instrumental in this increase in adult employment (Bingley et al., 2010, p. 99-117). Baker et al. examined the substitution relationship between young, adult, and older workers in their study on Canada, looking at variables such as the youth unemployment rate, youth employment rate, adult unemployment rate, adult employment rate, youth school attendance rate, and older employment rate. A strong relationship was found between older employment and the youth unemployment rate. Meanwhile, the study also revealed that an increase in elderly employment leads to an increase in both youth and adult employment (Baker et al., 2010. p. 77-97). Gruber and Wise, in their study covering 12 OECD countries, determined that measures aimed at increasing the employment of people aged 55-64 did not have a negative effect on the employment of people aged 15-24. Furthermore, they found that in six countries where there was a large increase in the employment rate of older workers, young people's employment rate also increased significantly (Gruber & Wise, 2010). Thießen studied the effects of ageing on sectoral employment in selected 55 countries. According to the study, it was determined that population ageing leads to an increase in relative employment in sectors such as manufacturing, finance, wholesale and retail trade, etc., and a decrease in relative employment in agriculture and mining sectors. Moreover, no clear impact of population ageing on employment was found in sectors such as electricity, gas, water, construction, transportation, and communications (Thießen, 2007, p. 1-24). Based on data from 1968-2005, Salem and colleagues investigated the long-term relationship between the increase in the labor force participation of older people and the unemployment of young people and adults (people of mature age) in their study for France. Results of the study revealed that higher participation of older individuals in the workforce led to an increase in youth employment rates and a decrease in youth unemployment rates. Nonetheless, caution was advised regarding the findings, as the correlations identified did not necessarily indicate a causal relationship between older and youth employment. In addition, they found that an increase in the labor force participation of older leads to a decrease in the employment rates of adults (the 25-54 age group). On top of that, the findings did not provide evidence that a decrease in the labor force participation of older leads to an employment increase among young people (Salem et al., 2008, p. 1-40).

Based on workforce projections from 25 European Union member states, Carone analyzed the impact of population ageing on the workforce market and economic growth rates in these countries. Results revealed that population ageing and the increase in the share of older workers in the total workforce will have a negative impact on workforce supply, causing a slowdown in growth in economy. They also pointed out that the increasing employment growth rate between 2004 and 2017 is likely to decline between 2018 and 2050 due to the increasing share of older workers (Carone, 2005, p. 1-57). Lisenkova et al. noted in their study for Scotland that the decrease in the workforce supply caused by population ageing and a decline in the population would have negative effects on the level of employment and growth in economy. Meanwhile, they found that the working-age population is going down, but this is mostly balanced out because most immigrants coming to the country are working-age people. Basically, the drop in employment is less than the drop in the working-age population (Lisenkova et al., 2010, p. 1351-1368). In their study for the European Union, the United States, and China, Didžgalvytė and Lukšaitė examined the impact of population ageing on labor force participation, employment, growth of the labor, savings, and healthcare spending. They found that population ageing has a negative impact on labor force participation, employment, and growth of the labor (Didžgalvytė & Lukšaitė, 2014, p. 65-81). In Japan, Kondo examined the impact of the increase in elderly employment resulting from the legal requirement for permanent employment put into effect in 2006 on the employment of other workers. As a result of the study, it was established that there was no substitution relationship between the increase in elderly employment resulting from this practice and full-time youth employment. Furthermore, it was noted that some companies terminated the employment of part-time women workers during the period of the policy (Kondo, 2016, p. 1-23).

Dixon investigated the effect of population ageing on the young and old workforce in his study for the United Kingdom. Based on the results of the study, it was found that population ageing could have an effective impact on both the total employment rate and the employment rates of different age groups (Dixon, 2003, p. 67-76). The study conducted by Kasnauskienė and Andriuškaitė for Lithuania examined the impact of population ageing on the employment rate, growth, household consumption and savings. They found that the old-age dependency index, used as an indicator of population ageing, had no statistically significant effect on the employment rate in the short run (Kasnauskienė & Andriuškaitė, 2017, p. 44-62).

The study by Henkens et al. demonstrated that there is a decline in the workforce supply due to population ageing. To compensate for this decline in the workforce supply, priority is given to the employment of women, ethnic minorities, and younger individuals (Henkens et al., 2008, p. 1314-1329). Irmen and Litina studied the impact of population ageing on immigrants and gender attitudes. They found that population ageing leads to a decline in the working-age population, an increase in the number of economically dependent elderly people, and a decline in total production. They also point out that increasing the labor supply is necessary for increasing total production. However, they emphasize that policies attracting both immigrants and women to the workforce supply are needed to increase the workforce supply (Irmen & Litina, 2022, p. 1009-1032). It is suggested by Guzmán et al. that the decrease in the workforce due to population ageing can be mitigated by the participation of the older workforce (people aged 60-64 and 65 and above) and women in the workforce. It is also possible to enable older workers and women to join the workforce only through the provision of childcare services, flexible working hour arrangements, by eliminating tax and social assistance disincentives for second earners in the family, by abandoning wage policies based on gender-based wage discrimination, by gradually increasing the retirement age, and by creating equal lifelong learning opportunities for women and men (Guzmán et al., 2025). Austen and Giles analyzed the impact of population ageing on women's paid employment opportunities in their study on Australia. Results of the research revealed that population ageing will lead to an increase in the labor force participation of women. Additionally, the study highlighted that women's employment will play a crucial role in compensating for the decline in workforce supply caused by population ageing. They also point out that population ageing will create additional demand for the type of workforce traditionally provided by women (domestic work, elderly care, nursing, childcare, etc.) (Austen & Giles, 2003, p. 257-278). In their study, Brown and Guttmann investigated the impact of population ageing on the workforce supply. The finding of the study shows that population ageing is causing a decline in the workforce supply, while this decline can be balanced by increasing the labor force participation of women and older people (Brown & Guttmann, 2017, p. 37-46). Hu analyzed the impact of population ageing on the workforce supply in his study on Japan. Findings from the study reveal that the decline in workforce supply associated with ageing is increasing and becoming progressively more severe. Hu emphasizes that increasing women's employment is necessary to mitigate the decline in workforce supply and boost economic growth (Hu, 2024, p. 692-701). The study by Rensburg et al. examined the economic impacts of population ageing in New Zealand. They concluded that the decline in labor supply associated with population ageing could be mitigated by increasing the labor force participation rates of women and older labor (Rensburg et al., 2021, p. 1-73). The study conducted by Zuo et al. for China looked into the impact of population ageing on employment. It was found that population ageing reduces the labor supply by causing a decline in the working-age population. To mitigate this decline in the labor supply, the study highlights the need to increase labor force participation (Zuo et al., 2017, p. 107-123).

In a study covering 22 OECD countries, Kalwij et al. explored how the employment of young people could change in the event of older workers retiring later. As a result of the research, it was determined that the changes in older employment (the 55-64 age group) had a small but positive effect on youth (the 15-24 age group) and adult (the 25-54 age group) employment (Kalwij et al., 2010, p. 341-359). Munnel and Wu investigated the effect of an increase in the retirement age on youth unemployment in their study. They observed that as a result of an increase in the retirement age, the rise in the employment rate of older workers led to an improvement in youth employment and a decrease in youth unemployment (Munnel & Wu, 2012, p. 1-54). Zhang analyzed how raising the retirement age affects youth and adult employment in China. In the study, it was shown that because the Chinese population is ageing fast, raising the retirement age leads to an increase in the employment rate of older people. The analysis also determined that the increase in the employment rate of older workers did not cause a decrease in the employment rate of young workers. Conversely, an increase in the employment rate of older workers was found to have a positive effect on both the employment rates of young and adult workers (Zhang, 2012, p. 1-25).

In their study, Kinoshita and Kochhar reveal that women, comprising more than half of the global population and having a longer life expectancy than men, will play important roles in counteracting the decline in economic growth potential that will arise with population ageing. Specifically, the study points out that the women's workforce is vital in countries with rapidly ageing populations, such as Japan and Korea. Particular attention is paid to the fact that women outnumber men in terms of third-level education enrollment rates, indicating that the absence of these highly educated women from the workforce would represent a major economic loss. As such, an important role falls to both the state and the private sector in increasing labor force participation rates of women. For this purpose, it will be important for the government to reduce gender disparities in access to education, health, infrastructure, and financial services through government policies, to establish and promote child-care facilities, and to enact legislation that includes flexible working conditions for women. Such measures will help increase labor force participation rates of women. If the private sector provides both contract and work environment flexibility and uses performance-based reward systems instead of seniority and working hours, it will make a big difference in getting more women into the workforce. With this in mind, increasing women's participation in the workforce is critically important in developed Asian countries such as Japan and Korea (whose populations are ageing rapidly), not only for sustaining growth but also for counterbalancing the burden caused by an ageing and declining population. Engaging highly educated women in the workforce will make a significant contribution to sustaining economic growth (Kinoshita & Kochhar, 2016, p. 1-3).

The study conducted by Liu and Zhao focused on China, using data from the 2013-2022 period to evaluate the impact of population ageing on the workforce. The study found that as the population ages, the workforce supply will decrease, leading to higher workforce costs and lower labor force participation levels. Furthermore, population ageing will also lead to a decline in the quality of the workforce. Regarding workforce demand, with the ageing of the population, significant growth will occur in industries targeting the elderly (such as healthcare, entertainment, financial services focused on retirement systems, personal care, domestic services, etc.) (Liu & Zhao, 2024, p. 65-70).

Advanced technology sectors are experiencing a decline in productivity due to ageing workers' inability to adapt to the technological advances resulting from globalization, or the difficulties they face in adapting, thereby preventing these sectors from developing. Accordingly, it is necessary to ensure that workers who will become elderly in the future undergo an educational process that facilitates their adaptation to technological developments during their youth in order to ensure the development of technology-intensive sectors. Meanwhile, demographic ageing may facilitate the development of low-productivity sectors that are not technology-intensive and where cognitive skills are not a priority. Population ageing will inhibit the development of high-tech sectors and high-efficiency sectors where cognitive skills are at the forefront (Serban, 2012, p. 356-364).

A review of the literature reveals that studies in Denmark, 12 OECD countries (especially those with significant increases in the employment of the elderly population) and Canada that increases in the employment of the elderly lead to increases in the employment of the youth. Studies in Japan and France have shown that increased participation of the elderly in the workforce leads to increases in the employment of the youth (Bingley et al., 2010; Baker et al., 2010; Gruber and Wise, 2010; Oshio et al., 2010; Salem et al., 2008 and Thießen, 2007). These findings indicate a complementary relationship between the employment of the elderly and the employment of the youth in these countries. This conclusion is attributed to the fact that, as a result of the older population in these countries, the less experienced younger workforce complements the more experienced older workforce.

Other studies conducted in Scotland, the EU, the US, and China indicate that an ageing population leads to a decline in employment. While the study conducted in France found that the increase in the labor force participation of older people leads to a decrease in adult employment, the study conducted in 25 EU countries found that the increase in the labor force participation of older people slows down the growth rate of employment, and the study conducted in Japan determined that the increase in the employment of older people leads to a decrease in the women's employment rate (Lisenkova et al., 2010; Didžgalvytė & Lukšaitė, 2014; Salem et al., 2008; Carone, 2005 and Kondo, 2016).

Also, in studies on Australia, Japan, China, and New Zealand, it has been pointed out that population ageing reduces the workforce supply and that this reduction in the workforce supply can be mitigated by getting more women and older people into the workforce and increasing their employment (Austen & Giles, 2003; Hu, 2024; Zuo et al., 2017 and Rensburg et al., 2021).

On the other hand, women in fast-ageing countries, particularly Japan and Korea, play an important role in achieving sustainable growth by filling the gap in the workforce due to the ageing population, and they are expected to play a significant role in compensating for the burden that the passive workforce (retired workforce) places on the social security system through healthcare expenditures and retirement pension payments (by entering the workforce and paying premiums) on the other (Kinoshita & Kochhar, 2016).

4. METHODOLOGY AND MODEL

Both employment and labor force participation rates of age groups are classified in the literature with respect to population ageing and retirement age. In this regard, the labor force participation rates of Türkiye are evaluated in the context of the age groups identified in the literature. Therefore, labor force participation rate of the population aged 55-64, which is taken into account in the classification of older workers related to population ageing, is considered in this study (Ghosheh vd., 2006; Maestas vd., 2016). On the other hand, in Türkiye, there are also many people who have retired but returned to work due to the insufficient level of income they receive. Some of these workers retired early due to early retirement policies, whereas others are aged 65 and over (especially in recent years, when the level of retirement pensions has remained at the poverty or even starvation level, forcing people aged

65 and over back into the workforce). For this reason, it is essential to include the labor force participation rate of the population aged 65 and over in the study.

The aim of this study is therefore to examine data from 1988 to 2022 in Türkiye, which is ageing as a result of demographic change, in order to determine whether the effect of population ageing and the elderly workforce on women's employment is substitutive or complementary. In the analysis, employment rate of women aged 15-64, labor force participation rate of the population aged 55-64, labor force participation rate of the population aged 65 and over, life expectancy at age 65 for men, life expectancy at age 65 for women, rate of growth in the service sector, growth in the urban population, and long-term correlation with the gender exclusion index will be investigated. In order to identify the long-term relationship between these variables, the ARDL Bound Test (Autoregressive Distributed Lag Bound Test) developed by Pesaran et al. (2001) was used. The ARDL Bound Test was used in this study for two main reasons. One reason is that this test makes it possible to test for cointegration relationships even if the series have different stationary levels. The second reason is that the test works better with small sample sizes (Narayan & Narayan, 2004; Pesaran et al., 2001).

When empirical literature is evaluated, it can be seen that there are multiple variables that affect employment. The models included in this study were developed on the basis of the models by Oshio et al. (2010), Baker et al. (2010) and Salem et al. (2008).

In this study, WOMENEMP1564 is the dependent variable, and LFP5564, LFP65, LE65M, LE65F, SERVICE, URBANPOP, and EXCLUSION are the independent variables. In the study, correlation analysis was conducted first to establish the correlation relationship among the variables. Highly correlated regressors were separated across two models to reduce multicollinearity concerns and the models below were developed.

$$WOMENEMP1564_{it} = \beta_0 + \beta_1 LFP5564_{it} + \beta_2 LFP65_{it} + \beta_3 LE65M_{it} + \beta_4 SERVICE_{it} + \beta_5 URBANPOP_{it} + \beta_6 EXCLUSION_{it} + \varepsilon_{it} \quad (1)$$

$$WOMENEMP1564_{it} = \beta_0 + \beta_1 LFP5564_{it} + \beta_2 LFP65_{it} + \beta_3 LE65F_{it} + \beta_4 SERVICE_{it} + \beta_5 URBANPOP_{it} + \beta_6 EXCLUSION_{it} + \varepsilon_{it} \quad (2)$$

4.1. ARDL Bound Test (Autoregressive Distributed Lag Bound Test)

First, the time series properties of the variables must be determined in order to establish the long-term relationship between the variables using the ARDL Bound Test. The stability properties of the series are examined for this purpose. To determine the stationary properties of the series in this study, the ADF (Augmented Dickey Fuller) (1981) and PP (Phillips Perron) (1988) unit root tests were used. Because of its advantages, the ARDL model developed by Pesaran et al. (2001) will be used in this study. There are two stages to the ARDL Bound Test. The first stage examines whether there is a long-term relationship between the variables in the model. During the second stage, estimates of the short and long-term coefficients for the series found to be cointegrated in the first stage are calculated. Similar to unit root tests, the AIC and SC criteria are used in the ARDL Bound Test to determine the length of the lag. Furthermore, to obtain reliable results from the ARDL Bounds Test, there should be no autocorrelation problem among the error terms. Following the determination of the appropriate lag length, if the specified lag length does not contain autocorrelation, presence of a long-term relationship between the variables will be examined using the F-Test (Wald Test).

In the ARDL Bound Test, the ARDL model used to reveal the long-term relationship between variables is as follows:

ARDL Model for Equation Numbered (1)

$$\Delta WOMENEMP1564_t = \beta_0 + \sum_{i=1}^{p} \beta_{1i} \Delta WOMENEMP1564_{t-i} + \sum_{i=0}^{p} \beta_{2i} \Delta LFP5564_{t-i} + \sum_{i=0}^{p} \beta_{3i} \Delta LFP65_{t-i} + \sum_{i=0}^{p} \beta_{4i} \Delta LE65M_{t-i} + \sum_{i=0}^{p} \beta_{5i} \Delta SERVICE_{t-i} + \sum_{i=0}^{p} \beta_{6i} \Delta URBANPOP_{t-i} + \sum_{i=0}^{p} \beta_{7i} \Delta EXCLUSION_{t-i} + \lambda_1 WOMENEMP1564_{t-1} + \lambda_2 LFP5564_{t-1} + \lambda_3 LFP65_{t-1} + \lambda_4 LE65M_{t-1} + \lambda_5 SERVICE_{t-1} + \lambda_6 URBANPOP_{t-1} + \lambda_7 EXCLUSION_{t-1} + \gamma TREND + \varepsilon_t \quad (3)$$

In equation (3), Δ represents the first difference operator, p represents the optimal lag lengths, *TREND* represents the trend, and ε represents the equation error term. By estimating the econometric model in equation (3), the F-test statistic is calculated. A long-term relationship between the variables is tested using the F-test (Wald Test). If the F-test statistic indicates that there is a long-term relationship between the variables in the model, Equations (4) and (5) are estimated to determine the long and short-term coefficients among the variables.

$$WOMENEMP1564_t = \Upsilon_0 + \sum_{i=1}^{n}\Upsilon_{1i} WOMENEMP1564_{t-i} + \sum_{i=0}^{n}\Upsilon_{2i} LFP5564_{t-i} + \sum_{i=0}^{n}\Upsilon_{3i} LFP65_{t-i} + \sum_{i=0}^{n}\Upsilon_{4i} LE65M_{t-i} + \sum_{i=0}^{n}\Upsilon_{5i} SERVICE_{t-i} + \sum_{i=0}^{n}\Upsilon_{6i} URBANPOP_{t-i} + \sum_{i=0}^{n}\Upsilon_{7i} EXCLUSION_{t-i} + \gamma TREND + \varepsilon_t \quad (4)$$

$$\Delta WOMENEMP1564_t = \alpha_0 + \alpha_1 ECT_{t-1} + \sum_{i=1}^{n}\alpha_{1i}\Delta WOMENEMP1564_{t-i} + \sum_{i=0}^{n}\alpha_{2i}\Delta LFP5564_{t-i} + \sum_{i=0}^{n}\alpha_{3i}\Delta LFP65_{t-i} + \sum_{i=0}^{n}\alpha_{4i}\Delta LE65M_{t-i} + \sum_{i=0}^{n}\alpha_{5i}\Delta SERVICE_{t-i} + \sum_{i=0}^{n}\alpha_{6i}\Delta URBANPOP_{t-i} + \sum_{i=0}^{n}\alpha_{7i}\Delta EXCLUSION_{t-i} + \gamma TREND + \varepsilon_t \quad (5)$$

Error Correction Model (ECM) is shown in Equation (5). ECT_{t-1} represents the error correction term, the coefficient α_1 represents the coefficient of the error correction term, and *TREND* represents the trend in Equation (5). This coefficient α_1, indicates that deviations occurring in the short term will be corrected in the long term. In other words, it shows that deviations occurring at equilibrium will be corrected in the next period. The coefficient is expected to have a negative sign (between 0 and -1) and be statistically significant at the 5% significance level.

5. DATA AND RESULTS OF THE STUDY

5.1. Definitions of the Variables

The main objective of this study is to analyze the cointegration relationship between the employment rate of women aged 15-64, the labor force participation rate of the population aged 55-64, the labor force participation rate of the population aged 65 and over, life expectancy at age 65 for men, life expectancy at age 65 for women, service sector growth rate, urban population growth, and exclusion index by gender in Turkey. In this study, WOMENEMP1564 is the dependent variable, while LFP5564, LFP65, LE65M, LE65F, SERVICE, URBANPOP, and EXCLUSION are the independent variables. We used annual data from 1988 to 2022 in this study. Table 1 provides definitions of the variables used in the analysis and their sources.

Table 1. Definitions of the Variables

SYMBOL	VARIABLE	SOURCE
WOMENEMP1564	Employment rate of women aged 15-64 (Employment/population ratio) (percentage of the population in the same subgroup)	OECD Database
LFP5564	Labor force participation rate of the population aged 55-64 (percentage of the population in the same subgroup)	OECD Database
LFP65	Labor force participation rate of the population aged 65 and over (percentage of the population in the same subgroup)	OECD Database
LE65M	Life expectancy at age 65 (men)	OECD Database
LE65F	Life expectancy at age 65 (women)	OECD Database
SERVICE	Annual growth rate of the service sector (%)	Presidency of the Republic of Türkiye, Strategy and Budget Presidency (2026a, 2026b)
URBANPOP	Urban population growth (annual %)	World Bank Database
EXCLUSION	Exclusion index by gender	The V-Dem Institute Database

Table 2 provides the descriptive statistics for the variables.

Table 2. Descriptive Statistics for the Variables

Variable	Mean	Maximum	Minimum	S.D.	S	K	Normality
WOMENEMP1564	28.739	34.500	22.319	3.612	1.937	1.451	^{2}(02)=1.937*
LFP5564	36.773	47.11	28.290	5.287	1.937	1.451	^{2}(02)=1.451*
LFP65	15.796	23.590	9.977	4.394	1.937	1.451	^{2}(02)=4.110*
LE65M	14.131	16.300	12.400	1.242	1.937	1.451	^{2}(02)=3.063*
LE65F	16.280	19.600	13.800	1.995	1.937	1.451	^{2}(02)=4.707**
SERVICE	4.768	12.900	-6.577	4.647	1.937	1.451	^{2}(02)=3.060*
URBANPOP	2.406	4.353	1.255	0.703	1.937	1.451	^{2}(02)=13.788***
EXCLUSION	0.491	0.530	0.460	0.023	1.937	1.451	^{2}(02)=2.717*

(1) ***, **, and *, symbols represent significance at the 1%, 5% and 10% levels respectively.

(2) S.D: Standard Deviation S: Skewness, K: Kurtosis

When examining the descriptive statistics for the variables, it is observed that the WOMENEMP1564 variable, which serves as the dependent variable in the model, is normally distributed with a mean of 28.739 at the 10% significance level. The LFP5564 variable, treated as an independent variable, has a mean of 36.773; the LFP65 variable has a mean of 15.796; the LE65M variable has a mean of 14.131;

the SERVICE variable with a mean of 4.768, and the EXCLUSION variable with a mean of 0.491, all follow a normal distribution at the 10% significance level. On the other hand, the LE65F variable shows a normal distribution with a mean of 16.280 at the 5% significance level, and the URBANPOP variable shows a normal distribution with a mean of 2.406 at the 1% significance level.

Graph 1 shows the time series graphs of the variables.

Figure 1. Time Series Graphs of the Variables

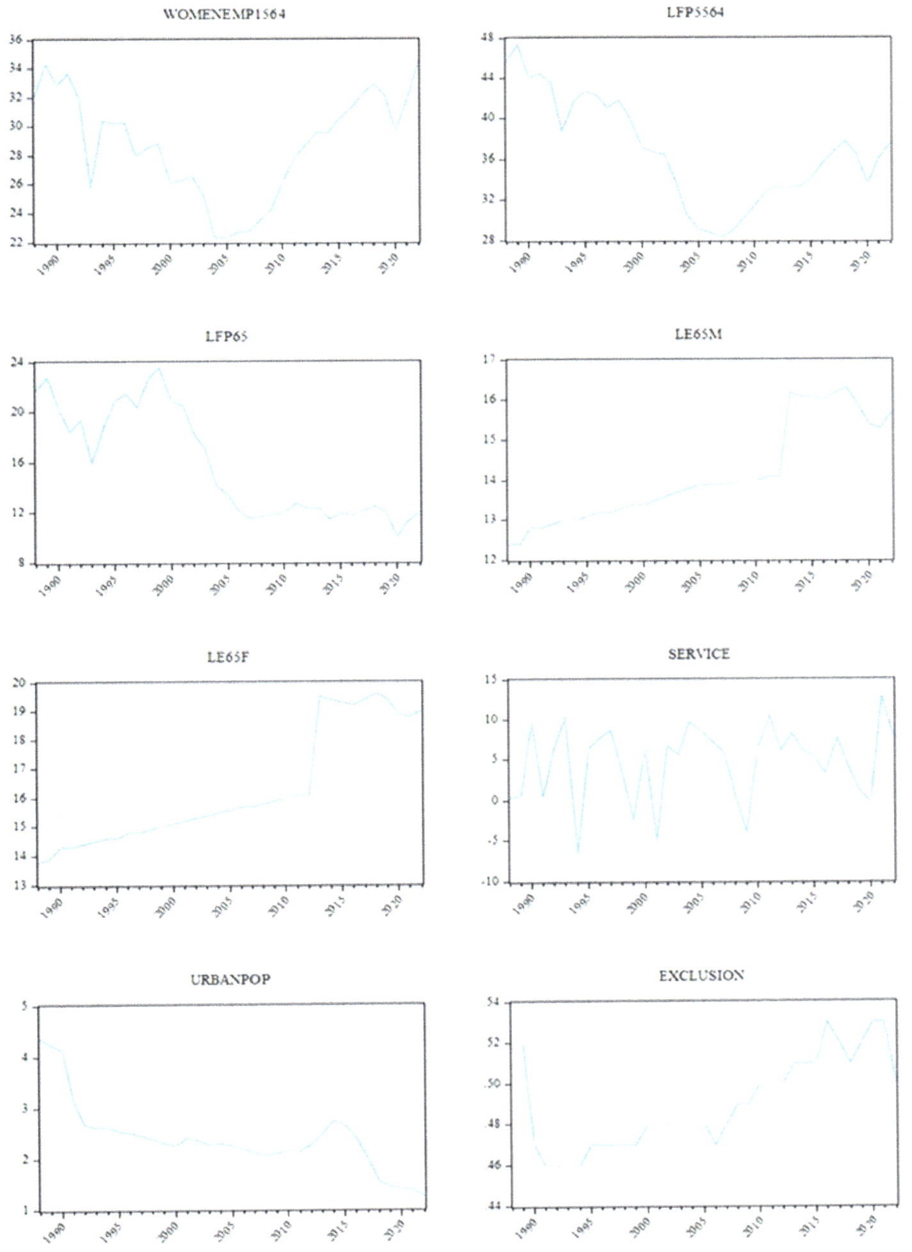

When we analyses the time series graphs of the variables, we observe that the WOMENEMP1564 variable has two different trend patterns during the study period, a decreasing trend followed by an increasing trend. Meanwhile, the WOMENEMP1564 variable demonstrates structural break characteristics in both the mean and trend. It can be observed that the LFP5564 and LFP65 variables first had a declining trend but later had two different trend structures, an increasing trend and a steady course, respectively. Furthermore, the variables LFP5564 and LFP65 are found to show structural break characteristics in the mean trend. It is observed that the variables LE65M and LE65F have an upward trend throughout the study period. Nevertheless, the LE65M and LE65F variables have shown a deep upward structural break in the average, particularly in recent periods, followed by the end of the upward trend. Despite not having a clear trend, the SERVICE variable often shows structural breaks in the mean. While the URBANPOP variable has a declining trend, it shows slight structural breaks. As for the EXCLUSION variable, it is observed that it has a decreasing trend at first and then an increasing trend, demonstrating structural break characteristics in the mean trend. Based on the fact that current structural breaks may lead to misleading results in classical unit root tests, it is thought that it would be useful to also apply structural break unit root tests in order to provide a basis for classical unit root tests.

5.2. Unit Root Test Results

For the purpose of investigating the stationary status of the series of the variables WOMENEMP1564, LFP5564, LFP65, LE65M, LE65F, SERVICE, URBANPOP, and EXCLUSION, which were covered in the study, both ADF and PP unit root tests and a structural break ADF unit root test were carried out. Table 3 shows the results of the ADF and PP unit root tests, and Table 4 shows the results of the structural break ADF unit root test.

Table 3. ADF and PP Unit Root Test Results

VARIABLES	Level/ First Difference	ADF Test Statistic		PP Test Statistic		RESULT
		Constant	Constant and Trend	Constant	Constant and Trend	
WOMENEMP1564	Level	1.304(0)	-1.212(0)	-1.263(1)	-0.906(3)	I(1)
	First Difference	-6.089(0)***	-6.692(0)***	-6.089(0)***	-7.477(0)***	
LFP5564	Level	-1.759(0)	-0.842(0)	-1.761(2)	-0.798(2)	I(1)
	First Difference	-5.155(0)***	-5.754(0)***	-5.183(3)***	-5.749(1)***	
LFP65	Level	-1.291(0)	-1.725(0)	-1.341(3)	-1.975(3)	I(1)
	First Difference	-5.732(0)***	-5.719(0)***	-5.756(3)***	-5.745(3)***	
LE65M	Level	-1.013(0)	-2.329(0)	-0.953(4)	-2.411(1)	I(1)
	First Difference	-5.819(0)***	-5.731(0)***	-5.848(5)***	-5.749(5)***	
LE65F	Level	-0.764(0)	-2.196(0)	-0.691(3)	-2.196(0)	I(1)
	First Difference	-5.973(0)***	-5.878(0)***	-6.015(4)***	-5.914(4)***	
SERVICE	Level	-6.139(0)***	-6.157(0)***	-7.661(8)***	-8.969(10)***	I(0)
	First Difference	-9.545(0)***	-9.387(0)***	-19.978(13)***	-19.547(13)***	
URBANPOP	Level	-3.436(2)**	-3.816(1)**	-2.584(0)	-2.577(0)	I(1)
	First Difference	-3.442(1)**	-3.500(1)**	-3.209(4)*	-3.269(4)*	
EXCLUSION	Level	-1.845(0)	-4.069(0)**	-1.941(2)	-4.653(7)***	I(1)
	First Difference	-5.704(1)***	-4.883(1)***	-4.583(1)***	-4.621(1)***	

(1) ***, **, and *, symbols represent significance at the 1%, 5% and 10% levels and the variables are stationary at 1%, 5% and 10% levels, respectively.

When we look at Table 3, all the variables other than SERVICE are not stationary at the level, but they become stationary when we take the first differences. In other words, it can be observed that the series for the SERVICE variable are stationary at level (I(0)), while the series for the WOMENEMP1564, LFP5564, LFP65, LE65M, LE65F, URBANPOP, and EXCLUSION variables are stationary at the first difference (I(1)). Upon comprehensive analysis of the ADF and PP unit root test results, it can be seen that all variables meet the stability condition at the maximum (I(1)) level.

Table 4. ADF Unit Root Test With Structural Break Results

VARIABLES	Level/ First Difference	ADF Unit Root Test With Structural Break Results				RESULT
		Model Specifications				
		Constant	Constant and Trend			
			Break Specifications			
			Constant	Trend	Constant and Trend	
WOMENEMP1564	Level	-1.943(0)	-2.343(0)	-4.662(0)**	-4.838(0)	I(1)
	First Difference	-7.940(0)***	-8.073(0)***	-6.829(0)***	-7.933(0)***	
LFP5564	Level	-3.205(3)	-2.509(0)	-3.575(0)	-4.541(0)	I(1)
	First Difference	-6.264(0)***	-6.293(0)***	-5.769(0)***	-6.197(0)***	
LFP65	Level	-4.002(0)	-3.776(0)	-2.017(0)	-3.596(0)	I(1)
	First Difference	-6.171(0)***	-7.186(0)***	-5.956(0)***	-7.836(0)***	
LE65M	Level	-4.233(0)*	-7.248(2)***	-2.533(0)	-12.494(0)***	I(1)
	First Difference	-13.528(0)***	-13.406(0)***	-6.089(0)***	-11.232(3)***	
LE65F	Level	-5.623(0)***	-13.084(2)***	-2.525(0)	-16.418(3)***	I(1)
	First Difference	-24.196(0)***	-23.869(0)***	-6.376(0)***	-13.339(3)***	
SERVICE	Level	-6.751(0)***	-6.581(0)***	-6.321(0)***	-6.524(0)***	I(0)
	First Difference	-10.238(0)***	-9.978(0)***	-9.489(0)***	-9.797(0)***	
URBANPOP	Level	-8.703(2)***	-7.334(2)***	-6.643(2)***	-7.025(2)***	I(0)
	First Difference	-4.799(1)**	-5.142(1)**	-6.153(1)***	-5.651(1)***	
EXCLUSION	Level	-3.978(0)	-7.812(1)***	-5.612(0)***	-7.013(1)***	I(1)
	First Difference	-7.855(0)***	-7.812(1)***	-7.921(0)***	-7.488(0)***	

(1) ***, **, and *, symbols represent significance at the 1%, 5% and 10% levels and the variables are stationary at 1%, 5% and 10% levels, respectively.

When we look at Table 4, we see that the SERVICE and URBANPOP variables are stationary at level (I(0)), while the WOMENEMP1564, LFP5564, LFP65, LE65M, LE65F, and EXCLUSION variables become stationary after taking their first differences (I(1)). The results of the ADF and PP Unit Root tests show that the test results for all variables except URBANPOP are parallel when compared with the results of the Structural Break ADF Unit Root test. While the URBANPOP variable series is stationary at the first difference (I(1)) according to the ADF and PP Unit Root test results, it becomes stationary at the level (I(0)) according to the Structural Break ADF unit root test results.

Considering the ADF and PP unit root test results together with the Structural Break ADF unit root test results as a whole, it can be observed that some variables in the models are stationary at level (I(0)), while others are stationary at the first difference (I(1)). Meanwhile, there are no variables that are stationary at the second difference level (I(2)). Based on these results, it was decided to use the ARDL Bound Test in the analysis. Since, the ARDL Bound Test allows for testing the cointegration relationship even if the series have different levels of stationarity. Furthermore, the ARDL Boundary Test provides more effective results in data with fewer observations than similar cointegration tests (Narayan & Narayan, 2004; Pesaran et al, 2001).

Graph 2 presents the Akaike Information Criterion comparisons performed to identify the optimal lag lengths for the ARDL models in the study.

Figure 2. Akaike Information Criterion Comparisons for Optimal Lag Selection

Model 1

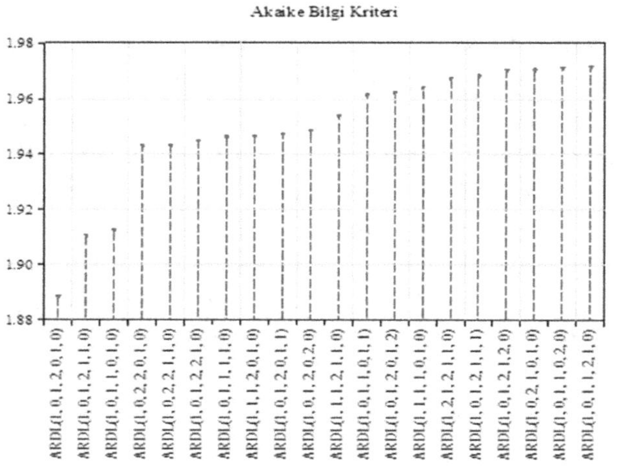

Model 2

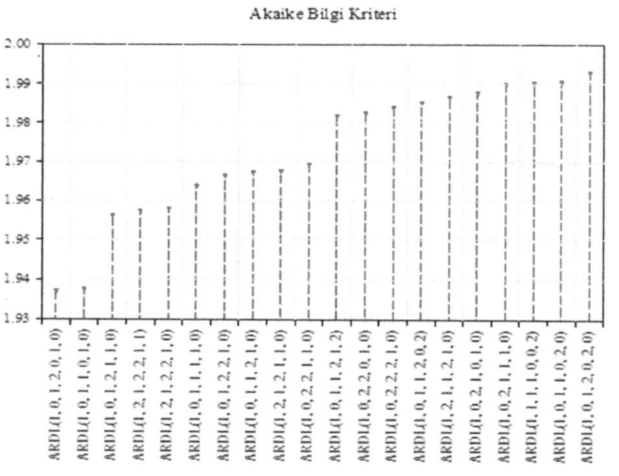

When the graphs are analyzed, we see that the smallest Akaike Information Criterion values for both Model 1 and Model 2 are calculated for models with the same lag structure. That means the model with the ARDL (1, 0, 1, 2, 0, 1, 0) lag structure is optimal for both research models.

5.3. ARDL Bounds Test Results

After ADF and PP stationarity tests, we moved on to the ARDL test (Autoregressive Distributed Lag Bound Test). In order to identify the cointegration relationship among the variables WOMENEMP1564, LFP5564, LFP65, LE65M, LE65F, SERVICE, URBANPOP, and EXCLUSION contained in the model, the F-Test (Wald Test) was used. Table 5 presents the results of the F-Test.

Table 5. Long-Term Cointegration Relationship Test Results

Models	F Statistic	Lag Lengths	Cointegration Relationship		
			%1	%5	%10
f(WOMENEMP1564| LFP5564, LFP65, LE65M, SERVICE, URBANPOP, EXCLUSION)	F=19.631***	(1, 0, 1, 2, 0, 1, 0)	Yes	Yes	Yes
f(WOMENEMP1564| LFP5564, LFP65, LE65F, SERVICE, URBANPOP, EXCLUSION)	F=18.954***	(1, 0, 1, 2, 0, 1, 0)	Yes	Yes	Yes

(1) ***, **, and *, symbols represent significance at the 1%, 5% and 10% levels, respectively.

(2) Due to the small number of observations, the maximum lag length was set to 2, and AIC criteria were used to determine the optimal lag length.

(3) Lower and upper critical limit values recommended by the EViews software package for the current sample using Bootstrap,

Lower and upper critical limit values at a 10% significance level are respectively 2.977 and 4.260

Lower and upper critical limit values at a 5% significance level are respectively 3.576 and 5.065

Lower and upper critical limit values at a 1% significance level are respectively 5.046 and 6.930

As shown in Table 5, there is a statistically significant long-term cointegration relationship among the variables in the model at the 1% significance level for both model 1 and model 2. To put it another way, it can be seen that the variables included in both models have a statistically significant long-term equilibrium at the 1% significance level. The results, therefore, confirm the existence of a long-term relationship among the variables included in the models.

5.4. ARDL Model Results

As a result of the F-test, it was determined that there is a cointegration relationship between the variables WOMENEMP1564, LFP5564, LFP65, LE65M, LE65F, SERVICE, URBANPOP, and EXCLUSION, and then the coefficients of the variables in the models were estimated. Table 6 presents the long-term coefficients of the ARDL models, assumption tests, and error correction model results.

Table 6. ARDL Model Results

Model	Model 1	Model 2
ARDL Specification	**f(WOMENEMP1564| LFP5564, LFP65, LE65M, SERVICE, URBANPOP, EXCLUSION)**	**f(WOMENEMP1564| LFP5564, LFP65, LE65F, SERVICE, URBANPOP, EXCLUSION)**
	ARDL((1, 0, 1, 2, 0, 1, 0)	**ARDL(1, 0, 1, 2, 0, 1, 0)**
LFP5564	0.921***	0.965***
	[0.000]	[0.000]
LFP65	-0.238***	-0.259***
	[0.006]	[0.003]
LE65M	-1.273**	-
	[0.018]	
LE65F	-	-0.784**
		[0.028]
SERVICE	-0.071**	-0.064*
	[0.042]	[0.056]
URBANPOP	2.796***	2.759***
	[0.000]	[0.000]
EXCLUSION	-27.352	-31.979
	[0.214]	[0.142]
Sabit	10.871***	7.545***
	[0.000]	[0.000]
Trend	0.452***	0.466***
	[0.000]	[0.000]
ECT_{t-1}	-0.792***	-0.806***
	[0.000]	[0.000]
Diagnostic Statistics		
Autocorrelation	$\chi^2(2)=2.854$	$\chi^2(2)=2.097$
	(0.240)	(0.351)
Functional Form	F(1,28)=2.734	F(1,28)=1.413
	(0.108)	(0.243)
Normality	$\chi^2(2)=6.939$**	$\chi^2(2)=8.459$**
	(0.031)	(0.015)
Changing Variance	$\chi^2(12)=4.215$	$\chi^2(2)=5.029$
	(0.979)	(0.957)

(1) ***, **, and *, symbols represent significance at the 1%, 5% and 10% levels, respectively.

When we look at the diagnostic statistics in Table 6, we see that we don't have any problems with autocorrelation, heteroscedasticity, or functional form for Model 1 and Model 2. In addition, we see that the error terms are normally distributed at the 5% significance level, even if they are not 1%.

Upon examining the long-term prediction coefficients and t-statistic values presented in Table 6, a positive and statistically significant relationship at the 1% significance level was found between the LFP5564 variable and the WOMENEMP1564 variable in both Model 1 and Model 2. This result indicates a statistically significant and positive relationship at the 1% significance level between the LFP5564 and WOMENEMP1564 variables in the long term. This indicates that, in the long term, an increase (or decrease) in the employment rate of women aged 15–64 is associated with an increase (or decrease) in the labor force participation rate of the population aged 55–64.

On the other hand, a positive and statistically significant relationship at the 1% significance level was detected between the URBANPOP variable and the WOMENEMP1564 variable in both Model 1 and Model 2. This indicates the existence of a positive and statistically significant long-term relationship at the 1% significance level between the URBANPOP variable and the WOMENEMP1564 variable. This result implies that, in the long term, an increase (or decrease) in the employment rate of women aged 15–64 is associated with an increase (or decrease) in the urban population.

In both Model 1 and Model 2, a negative and statistically significant relationship at the 1% significance level was identified between the LFP65 variable and the WOMENEMP1564 variable. This result reveals that, in the long term, there is a statistically significant negative relationship between the LFP65 and WOMENEMP1564 variables at the 1% significance level. This suggests that, in the long term, a decrease (or increase) in the employment rate of women aged 15-64 is linked to an increase (or decrease) in the labor force participation rate of the 65 and over age group.

In Model 1, A negative and statistically significant relationship at the 5% significance level was found between the LE65M variable and the WOMENEMP1564 variable. This result demonstrates the existence of a statistically significant negative relationship at the 5% significance level between the LE65M and WOMENEMP1564 variables in the long term. This indicates that the decline (or increase) in the employment rate of women aged 15–64 is associated with an increase (or decrease) in life expectancy at age 65 among men.

In Model 2, a negative and statistically significant long-term relationship at the 5% significance level was observed between the LE65F variable and the WOMENEMP1564 variable. This result demonstrates the existence of a statistically significant and negative relationship at the 5% significance level between the LE65F and

WOMENEMP1564 variables in the long term. This finding suggests that, women in the long-term, a decrease (or increase) in the employment rate of women aged 15–64 is associated with an increase (or decrease) in life expectancy at age 65 among.

A negative and statistically significant long-term relationship was found between the SERVICE variable and the WOMENEMP1564 variable at a significance level of 5% for Model 1 and 10% for Model 2. In more clearly terms, in both models there is a statistically significant negative relationship between the SERVICE and WOMENEMP1564 variables in the long term. This finding suggests that, in the long term, a decrease (or increase) in the employment rate of women aged 15–64 is associated with an increase (or decrease) in the annual growth rate of the service sector.

In both models, a negative but statistically insignificant relationship was obtained between the EXCLUSION variable and the WOMENEMP1564 variable. In other words, there is no statistically significant relationship between the EXCLUSION variable and the WOMENEMP1564 variable in the long term. This result indicates that, in the long term, the decline (or increase) in the employment rate of women aged 15–64 is not related with an increase (or decrease) in exclusion index by gender. However, the most notable point here is that although statistically insignificant, the coefficient value is quite large in both models. The fact that the coefficient value is negative and quite large is largely consistent with the reality of "female workforce is driven out of the work life".

In both models, "the trend" is positive and highly significant. This result can be interpreted as an indication that strong structural transformations are taking place in Turkey. Specifically, it can be said that factors such as the decrease in the share of agriculture in the economy, the increase in education levels, changes in demographic structure, increasing urbanization and the increase in women's participation in the workforce due to increased education levels, changes in cultural structure, increasing informal employment in agricultural and non-agricultural sectors, and the prominence of non-employment-based growth played a significant role in this outcome (Acar, 2016, p. 53-72; Meçik & Afşar, 2014, p. 1-23).

When Table 6 is examined, it is observed that the ECT_{t-1} error correction coefficient is statistically significant at the 1% significance level for both Model 1 and Model 2, with a negative sign in the expected direction and an absolute value less than 1. For both models, this result means that the error correction mechanism is working and that deviations from long-term equilibrium (caused by shocks, etc.) are corrected over time. To put it more clearly, the result obtained here indicates that any deviation from equilibrium will be corrected by a movement back towards equilibrium. Furthermore, it shows that deviations from equilibrium will be corrected within a period of 1 to 2 years in both models, returning to long-term equilibrium. The ECT_{t-1} error correction coefficient in Model 1 and Model 2 shows that deviations occurring in equilibrium will be corrected at rates of 79% and 80% in the following period, respectively.

Graph 3 shows the CUSUM and CUSUMSQ tests developed by Brown et al. (1975) to verify the stability of long-term models and/or estimated coefficients.

Figure 3. CUSUM and CUSUMSQ Graphs for Long-Term Models

CUSUM Graph	**CUSUMSquare Graph**

Model 1

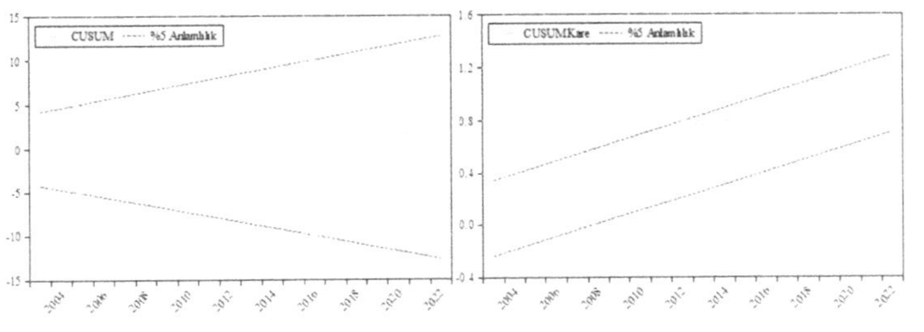

Model 2

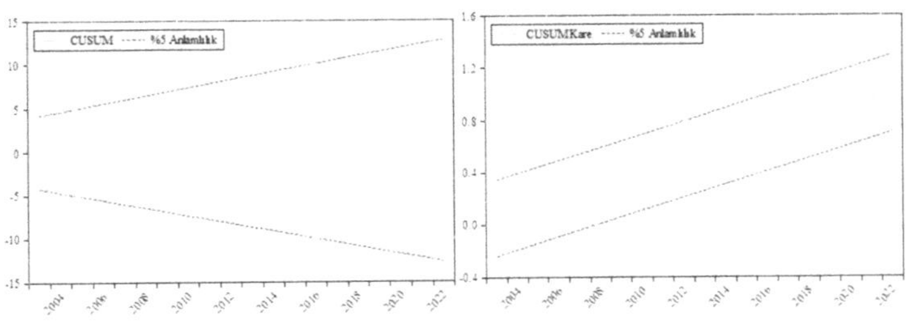

As can be seen in Graph 3, stability conditions are met at the 5% significance level for Model 1's CUSUM graph. Nevertheless, although Model 1's CUSUM Square graph slightly exceeds the 5% significance band after 2006, it does not exceed the 10% significance level. In other words, Model 1's long-term coefficients satisfy the stability conditions at the 10% significance level, but not at the 5% significance level. Both the CUSUM and CUSUMQ graphs for Model 2 are within the critical limits at the 5% significance level, meaning they are within the desired confidence interval. This result signifies that the long-term coefficients of the models satisfy the stability conditions at the 5% significance level.

6. CONCLUSIONS AND RECOMMENDATIONS

It can be seen that the population of Türkiye is ageing very quickly, despite having a slightly younger working-age population structure than EU countries. This ageing phenomenon is primarily driven by three key factors. First, most families prefer to have one or two children at most, mainly for economic reasons, which leads to a significant decline in birth rates and as a result, population growth rates. Second, due to advances in medicine, mortality rates have decreased. Third, again due to advances in medicine, there has been an increase in life expectancy (in particular, life expectancy at age 65). When we take into account that the share of the population aged 0-14 in the total population of Türkiye is falling fast and this decline is expected to increase in the coming years (which is expected to fall from 23.5% in 2018 and 22.6% in 2023, 19.3% in 2040, 16.9% in 2060 and 15.7% in 2080), we can say that the young population in Türkiye will continue to decrease. On the other hand, as the share of the population aged 65 and over in the total population of Türkiye is increasing quickly and this increase is expected to continue in the coming years (this share will be 12.7% in 2030, 16.2% in 2040, 20.1% in 2050, 22.6% in 2060, 24.2% in 2070 and 25.6% in 2080), we can say that the number of elderly people will increase further. The share of the population aged 65 and over in the total population of Türkiye in 2024 is 10.4%. Based on this rate, Türkiye is currently classified as a "very old society". But this share is expected to reach 12.7% in 2030, 16.2% in 2040, 20.1% in 2050, 22.6% in 2060, 24.2% in 2070, and 25.6% in 2080, and keeping this in mind, it is clear that in the coming years, Türkiye will be classified as a "significantly older society". Based on this population structure and projection, it can be said that the share of the 0-14 age group in the total population of Türkiye is decreasing, but the share of the population aged 65 and over (especially the share of women compared to men) is increasing, in short, the population of Türkiye is ageing very quickly, and within the ageing population, the share of the elderly women will increase more than that of men. Both at birth and at age 65, life expectancy in Türkiye is longer for women than for men. Together with the ageing of the population, this means that the share of women in the older labor supply (aged 55-64 and 65+) will be significantly higher than that of men in the ageing labor market of the future. Decreases in the share of the 0-14 age group in the total population result in a decrease in the ratio of dependent children, whereas an increase in the share of the 65 and over age group in the total population results in an increase in the ratio of dependent elderly (World Bank, 2025a; World Bank, 2025b; World Bank, 2025c; TÜİK, 2025; OECD, 2025c; OECD, 2025b). In the population structure, this change indicates that the share of young and working-age people in the total population of Türkiye is decreasing, while the share of the elderly population is increasingly growing. This result indicates that the labor supply in Turkey will decrease in the coming years, and the share of the elderly workforce in the total labor supply will further increase (especially with the gradual increase in the retirement age following the regulation in 2008, raising the retirement age to 65 for both women and men. Looking at labor force participation rates, it is evident that especially after 2008, the labor force participation rate of the population aged 55-64 has been steadily increasing for both women and men. Meanwhile, we can see that the labor force participation rate of the population aged 65 and over, which had been going up and down until 2016, began to rise starting in 2017, and this is pretty interesting. The reason for this could be that the retirement pensions or incomes of people 65 and older are below the poverty threshold or even the starvation threshold.

As the population ages, the decline in the working-age population will not only negatively impact economic growth but will also make it difficult to sustain growth in economy. The ageing of the population will also cause an increase in public spending on health, care and pensions for the ageing population in the years to come. The ageing of the population will therefore increase the financial burden on the public sector. Currently, the negative effects of this financial burden on the public sector caused by population ageing are being felt in many developed countries. But these negative effects are not yet fully felt in Türkiye. Population projections for Türkiye show when analyzed that the share of the 65 and older age group in the total population will begin to increase, especially after 2045, and that this share will exceed the share of the 50-64 age group (Ministry of Development of the Republic of Türkiye, 2018, p. 44; OECD, 2025c). As such, Germany and many other European Union countries, where the elderly population is increasing day by day, have raised the retirement age because of the increase in healthcare spending that population ageing will cause and the burden it will put on the social security system with retirement pension payments. By doing so, these countries have managed to keep the elderly workforce in the working life for more years.

Considering the negative impact on economic growth of the decrease in the working-age population as a result of population aging, and the financial burden that an aging population will place on the public, the inclusion of women in the workforce will make a significant contribution to offsetting these two negative consequences. In this demographic structure, female force has two crucial roles to play. Firstly, they contribute to sustained growth by employing to replace employees who leave the labor force due to aging. Secondly, they play a role in offsetting the increased healthcare costs associated with aging, as well as mitigating the burden that pension payments after retirement will place on the social security system. In other words, women who unable to participate the working life will play an important role on the one hand in achieving sustainable growth by filling the gap in the labor supply created by the aging population and, and in compensating for the burden that passive labor force (retired labor force) places on the social security system through healthcare expenditures and pension payments (by starting work and paying premium).

However, in many countries, including developed ones, serious discrimination against women in employment is observed, and women are pushed out of the working life. Therefore, keeping young and female workers, who constitute a significant portion of the total workforce, out of production hinders their growth on the one hand and causes to realize growth below their potential on the other. When looking at the age groups with the highest women's employment rates in Türkiye, we see that the 25-54 age group ranks first, the 15-24 age group ranks second, the 55-64 age group ranks third, and the 65 and older age group ranks fourth. Considering the employment of women by sector in Türkiye, it can be seen that the service sector ranks first in terms of employment between 2005 and 2022, agriculture ranks second, and manufacturing within the industrial sector ranks third. As for the areas of activity and employment of women in the service sector, it is observed that health and social services, wholesale and retail trade, education, accommodation and food service activities, public administration and defense, administrative and support service activities, professional, scientific, and technical activities, transportation and storage, financial and insurance activities, information and communication, real estate activities, and culture, arts, entertainment, recreation, and sports rank at the top respectively (OECD, 2025d; TURKSTAT, 2023; TURKSTAT 2025). In this context, it is of great importance to implement regulations that will increase women's participation in the workforce, especially in countries like Turkey, which has a somewhat younger working-age population compared to many EU countries with aging populations, during periods of declining birth rates. With these regulations, women, who constitute more than half of the total population but pushed out of the working life, will be included in the workforce, thus ensuring the sustainability of economic growth on the one hand and offsetting the financial burden that the aging population places on the public on the other.

Based on data from 1988 to 2022, we looked in this study at the impact of population ageing and the ageing workforce on women's employment in Türkiye, which is a result of demographic change. In the analysis focused on the employment rate of women aged 15-64, the labor force participation rate of the population aged 55-64, the labor force participation rate of the population aged 65 and over, life expectancy at age 65 for men, life expectancy at age 65 for women, service sector annual growth rate, increase in urban population, and exclusion index by gender variables are in order to explore the long-term relationship among these variables. In order to reveal this relationship, the ARDL Bound Test (Autoregressive Distributed Lag Bound Test) developed by Pesaran et al. (2001) were used. This study analyzed created models based on the models developed by Oshio et al. (2010), Baker et al. (2010) and Salem et al. (2008).

According to the empirical findings of the analysis;

(I) Positive and statistically significant relationship at the 1% significance level were detected between the labor force participation rate of the population aged 55-64 (LFP5564) and the employment rate of women aged 15-64 (WOMENEMP1564) in both models. This result is in line with the studies by Oshio et al. (2010) and Salem et al. (2008), who analyzed the relation between the labor force participation of older people and the employment of young people. This result suggests that in the long term, an increase (decrease) in the labor force participation rate of the population aged 55-64 will cause an increase (decrease) in the employment rate of women aged 15-64. When the figures for the period 1988-2022 are examined, it is seen that in this period, the labor force participation rate of the population aged 55-64 and employment rates of the same age group, as well employment rates of the 55-64 age group and employment rates of women in the 15-64 age group, show a parallel trend (OECD, 2025d). Therefore, this result can be explained by parallelism of increase in employment rates for the 55-64 age group (especially after 2008) and the increase in employment rates for women aged 15-64 (especially after 2008) during the period in question. This is because a complementary relationship is observed between employment for the 55-64 age group and employment for women aged 15-64, both for the 1988-2008 period, which covers the early retirement period, and for the 2008-2022 period, which covers the increase in the retirement age. In this case, it can be said that the employment rate for the 55-64 age group increased in response to the increase in the labor force participation rate of the 55-64 age group, and in response to the increase in the employment rate for women aged 15-64, the employment rate for women aged 15-64 increased (as a result of the complementary relationship).

(II) A statistically significant positive relationship at the 1% significance level was found between the urban population growth rate (URBANPOP) and the employment rate of women aged 15-64 (WOMENEMP1564) in both Model 1 and Model 2. It shows that in the long term, an increase (decrease) in the urban population growth rate will lead to an increase (decrease) in the employment rate of women aged 15-64. It is possible to account for this result by the fact that the labor force participation rates of women (especially women with college and university degrees) in cities are on a steady upward trend and that there is a parallel trend between the labor force participation rate of women aged 15-64 and the employment rates of women in the same age group in the period 1988-2022 (Republic of Türkiye Ministry of Family and Social Policies, General Directorate of Women's Status, 2014, p. 23; OECD, 2025d; Kaygusuz et al., 2024, p. 1-46). It is also possible to say that transition to an export-based industrialization strategy in Türkiye after 1980 was a contributing factor. Specifically, there was a shift toward export-oriented manufacturing production after 1980, which increased demand for low-skilled, labor-intensive workers in this industry. With the decline in the share of the agricultural sector in the economy as a result of the policies implemented after 1980, migration from rural to urban areas increased, and women who came to the cities began to work in labor-intensive sectors such as textiles due to their low level of education. As a result, population migration from rural to urban areas increased the urban population, causing an increase in the employment rate of low-educated, labor-intensive working women. Lastly, we can see that the service sector has the highest rate of women's employment in Türkiye. It is clear that the reason for this increase in women's employment is that the service sector has the highest rate of employment for women in Türkiye and that the activities and jobs in the service sector are mostly located in cities.

(III) A statistically significant negative relationship at the 1% significance level were determined between the labor force participation rate of the population aged 65 and over (LFP65) and the employment rate of women aged 15-64 (WOMENEMP1564) in both models. This means that, if the labor force participation rate of the population aged 65 and over increases (decreases) in the long term, the employment rate of women aged 15-64 will decrease (increase). Considering the figures for the period 1988-2022, a parallel trend is observed between the labor force participation rate of the population aged 65 and over and the employment rates of the same age group during this period, whereas the opposite trend is seen between the employment rate of the population aged 65 and over and the employment rates of women aged 15-64 (OECD, 2025d). This finding can be explained by structural economic and social factors specific to Turkey. Within the framework of the gender-based division of labor in Turkey, the fact that the role of providing "care for the elderly and children" within the household has been left to women negatively affects women's labor force participation and employment (Karabıyık, 2012, p. 256; Serel & Özdemir, 2017, p. 137). On the other hand, the fact that pension benefits in Turkey are insufficient to cover basic living expenses is prompting older adults aged 65 and older to re-enter the labor market. Elderly men aged 65 and over tend to work in jobs that require low skills or jobs with flexible work models. These jobs, in turn, constitute the sectors where young and middle-aged women are primarily employed (Önder, 2013, p. 35-61). The shift of older men toward these sectors is causing young and middle-aged women to be excluded from the workforce. Furthermore, it is observed that men aged 65 and older predominantly enter low-wage, informal, and agricultural sectors. These sectors, however, are precisely where female employment—particularly among those with low levels of education—is most concentrated. The shift of men aged 65 and older toward these sectors is narrowing the employment opportunities available to women, thereby causing them to be excluded from the workforce (Padhi & Triveni, 2025, p. 2013-2034). Additionally, raising the retirement age forces older people to remain in the workforce longer. This, in turn, hinders the employment of women (especially young and middle-aged women) in job opportunities that will become vacant after retirement. Furthermore, older women who previously cared for their grandchildren are forced to re-enter the labor market due to insufficient pension payments and the increased retirement age. In this situation, young and middle-aged working women are forced to leave their jobs due to the lack of adequate and affordable childcare facilities (Chevalier & Viitanen, 2002, p. 915-918).

(IV) A negative and statistically significant relationship at the 5% significance level was determined between life expectancy at age 65 for men (LE65M) and the employment rate of women aged 15-64 (WOMENEMP1564) in Model 1. In the long term, an increase (decrease) in life expectancy at age 65 for men implies a decrease (increase) in the employment rate of women aged 15-64. Considering the data for the period 1988-2022, there has been a continuous increase in the life expectancy of men at age 65 during this period (OECD, 2024). This increase means that the number of elderly men requiring care is rising. Therefore, the increase in life expectancy at age 65 for men, which leads to a decrease in the employment rate of women aged 15-64, can be explained by the fact that in Turkey, the responsibility for caring for elderly family members is traditionally left to women as a societal role. Therefore, in Turkey, the societal responsibility of providing elderly care within the family is left to women, leading to women to remain outside of the working life. On the other hand, both educated women working in career professions and families who have no one to care for their elderly family members try to obtain care services from the relevant market. In other words, these families employ female labor to undertake the care of their elderly family members. However, since this employed female workforce is mostly working in the informal sector, it is not reflected in female employment rates.

(V) A negative and statistically significant relationship at the 5% significance level was found between life expectancy at age 65 for women (LE65F) and the employment rate of women aged 15-64 (WOMENEMP1564) in Model 2. This result indicates that, in the long term, an increase (decrease) in life expectancy at age 65 for women leads to a decrease (increase) in the employment rate of women aged 15-64. Examining the figures for the period 1988-2022, it is seen that life expectancy at age 65 for women has continuously increased during this period (OECD, 2024). This increase implies an increase in the number of elderly women requiring care. Therefore, the fact that the increase in life expectancy at age 65 for women leads to a decrease in the employment rate of women aged 15-64 can be explained by the fact that in Turkey, the responsibility for caring for elderly family members is traditionally left to women as a societal role. In other words, in Turkey, the societal responsibility of providing elderly care within the family is left to women, leading to women to remain outside of the working life. On the other hand, both educated women working in career professions and families who have no one to care for their elderly family members try to obtain care services from the relevant market. In other words, these families employ female labor to undertake the care of their elderly family members. However, since this employed female workforce is mostly working in the informal sector, it is not reflected in female employment rates.

(VI) A negative and statistically significant relationship was found between the annual growth rate of the service sector (SERVICES) and the employment rate of women aged 15-64 (WOMENEMP1564), at the significance level of 5% for Model 1 and 10% for Model 2. This result indicates that, in the long term, an increase (decrease) in the annual growth rate of the service sector leads to a decrease (increase) in the employment rate of women aged 15-64. Examining the figures for the period 1988-2022, it is observed that the annual growth rate of the service sector has followed a rather unstable and fluctuating course. On the other hand, the downward trend in the annual growth rate of the service sector is more pronounced than its upward trend. The declines observed, particularly during the economic crises and the COVID-19 pandemic, are much sharper. Furthermore, it is observed that the employment rate of women aged 15-64, although fluctuating, generally shows a decrease between 1988-2008 but an increase after 2008. When graphs for both variables are plotted for the study period, it is seen that, as a general trend, the employment rate of women aged 15-64 increases (decreases) in the years when the annual growth rate of the service sector decreases (increases) (Presidency of the Republic of Türkiye, Strategy and Budget Presidency, 2026a, 2026b). This finding can be explained by several factors specific to Turkey. In Turkey, it is observed that women have a larger share than men in informal employment. Women working in the informal sector are often employed in jobs lacking job security and social security, in temporary positions, in unskilled informal service sectors, and for low wages (Karabıyık, 2012, p. 247-248; Serel & Özdemir, 2017, p. 137). Furthermore, because retirement pensions are insufficient for subsistence levels, the inclination of elderly men aged 65 and over to work for low wages and informally in unskilled, informal service sectors, where women's employment is traditionally prevalent, negatively impacts women's employment (Padhi & Triveni, 2025, p. 2013-2034).

(VII) In both models, a negative but statistically insignificant relationship was obtained between the exclusion index by gender (EXCLUSION) and the employment rate of women aged 15–64 (WOMENEMP1564). In the long term, this result reveals that exclusion index by gender has no statistically significant impact on the employment rate of women aged 15-64. Nevertheless, a noteworthy point is that the coefficient value is quite high in both models, in spite of being statistically insignificant. A negative and quite high coefficient value is in line with the fact that "exclusion of women from the working life" in Türkiye.

Recommendations

1- Currently classified as a "very old society" it is clear that Turkey will be classified as an "significantly older society" in the coming years. While the share of the population of working age will decrease in the total population with the ageing of the population, the share of the elderly population will increase significantly. This situation indicates that, along with the aging population, Turkey will experience a significant contraction in the labor supply in the coming years. Furthermore, an increase in the number of elderly workers within the total labor force supply will become a concern. This result reveals that in Turkey will become much more apparent that decrease in the labor supply and an increase in the number of older workers within the total labor supply in the coming years, hereby is negatively impacting economic growth and even jeopardizing its sustainability. On the other hand, with population aging, the financial burden on the public sector is expected to increase further in the coming years due to rising healthcare, care, and pension expenditures for the aging population. And Turkey is quite unprepared for all these negative consequences. The results of this study reveal that both the inclusion of women and those who are not very old (55-64 years old) in the working life is crucial both for achieving a sustainable growth and for mitigating the financial burden that aging has brought and will bring to the public sector. Notably, the exclusion of highly educated women from the working life will result in a significant economic loss. Therefore, considering the negative consequences of aging, it makes it mandatory to include that the inclusion of the female labor force into working life, which makes up about half of the total population but pushed out of working life in Türkiye. To this end, both the government and the private sector must make regulations now to increase women's participation in the workforce. Otherwise, it will be too late. To this end, the state needs to reduce gender disparities in access to education, health, infrastructure, and financial services through government policies; ensure and encourage the establishment of childcare facilities; implement legal regulations that include flexible working conditions for women; provide financial support (micro credit) for female entrepreneurs; eliminate tax and social assistance deterrents for those earning a second income in the family; and create equal lifelong learning opportunities for women and men. The private sector, on the other hand, abandoning gender-based wage discrimination policies, providing flexibility in both contracts and work environment, and adopting performance-based reward methods instead of seniority and working hours will significantly contribute to increasing labor force participation rates of women.

2- The study's findings, revealing a complementary relationship between the employment rate of the 55-64 age group and the employment rate of women aged 15-64, and the fact that the share of the older labor force in the total labor force will increase due to aging in the coming years. Therefore, working conditions need to be adjusted for the aging workforce now, and the necessary steps need to be taken in this regard. Furthermore, in technology-intensive sectors, the aging workforce should be subject to a continuous learning process (lifelong learning process) to facilitate their adaptation to changing technological developments.

3- The study revealed a negative relationship between the employment rate of women aged 15-64 and life expectancy at age 65 for both men and women. This result indicates that, depending on the increase number of elderly individuals in Turkey in the coming years, women's employment will decrease even further. in Turkey, considering that the responsibility of caring for elderly family members is traditionally left to women as a societal role, this burden on women must be removed in order for them to remain in and/or participate in the working life. To this end, it is necessary to find new, low-cost elderly care solutions that encompass the entire society, to create the necessary policies, and to implement these policies.

4- The study revealed a positive relationship between the urban population growth rate and the employment rate of women aged 15-64. Considering that the service sector has the highest female employment rate in Turkey, and that the vast majority of activities and jobs within this sector are located in cities, it is expected that increasing (decreasing) urbanization will lead to an increase (decrease) in female employment. The labor force participation rates of women living in cities (in particular, women with college and university degrees) are higher than those of women living in rural areas. Therefore, the inclusion of highly educated women, the majority of whom live in cities, into the working life is of great importance for sustaining economic growth.

5- Currently in Turkey, it is observed that human health and social services are the sector with the highest employment rate for women within the service sector. Taken into consideration the aging population and the expected increase in the number of elderly individuals, the demand for female labor in these sectors (especially in human health and social services for the elderly, and for jobs that women traditionally do, such as elderly care, nursing etc.) is projected to increase further. This indicates a growing need for trained personnel in these fields in the coming years. This too, shows that many more people need to be trained and educated to work in these fields now.

REFERENCES

Acar, E. Ö. (2016). Türkiye'de Yapısal Dönüşüm ve İşgücü Piyasaları Üzerine Bir İnceleme. *Pamukkale Üniversitesi Sosyal Bilimler Enstitüsü Dergisi, 25*, 53–72.

Austen, S., & Giles, M. (2003). The Likely Effects of Ageing on Women's Involvement in the Paid Workforce. *Australian Bulletin of Labour, 29*(3), 257–278.

Baker, M., Gruber, J., & Milligan, K. (2010). The Interaction of Youth and Elderly Labor Markets in Canada. In Gruber, J., & Wise, D. A. (Eds.), *Social Security Programs and Retirement around the World: The Relationship to Youth Employment* (pp. 77–97). University of Chicago Press., https://www.nber.org/system/files/chapters/c8252/c8252.pdf DOI: 10.7208/chicago/9780226309507.003.0003

Baybora, D. (2010). Çalışma Yaşamında Yaş Ayrımcılığı ve Amerika Birleşik Devletleri'nde Yaş Ayrımcılığı Düzenlemesi Üzerine. *Çalışma ve Toplum*, 1(24), 1-30.

Bingley, P., Gupta, N. D., & Pedersen, P. J. (2010). Social Security, Retirement and Employment of the Young in Denmark. In Gruber, J., & Wise, D. A. (Eds.), *Social Security Programs and Retirement around the World: The Relationship to Youth Employment* (pp. 99–117). University of Chicago Press., https://www.nber.org/system/files/chapters/c8253/c8253.pdf DOI: 10.7208/chicago/9780226309507.003.0004

Bloom, D. E., Canning, D., & Fink, G. (2011). Implications of Population Aging for Economic Growth. *National Bureau of Economic Research Working Paper Series, No:16705* (p. 1-38). https://www.nber.org/system/files/working_papers/w16705/w16705.pdf

Bloom, D. E., Canning, D., Fink, G., & Finlay, J. E. (2007). Fertility, Female Labor Force Participation, and the Demographic Dividend. *Working Paper Series (National Bureau of Economic Research), 13583*, 1–43. https://www.nber.org/system/files/working_papers/w13583/w13583.pdf. DOI: 10.3386/w13583

Bloom, D. E., & Finlay, J. E. (2008). Demographic Change and Economic Growth in Asia. *PGDA Working Paper No. 41* (p. 1-31). https://www.hsph.harvard.edu/wp-content/uploads/sites/1288/2013/10/PGDA_WP_41.pdf

Brown, A., & Guttmann, R. (2017). Ageing and Labour Supply in Advanced Economies. *Reserve Bank of Australia, Bulletin*, December Quarter, 37-46. https://www.rba.gov.au/publications/bulletin/2017/dec/pdf/bu-1217-5-ageing-and-labour-supply-in-advanced-economies.pdf

Brown, R. L., Durbin, J., & Evans, J. M. (1975). Techniques for Testing the Constancy of Regression Relationships over Time. *Journal of the Royal Statistical Society. Series B, Statistical Methodology*, *37*(2), 149–192. DOI: 10.1111/j.2517-6161.1975.tb01532.x

Carone, G. (2005). Long-term Labour Force Projections for the 25 EU Member States: A Set of Data for Assessing the Economic Impact of Ageing. *European Economy. European Commiıssion Economic Papers Number 235.* November 2005, ISBN: 92-894-8874-3. https://ec.europa.eu/economy_finance/publications/pages/publication576_en.pdf

Chevalier, A., & Viitanen, T. K. (2002). The Causality between Female Labour Force Participation and The Availability of Childcare. *Applied Economics Letters*, *9*(14), 915–918. DOI: 10.1080/13504850210138469

Didžgalvytė, M., & Lukšaitė, I. (2014). Demografinio Senėjimo Itaka Ekonominiams Rodikliams. *Taikomoji Ekonomika: Sisteminiai Tyrimai,* 65-81. https://portalcris.vdu.lt/server/api/core/bitstreams/9844c052-3a67-4ccb-87d5-574574517df6/content

Dixon, S. (2003). Implications of Population Ageing for the Labour Market. In Flowers, A. (Ed.), *Labour Market Trends, Organisation for Economic Co-operation and Development* (pp. 67–76). Special Feature., http://www.re-integrate.eu/resources/webre--implications-of-population-ageing-for-the-labour-market.pdf

Erol, M. T. (2012). Avrupa Birliği'nde Nüfusun Yaşlanması ve Sağlık Harcamalarına Etkisi. *Sosyal Güvence*, *0*(1), 54–81.

Faruqee, H. (2002). Population Aging and Its Macroeconomic Implications: A Framework for Analysis. *IMF Working Paper*, *02/16*(16), 1–32. DOI: 10.5089/9781451843415.001

Gavrilov, L. A., & Heuveline, P. (2003). Aging of Population. In Demeny, P., & McNicoll, G. (Eds.), *The Encyclopedia of Population* (pp. 32–37). Macmillan Reference USA.

Ghosheh, N. S.Jr, Lee, S., & McCann, D. (2006). Conditions of Work and Employment for Older Workers in Industrialized Countries: Understanding the Issues. *SSRN*, (15), 1–60. DOI: 10.2139/ssrn.2932201

Grimshaw, D. (2014). At Work But Earning Less: Trends in Decent Pay and Minimum Wages For Young People. *Employment Working Paper No. 162* (p. 1-69.)

Gruber, J., & Wise, D. A. (2010). *Social Security Programs and Retirement Around the World: The Relationship to Youth Employment.* Chicago University Press, Chicago, National Bureau of Economic Research Conference Report. DOI: 10.7208/chicago/9780226309507.001.0001

Guzmán, P. C., Coelli, F., & Nilsson, E. (2025). Raising Employment among Women and Older Workers: A policy Lever for Ageing Economies. *The Centre for Economic Policy Research (CEPR).* https://cepr.org/voxeu/columns/raising-employment-among-women-and-older-workers-policy-lever-ageing-economies

Henkens, K., Remery, C., & Schippers, J. (2008). Shortages in an ageing labour market: An analysis of employers' behaviour. *International Journal of Human Resource Management, 19*(7), 1314–1329. https://data.worldbank.org/indicator/SP.POP.0014.TO?end=2024&locations=TR&start=1966. DOI: 10.1080/09585190802110117

Hu, Y. (2024). A Study on the Correlation Between Women's ReEmployment Problems and Economic Growth in Japan in The Context of Population Aging. In P. Dou and K. Zhang (Eds.), *Proceedings of the 2023 International Conference on Economic Management, Financial Innovation and Public Service (EMFIPS 2023)* (p. 692-701), Advances in Economics, Business and Management Research 287. https://www.atlantis-press.com/proceedings/emfips-23/126000880

Irmen, A., & Litina, A. (2022). The Implications of Population Aging for Immigrant- and Gender-Related Attitudes. In Bloom, D. E., Sousa-Poza, A., & Sunde, U. (Eds.), *The Routledge Handbook of the Economics of Ageing* (pp. 1009–1032). Routledge Taylor & Francis Group.

Kalwij, A., Kapteyn, A., & de Vos, K. (2010). Retirement of older workers and employment of the young. *De Economist, 158*(4), 341–359. https://d-nb.info/119241893X/34. DOI: 10.1007/s10645-010-9148-z

Karabıyık, İ. (2012). Türkiye'de Çalışma Hayatında Kadın İstihdamı. *Marmara Üniversitesi İ.İ.B.F. Dergisi, XXXII*(I), 231–260.

Karakaş, Ö. (2020). Dijitalleşme ve Kadın Emeği. *Terrabayt,* Nisan 30, 2020. https://terrabayt.com/yasam/dijitallesme-ve-kadin-emegi/

Kasnauskienė, G., & Andriuškaitė, M. (2017). Economic Implications of Ageing Lithuanian Population. *Organizations and Markets in Emerging Economies, 8*(1), 44–62. https://www.journals.vu.lt/omee/article/view/14196/13091. DOI: 10.15388/omee.2017.8.1.14196

Kaygusuz, E. D., Filiztekin, A., & Göker, Z. G. (2024). Türkiye'de Kadınların İşgücüne Katılımı: Genel Eğilimler, Bölgesel ve Demografik Farklar, Tutumlar. *TÜBİTAK Projesi Aralık 2024,* 1-46. https://kagider.s3.eu-central-1.amazonaws.com/uploads/projectPictures/cc50b333-266d-4198-bf95-ab0d383a8440.pdf

Kinoshita, Y., & Kochhar¸, K. (2016). Women can help offset the problems of an aging population and a shrinking workforce. *Finance & Development*, *53*(1), 1–3. https://www.imf.org/external/pubs/ft/fandd/2016/03/kinoshita.htm

Kondo, A. (2016). Effects of Increased Elderly Employment on Other Workers' Employment and Elderly's Earnings in Japan. *IZA Journal of Labor Policy*, *5*(2), 1–23. https://www.researchgate.net/publication/292187914_Effects_of_increased_elderly_employment_on_other_workers'_employment_and_elderly's_earnings_in_Japan. DOI: 10.1186/s40173-016-0063-z

Lisenkova, K., McGregor, P. G., Pappas, N., Swales, J. K., Turner, K., & Wright, R. E. (2010). Scotland the Grey: A Linked Demographic-Computable General Equilibrium (CGE) Analysis of the Impact of Population Ageing and Decline. Regional Studies. *Regional Studies*, *44*(10), 1351–1368. DOI: 10.1080/00343400701654228

Liu, D., & Zhao, R. (2024). The Impact of Population Aging on Employment. *Journal of Education. Humanities and Social Sciences*, *36*, 65–70.

Maestas, N., Mullen, K. J., & Powell, D. (2016). The Effect of Population Aging on Economic Growth, Whe Labor Force and Productivity. *RAND Working Paper* (p. 1-55). https://papers.ssrn.com/sol3/papers.cfm?abstract_id=2533260

Meçik, O., & Afşar, M. (2014). Türkiye Ekonomisinde Yapısal Dönüşümler ve İşgücü Piyasasındaki Gelişmeler. *Optimum Ekonomi ve Yönetim Bilimleri Dergisi*, *1*(2), 1–23.

Ministry of Development of the Republic of Türkiye. (2018). *On Birinci Kalkınma Planı (2019-2023), Sosyal Güvenlik Sisteminin Sürdürülebilirliği*. Özel İhtisas Komisyonu Raporu, Ankara 2018. https://www.sbb.gov.tr/wp-content/uploads/2020/04/SosyalGuvenlikSismininSurdurulebilirligiOzelIhtisasKomisyonuRaporu.pdf

Munnel, A. H., & Wu, A. Y. (2012). Will Delayed Retirement by the Baby Boomers Lead to Higher Unemployment Among Younger Workers? *Center for Retirement Research at Boston College Working Paper No: 2012-22* (p. 1-54). https://papers.ssrn.com/sol3/papers.cfm?abstract_id=2162093

Narayan, P. K., & Narayan, S. (2004). Estimating Income and Price Elasticities of Imports for Fiji in a Cointegration Framework. *Economic Modelling*, *22*(3), 423–438. DOI: 10.1016/j.econmod.2004.06.004

Nordin, N., Nordin, N. N., & Ahmad, N. A. (2015). The Effects of the Ageing Population on Healthcare Expenditure: A Comparative Study of China and India. *First International Conference on Economics and Banking (ICEB-15)*, 297-310. https://www.researchgate.net/publication/299963935_The_Effects_of_the_Ageing_Population_on_Healthcare_Expenditure_A_Comparative_Study_of_China_and_India

OECD. (2024). *Life Expectancy at 65 (indicator)* [Data set]. https://data.oecd.org/healthstat/life-expectancy-at-65.htm

OECD. (2025a). *Elderly population (indicator)* [Data set]. https://data-explorer.oecd.org/vis?lc=en&pg=0&snb=1&vw=tb&df[ds]=dsDisseminateFinalDMZ&df[id]=DSD_POPULATION%40DF_POP_HIST&df[ag]=OECD.ELS.SAE&df[vs]=&pd=1988%2C2024&dq=TUR.POP.PT_POP._T.Y_LT15%2BY15T24%2BY15T64%2BY_GE65.&ly[rw]=AGE&ly[cl]=TIME_PERIOD&to[TIME_PERIOD]=false

OECD. (2025b). *Population Projections* [Data set]. https://data-explorer.oecd.org/vis?df[ds]=DisseminateFinalDMZ&df[id]=DSD_POPULATION%40DF_POP_PROJ&df[ag]=OECD.ELS.SAE&dq=TUR.POP.PT_POP.M%2BF%2B_T.Y_GE65.&pd=2024%2C2070&to[TIME_PERIOD]=false&vw=tb

OECD. (2025c). *Historical Population Data* [Data set]. https://data-explorer.oecd.org/vis?lc=en&pg=0&snb=1&vw=tb&df[ds]=dsDisseminateFinalDMZ&df[id]=DSD_POPULATION%40DF_POP_HIST&df[ag]=OECD.ELS.SAE&df[vs]=&pd=1960%2C2025&dq=TUR.POP.PT_POP%2BPS.F%2BM%2B_T.Y_LT15%2BY15T24%2BY15T64%2BY_GE65.&ly[rw]=AGE&ly[cl]=TIME_PERIOD&to[TIME_PERIOD]=false

OECD. (2025d). *Labour Force Participation Rate, Employment and Unemployment by five-year age group and sex – indicators* [Data set]. https://data-explorer.oecd.org/vis?df[ds]=DisseminateFinalDMZ&df[id]=DSD_LFS%40DF_LFS_INDIC&df[ag]=OECD.ELS.SAE&dq=TUR.UNE_RATE%2BLF_RATE%2BEMP_RATIO.PT_POP_SUB%2BPT_LF_SUB.F%2BM%2B_T.Y15T24%2BY25T54%2BY55T64%2BY_GE65.LF%2BEMP%2BUNE&pd=1960%2C2024&to[TIME_PERIOD]=false&vw=tb

Öğütoğulları, E., & Kılıç, C. (2016). Türkiye İşgücü Piyasasında Yeni Bir Problem Alanı: 40 Yaş ve Üstü İşsizler. *Çalışma İlişkileri Dergisi*, 7(1), 85-97.

Önder, N. (2013). Türkiye'de Kadın İşgücünün Görünümü. *Çalışma ve Sosyal Güvenlik Bakanlığı Çalışma Dünyası Dergisi*, 1(1), p. 35-61.

Oshio, T., Shimizutani, S., & Oishi, A. S. (2010). Does Social Security Induce Withdrawal of the Old from the Labor Force and Create Jobs for the Young? The Case of Japan. In Gruber, J., & Wise, D. A. (Eds.), *Social Security Programs and Retirement around the World: The Relationship to Youth Employment* (pp. 217–241). The National Bureau of Economic Research, University of Chicago Press., https://www.nber.org/system/files/chapters/c8257/c8257.pdf DOI: 10.7208/chicago/9780226309507.003.0008

Padhi, B., & Triveni, T. (2025). The Indian Labor Market and Elderly: Acclimatizing to an Aging Population in the Workplace. İn S. Irudaya Rajan (Ed.), *Handbook of Aging, Health and Public Policy* (p. 2013–2034). Springer Nature. https://link.springer.com/rwe/10.1007/978-981-99-7842-7_26

Pesaran, M. H., Shin, Y., & Smith, R. J. (2001). Bounds Testing Approaches to the Analysis of Level Relationships. *Journal of Applied Econometrics*, *16*(3), 289–326. DOI: 10.1002/jae.616

Presidency of the Republic of Türkiye, Strategy and Budget Presidency (2026a). *1924-2017 Sektörel Büyüme Hızları ve GSYH Deflatörü* [Data set]. tab1-10

Presidency of the Republic of Türkiye, Strategy and Budget Presidency (2026b). *GSYH ve Alt Bileşenlerinin Ortalama Büyüme Hızı, Temel Ekonomik Göstergeler Veritabanı* [Data set]. https://www.sbb.gov.tr/temel-ekonomik-gostergeler-veritabani/

Republic of Türkiye Ministry of Family and Social Policies. General Directorate of Women's Status (2014). Türkiye'de Kadın İşgücü Profili İstatistiklerinin Analizi. Duygu Matbaacılık, 1-192. https://www.aile.gov.tr/uploads/ksgm/uploads/pages/dagitimda-olan-yayinlar/turkiye-de-kadin-isgucu-profili-ve-istatistiklerinin-analizi-nihai-rapor.pdf

Şahin, L., & Yıldırım, K. (2015). On Dokuzuncu Yüzyıldan Günümüze Türkiye'de İşsizlikle Mücadele Politikaları. *Çalışma ve Toplum*, 2015/2, 111-152.

Salem, M. B., Blanchet, D., Bozio, A., & Roger, M. (2008). Labor Force Participation by the Elderly and Employment of the Young: The Case of France. *Paris School of Economics Working Paper No: 2008–57* (p. 1-40). https://halshs.archives-ouvertes.fr/halshs-00586064/document

Samorodov, A. (1999). Ageing and Labour Markets for Older Workers. *Employment and Training Papers 33* (p. 1-38). https://www.ilo.org/sites/default/files/wcmsp5/groups/public/%40ed_emp/documents/publication/wcms_120333.pdf

Satı, Z. E., & Yılmaz, B. O. (2020). Endüstri 4.0 Ortamında Değişen İş ve Mesleklerin Türkiye'de Kadın İstihdamına Etkileri. *Strategic Public Management Journal,* 6(11), 54-76. https://dergipark.org.tr/tr/download/article-file/1129246

Şen, M. (2018). Geçmişten Günümüze Türkiye'de İşsizliğin Seyri: İşsizlikle Mücadelede Türkiye İş Kurumu (İşkur). *2 nd International Symposium Humanities and Social Sciences 04-07 August 2018 / COMRAT* (p. 96-116)

Serban, A. C. (2012). Aging Population and Effects on Labour Market. *Procedia Economics and Finance. International Conference on Applied Economics (ICOAE)*, 1, 356-364.

Serel, H., & Özdemir, B. S. (2017). Türkiye'de Kadın İstihdamı ve Ekonomik Büyüme İlişkisi. *Yönetim ve Ekonomi Araştırmaları Dergisi / Journal of Management and Economics Research,* 15(3), p. 132-148

The V-Dem Institute. (2023). *V-Dem (Varieties of Democracy) (Global Standards Local knoeledge)* [Data set]. https://www.v-dem.net/data/the-v-dem-dataset/

Thießen, U. (2007). *Aging and Structural Change. DIW Discussion Papers, No. 742*. German Institute for Economic Research., https://www.econstor.eu/bitstream/10419/27266/1/550070923.PDF

TÜİK. (2025). *Nüfus Projeksiyonları, 2018-2080* [Data set]. https://data.tuik.gov.tr/Bulten/Index?p=Nufus-Projeksiyonlari2018-2080-30567

TURKSTAT. (2023). *Sektöre göre İstihdam Edilenler, İşgücü İstatistikleri* [Data set]. https://data.tuik.gov.tr/Bulten/Index?p=Isgucu-Istatistikleri-2022-49390, TURKSTAT (2025). *Ekonomik Faaliyete Göre İstihdam Edilenler. İşgücü İstatistikleri* [Data set]. https://veriportali.tuik.gov.tr/tr/press/49390 *Erişim tarihi: 30.07.2023.*

Uğur, S. (2002). Sosyal Güvenliğimizdeki Son Değişikliklerin Değerlendirilmesi. *Dokuz Eylül Üniversitesi Sosyal Bilimler Enstitüsü Dergisi*, *4*(2), 131–146.

Uyanık, Y., & Başyiğit, R. (2018). Demografik Yapı İçinde Yaşlı Nüfusun Görünümü ve Aktif Yaşlanma Yaklaşımı Perspektifinde Politika Örnekleri. *İş ve Hayat,* 4(8), 273-310.

van Rensburg, M. Domican, S., & Kennedy, A. (2021). *The Economic Impacts of an Ageing Population in New Zealand, Background Paper for the 2021 Statement on the Long-term Fiscal Position.* New Zealand Treasury, 1-73. https://www.treasury.govt.nz/sites/default/files/2021-09/ltfs21-bp-economic-impact-ageing-population-nz.pdf

WAPES. (World Association of Public Employment Services) (2023). Impact of Global Population Ageing on Employment and the Labour Market. *STUDIES & SURVEYS*, 1-10. https://wapes.org/wp-content/uploads/2023/02/Impact-of-global-population-ageing.pdf

World Bank. (2025a). *World Development Indicators, Birth Rate, crude (per 1,000 people)* [Data set]. https://data.worldbank.org/indicator/SP.POP.0014.TO?end=2024&locations=TR&start=1966

World Bank. (2025b). *World Development Indicators, Death Rate, crude (per 1,000 people)* [Data set]. https://data.worldbank.org/indicator/SP.DYN.CDRT.IN?locations=TR

World Bank. (2025c). *World Development Indicators, Population Ages 0-14 (% of total Population)* [Data set]. https://data.worldbank.org/indicator/SP.POP.0014.TO.ZS?locations=TR

World Bank. (2025d). *World Development Indicators, Population Ages 65+ ((% of total Population)* [Data set]. https://data.worldbank.org/indicator/SP.POP.0014.TO.ZS?locations=TR

Zhang, C. (2012). The Relationship between Elderly Employment and Youth Employment: Evidence from China. *MPRA Paper No.37221* (p. 1-25). https://mpra.ub.uni-muenchen.de/37221/1/MPRA_paper_37221.pdf

Žnidaršič, J., & Dimovski, V. (2010). Reluctance Towards Older Workers in Slovenia. *The International Business & Economics Research Journal*, *9*(2), 83–100. DOI: 10.19030/iber.v9i2.525

Zuo, X., Chen, G., & Sun, X. (2017). Population Aging and Its Impact on Employment. In Tian, X. (Ed.), *China's Population Aging and the Risk of 'Middle-income Trap', Research Series on the Chinese Dream and China's Development Path* (pp. 107–123). Springer., DOI: 10.1007/978-981-10-4941-5_4

Zweifel, P., & Ferrari, M. (1992). Is There a Sisyphus Syndrome in Health Care. *Developments in Health Economics and Public Policy*, *1*, 311–330. DOI: 10.1007/978-94-011-2392-1_15 PMID: 10172497

KEY TERMS AND DEFINITIONS

ARDL Bounds Test: A test used to determine the long-term relationship between variables.

EXCLUSION: Exclusion index by gender.

LE65F: Life expectancy at age 65 (women), and life expectancy at age 65 for women.

LE65M: Life expectancy at age 65 (men), and life expectancy at age 65 for men.

LFP5564: Labor force participation rate of the population aged 55-64 (percentage of the population in the same subgroup), and labor force participation rate of the population aged 55-64.

LFP65: Labor force participation rate of the population aged 65 and over (percentage of the population in the same subgroup), and the labor force participation rate of the population aged 65.

Mature Society: A society where the population aged 65 and over is between 4% and 7% of the proportion of the total population.

Old Society: A society where the population aged 65 and over is between 7% and 10% of the proportion of the total population.

SERVICE: Annual growth rate of the service sector (%), and, rate of growth in the service sector.

URBANPOP: Urban population growth (annual %), and growth in the urban population.

Very Old Society: A society where the population aged 65 and over accounts for more than 10% of the proportion of the total population.

WOMENEMP1564: Employment rate of women aged 15-64 (Employment/population ratio) (percentage of the population in the same subgroup).

Young Society: A society where the population aged 65 and over is less than 4% of the proportion of the total population.

Chapter 6
Age Matters:
Factors Influencing Retirement Decisions Among Private Sector Employees

Wasantha Rajapakshe
http://orcid.org/0000-0002-0757-9030
Sri Lanka Institute of Information Technology, Sri Lanka

H. G. S. M. Hapurugala
Sri Lanka Institute of Information Technology, Sri Lanka

ABSTRACT

Assessing workforce dynamics based solely on chronological age remains a complex endeavor, particularly amidst international debates questioning age as the exclusive determinant of retirement eligibility. Contrary to conventional assumptions that older individuals are both unwilling and unable to continue working post-retirement, recent studies underscore a growing willingness among many seniors to extend their careers beyond statutory retirement ages. This study aims to delve into the multifaceted influences shaping retirement decisions, focusing on factors beyond age alone, including mental and physical health and employee competencies. The study finds compelling evidence that mental and physical health significantly influence retirement choices. Furthermore, insights from respondents' open-ended responses suggest a nuanced subjective perspective, with age often perceived as a predominant factor despite statistical insignificance.

DOI: 10.4018/979-8-3373-7483-3.ch006

INTRODUCTION

In Sri Lanka, retirement in the private sector is primarily determined by statutory age thresholds, organizational policy, and Employees' Provident Fund (EPF) regulations. However, the assumption that chronological age alone should determine retirement remains conceptually and practically debatable. Internationally, retirement practices are evolving due to demographic shifts, increased life expectancy, and changing labor market dynamics (Wu et al., 2016). For example, several Western countries, including the Netherlands, have encouraged delayed retirement to reduce social security burdens and sustain workforce participation (Sewdas et al., 2017). These global developments raise important questions regarding whether retirement decisions should rely solely on age or incorporate broader determinants such as health and competencies.

Retirement represents a major life transition with financial, social, and psychological implications. While retirement may provide relief from work-related stress, it may also generate financial insecurity and health vulnerabilities. Evidence suggests that retirees often exhaust legally mandated funds on immediate expenditures and later seek additional income opportunities (Ali & Frank, 2018). Moreover, reduced financial capacity during retirement has been associated with declining physical and mental well-being (Cupák et al., 2019). These consequences have implications not only for individuals but also for governments tasked with supporting aging populations.

At the organizational level, mandatory retirement may lead to the premature loss of tacit knowledge—defined as the unwritten and experience-based expertise accumulated over time—which is particularly valuable in sector-specific operations. When firms lack effective succession planning, enforced retirement can disrupt continuity and productivity. Although aging may be associated with cognitive or physical decline in some cases (Tian & Shi, 2022), termination decisions should ideally be grounded in demonstrated competency or health limitations rather than age alone (Carmel & Tur-Sinai, 2021). Performance enhancement should be based on objective evaluation mechanisms rather than assumptions about aging (Tang et al., 2013).

The Sri Lankan context provides a unique institutional setting for examining these issues. The Minimum Retirement Age of Workers Act (2021) sets the minimum retirement age at 60, while the compulsory retirement age for government employees is 65 (Department of Labor Sri Lanka, 2023). However, many private sector organizations continue to apply retirement ages between 55 and 60 for men and 50 and 55 for women, influenced partly by EPF withdrawal regulations (EPF, 2023). This divergence between statutory provisions and organizational practices creates an environment where retirement decisions are shaped by legal, financial, organizational, and individual factors.

Theoretically, retirement decisions are framed within life-span and career development perspectives. Super's career development theory emphasizes career stages and the alignment of competencies with occupational roles across the life cycle (Kosine & Lewis, 2008). Career construction theory extends this view by conceptualizing careers as dynamic and influenced by health, financial resources, family responsibilities, and cultural expectations (Lytle et al., 2015). Despite these theoretical insights, limited research has simultaneously examined mental health, physical health, age, and competencies as integrated determinants of retirement decisions within the Sri Lankan private sector.

Accordingly, the primary objective of this chapter is to examine the determinants of retirement decisions among private sector employees in Sri Lanka by investigating the influence of mental health, physical health, age, and competencies. By integrating health-related, demographic, and competency-based predictors within a single analytical framework, this study contributes to a more comprehensive understanding of retirement decision-making in emerging economies.

LITERATURE REVIEW

Retirement as a Career Transition

Retirement is commonly understood as the transition from sustained employment to partial or complete withdrawal from paid work. Super's career development theory conceptualizes career progression across life stages and highlights how age influences the alignment between abilities, interests, and occupational roles (Kosine & Lewis, 2008). Career construction theory similarly views career development as a continuous, context-driven process influenced by life roles, health, financial security, and cultural norms (Lytle et al., 2015). These frameworks suggest that retirement is not simply a chronological event but a multidimensional transition shaped by personal and contextual factors.

Mental Health and Retirement Decisions

The relationship between retirement and mental health remains contested in the literature. Early assumptions that retirement universally improves well-being have been challenged (Salokangas & Joukamaa, 1991; Kolodziej & García-Gómez, 2019). Some studies report reductions in anxiety and improved emotional states following retirement (Drentea, 2002), while others show that depressive symptoms may increase after retirement (Mosca & Barrett, 2014). Dave et al. (2008) found that retirement can influence mental health outcomes by 6%–9% over time.

Employment beyond age 55 has been associated with better psychological outcomes in certain populations (Vo et al., 2014; Lindwall et al., 2017). Bossé et al. (1987) reported that men working between ages 62–65 were healthier than early or late retirees. Similarly, Negrini et al. (2013) found that voluntary retirement was associated with better mental health compared to retirement driven by organizational pressure. Minami et al. (2015) observed declines in mental health among retirees in Japan, while Picchio and Ours (2020) showed positive mental health spillovers within households. However, Maimaris et al. (2010) reported inconclusive evidence regarding the benefits of working beyond retirement age.

Given these mixed findings, mental health appears to function as both a predictor and consequence of retirement. Therefore:

> H1: Mental health significantly influences retirement decisions among private sector employees in Sri Lanka.

Physical Health and Retirement Decisions

Physical health is widely acknowledged as a determinant of retirement timing. Amorim and França (2019) found that poor health frequently precipitates involuntary retirement. Shultz and Wang (2007) similarly identified health as a strong predictor of retirement decisions. Kolodziej and García-Gómez (2019) demonstrated that disability pensioners exhibit poorer physical health outcomes compared to other groups.

However, findings are inconsistent. Hill and Weston (2017) reported that retirement did not uniformly predict changes in physical health when age was controlled. Johnston and Lee (2009) found improvements in well-being post-retirement but limited evidence of significant physical health changes. Szabó et al. (2018) identified heterogeneous health trajectories among retirees, suggesting that pre-retirement conditions shape post-retirement outcomes. Mizuochi and Mizuochi (2021) argued that perceived health status may influence retirement decisions more strongly than objective health measures. Thus: H2: Physical health significantly influences retirement decisions among private sector employees in Sri Lanka.

Age and Retirement Expectations

Age remains a central variable in retirement policy and organizational practice. Perceived age discrimination can reduce work engagement and influence retirement intentions (Bayl-Smith & Griffin, 2014). Age anchors embedded in pension systems significantly affect expected retirement age, particularly among women (Vermeer,

2016; Opatha, 2022). Coppola and Wilke (2014) found that education and income influence retirement expectations, with more educated individuals tending to delay retirement.

Scholars such as Romaioli and Contarello (2019), Akkermans et al. (2016), Nagy et al. (2022), and Vickerstaff and Van der Horst (2021) argue that age operates not only biologically but also socially and institutionally. These findings suggest that age influences retirement decisions through policy frameworks, discrimination perceptions, and socioeconomic conditions. Therefore, H3: Age significantly influences retirement decisions among private sector employees in Sri Lanka.

Competencies and Retirement Decisions

Competencies refer to the practical application of skills, knowledge, and abilities in workplace tasks. Saba and Guerin (2005) observed that older managers may consider early retirement when satisfied with their skills and work relationships. Wiktorowicz (2017) found that highly skilled Polish workers over 50 sometimes retire early despite strong competencies. Jalatieo (2014) demonstrated that competencies shape readiness and task suitability among pre-retirees.

Training motivation and self-perceived job ability are positively associated with sustained employability (Krapp, 2005; Beier & Kanfer, 2009). Thieme et al. (2015) emphasized that work ability encompasses both physical and cognitive competencies. Cahill et al. (2021) and Amani and Fussy (2022) highlighted the importance of meaningful engagement post-retirement.

These findings indicate that competencies influence whether employees perceive themselves—and are perceived by employers—as capable of extending their working lives. Accordingly, H4: Competencies significantly influence retirement decisions among private sector employees in Sri Lanka.

METHODOLOGY

Research Philosophy and Approach

This study is grounded in a pragmatic research philosophy and uses an embedded mixed-methods approach to examine factors influencing retirement decisions among private-sector employees in Sri Lanka. Pragmatism assumes that complex human decisions—such as retirement—cannot be fully understood using a single method; therefore, combining quantitative testing with qualitative explanation improves interpretive depth and practical relevance (Creswell, 2014). Accordingly, the quantitative component tests hypothesized relationships between key predictors and retirement decisions, while the qualitative component (open-ended responses) is used to explain and contextualize the statistical patterns observed.

Research Design

A cross-sectional survey design was employed. Data were collected from full-time private-sector employees in Sri Lanka's Western Province, which hosts a high concentration of formal private employment and diverse organizational activity. The target population comprised employees aged 35 years and above, as this group includes mid-career and late-career employees who are more likely to hold informed views about retirement planning, intentions, and post-retirement pathways. The conceptual model included four independent variables—mental health, physical health, age, and competencies—and one dependent variable—retirement decision (intention toward retirement/continued employment).

Sector Selection Rationale

Participants were drawn from four private-sector categories: finance, manufacturing, information technology (IT), and services. These sectors were selected deliberately to ensure heterogeneity in work characteristics and retirement-related conditions. First, the sectors differ in the nature of work demands and human capital dependence: manufacturing includes comparatively higher physical demands, whereas finance and IT are more cognitively intensive and knowledge-based. This distinction is central to a model that tests health and competency influences on retirement decisions. Second, the sectors differ in employment arrangements and career structures (e.g., performance evaluation routines, promotion systems, and perceived post-retirement opportunities). Third, they offer varied pathways for post-retirement engagement such as consulting, entrepreneurship, and self-employment, which may shape retirement motivations and attitudes. Selecting these sectors therefore strengthened the study's capacity to examine retirement decisions across structurally different work environments rather than limiting inference to a single occupational setting.

Sampling Strategy and Sample Size

Sample size was determined using Krejcie and Morgan's (1970) table. Based on this approach, a minimum sample of 351 respondents was targeted to support statistically meaningful inference for the study population. The study initially distributed questionnaires to achieve this target, and 323 usable responses were retained for analysis (valid response rate: 92%).

A probability-based sampling method was adopted to minimize selection bias. Simple random sampling was used because participating organizations provided access to employee lists, allowing each eligible employee an equal chance of selection. Simple random sampling was considered appropriate given the primary analytical aim: testing relationships among predictors and retirement decisions across a heterogeneous private-sector sample, rather than producing sector-specific prevalence estimates.

Stratified sampling was considered but not adopted for two reasons. First, proportional stratification requires complete and consistent sampling frames across sectors and firms (e.g., accurate totals by sector, job grade, and job family), which were not uniformly available across participating organizations. Second, stratification would require sufficient observations within each stratum to enable meaningful stratum-level inference and stable parameter estimation, potentially increasing sample size requirements. Within these practical constraints, simple random sampling offered a defensible and efficient probability approach aligned with the study's objectives.

Instrument Development

The questionnaire comprised three main components. The first section collected demographic information, including gender, age, marital status, income, and job position. The second section consisted of Likert-scale items measured on a five-point scale (1 = Strongly Disagree to 5 = Strongly Agree), assessing the four predictor variables—mental health, physical health, age perceptions, and competencies—along with the dependent variable, retirement decision. These scale items were adapted from established instruments in occupational and retirement research, including studies on retirement and psychological well-being (Drentea, 2002) and retirement determinants and work ability (Shultz & Wang, 2007). The third section included five open-ended questions (Items 36–40), which invited respondents to elaborate on factors motivating or discouraging retirement, reasons for remaining employed, and qualities that justify post-retirement retention. This structure enabled the study to examine retirement decisions from complementary quantitative and qualitative perspectives.

Data Collection and Ethical Considerations

Data were collected via both physical and online questionnaires after obtaining ethical clearance from the SLIIT Business School Ethical Review Committee (RE/MBA/2021/14). Respondents were informed of the study's purpose, confidentiality assurances, and voluntary participation. No monetary incentives were provided, and participants could withdraw at any stage. The study adhered to ethical standards for human research, including informed consent and data anonymity.

Analytical Procedures

Quantitative data were analyzed using Stata software. The analysis began with descriptive statistics to summarize demographic characteristics and the distribution of key study variables. Internal consistency of the measurement scales was assessed using Cronbach's alpha coefficients. To test the proposed hypotheses, an ordered probit regression model was employed to estimate the effects of mental health, physical health, age, and competencies on retirement decisions categorized into three levels—low, moderate, and high. Marginal effects analysis was subsequently conducted to interpret the practical significance of the results by estimating how a one-unit change in each predictor variable alters the probability of selecting a particular retirement category. In addition, qualitative responses from the open-ended questions were analyzed using frequency-based text analysis and visualized through a word cloud to identify recurring themes and dominant perceptions. This integrated analytical strategy enabled the study to triangulate statistical findings with participants' subjective explanations, thereby enhancing interpretive depth and supporting the pragmatic mixed-method research design.

RESULTS

Descriptive statistics are employed to characterize the fundamental characteristics of the data in this research, providing quick summaries of the sample and the metrics. These statistics offer a concise overview of the demographic profile of the respondents who participated in the study, as presented in Table 1.

Table 1. Demographic profile of the respondents

Demographics	Categories	N	Percentage (%)
Gender	Female	183	57
	Male	140	43
	Total	323	100
Marital status	Married	286	89
	Single	34	11

continued on following page

Table 1. Continued

Demographics	Categories	N	Percentage (%)
	Other	3	1
	Total	323	100
Age	35 years to 45 years	81	25
	46 years to 55 years	175	54
	Above 55 years	67	21
	Total	323	100
Position	Non - Executive	22	7
	Executive	189	59
	Manager and above	112	35
	Total	323	100
Income	Less than 25,000	0	0
	25,000 - 35,000	4	1
	35,000 - 45,000	46	14
	45,000 - 55,000	109	34
	Above 55,000	164	51
	Total	323	100

Sources: Authors' calculations based on the survey

These descriptive statistics provide an essential baseline understanding of the sample's demographic composition. This understanding is critical for contextualizing the findings and ensuring the robustness of the study's analyses. The sample includes a balanced representation of gender, a range of ages predominantly centered around mid to late career stages, and varying position and income. This diversity allows for a comprehensive analysis of the factors influencing retirement decisions among employees in the Western Province of Sri Lanka.

Reliability results

The accuracy and reliability of the data substantially impact the study's outcomes. To ensure that the questionnaire provides standardized and high-quality information, it was tested for reliability. Cronbach's alpha was used to measure internal consistency, indicating how well a set of questions is linked. Cronbach's alpha is widely recognized as a scale of dependability (Hinton, McMurray, & Brownlow, 2014).

The researcher calculated Cronbach's alpha for all dependent and independent variables, with findings exceeding 0.7, demonstrating high internal consistency. Table 2 presents the results of the reliability test. Since all the variables have Cronbach's alpha values greater than 0.70, the reliability of all variables is considered highly acceptable. This indicates a high level of internal consistency for all questionnaire scales. The robust reliability results reinforce the dependability of the collected data, ensuring that the findings of the study are based on a reliable measurement framework.

Table 2. Results of the Reliability Test

Variable	Cronbach's alpha	Cronbach's alpha if the item deleted	No. of question items
Retirement	.889	.719	07
Mental Health	.820	.600	07
Physical Health	.799	.631	07
Age	.851	.702	07
Competencies	.821	.718	07

Sources: Authors' calculations based on the survey

Results of Descriptive Statistics

Table 3 elucidates the respondents' perspectives on the dependent and independent variables of the study. The descriptive analysis underscores the probable relationships between these variables. Respondents exhibit a neutral attitude towards most criteria, with the exception of age and competencies, which have mean scores of 4.061 and 4.045, respectively. The average responses for retirement decisions (3.7978), and mental health (3.9110) are also neutral. In contrast, physical health, age, and competencies are rated higher, with mean values of 4.0177, 4.1414, and 4.1556, respectively. The most frequent response across the questionnaire is 4.14, indicating a generally positive perspective on the elements specified in the questionnaire.

The high standard deviation in the responses suggests a broad range of views among participants, reflecting considerable variability in perceptions of the factors. Notably, retirement exhibits significant variance, similar to the standard deviation, while other components demonstrate closer variances and means, which is a positive indication of consistency.

Skewness assesses the symmetry of a variable's distribution (Hair Jr, Sarstedt, Ringle, & Gudergan, 2017). A skewed distribution implies that the responses are not symmetrically distributed around the mean, leaning either to the right or left. Kurtosis, on the other hand, measures the peakedness of a distribution. All variables exhibit negative skewness, except for the retirement variable, which has a symmetric distribution, as presented in Table 3. The distributions for mental health, physical health, and competencies are substantially skewed, while the distribution for age is mildly skewed.

Kurtosis values fall within acceptable ranges. The distributions for retirement (-0.738) and mental health (-0.112) are platykurtic and mesokurtic, respectively. The other three independent variables have positive kurtosis values of 0.500, 1.965, and 0.765, indicating platykurtic distributions with broader and flatter peaks. These findings offer a nuanced understanding of the respondents' perceptions and highlight the importance of age and competencies as significant factors. The high variability and distribution characteristics of the responses provide insights into the complexity and diversity of opinions among the participants.

Table 3. Descriptive statistics

Variable	Mean	Mode	Median	SD	Skewness		Kurtosis	
					Statistic	Std. Error	Statistic	Std. Error
Retirement	3.5958	4.14[b]	3.7978[a]	0.7411	-0.506	0.136	-0.738	0.271
Mental Health	3.7966	4.14[b]	3.9110[a]	0.5817	-0.604	0.136	-0.112	0.271
Physical Health	3.9115	4.14	4.0177[a]	0.5473	-0.818	0.136	0.5	0.271
Age	4.0615	4.14	4.1414[a]	0.5209	-1.122	0.136	1.965	0.271
Competencies	4.0456	4.14	4.1556[a]	0.5091	-0.949	0.136	0.761	0.271

N =323

Sources: Authors' calculations based on the survey

Result of Hypothesis Testing

The initial ordered probit estimation findings and variable marginal effects are presented in Table 4. Statistically significant retirement factors include all variables except age ($p = 0.37$) and competencies ($p = 0.70$), leading the researcher to reject the null hypotheses for mental and physical health ($p < 0.01$ and $p < 0.05$, respectively). Marginal effects were calculated at the mean using the categorical model where low = 1, moderate = 2, and high = 3. The marginal effect represents the change in the dependent variable (retirement) relative to the independent factors (mental health, physical health, age, and competencies).

The analysis of marginal effects reveals significant insights into the factors influencing retirement decisions among the study's participants. Mental health demonstrates a substantial impact, where a one-unit improvement decreases the likelihood of retirement by 0.19 in the low group and by 0.05 in the moderate group. Similarly, physical health plays a crucial role, with a one-unit increase lowering retirement likelihood by 0.07 in the low group and by 0.02 in the moderate group. In contrast, age and competencies did not show statistically significant effects on retirement decisions, as indicated by p-values of 0.37 and 0.70, respectively. These findings underscore the importance of health status, particularly mental and physical well-being, in shaping retirement preferences and highlight potential avenues for policy and intervention aimed at prolonging workforce participation among older adults.

The results suggest that improvements in mental and physical health have a significant impact on reducing the likelihood of retirement, particularly in the low and moderate categories. The marginal effects decrease as the health variables move from low to moderate, indicating a diminishing impact on retirement decisions in these categories. Further analysis is needed to explore robust categorical outcome changes and their implications for retirement decisions.

These findings provide valuable insights into the factors influencing retirement decisions among the study's participants, highlighting the nuanced role of health and competency levels in shaping these decisions.

Table 4. Initial ordered probit estimation results

Variables	Coef.	Std. Err.	z	P>z	Marginal effects in percentage		
					Low=1	Moderate=2	High=3
Mental health	0.6443***	0.1065	6.05	0	-0.1944***	-0.0553***	0.2497***
Physical health	0.2524**	0.1131	2.23	0.026	-0.0762**	-0.0217*	0.0978**
Age	0.1007	0.1124	0.9	0.37	-0.0304	-0.0086	0.0390
Competencies	-0.0436	0.1163	-0.38	0.707	0.0132	0.0037	-0.0169
	Ancillary parameters				Marginal effects after stepwise		
Low	1.5633		0.4023		0.2274	0.3675	0.4050
Moderate	2.5510		0.4123				
Pseudo R2 = 0.0964							
Log likelihood = -314.94							
Number of obs= 323							

Note: ***Significant at the 1% level; **Significant at the 5% level; *Significant at the 10% level
Source: Researcher's calculation

Low and moderate mental health outcomes are negative under marginal influence, as shown in Table 5. If respondents' mental health improves by one unit, their retirement likelihood will decrease by 0.20. Respondents believe mental health has little effect on retirement if it is good or improves by one unit. However, mental health's marginal effect under low conditions was -0.15. These also state that strong mental health does not affect retirement. The moderate group has a 0.05 chance of harming retirees' mental health. In the high category, a 1% rise in employee mental health increases the probability of positively affecting mental health as a factor in retirement by 0.25 (Table 5).

Good physical fitness is associated with a favorable association between physical health and retirement. One percent improvement in the employee's physical health reduces the probability of unfavorable physical health affecting retirement by 0.07. That implies that if physical health is good, it is unlikely to negatively impact retirement. The marginal impact results show that respondents with good physical health are likelier to choose physical health as a retirement factor. A one percent rise in the employee's physical health increases the probability of affecting physical health as a favorable retirement factor by 0.09 (Table 5).

These findings underscore the significant role of both mental and physical health in shaping retirement preferences, highlighting the importance of maintaining good health as individuals approach retirement age.

Table 5. Ordered Probit Results

Variables	**Estimation Coef.**	**Robust SE Std. Err.**	**Marginal effects in percentage**		
			Low Y=1	**Moderate Y=2**	**High Y=3**
Mental Health	0.6677*	0.102428	-0.2015*	-0.0572***	0.2588***
Physical Health	0.2430**	0.104963	-0.0733**	-0.0208*	0.0941**
Ancillary parameters			Marginal effects after stepwise		
Low	1.4448	0.2945	0.2276	0.3673	0.4051
Moderate	2.4317	0.3081			
Pseudo R2 = 0.0951					
Log-likelihood = -315.3992					
Number of obs= 323					

Note: ***Significant at the 1% level; **Significant at the 5% level; *Significant at the 10% level
Source: Researcher's calculation

Word Cloud analysis

Word cloud analysis examined the most frequently used words in open-ended inquiries from a diverse group of 323 respondents. However, it's important to note that only five of these respondents answered questions 36–40.

Health, mental performance, physical fitness, and knowledge emerged as the most prevalent factors influencing retirement decisions among private-sector employees (Fig. 1, *Question 36*). This question garnered 60 responses, with 15% of employees emphasizing the importance of health in their retirement planning. The researcher noted that pensioners who continue to work tend to have better mental health than those who fully retire (Lindwallet al., 2017). This underscores the crucial role of good mental health in post-retirement work, highlighting the urgency of addressing health-related issues in retirement planning.

Respondents most wanted to retire for freedom, start a business, and reduce stress. Freedom and company start-up considerations account for 8% of the 229 words (Fig. 1, *Question 37*). For the question, 37 out of 107 responded. According to respondents, retirement incentives include quiet retirement or starting a business. Stress motivates 4% of retirees; therefore, they may want a stress-free life. According to Rosen & Jerdee (1989), word cloud data suggests that some people consider retirement owing to job pressure, stress, workplace conflict, etc. Even Negrini, Panari, Simbula, and Alcover (2013) found that work-related stress motivates early retirement, suggesting that mental freedom is a motivator.

Financial considerations emerged as a significant factor that deters retirement, as cited by most respondents. Beyond finances, socialization was another significant word (Fig. 1, *Question 38*). This finding, along with the influence of good health, working arrangements, everyday activities, and financial gain on retirement decisions, as found by Sewdas et al. (2017), underscores the complex interplay of economic and social factors in retirement planning. The observation that less productive workers in households with more significant gains are more eager to retire early than those without income further highlights the strong influence of financial variables on retirement decisions (Coppola & Wilke, 2010).

Performance and dedication emerged as frequent terms in queries concerning employee attributes that the organization should retain beyond retirement, accounting for 10% of other replies (Fig. 1, *Question 39*). This finding underscores the importance of these qualities in retaining valuable employees. However, it's worth noting that performance-related phrases were more prevalent than committed employees, indicating that respondents expect good performance to be the primary factor in retaining an employee after retirement. This insight is valuable for organizations seeking to maintain a high-performing workforce even after employees reach retirement age.

The qualitative investigation examined honest opinions about retiring employees based on age. Age was 11% of the 184 generated words. However, only some respondents consider performance, quality, delivery, and healthiness more important than age when selecting Sri Lanka's retirement (Fig. 1, *Question 40*). Most countries and organizations seek to use flexible retirement and raise the retirement age since healthcare services have developed. According to the literature evaluations, some countries propose to raise the legal retirement age and implement flexible retirement ages since elderly communities indirectly affect the economy (Baruch et al., 2014).

Figure 1. Word Cloud Analysis (Questions 36–40)

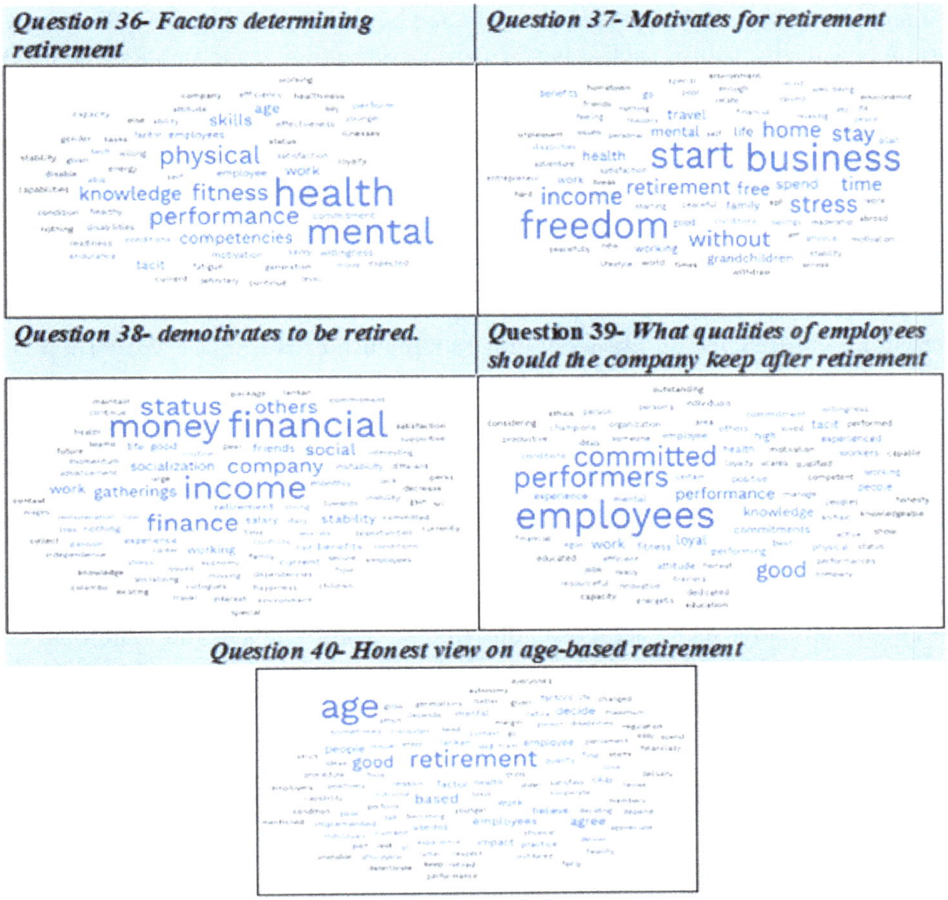

Source: Researchers' work

Data Triangulation

Based on the comparison between quantitative and qualitative findings, age initially emerged as a significant factor influencing retirement decisions in the nominal data analysis. However, in the ordered probit analysis following the stepwise model, age was found to impact retirement choices no longer significantly. This discrepancy underscores the subjective nature of employees' perspectives on retirement, highlighted by their emphasis on age as a relevant factor in open-ended questionnaire responses. In contrast, both quantitative and qualitative data consistently indicate that mental and physical well-being are pivotal considerations for retirement. Additionally, financial factors play a crucial role, with financial benefits identified as a primary reason for delayed retirement, as noted by Sewdas et al. (2017). The study further reveals that factors such as performance, commitment, and stable mental and physical health also exert influence over retirement decisions among employees in the Western Province of Sri Lanka.

DISCUSSION

This study delves into the profound impact of mental health, physical health, age, and competencies on private-sector retirement in Sri Lanka's Western area, transcending industry boundaries. A robust quantitative study unveiled respondent perceptions and tested the hypotheses, while word cloud research provided insights from respondents' open-ended questions. The findings, which validate two of the four hypotheses, are not just significant but also enlightening. They reveal that employees' decisions to resign are primarily influenced by mental and physical health, rather than age and skills. Notably, physical health emerges as a more critical retirement consideration in the high group than mental health.

The first hypothesis, which posits that Mental health impacts the retirement of private sector employees in Sri Lanka, is robustly validated with a confidence level of 95 percent and a p-value of 0.000 (Table 3). This validation instills confidence in the study's findings, which are further bolstered by the findings of other studies. For instance, the evidence supports research by Fennell et al. (2018), who found that stigma and subsequently reduced help-seeking had more of an impact on mental health concerns than physical health concerns in both rural men and women.

When examining the impact of the mental health factor using marginal effect analysis, it is observed that both low and moderate outcomes yielded negative results. These findings have significant implications, suggesting that individuals who report good mental health or experience an increase in mental health tend to perceive a lower influence of mental health on retirement. The calculated marginal effect of mental health in the low category was -0.2015, indicating a minimal impact of mental health on retirement when the mental well-being of the individuals surveyed is favorable. The moderate category exhibits a marginal likelihood of influencing mental health as a variable in retirement, with a coefficient of 0.05. In the high category, a mere one percent improvement in employees' mental health is associated with a 0.25 increase in the likelihood of mental health contributing to retirement. These implications underscore the potential impact of mental health on retirement decisions.

The second hypothesis, which suggests that Physical health impacts the retirement of private sector employees in Sri Lanka, is also validated with a confidence level of 95 percent and a p-value of 0.026 (Table 3). This validation further strengthens the Robustness of our study.

Retirement affects older adults' physical fitness (Rai et al., 2020). Rai et al. (2020) examined older worker retirement factors. Accelerometers measured physical activity in 60-year-old Australian retirees. Two types of retirement considerations are physical and psychological changes in later life that can stimulate or discourage physical exercise and older people's adaptability to these changes. The retirement outlook was the most significant adaptive factor affecting physical fitness.

When examining the outcomes of the physical health variable, a notable correlation is observed, indicating a substantial likelihood of a favorable influence on retirement when individuals possess good physical fitness. A 1% increase in an employee's physical health is associated with a 0.07 decrease in the likelihood of physical health negatively impacting retirement. This evidence implies that individuals with good physical health are doubtful to hold a negative perspective regarding the impact of physical health on retirement. The findings regarding the marginal effect of physical health further explain that when the respondents' physical health is favorable, there is a higher likelihood of selecting physical health as a determining factor in retirement decisions. According to the higher category, a positive correlation exists between a one percent increase in an employee's physical health and an increased likelihood of physical health being a significant factor in retirement, with a coefficient of 0.09.

When examining the marginal effect of both factors, it is evident that respondents perceive physical health as having a more significant impact on retirement than mental health when considering values in the high category.

The impact of retirement on the physical fitness levels of older persons has been emphasized in scholarly literature (Rai et al., 2020). Furthermore, scholars investigate the factors that impact the retirement decisions of elderly individuals. The study involved interviews with a sample of retired individuals aged 60 years and older in Australia. Accelerometers are used to obtain an objective measure of their physical activity. Two categories of factors that impact retirement are identified: the physical and psychological changes in later life that can encourage or discourage physical activity and the adaptation processes undertaken by older individuals in response to these changes. Adopting a gain or loss perspective toward retirement has been identified as the most influential adaptive factor impacting physical fitness (Rai et al., 2020).

The third hypothesis is that age influences the retirement of private sector employees in Sri Lanka. The p-value of 0.37 (Table 3) between age and retirement indicated that Hypothesis 3 (H3) is rejected with a confidence level of 95%. Age is shown to be insignificant in this investigation. The findings are reinforced by Sewdas et al. (2017), who discovered that employees prefer working past retirement age; Bayl-Smith and Griffin (2014); and Vermeer (2016), who discovered that age is one of the identified workplace discriminations. Coppola (2014) reveals that they plan to retire later.

However, after analyzing the survey's open-ended questions, it has been revealed that age is a more important factor for retirement, which provides a contradictory opinion compared with the statistical results of the same respondents. Many other researchers supported this finding. Bahrami (2001) found that age is a significant component in teacher retirement decisions. The age variable is significant at .01 because faculty seniority increases retirement age.

While age was determined to have no significant impact in the present study, the research conducted by Bahrami (2001) on the determinants of faculty retirement decisions demonstrates that age plays a significant role. Nevertheless, the conclusive results directly oppose the discoveries made in the studies. The age variable has achieved statistical significance at an alpha level of .01, indicating a significant relationship between seniority level at the faculty and retirement age, with retirement age increasing as seniority level increases. This study supports Magammulla et al.'s (2023) study on public sector employees in Sri Lanka, showing that health can negatively affect the perception of extending the retirement age.

The last hypothesis is that Competencies impact the retirement of private-sector employees in Sri Lanka. With a confidence level of 95 percent, the p-value of .707 (Table 3) between competencies and retirement proved that Hypothesis 4 (H4) is rejected. This finding is supported by the works of Kuiate & Noland (2019), Lee (2023), Cahill, Galvin, & Pettigrew (2021), and Amani & Fussy (2022). However, respondents emphasized in their responses to the open-ended question that knowledge could be a determining factor, which contradicts the statistical findings. This idea is supported by Jakštienė, Purvinis, and Narbutas (2014), revealing that preretirement age impacts competencies.

CONCLUSION

In conclusion, this study underscores a pivotal shift in understanding retirement dynamics among private-sector employees in Sri Lanka's Western Province. Unlike conventional wisdom that emphasizes age and competencies as primary determinants of retirement decisions, this research reveals that mental and physical health play more substantial roles. The findings challenge existing retirement policies in Sri Lanka, which predominantly consider age in retirement determinations. Instead, they highlight the urgent need to integrate broader health assessments into retirement frameworks, recognizing the positive impact that good mental and physical health can have on extending work-life and enhancing labor force participation among older adults. These insights are crucial for policymakers, emphasizing the importance of aligning retirement policies with evolving demographic and economic realities, fostering a more inclusive and sustainable approach to workforce management in Sri Lanka's private sector.

Limitations and future directions

The data for this study is collected from the population through a survey method incorporating open-ended questions. The qualitative questions had a significantly low respondent rate and yielded contradictory answers compared to the statistical findings. The proposed methodology employs a mixed-method approach combining multi-wave and experimental research. This approach will involve utilizing two distinct samples of older workers from various industries, ensuring high diversity. Furthermore, the data collection process is constrained to a brief time frame, and the sample size is restricted to a single cultural group, Sri Lanka. The proposal strongly suggests that future researchers should consider covering a larger population to enhance their findings' generalizability, thereby making significant contributions to the field of social sciences.

Policy Implications

Given the prevailing trend of an aging global workforce, it is crucial for organizations to adopt suitable strategies that focus on retaining older employees, particularly those aged 55 and above, in order to encourage them to continue working beyond the traditional retirement age. This study's findings indicate that beliefs about aging do not exert a substantial impact, whereas physical and mental health emerges as more influential factors. Hence, it is advisable for organizations to embrace the notion that aging can be altered and that careers may not necessarily come to an end upon retirement. To foster nonessentialist aging beliefs, it is imperative for senior executives and leaders to assume a pivotal role in shaping the organizational culture to facilitate this objective. In addition to advocating for a nonessentialist aging mindset, organizations should also leverage employees who already embrace nonessentialist beliefs about aging and are motivated to work beyond retirement age, thereby making valuable contributions to their organization if they are physically and mentally fit.

Theoretical Implications

The study's findings enhance comprehension of the decision to extend one's working years beyond the traditional retirement age. Previous studies have emphasized the significance of age as a determining factor in retirement decision-making. The study's empirical findings demonstrate that mental and physical health influence retirement decisions more than age. Although not consistently observed, the impact of these predictors has prompted researchers to advocate for further understanding of individual differences that may influence workers near retirement. Nevertheless, the impact of these predictors could have been more consistently observed, prompting researchers to advocate for further understanding of individual variances that may influence workers' retirement strategies.

REFERENCES

Akkermans, J., de Lange, A. H., van der Heijden, B. I., Kooij, D. T., Jansen, P. G., & Dikkers, J. S. (2016). What about time? Examining chronological and subjective age and their relation to work motivation. *Career Development International*, *21*(4), 419–439. DOI: 10.1108/CDI-04-2016-0063

Ali, S. B., & Frank, H. A. (2018). Retirement Planning Decisions: Choices Between Defined Benefit and Defined Contribution Plans. *American Review of Public Administration*, *49*(2), 218–235. DOI: 10.1177/0275074018765809

Amani, J., & Fussy, D. S. (2022). Retirement planning mistakes undermining the post-retirement adjustment and well-being. *Educational Gerontology*, *49*(2), 158–173. DOI: 10.1080/03601277.2022.2096306

Amorim, S. M., & França, L. H. (2019). Reasons for Retirement and Retirement Satisfaction. Psicologia: Teoria E Pesquisa, 35. https://doi.org/DOI: 10.1590/0102.3772e3558

Bahrami, B. (2001). Factors affecting faculty retirement decisions. *The Social Science Journal*, *38*(2), 297–305. DOI: 10.1016/S0362-3319(01)00114-8

Baruch, Y., Sayce, S., & Gregoriou, A. (2014). Retirement in a global labour market: A call for abolishing the fixed retirement age. *Personnel Review*, *43*(3), 464–482. DOI: 10.1108/PR-04-2013-0059

Bayl-Smith, P. H., & Griffin, B. (2014). Age discrimination in the workplace: Identifying as a late-career worker and its relationship with engagement and intended retirement age. *Journal of Applied Social Psychology*, *44*(9), 588–599. DOI: 10.1111/jasp.12251

Beier, M., & Kanfer, R. (2009). *Motivation in Training and Development*. Taylor & Francis.

Bossé, R., Aldwin, C. M., Levenson, M. R., & Ekerdt, D. J. (1987). Mental health differences among retirees and workers: Findings from the normative aging study. *Psychology and Aging*, *2*(4), 383–389. DOI: 10.1037/0882-7974.2.4.383 PMID: 3268232

Cahill, M., Galvin, R., & Pettigrew, J. (2021). The retirement experiences of women academics: A qualitative, descriptive study. *Educational Gerontology*, *47*(7), 297–311. DOI: 10.1080/03601277.2021.1929266

Carmel, S., & Tur-Sinai, A. (2021). Cognitive decline among European retirees: Impact of early retirement, nation-related and personal characteristics. *Ageing and Society*, *42*(10), 2343–2369. DOI: 10.1017/S0144686X21000064

Coppola, M., & Wilke, C. B. (2010). How Sensitive are Subjective Retirement Expectations to Increases in the Statutory Retirement Age? The German Case. SSRN Electronic Journal. DOI: 10.2139/ssrn.1701630

Coppola, M., & Wilke, C. B. (2014). At What Age Do You Expect to Retire? Retirement Expectations and Increases in the Statutory Retirement Age. *Fiscal Studies*, *35*(2), 165–188. DOI: 10.1111/j.1475-5890.2014.12027.x

Cupák, A., Kolev, G. I., & Brokešová, Z. (2019). Financial literacy and voluntary savings for retirement: Novel causal evidence. *European Journal of Finance*, *25*(16), 1606–1625. DOI: 10.1080/1351847X.2019.1641123

Dave, D., Rashad, I., & Spasojevic, J. (2008). The Effects of Retirement on Physical and Mental Health Outcomes. *Southern Economic Journal*, *75*(2), 497–523. DOI: 10.1002/j.2325-8012.2008.tb00916.x

Department of Labor Sri Lanka. (2023). Minimum Retirement Age of Workers Act, No. 28 Of 2021. https://labourdept.gov.lk/images/PDF_upload/NewAmendments/28-2021_e.pdf

Drentea, P. (2002). Retirement and Mental Health. *Journal of Aging and Health*, *14*(2), 167–194. DOI: 10.1177/089826430201400201 PMID: 11995739

EPF. (2023). *Annual report. 2020*. Retrieved from https://epf.lk/wp-content/uploads/2023/03/annualreport_2020_english.pdf

Hair Jr, J. F., Sarstedt, M., Ringle, C. M., & Gudergan, S. P. (2017). Advanced issues in partial least squares structural equation modeling. saGe publications.

Hill, P. L., & Weston, S. J. (2017). Evaluating eight-year trajectories for sense of purpose in the health and retirement study. *Aging & Mental Health*, *23*(2), 233–237. DOI: 10.1080/13607863.2017.1399344 PMID: 29212348

Hinton, P. R., McMurray, I., & Brownlow, C. (2014). *SPSS explained*. Routledge. DOI: 10.4324/9781315797298

Jakštienė, S., Purvinis, O., & Narbutas, V. (2014). Assessment of the Impact of Competencies for the Employment of Pre- retirement age people in Lithuania (applying the method of fuzzy logics). https://www.semanticscholar.org/paper/Assessment-of-the-Impact-of-Competencies-for-the-of-Jak%C5%A1tien%C4%97-Purvinis/7fca494639d42793e9683472d2f548b40b3126ed

Johnston, D. W., & Lee, W. S. (2009). Retiring to the good life? The short-term effects of retirement on health. *Economics Letters*, *103*(1), 8–11. DOI: 10.1016/j.econlet.2009.01.015

Kolodziej, I. W., & García-Gómez, P. (2019). Saved by retirement: Beyond the mean effect on mental health. *Social Science & Medicine*, *225*, 85–97. DOI: 10.1016/j.socscimed.2019.02.003 PMID: 30822608

Kosine, N. R., & Lewis, M. V. (2008). Growth and Exploration: Career Development Theory and Programs of Study. *Career and Technical Education Research*, *33*(3), 227–243. DOI: 10.5328/CTER33.3.227

Krapp, A. (2005). Basic needs and the development of interest and intrinsic motivational orientations. *Learning and Instruction*, *15*(5), 381–395. DOI: 10.1016/j.learninstruc.2005.07.007

Krejcie, R. V., & Morgan, D. W. (1970). Determining Sample Size for Research Activities. *Educational and Psychological Measurement*, *30*(3), 607–610. DOI: 10.1177/001316447003000308

Kuiate, C., & Noland, T. R. (2019). Attracting and retaining core competency: A focus on cost stickiness. *Journal of Accounting & Organizational Change*, *15*(4), 678–700. DOI: 10.1108/JAOC-04-2018-0038

Lee, Z. (2023). The Skill-Specific Automatability of Aging Workers and Its Impact on Retirement Decisions. *Work, Aging and Retirement*. Advance online publication. DOI: 10.1093/workar/waad008

Lindwall, M., Berg, A. I., Bjälkebring, P., Buratti, S., Hansson, I., Hassing, L., Henning, G., Kivi, M., König, S., Thorvaldsson, V., & Johansson, B. (2017). Psychological Health in the Retirement Transition: Rationale and First Findings in the HEalth, Ageing and Retirement Transitions in Sweden (HEARTS) Study. *Frontiers in Psychology*, *8*, 1634. Advance online publication. DOI: 10.3389/fpsyg.2017.01634 PMID: 29018374

Lytle, M. C., Foley, P. F., & Cotter, E. W. (2015). Career and Retirement Theories. *Journal of Career Development*, *42*(3), 185–198. DOI: 10.1177/0894845314547638 PMID: 26101455

Magammulla, C. C., Fernando, M. A. C. S. S., & Silva, C. W. C. (2023). Factors Affecting The Perception Towards The Retirement Age: A Case Of Public Sector Employees In Western Province, Sri Lanka. 1st International Conference On Social Sciences And Languages (Icssl - 2023) Sri Lanka, Sabaragamuwa University (2023-01-12) http://repo.lib.sab.ac.lk:8080/xmlui/handle/susl/3219

Maimaris, W., Hogan, H., & Lock, K. (2010). The Impact of Working Beyond Traditional Retirement Ages on Mental Health: Implications for Public Health and Welfare Policy. *Public Health Reviews*, *32*(2), 532–548. DOI: 10.1007/BF03391615

Minami, U., Nishi, M., Fukaya, T., Hasebe, M., Nonaka, K., Koike, T., Suzuki, H., Murayama, Y., Uchida, H., & Fujiwara, Y. (2015). Effects of the Change in Working Status on the Health of Older People in Japan. *PLoS One*, *10*(12), e0144069. DOI: 10.1371/journal.pone.0144069 PMID: 26633033

Mizuochi, M. (2021). Effect of Retirement Timing on Health. In *Exploring the Effect of Retirement on Health in Japan. SpringerBriefs in Population Studies*. Springer., DOI: 10.1007/978-981-16-2638-8_4

Mosca, I., & Barrett, A. M. (2014). The Impact of Voluntary and Involuntary Retirement on Mental Health: Evidence from Older Irish Adults. SSRN Electronic Journal. DOI: 10.2139/ssrn.2543918

Nagy, N., Rudolph, C. W., & Zacher, H. (2022). Reciprocal relationships between subjective age and retirement intentions. *European Journal of Work and Organizational Psychology*, *31*(4), 583–595. DOI: 10.1080/1359432X.2021.2016700

Negrini, A., Panari, C., Simbula, S., & Alcover, C. M. (2013). The push and pull factors related to early retirees' mental health status: A comparative study between Italy and Spain. *Journal of Work and Organizational Psychology*, *29*(2), 51–58. DOI: 10.5093/tr2013a8

Opatha, H. H. D. N. P. (2022). The Retirement Age: An Informative Analysis. *Sri Lankan Journal of Human Resource Management*, *12*(1), 39. Advance online publication. DOI: 10.4038/sljhrm.v12i1.5679

Picchio, M., & Ours, J. C. V. (2020). Mental health effects of retirement. *De Economist*, *168*(3), 419–452. DOI: 10.1007/s10645-020-09369-8

Rai, R., Jongenelis, M. I., Jackson, B., Newton, R. U., & Pettigrew, S. (2020). Retirement and Physical Activity: The Opportunity of a Lifetime or the Beginning of the End? *Journal of Aging and Physical Activity*, *28*(3), 365–375. DOI: 10.1123/japa.2019-0023 PMID: 31743090

Romaioli, D., & Contarello, A. (2019). "I'm Too Old for …" Looking into a Self-Sabotage Rhetoric and its Counter-narratives in an Italian Setting. *Journal of Aging Studies*, *48*, 25–32. DOI: 10.1016/j.jaging.2018.12.001 PMID: 30832927

Rosen, B., & Jerdee, T. H. (1989). Retirement policies: Evidence of the need for change. *Human Resource Management*, *28*(1), 87–103. DOI: 10.1002/hrm.3930280106

Saba, T., & Guerin, G. (2005). Extending Employment beyond Retirement Age: The Case of Health Care Managers in Quebec. *Public Personnel Management*, *34*(2), 195–214. DOI: 10.1177/009102600503400205

Salokangas, R. K., & Joukamaa, M. (1991). Physical and Mental Health Changes in Retirement Age. *Psychotherapy and Psychosomatics*, *55*(2–4), 100–107. DOI: 10.1159/000288415 PMID: 1891555

Sewdas, R., de Wind, A., van der Zwaan, L. G., van der Borg, W. E., Steenbeek, R., van der Beek, A. J., & Boot, C. R. (2017). Why older workers work beyond the retirement age: A qualitative study. *BMC Public Health*, *17*(1), 672. Advance online publication. DOI: 10.1186/s12889-017-4675-z PMID: 28830399

Shultz, K. S., & Wang, M. (2007). The Influence of Specific Physical Health Conditions on Retirement Decisions. *International Journal of Aging & Human Development*, *65*(2), 149–161. DOI: 10.2190/AG.65.2.c PMID: 17957985

Szabó, G., Allen, J., Stephens, C., & Alpass, F. (2018). Is retirement associated with physical health benefits? A longitudinal investigation with older New Zealanders. *Age and Ageing*, *48*(2), 267–272. DOI: 10.1093/ageing/afy176 PMID: 30379990

Tang, F., Choi, E., & Goode, R. (2013). Older Americans Employment and Retirement. *Ageing International*, *38*(1), 82–94. DOI: 10.1007/s12126-012-9162-3

Thieme, P., Brusch, M., & Büsch, V. (2015). The role of continuing training motivation for work ability and the desire to work past retirement age. European journal for Research on the Education and Learning of Adults, 6(1), 25-38. https://opus4.kobv.de/opus4-srh/frontdoor/index/index/docId/768

Tian, Y., & Shi, Z. (2022). Effects of physical activity on daily physical function in Chinese middle-aged and older adults: A longitudinal study from CHARLES. *Journal of Clinical Medicine*, *11*(21), 6514. DOI: 10.3390/jcm11216514 PMID: 36362742

Vermeer, N. (2016). Age Anchors and the Expected Retirement Age: An Experimental Study. *De Economist*, *164*(3), 255–279. DOI: 10.1007/s10645-016-9276-1

Vickerstaff, S., & Van der Horst, M. (2021). The Impact of Age Stereotypes and Age Norms on Employees' Retirement Choices: A Neglected Aspect of Research on Extended Working Lives. *Frontiers in Sociology*, *6*, 686645. DOI: 10.3389/fsoc.2021.686645 PMID: 34141736

Vo, K., Forder, P. M., Tavener, M., Rodgers, B., Banks, E., Bauman, A., & Byles, J. E. (2014). Retirement, age, gender and mental health: Findings from the 45 and Up Study. *Aging & Mental Health*, *19*(7), 647–657. DOI: 10.1080/13607863.2014.962002 PMID: 25271125

Wiktorowicz, J. (2017). Extending Working Life: Which Competencies are Crucial in Near-Retirement Age? *Journal of Adult Development*, *25*(1), 48–60. DOI: 10.1007/s10804-017-9274-9 PMID: 29527111

Wu, C., Odden, M. C., Fisher, G. G., & Stawski, R. S. (2016). Association of retirement age with mortality: A population-based longitudinal study among older adults in the USA. *Journal of Epidemiology and Community Health*, *70*(9), 917–923. DOI: 10.1136/jech-2015-207097 PMID: 27001669

KEY TERMS AND DEFINITIONS

Active Aging: A policy and practice framework that promotes health, participation, and security to enhance quality of life as people age.

Capability-Based Retirement: A model emphasizing health, competence, and performance as determinants of retirement eligibility rather than age.

Competency: The combination of knowledge, skills, and abilities that determine work effectiveness and adaptability.

Mental Health: Psychological well-being encompassing emotional stability, resilience, and cognitive function that affect work motivation and satisfaction.

Ordered Probit Model: A regression technique used to model relationships between ordinal dependent variables and independent predictors.

Physical Health: Functional ability and physiological well-being that enable sustained work performance.

Retirement Decision: The process through which an employee determines the timing and manner of exiting the workforce, influenced by health, financial, and psychosocial factors.

Chapter 7
Health System Sustainability and Labor Market Participation in an Aging Workforce:
Economic Implications and Policy Options

Lawal Olamilekan Abdulwahab
http://orcid.org/0000-0003-4955-244X
School of Business and Economics, Universiti Brunei Darussalam, Brunei

ABSTRACT

This chapter examines the interdependence between health system sustainability and labor market participation in the context of global population aging. Using an integrated framework based on health capital, human capital, lifecycle labor supply, and systems theories, it analyzes how health, productivity, and fiscal dynamics interact across individual, institutional, and macroeconomic levels. While aging raises dependency ratios, healthcare costs, and pension burdens, it can drive growth through preventive health, lifelong learning, and inclusive labor markets. Drawing on OECD and emerging economy cases, including Japan's productive aging model, Nordic health–labor integration, and China's pension reforms, the chapter proposes an Integrated Health–Labor–Fiscal (IHLF) Framework. It emphasizes cross-sectoral governance, preventive care, flexible employment, and fiscal adaptability, arguing that health must be treated as productive capital to turn longevity into a source of sustainable prosperity.

DOI: 10.4018/979-8-3373-7483-3.ch007

1. INTRODUCTION

1.1 Demographic Transition and the Aging Workforce

The 21st century sees a demographic shift marked by declining fertility, longer life expectancy, and an aging population. By 2050, over two billion will be aged 60+, double the 2020 figure. This impacts labor, health, and fiscal systems by changing the economic dependency ratio and workforce balance (Malik et al., 2022). In many developed economies, the aging workforce contributes to labor shortages and skill deficits, while in emerging economies, the fiscal strain arises primarily from inadequate pension systems and underfunded healthcare sectors (Michaeli et al., 2024). The aging process, if approached strategically, can generate opportunities through the 'silver economy,' a sector driven by older consumers, lifelong learning, and age-inclusive labor markets, encouraging policymakers to see aging as a growth driver (Yolusever, 2025). The link between health system sustainability and labor participation is crucial. Poor health limits work and increases public costs, while a healthy workforce boosts productivity and fiscal stability (Abdulwahab et al., 2026; Tang & Li, 2021). This mutual dependence forms the central axis of this chapter's analysis.

1.2 Theoretical Framework

This chapter explores the link between health system sustainability and labor participation in aging societies using an integrative, multi-level framework from economics, public health, and policy analysis. At the micro level, it examines individuals' health, human capital, and labor decisions affecting workforce participation and retirement. At the meso level, it examines organizational and institutional factors, such as workplace health programs and labor policies, that enable longer, healthier work lives. At the macro level, it analyzes demographic changes, fiscal sustainability, and national policies shaping interactions among health systems, labor markets, and public finances. By combining these levels, the chapter highlights the interconnectedness of health outcomes, institutions, and economic sustainability in aging populations.

1.2.1 Health Capital Theory

The Health Capital Theory, introduced by (Grossman, 1972), conceptualizes health as a durable form of capital that individuals both accumulate and depreciate over the life course. Investments in health through medical care, nutrition, preventive interventions, and healthy behaviors enhance productivity, reduce absenteeism, and extend working life. As individuals age, their stock of health capital depreciates more rapidly, influencing labor supply decisions, wage trajectories, and retirement timing (Crossdale & Penning, 2024). Maintaining health capital, therefore, becomes a strategic lever for sustaining labor market participation among older adults and mitigating productivity losses associated with aging.

1.2.2 Human Capital Theory

Building upon Becker's Human Capital Theory (Becker, 1975). This perspective acknowledges that education, skills, and health collectively determine an individual's productivity and adaptability in the labor market. In aging economies, continuous investment in human capital through lifelong learning, reskilling, and access to healthcare is critical for maintaining employability and ensuring that older workers remain competitive in evolving sectors (Abrha & Weldeyohans, 2025). Empirical evidence consistently shows that the interaction between health and education is pivotal for extending working lives and supporting inclusive economic growth amid demographic transition.

1.2.3 Lifecycle Labor Supply Model

The Lifecycle Labor Supply Model provides a microeconomic foundation for understanding how individuals allocate time between labor and leisure across their lifespan. Decisions regarding work participation, retirement, and savings are influenced by expected lifetime utility, which depends on factors such as income, health status, and institutional factors, including pension design and healthcare coverage. As health deteriorates, the marginal utility of leisure typically rises, prompting earlier retirement or reduced labor engagement. Conversely, good health extends both the capacity and willingness to work, thereby influencing aggregate labor participation rates and the economic dependency ratio (Y.-T. Liu et al., 2023). This model thus underscores the dynamic link between health status and labor supply behavior in aging societies.

1.2.4 Political Economy of Welfare and Fiscal Sustainability

The political economy perspective situates the health–labor nexus within broader questions of fiscal sustainability and intergenerational equity. As populations age, rising expenditures on healthcare, pensions, and long-term care intensify pressure on public finances. Fiscal sustainability theory examines whether government spending, taxation, and borrowing patterns remain viable in the face of demographic strain. Without structural reforms, age-related spending can erode fiscal balance and exacerbate intergenerational inequities (Chłoń-Domińczak, 2021). Consequently, prudent fiscal management through adaptive tax systems, efficient healthcare financing, and pension reform is essential to preserve social protection solvency and macroeconomic stability (Gunarsa, 2020).

1.2.5 Systems Theory of Health, Labor, and Fiscal Interdependence

Systems Theory connects health, labor, and fiscal systems as parts of a socioeconomic ecosystem. Challenges like fragmentation, data silos, and political resistance hinder implementation. Overcoming these barriers is vital for policy coordination and system resilience in aging societies (Crawshaw et al., 2024). This systems perspective underpins the chapter's approach, emphasizing cross-sector coordination and adaptive policy for sustainable aging. The framework links individual behavior, institutions, and macroeconomic outcomes. Health and human capital theories explain micro-level productivity factors; lifecycle and political economy models address behavioral and fiscal aspects, while systems theory unites these insights. This foundation supports subsequent sections with empirical evidence, fiscal modeling, and policy comparison analysis.

Figure 1 shows the integrated framework for analyzing health system sustainability and labor participation in aging societies. It models three interconnected levels: micro (individual health and human capital), meso (labor market and institutional structures), and macro (fiscal and policy systems). At the micro level, health and human capital influence productivity and employability. The meso level includes labor-market design, workplace systems, and health-service access that shape participation. The macro level covers fiscal sustainability, welfare, and intergenerational equity, showing how policies impact health and labor systems. Arrows depict bidirectional feedback: better health boosts productivity and revenues, while strong fiscal and labor systems improve health and participation. The outer ring, based on Systems Theory, emphasizes cross-sectoral policy coherence for sustainable aging. This framework underpins the subsequent empirical and policy analysis sections.

Figure 1. Integrated Theoretical Framework of Health–Labor–Fiscal Interdependence

Source: Author's design based on Grossman (1972) and Becker (1975).

1.3 Objectives, Scope, and Contribution

The overarching objective of this chapter is to analyze how health system sustainability influences labor force participation among aging populations and to identify economically viable, socially inclusive policy options. Specifically, the chapter aims to:

1. Examine how age-related health conditions affect labor market engagement and productivity.
2. Assess the fiscal consequences of healthcare and long-term care expenditures on national budgets.
3. Evaluate the cost-effectiveness of health and workplace interventions that promote extended working lives.
4. Compare international policy responses across high-income and emerging economies.
5. Develop an integrated policy framework linking health, labor, and fiscal systems for sustainable aging.

This chapter advances a systems-based health economics perspective that links individual health outcomes to macroeconomic performance. It aligns with aging and labor-market sustainability research and introduces an original model that integrates health economics with fiscal and labor policy, a less-explored area of current research (Nagarajan et al., 2019). This framework outlines demographic urgency, theory, and scope for analyzing how sustainable health systems support productive, inclusive labor markets in aging societies. The following sections will use empirical data, fiscal modeling, and policy to apply these theories for analysis.

2. GLOBAL DEMOGRAPHIC AND ECONOMIC

2.1 Demographic Aging and Economic Dependency

The global demographic landscape is undergoing an extraordinary transformation. Declining fertility rates, increasing longevity, and structural changes in population composition are converging to create an age distribution never observed in human history. By 2050, nearly one in six people globally will be aged 65 or older, compared to one in eleven in 2019 (Boodoo & Hosein, 2024). Figure 2 shows the global distribution of populations aged 65+ by 2050, highlighting geographic differences. Europe, East Asia, and North America will have the highest elderly rates, with over 30% in countries such as Japan, Italy, and Germany. These regions will face major fiscal and labor pressures from pensions and healthcare (Doling et al., 2018; Lunenfeld et al., 2021). Sub-Saharan Africa, South Asia, and parts of the Middle East are likely to maintain younger populations, with elderly shares below 15%. This reflects ongoing demographic dividends, but also future aging risks if policies are delayed (Nair, 2014). The map shows the uneven pace of global demographic transition, emphasizing the need for region-specific fiscal and labor policies to maintain economic productivity and intergenerational equity. This evidence supports the chapter's point that aging's economic and fiscal effects are not uniformly negative but depend on timing, policy adaptability, and institutional readiness of regions.

Figure 2. Global Aging Map (Projected Share of Population 65+ by 2050)

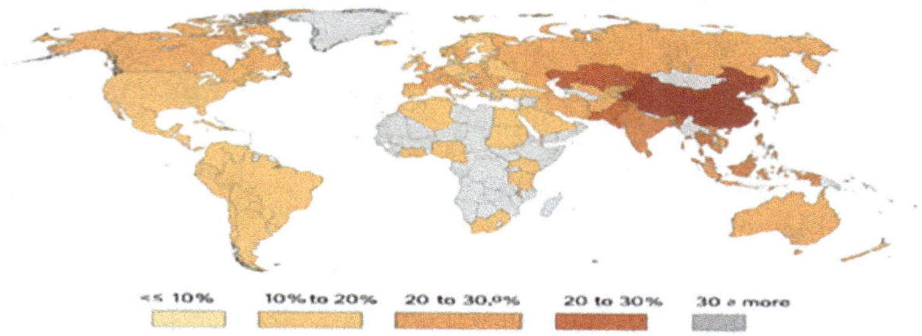

Source: Adapted from (OECD, 2023).

This demographic transition carries profound economic and social consequences, particularly for labor markets, productivity, and fiscal sustainability (Yolusever,

2025). The old-age dependency ratio (OADR), which measures the elderly (65+) to the working-age population (15–64), indicates demographic pressure. In countries like Japan, Italy, and Germany, OADR exceeds 45%, with emerging economies following. Rising ratios mean fewer workers support more retirees, stressing pensions, healthcare, and fiscal transfers (Mihajlović & Miladinov, 2024). The fiscal and economic effects of aging vary across regions. Some Asian and African economies benefit from a demographic dividend due to large working-age populations, while others, like those in Eastern Europe, face fiscal tightening from population aging. A country's fiscal vulnerability depends on initial debt, productivity growth, and labor-market adaptability (Meka'a & Moneboulou, 2024; Yaqoob et al., 2024).

Table 1 presents a comparative snapshot of old-age dependency ratios (OADR) and associated fiscal vulnerabilities across selected economies. The data illustrate that advanced economies, such as Japan and Germany, face the most acute demographic pressures, with OADR values exceeding 60% by 2050, thereby intensifying demands on pension and health systems. Conversely, emerging economies like India and Nigeria still benefit from a demographic dividend but risk future fiscal strain due to weak social protection and informal labor structures. The comparative perspective underscores the importance of early reform, preventive health investments, and labor-market adaptability as key levers for mitigating the fiscal consequences of aging.

Table 1. Comparative Old-Age Dependency Ratios and Fiscal Vulnerability by Region

Country	Old-Age Dependency Ratio (OADR) 2020	Projected OADR 2050	Key Fiscal Risk	Primary Mitigation Strategy
Japan	48%	73%	Pension burden, labor shortages	Raising retirement age, automation, and lifelong employment policies
Germany	45%	67%	Rising healthcare and LTC expenditure	Efficiency reforms and migrant labor integration
Sweden	35%	49%	Moderate pension pressure	Flexible retirement and preventive health investment
Brazil	19%	36%	Pension imbalance and fiscal rigidity	Tax reform and gradual retirement restructuring
China	20%	44%	Declining labor supply	Gradual pension reform and health system expansion
India	10%	22%	Informal labor market and low coverage	Expanding universal pensions and health access
Nigeria	6%	14%	Low institutional coverage, rising informality	Strengthening community-based care and informal sector inclusion

Source: Compiled from the Global reports (UN DESA, OECD, IMF, and World Bank).

Countries with early pension and healthcare reforms, notably Sweden, Germany, and Denmark, tend to maintain fiscal stability despite demographic aging. Conversely, economies delaying reforms face compounding debt and healthcare burdens due to both demographic inertia and political economy constraints (Vučković & Banović, 2021).

2.2 Health-Adjusted Life Expectancy and Workforce Capacity

Aging should be viewed in terms of functional capacity rather than solely in terms of chronological age. The concept of Health-Adjusted Life Expectancy (HALE), showing the average healthy years a person can expect, offers a nuanced view of the economic impact of aging. In high-income countries, HALE often exceeds 70 years, but in lower-income regions, poor health shortens the effective working years. Studies show that healthier aging populations maintain higher labor participation among older adults. Japan's strategy, combining preventive health and flexible work policies, has helped people aged 60–69 stay active, reducing some fiscal challenges of aging (J.-W. Lee, 2025). Similarly, in China, population aging has paradoxically improved firm-level labor productivity, mainly through capital deepening and technological adaptation (Wu et al., 2025). In emerging economies like India and Central/Eastern European countries, weak healthcare and limited re-skilling worsen early labor exit, reducing productivity (Mihajlović & Miladinov, 2024). The economic burden is magnified when health-adjusted life expectancy lags behind the statutory retirement age, compelling governments to subsidize rising health and pension expenditures.

2.3 Sectoral and Gender Dimensions of Aging Labor Markets

Population aging impacts labor markets unevenly. The service sector, especially healthcare, education, and eldercare, employs more older workers due to lower physical demands and flexible hours. In contrast, physically intensive sectors such as manufacturing, construction, and agriculture experience faster attrition among older workers (Grenčíková et al., 2023). Gender disparities influence labor outcomes in aging societies. Women, with longer life expectancy but lower lifetime earnings, face lower pensions and more unpaid care. Policies such as flexible work, caregiver credits, and pension reforms that recognize unpaid care are vital for sustainable participation (Profeta, 2023; Uścińska, 2023). Moreover, immigration policies and active aging programs can alleviate demographic pressure by augmenting the labor supply and sustaining productivity growth.

For example, Nordic countries and Germany have demonstrated that balanced migration inflows and continuous training programs for older workers significantly moderate dependency ratios and maintain labor market vitality (Abdulwahab & Azam, 2026; Caoyan et al., 2024). Demographic aging presents economic challenges, including rising dependency ratios that strain fiscal and labor markets. Strategies such as improving health, reskilling, and gender- and migration-sensitive policies can sustain productivity and reduce the fiscal burden. The next section will examine how health directly impacts labor participation and productivity, linking demographic trends with economic outcomes analysis.

3. THE HEALTH–LABOR MARKET NEXUS

This section examines the micro-level mechanisms through which individual health status influences labor market participation, productivity, and employment trajectories across the life course.

3.1 Linkages Between Health and Labor Market Outcomes

Health is crucial for labor market participation. Good health boosts productivity and skill development, and prolongs careers, while ill health, especially chronic conditions, lowers employability, increases absenteeism, and causes early exits. These issues are more common in aging societies with rising chronic diseases. Recent evidence shows that chronic illnesses like diabetes, cardiovascular issues, arthritis, and depression directly reduce employment, working hours, and increase early retirement (Qiao et al., 2021). Similarly, health deterioration is associated with a higher likelihood of work exit and absenteeism, particularly among older agricultural and manual workers (Chiang et al., 2025). This nexus extends beyond physical health to encompass mental and psychosocial well-being, as mental distress, anxiety, and depression substantially reduce work performance through both absenteeism and reduced productivity while present at work (Chodavadia et al., 2023). The dual impact of chronic and mental conditions thus constitutes a major pathway through which population health determines economic output.

3.2 Absenteeism, Presenteeism, and Productivity Losses

The productivity cost of ill health mainly comes from absenteeism and presenteeism, with research showing presenteeism often causes more loss, especially in chronic pain, headaches, or fatigue. For example, a Turkish manufacturing study found that 94% of productivity loss was due to presenteeism, costing 2.4% of workforce capacity each year (Selekler et al., 2015). Cross-national evidence from Hungary further reveals that presenteeism correlates more strongly with deteriorating self-rated health and aging than absenteeism, underscoring the hidden economic burden of suboptimal workplace health (Péntek et al., 2020). The Productivity-Adjusted Life Year (PALY) framework extends this understanding by integrating lifetime productivity losses, offering policymakers a metric that links workforce health directly to macroeconomic performance (Ademi et al., 2021). Furthermore, occupational health interventions have proven effective in mitigating both absenteeism and presenteeism. Evidence-based workplace programs, ranging from ergonomic adjustments to chronic disease self-management training, have yielded measurable improvements in worker well-being and firm productivity (Silvaggi et al., 2020).

Figure 3 shows how declining worker health causes productivity and fiscal losses. Chronic and mental health issues lead to absenteeism and presenteeism, reducing effective labor, which, at the firm level, results in decreased output, higher replacement costs, and lower competitiveness. On a macro scale, these losses reduce GDP, tax revenues, and fiscal space, while raising healthcare and social expenses. The feedback loop indicates that limited fiscal capacity hampers public health investment, worsening workforce health. The model emphasizes the importance of preventive and workplace health measures to maintain productivity and fiscal resilience in aging populations.

Figure 3. Productivity Loss Pathways – From Ill Health to Macroeconomic Impact

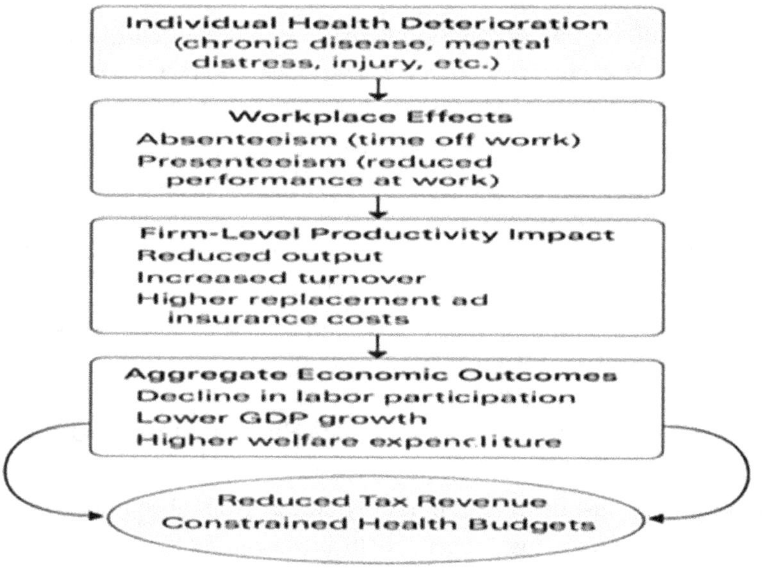

Source: Author's concept based on (Bloom et al., 2012; Bloom & Canning, 2000; Suhrcke et al., 2008).

3.3 Gender and Socioeconomic Differentials in Health–Work Linkages

Gender disparities substantially influence the relationship between health and the labor market. Women tend to exhibit a higher prevalence of chronic conditions such as arthritis and depression, leading to elevated risks of involuntary job loss or early retirement (Piłat et al., 2020). Men are more prone to cardiovascular and metabolic disorders that reduce physical work ability. Socioeconomic status influences these outcomes: higher-educated workers with access to healthcare tend to be more resilient to productivity shocks from illness.

Conversely, manual workers in low- and middle-income economies face hazardous conditions and limited health services, leading to greater declines in productivity (Mansyur, 2021). Moreover, geographic and occupational differences shape exposure to chronic disease risks. In China, rural workers exhibit stronger associations between poor health and workforce withdrawal than urban employees, primarily due to limited healthcare access and informal labor market structures (Y. Li et al., 2024). These inequalities necessitate targeted, equity-oriented interventions that address both healthcare access and labor market inclusion.

3.4 Chronic Conditions, Mental Health, and Workforce Sustainability

Chronic and mental health conditions reduce labor force participation and impose economic burdens. For instance, in Spain, indirect costs of chronic delta hepatitis, due to absenteeism, presenteeism, and early death, are estimated at €12.7 million yearly, showing the macroeconomic impact of productivity losses (Buti et al., 2025). Similarly, autoimmune diseases, chronic pain, and interstitial lung disorders markedly reduce work participation and increase disability claims across age groups (Cordeiro et al., 2022). Beyond physical illness, psychological distress exerts equally severe effects on economic performance, compounding other risk factors like occupational stress, poor nutrition, and inadequate workplace support structures (Keramat et al., 2025). Multidisciplinary workplace health programs, including physical therapists and occupational health experts, show strong potential to reverse negative trends.

A recent Japanese study found that targeted workshops for chronic pain prevention improved satisfaction and reduced presenteeism, strengthening the case for integrated health strategies (Oka et al., 2024). Table 2 presents estimated productivity losses and costs associated with various chronic and mental health conditions. Mental disorders like depression and anxiety cause the highest losses due to absenteeism and presenteeism. Chronic illnesses such as diabetes and cardiovascular disease also lead to early exit and reduced work capacity. Overall, the data highlight that preventive health and occupational interventions generate significant macroeconomic benefits by reducing productivity costs in aging workforces.

Table 2. Economic Impact of Selected Chronic and Mental Health Conditions

Condition	Average Productivity Loss (%)	Estimated Annual Economic Cost (€ millions)	Primary Impact Channel	Key Intervention Type
Diabetes	5–8	12,000	Absenteeism, early retirement	Preventive disease management, dietary monitoring
Cardiovascular diseases	6–9	15,400	Presenteeism, disability	Health screenings, lifestyle modification
Chronic pain (e.g., musculoskeletal disorders)	4–6	7,800	Presenteeism, reduced work performance	Ergonomic workplace interventions
Depression & anxiety disorders	6–10	18,500	Absenteeism and presenteeism	Workplace mental health programs, counseling
Autoimmune and inflammatory diseases	3–5	9,200	Work disability, absenteeism	Early diagnosis, occupational rehabilitation
Chronic respiratory conditions	4–7	6,100	Work absence, reduced stamina	Environmental controls, medical adherence

Source: Compiled by the author from the existing studies.

3.5 Policy Implications Toward a Health–Productivity Continuum

Empirical evidence shows a strong, bidirectional link between population health and labor market performance. Investing in preventive healthcare, mental health, and workplace ergonomics can extend working lives, boost productivity, and reduce the macroeconomic costs of aging. The concept of Productivity-Adjusted Life Year (PALY) helps policymakers quantify the economic benefits of health interventions and allocate resources better. As health systems move toward universal coverage and workplace wellness programs grow, aligning public health goals with employment strategies is key to fiscal stability and workforce vitality. Policy should integrate chronic disease management into labor frameworks, promote employer co-investment in health innovations, and reduce health inequities through social protection. Health is a vital part of economic capital, not just a medical outcome. By embedding health promotion in labor and fiscal policies, countries can turn longevity into a driver of productivity and resilience. In aging societies, creating a healthy, inclusive, and adaptable workforce is essential for long-term economic stability and sustainability.

4. FISCAL IMPLICATIONS OF POPULATION AGING AND HEALTH SYSTEM PRESSURES

This section analyzes the macro-level economic implications of population aging, including rising health expenditures, pension pressures, and broader fiscal sustainability challenges.

4.1 Public Expenditure Patterns and Fiscal Sustainability

Population aging puts significant strain on public finances, mainly due to rising healthcare, pensions, and LTC costs. Elderly population growth is expected to increase age-related public spending by 6–7% of GDP across OECD nations in the next fifty years, despite pension reforms (R. Lee, 2025). The fiscal vulnerability of aging societies stems from demographic trends, policy inertia, and institutional inefficiencies. In Spain, despite healthcare improvements, demographic changes could increase public health spending by up to 3% of GDP by 2050 (Mansouri et al., 2025). Similarly, Brazil's public spending on health and pensions is expected to surge from 18% to 27% of GDP by mid-century, potentially crowding out investments in education and infrastructure (de Castro & Toneto, 2019; Lanza Queiroz & Lobo Alves Ferreira, 2021). The Overlapping Generations (OLG) modeling approach offers critical insights into how demographic shocks affect fiscal sustainability over time.

A Japan-calibrated OLG model shows that financing age-related costs via gradual consumption tax increases improves macroeconomic performance and intergenerational equity more than debt or raising social security contributions (Yamamura, 2025). Likewise, evidence from Austria, France, and Spain demonstrates that welfare-state transfers, especially healthcare and pensions, redistribute income heavily toward older cohorts, raising concerns about intergenerational fairness and fiscal viability (Abio et al., 2021). Figure 4 shows how population aging affects government budgets and economic stability. Aging raises healthcare, pension, and long-term care costs, while shrinking the labor tax base and reducing revenues. These pressures constrain investment. The outer ring features policy feedback mechanisms, such as health, labor, and pension reforms, that can mitigate demographic impacts. The model stresses integrated fiscal planning for long-term stability and resilience.

Figure 4. Fiscal Channels of Population Aging

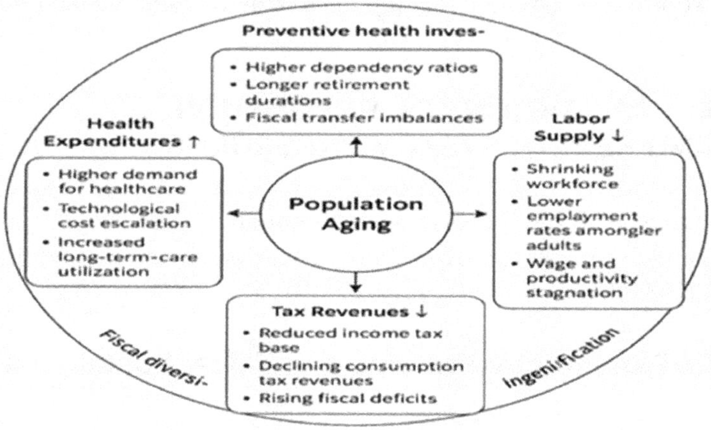

Source: Author's elaboration based on Global reports.

4.2 Health Expenditures and Long-Term Care Pressures

Health and long-term care costs are highly affected by demographic aging, as healthcare demand grows exponentially after age 65. In Switzerland, projections indicate health spending, especially on LTC, will outpace GDP, driven by demographic aging and non-demographic factors like medical tech and income growth (Lussi et al., 2024). Similarly, Finland's fiscal projections indicate that long-term care costs grow faster than healthcare costs, suggesting that the proximity-to-death effect, rather than chronological aging alone, drives expenditure escalation (Kosunen et al., 2025). Considering these factors in fiscal models yields slower expected growth in healthcare spending, offering policymakers a more accurate sustainability outlook (Lassila & Valkonen, 2019). China's experience shows that aging poses fiscal challenges. LTCI cut elderly out-of-pocket health costs by 5%, but inflation and rising systemic costs threaten long-term fiscal sustainability (Z. Liu et al., 2025). In developing economies lacking formal LTC systems, the fiscal burden appears indirectly through informal care and lost labor productivity. This hidden cost underscores the need for a multi-sectoral financing approach that combines social insurance, public health investments, and family support policies.

4.3 Pension Systems and Fiscal Balances

Public pension systems are the largest source of age-related fiscal pressure. As dependency ratios increase, PAYG systems in Europe and Asia face sustainability issues. Sweden's 1994 reform shifted to a notional defined contribution (NDC) system, tying benefits to lifetime contributions and stabilizing fiscal outcomes (Boado-Penas et al., 2020). In Italy, Generational Accounting analyses demonstrate that immigration and higher labor market participation among women can significantly improve fiscal sustainability by expanding the contributor base (Ambrosini, 2018; Bettin & Sacchi, 2020). Likewise, in India, simulations of universal pension schemes suggest that while short-term expenditure requirements rise sharply, long-term fiscal sustainability can be achieved under realistic assumptions of productivity growth and inflation control (Ranganathan, 2017). However, pension adequacy and intergenerational equity remain delicate trade-offs. Raising retirement ages and promoting voluntary savings may ease fiscal pressure, but risk worsening inequality if not paired with inclusive labor and health policies.

Table 3 compares pension reform strategies and their corresponding fiscal and equity outcomes across representative economies. Structural reforms that link benefits directly to lifetime contributions, such as Sweden's NDC system, have demonstrated long-term fiscal stability and intergenerational equity. In contrast, parametric or partial reforms in countries like Italy and Brazil yield only moderate sustainability gains, especially where informal labor or political resistance limits coverage. Hybrid systems in emerging economies, such as India, face the dual challenge of expanding social protection while maintaining fiscal prudence. Collectively, the evidence suggests that comprehensive, transparent, and equitable pension reforms are crucial to maintaining fiscal balance in aging societies.

Table 3. Pension Reform Models and Fiscal Outcomes

Country	Pension System Type	Reform Strategy	Fiscal Outcome	Equity Impact
Sweden	Notional Defined Contribution (NDC)	Shifted benefits to lifetime contributions; automatic stabilizers	Stabilized long-term fiscal balance; reduced intergenerational risk	High equitable contribution-benefit linkage
Italy	Pay-As-You-Go (PAYG)	Gradual parameter reform; partial NDC introduction	Moderate fiscal improvement; still exposed to demographic shifts	Medium partial fairness achieved
Germany	Earnings-Related PAYG	Adjusted retirement age and contribution rates	Maintained solvency; improved fiscal stability	High gender-inclusive reform outcomes
Brazil	Defined Benefit (DB)	Constitutional pension overhaul (2019)	Reduced public pension deficit by 1.5% of GDP over 10 years	Moderate limited informal sector inclusion
India	Hybrid (PAYG + Universal Pension)	Introduced targeted social pensions and parametric changes	Short-term cost increase; long-term fiscal balance under growth assumptions	Low informal sector undercoverage remains
Japan	Multi-Tier System	Gradual rise in retirement age; more vigorous contribution enforcement	Improved solvency ratio; delayed fiscal burden peak	High equitable benefit formula and gender balance

Source: Compiled by the author from the Global reports.

4.4 Macroeconomic Feedbacks and the Longevity Economy

Population aging affects macroeconomic variables, impacting fiscal sustainability. Declining labor supply and rising healthcare costs reduce GDP growth and tax revenues, increasing debt. But the longevity economy services and innovations for older consumers can partly offset these effects by creating new fiscal revenue (Stepanova, 2019). Evidence from OECD analyses suggests that countries adopting inclusive fiscal and labor strategies, such as expanding workforce participation among older adults, improving healthcare efficiency, and integrating migrant labor, achieve stronger long-term growth and fiscal outcomes (Rouzet et al., 2019). Meanwhile, stress testing of fiscal systems in emerging markets, such as Ukraine, reveals that demographic aging fundamentally alters public spending structures, requiring an expansion of fiscal space through improved tax collection, reallocation, and health financing reforms (Temsumrit, 2023).

4.5 Building Sustainable Fiscal Resilience

To ensure the sustainability of health and social spending amid demographic aging, it is essential to balance efficiency-enhancing reforms with measures that preserve equity and social justice. Diversifying financing mechanisms by combining consumption taxes, payroll contributions, and general revenues can more evenly spread the fiscal burden, as demonstrated by Japan's OLG model (Uchida & Ono, 2024). Enhancing preventive health and LTC efficiency, and prevention-oriented healthcare spending can moderate cost growth, improving both health outcomes and fiscal stability (Grimm et al., 2025). Adopt intergenerationally neutral policies and reforms that must ensure fairness between working-age taxpayers and retirees, avoiding excessive redistribution toward older cohorts (Bravo et al., 2023; Chybalski, 2018). Leveraging longevity economy opportunities to stimulate innovation in healthcare technology and the silver industries can expand fiscal space while promoting healthy aging (Sisubalan et al., 2025). Population aging strains health, pension, and care costs, but strategic reforms on prevention, efficiency, and fairness can sustain fiscal health amid demographic shifts. The next section reviews measures that promote productive aging and fiscal stability resilience.

5. EVALUATING HEALTH AND LABOR INTERVENTIONS

This section focuses on the meso-level institutional and organizational responses, including workplace health programs and occupational interventions designed to sustain labor force participation among aging workers.

5.1 Rationale for Integrated Health–Labor Interventions

As aging populations intensify fiscal and labor market pressures, evidence suggests that integrated workplace health and labor interventions, combining preventive healthcare, occupational health, and productivity-enhancing measures, yield significant economic and social benefits. Investments in health promotion, ergonomics, chronic disease management, and mental health contribute not only to improved well-being but also to extended workability and reduced public expenditure on sickness absence and disability. Economic evaluations have increasingly recognized occupational health as both a public good and a productivity driver, offering dual benefits: reducing healthcare costs and preserving labor supply. The evolving consensus among labor economists and public health researchers highlights that interventions targeting aging and workforce health must balance effectiveness, efficiency, and equity, ensuring cost-effectiveness while addressing diverse worker needs (Dongen & Beek, 2022).

5.2 Preventive Health Programs and Economic Returns

Preventive health measures such as screenings, vaccinations, and lifestyle programs are often cost-effective and can save money. A review of OECD countries showed that over half of aging population programs, especially for diabetes, obesity, and heart health, are either cost-saving or cost-effective (Demirtas & Flahault, 2025). Figure 5 shows ROI for preventive health interventions. Vaccination and chronic disease programs provide a €3–€5 benefit for every € 1 invested. Workplace ergonomic and mental health programs also offer strong fiscal benefits by reducing absenteeism and healthcare costs and boosting productivity. These findings support shifting public health spending from reactive care to prevention, especially in aging economies where costs and productivity losses grow with age. Preventive investments are vital for public health, economic stability, and resilience.

Figure 5. Economic Returns of Preventive Health Investments

Source: Data adapted from OECD, WHO, and McDaid.

A cost-benefit analysis of preventive healthcare found that it yields high long-term fiscal returns by reducing hospital admissions, chronic diseases, and productivity losses. Every euro spent produces multiple euros in societal benefits via lower healthcare costs and improved labor productivity (Mehboob, 2025). These findings reinforce the economic rationale for governments to reorient public health spending from reactive treatment to proactive prevention, particularly in aging economies, where the cost of inaction escalates exponentially over time.

5.3 Workplace Health Promotion and Occupational Interventions

5.3.1 Ergonomic and Physical Health Interventions

Work-related musculoskeletal disorders (WMSDs) cause absenteeism and early retirement among older workers. Systematic reviews show that organizational ergonomic interventions, such as better workstation design, participatory ergonomics, and adaptive scheduling, are cost-effective investments in health. Of nine studies, seven showed positive economic outcomes, especially where managerial support and worker involvement were high (Costa-Black & Arteberry, 2020). The INTEVAL_Spain project, a cluster-randomized trial with nursing staff, showed that interventions combining ergonomics, case management, and health promotion cut musculoskeletal pain and sick leave, improving work function. A cost-utility analysis confirmed strong cost-effectiveness for health systems and employers (Serra et al., 2019).

5.3.2 Occupational Disease Prevention and Screening

Early detection programs in the workplace, particularly for osteoporosis and other age-related conditions, have proven cost-effective. A screening program for healthcare workers identified high-risk individuals at minimal annual cost (€8,242), achieving a benefit-to-cost ratio of 2.07, thus preventing future productivity losses and healthcare expenses (Rinaldi et al., 2021). Similarly, engineering control programs for silicosis prevention in industrial settings have yielded exceptional cost-effectiveness, saving a healthy life year at a cost of roughly $105–$109 across diverse economies (Rahimi et al., 2021).

5.4 Mental Health and Psychosocial Interventions

Mental health interventions are crucial for sustainable labor, especially in aging and high-stress workforces. A trial of a problem-solving intervention (PSI) for employees with mental disorders showed PSI cut long-term sickness absence costs and provided societal benefits, even if not immediately profitable for employers (Poll et al., 2020). Organizational mental health programs offer high ROI, with meta-analyses showing values from −20% to 3560%. Leadership-focused, shorter interventions deliver the greatest financial benefits (Azadehyaei et al., 2025). Workplace suicide prevention programs effectively reduce suicide risk and absenteeism by combining education, leadership training, and stigma reduction, especially in high-risk industries like construction and emergency services (Hallett et al., 2024).

5.5 Institutional and Organizational Determinants of Success

Workplace health program success relies on culture, leadership, and the integration of policy. Studies show WHP interventions succeed more with active management involvement, tailored programs, and strong monitoring (Eriksson & Dellve, 2020). Implementation fidelity and worker engagement remain high over time. Moreover, economic incentive schemes such as insurance premium reductions or government subsidies for occupational health compliance have been shown to yield favorable return ratios between 1.01 and 4.81 per euro invested, confirming the feasibility and effectiveness of fiscal stimulus for workplace safety and health investment (Guerbaai et al., 2023).

5.6 Investing in Productive Aging

Evidence from cost-effectiveness and ROI studies shows investing in occupational and preventive health is an economic growth strategy, not just welfare. Policy recommendations include institutionalizing workplace health programs, mandating economic evaluations of public health and labor interventions, integrating health promotion into corporate social responsibility, incentivizing private-sector co-investment through tax benefits or lower insurance premiums, and establishing interministerial coordination among the labor, health, and finance ministries to sustain workforce health. Preventive and workplace interventions yield high returns, boost productivity, and extend working life. As the global workforce ages, health investment will be key to fiscal and economic stability and resilience.

Table 4 summarizes key workplace health interventions demonstrating measurable economic and productivity gains. Ergonomic redesign, chronic disease management, and mental health programs consistently yield positive returns on investment, particularly in physically and psychologically demanding sectors. Screening initiatives and comprehensive wellness programs further enhance long-term fiscal sustainability by reducing absenteeism, health costs, and turnover. The evidence underscores that workplace health promotion is both a social and economic imperative, forming a central component of sustainable aging workforce strategies.

Table 4. Summary of Effective Workplace Health Interventions

Intervention Type	ROI/Cost-Effectiveness Ratio	Target Group	Primary Outcomes
Ergonomic redesign and participatory ergonomics	ROI: 1.5–3.0	Manual and healthcare workers	Reduced musculoskeletal pain and absenteeism
Chronic disease management and workplace health promotion	ROI: 2.0–2.5	Older employees, shift workers	Extended work ability, improved productivity
Mental health interventions (e.g., problem-solving, leadership support)	ROI: 2.8–3.6	Service sector and high-stress occupations	Reduced long-term sickness absence; higher satisfaction
Occupational screening (osteoporosis, silicosis prevention)	Benefit–cost ratio: 2.0	Industrial and healthcare workers	Early disease detection, lower absenteeism
Comprehensive workplace wellness programs (WHP)	ROI: 3.0–4.8	Multisector organizations	Lower insurance premiums, improved morale
Workplace suicide prevention & psychosocial safety	ROI: up to 3.5	Construction, emergency services	Reduced absenteeism, lower suicide risk

Source: Compiled from Silvaggi et al. (2020), Costa-Black & Arterberry (2020), and Eriksson & Dellve (2020).

6. COMPARATIVE POLICY ANALYSIS: LESSONS FROM OECD AND EMERGING ECONOMIES

6.1 Divergent Pathways to Managing Aging Workforces

Globally, countries are converging on a demographic reality, an expanding elderly population with profound implications for labor markets, healthcare systems, and fiscal sustainability. However, their policy trajectories differ significantly based on economic maturity, institutional capacity, and the design of their welfare state. OECD nations have primarily pursued comprehensive, multi-sectoral aging strategies that integrate labor market reform, healthcare efficiency, and pension restructuring. In contrast, emerging economies are still in the early stages of developing integrated aging policies. Comparative evidence shows that success depends on how well health and labor reforms are synchronized within fiscal frameworks (Damasceno et al., 2021).

6.2 OECD Experiences: Coordinated Policy Innovation

6.2.1 Japan: Extending Healthy Working Life

Japan continues to lead in aging workforce innovation by combining labor flexibility, technology, and health initiatives, which improve fiscal and employment sustainability. Raising retirement age, retraining older workers, and linking pensions to health and productivity have increased participation among 60–74-year-olds. Social security reforms connecting pensions to health metrics are expected to raise older men's employment by 10 percentage points (Inukai, 2025). In addition, Japan's local government initiatives in health promotion, such as the Health Japan 21 framework, highlight how preventive health measures reduce long-term care costs and support continued labor participation (Tsuji, 2020).

6.2.2 The Nordic Model: Integrating Health, Labor, and Equity

The Nordic countries (Sweden, Denmark, Finland) provide a social-democratic model emphasizing universalism, equity, and active labor-market participation. Their success lies in three policy principles: Flexible retirement systems tied to life expectancy. Preventive and occupational health care integration into labor policy. Inclusive labor market programs for older and marginalized workers. These approaches maintain high participation rates among workers aged 60 and above while keeping old-age poverty rates low. Empirical studies demonstrate that coordinated social policies in these countries mitigate fiscal strain and preserve workforce capacity (Greve, 2018).

6.2.3 Australia: Reforming Aged Care and Workforce Systems

Australia exemplifies a mixed welfare model that balances public health, private insurance, and labor market flexibility. The aged care sector, currently undergoing reform, emphasizes home-based care, safety regulation, and workforce training. However, challenges persist, particularly workforce shortages and uneven quality standards. Policy analysts argue that sustainable reforms will require targeted funding mechanisms and the adoption of technology to enhance care efficiency and worker productivity (Alsaeed et al., 2025). Australia's JobKeeper and lifelong learning programs offer valuable templates for developing economies aiming to strike a balance between health investment and employment sustainability.

6.2.4 Slovenia and OECD Central Europe: Fiscal Adjustment through Longer Working Lives

In Central European OECD members, such as Slovenia, the policy focus is on extending working lives and improving healthcare efficiency to offset the pressures of an aging population. The OECD recommends aligning incentives through age-friendly labor institutions and efficient long-term care (LTC) management. Slovenia's reforms emphasize retraining older workers and leveraging technology to enhance productivity (Rozman & Cančer, 2021).

6.3 Emerging Economies: Adaptive, Resource-Constrained Strategies

6.3.1 China: Gradual Pension Reform and Health System Expansion

China faces dual challenges: rapid aging and incomplete welfare coverage. Pension reforms that combine parametric adjustments (such as increases in the retirement age and extensions of the contribution period) with the expansion of voluntary and rural pension schemes are crucial to both fiscal and social sustainability. Scholars emphasize integrating age management and poverty reduction in aging policy design (Nikolov & Adelman, 2018). Furthermore, the government's Healthy China 2030 initiative embeds preventive health into aging policy, highlighting a shift toward productive aging and fiscal prudence.

6.3.2 India and Malaysia: Inclusive Aging Policies amid Informal Labor Markets

India and Malaysia's experiences underscore the need for labor formalization and the design of inclusive pensions. In Malaysia, policy efforts aim to sustain labor participation by combining lifelong learning, flexible retirement, and workforce inclusivity. Policies that balance the retention of older workers with youth employment opportunities are vital for demographic stability (Azhar & Omar, 2025). India's gradual move toward a universal social pension and its focus on strengthening the health system reflect lessons learned from OECD welfare transitions. However, challenges in funding, coverage, and labor informality remain substantial.

6.3.3 Latin America: Leveraging Technology and Training

Latin American countries like Chile, Mexico, and Brazil are investing in lifelong learning and digital skills to address productivity decline driven by population aging. Policies focus on technology adoption, fiscal reforms, and mobilizing underused labor, especially older and low-skilled workers (Chavez & Vizuete-Sandoval, 2025; Duque & Otaegui, 2023). These strategies show how digital inclusion can maintain labor-market efficiency in aging economies. Table 5 highlights six key dimensions for successful aging policies: labor flexibility, preventive health, fiscal adaptability, gender equity, tech innovation, and migration. OECD countries like Japan, Sweden, and Finland succeed through long-term policy integration and fiscal governance, while emerging economies like Malaysia, China, and Brazil use adaptive, tech-driven approaches. Success mainly depends on coherence in aligning health, labor, and fiscal policies. These findings stress the need to adapt global best practices to local capacities and demographic trajectories.

Table 5. Core Attributes of Successful Aging Policies

Dimension	Policy Mechanism	OECD Example	Emerging Economy Example
Labor Flexibility & Incentives	Phased retirement, flexible work hours, and retraining subsidies	Japan, Sweden	Malaysia
Preventive Health Integration	Embedding health promotion into employment and welfare policy	Finland, Denmark	China
Fiscal Adaptability	Diversified pension funding and targeted LTC expenditure	Sweden	Brazil
Gender Equity & Inclusion	Pension credit for unpaid care work and caregiver benefits	Germany, Norway	India
Technology-Enabled Labor & Care	Use of digital tools, telemedicine, and online reskilling	Australia, Finland	Chile, Mexico
Migration & Workforce Renewal	Balanced migration policies to offset demographic pressure	Germany, Nordic states	Malaysia

Source: Compiled from Profeta (2023) and Caoyan et al. (2024).

Policy transferability, however, depends on institutional maturity and fiscal capacity. While OECD models offer strong frameworks, emerging economies must adapt reforms to their informal labor markets, fiscal limitations, and demographic timelines.

6.4 Policy Implications: Toward a Global Framework for Healthy Aging

Comparative evidence indicates that sustainable aging policies rest on five interconnected pillars. Health–Labor Integration involves embedding preventive healthcare in labor laws and employer mandates. Flexible Lifecourse Employment promotes phased retirement, part-time work, and lifelong learning to boost employability. Fiscal and Pension Reform Alignment ensures sustainability through transparent contribution–benefit connections. Technology-Enabled Work and Care utilizes digital health tools, telemedicine, and telework to include older workers. Finally, Equity and inclusion require gender-sensitive, accessible systems to reduce disparities. Countries like Japan, Nordic nations, and some middle-income economies show that population aging can drive growth, not just fiscal challenge (Nagarajan & Sixsmith, 2021). Integrating health system efficiency, labor market flexibility, and fiscal discipline is key to resilient aging policy. High-income nations refine their institutions, while emerging economies focus on inclusive reforms grounded in equity, digital innovation, and lifelong health. A coordinated global approach can turn demographic transition into a driver of inclusive, sustainable economic growth and development.

7. INTEGRATED POLICY FRAMEWORK FOR SUSTAINABLE AGING WORKFORCES

7.1 Conceptual Foundations of an Integrated Framework

Achieving health system sustainability and labor market vitality in aging societies requires a coordinated policy approach uniting health, labor, fiscal, and social care systems within an adaptive framework. Based on the WHO's model of Integrated, People-Centred Health Services, this emphasizes five strategies: empowering communities, strengthening governance, reorienting care toward prevention, cross-sector coordination, and creating supportive institutions (Huffstetler et al., 2023). These principles support the Integrated Health–Labor–Fiscal Framework (IHLF), aiming to align workforce participation, health investment, and fiscal sustainability. Evidence from the EU, Canada, and Singapore shows integrated systems improve health outcomes, extend healthy work life, and increase public expenditure efficiency through coordinated governance and shared accountability (Cristea et al., 2020). By aligning health and labor policies with fiscal planning, the IHLF provides a strategic foundation for turning demographic aging into inclusive growth. This integration helps nations sustain productivity, safeguard fiscal balance, and make longevity an asset for social well-being and economic resilience.

7.2 Pillars of the Integrated Policy Framework

7.2.1 Health System Integration

Integrated health systems focus on functional ability and intrinsic capacity rather than disease management. The WHO and the World Bank emphasize that reorienting clinical care toward functionality improves outcomes and efficiency (Zhou et al., 2023). Recent evidence from Singapore's Integrated Senior Health and Wellness (ISHW) Hub demonstrates that integrating preventive screening, nutrition, and social engagement within a community-driven model enhances physical capacity, reduces hospitalizations, and fosters intergenerational participation (Huang et al., 2025). Similarly, China's experience with coupling disease prevention, medical services, and financing between 2012 and 2021 reveals progress toward universal health coverage (UHC). However, it highlights the importance of regional coordination and efficient use of health resources (Tao et al., 2020).

7.2.2 Labor Market and Workforce Integration

Policies must promote lifelong labor participation, flexible retirement options, and continuous skill development. Studies from Australia indicate that successful workforce aging strategies require integration of health promotion with active labor policies, including retraining and workplace adaptation (Lu et al., 2025; Noone et al., 2018). Integrated systems that align occupational health, lifelong learning, and job redesign can reduce involuntary retirement and enhance the productivity of older workers, thereby directly supporting labor market resilience.

7.2.3 Fiscal and Financial Coordination

Fiscal sustainability must be embedded within health and labor policy design. The Learning Health System (LHS) framework adopted in Ontario, Canada, illustrates how data-driven feedback loops can align resource allocation, financial incentives, and health outcomes (Jarmain et al., 2025). Moreover, evidence from EU integrated care programs shows that scaling up telehealth and preventive models requires adaptive business models and stable reimbursement mechanisms (Gullslett et al., 2024). To enhance transparency and fiscal efficiency, adopting data-driven financial frameworks that integrate health, labor, and social expenditure into long-term projections is crucial. A 2024 framework for transparent, evidence-based decision-making advocates the use of predictive analytics to optimize national development and healthcare investment (Lawal et al., 2024).

7.3 Integrating Social and Community Care

Health and social care integration is particularly vital for aging populations. In Asia, connecting community-based social services with medical and preventive care enables a continuum of care that meets physical, emotional, and financial needs. A scoping review on social–health integration in Asia emphasizes the necessity of aligning cultural norms, community participation, and human resource competency within long-term care (LTC) systems (Alavi et al., 2022). China's provincial-level implementation of integrated elderly care using the Rainbow Model of Integrated Care (RMIC) also reveals that multi-sector collaboration between health, civil affairs, and family doctor teams improves coordination and reduces fragmentation (Yuan et al., 2022).

7.4 Governance, Data, and Multi-Sector Coordination

Governance mechanisms underpinning an integrated framework must ensure cross-sectoral accountability, data interoperability, and fiscal transparency. Successful systems share the following characteristics: Centralized health and labor data systems for real-time decision-making (as in Canada's LHS model), Multi-ministerial governance bodies coordinating aging-related initiatives across health, finance, labor, and social protection ministries, and Public-private partnerships (PPPs) that mobilize innovation, technology, and investment to expand health system capacity (Clarke et al., 2019). The European Union's experience demonstrates that policy coherence between pension systems, healthcare reform, and labor incentives fosters fiscal resilience, while fiscal misalignment creates compounding inefficiencies (Ramos-Herrera & Sosvilla-Rivero, 2020).

7.5 Implementation Strategies for Sustainable Outcomes

The transition from fragmented to integrated systems necessitates institutional readiness, robust digital infrastructure, and effective stakeholder engagement. Case evidence identifies several enabling factors, such as Intersectoral collaboration and mission alignment, which enhance implementation success; Data and technology integration improve service delivery efficiency and monitoring; Community-based capacity building fosters ownership and sustainability; and Fiscal incentives for healthy aging enterprises (e.g., tax credits for age-friendly workplaces) can align private sector incentives with public objectives (Ginting et al., 2025). To ensure resilience, integrated frameworks should incorporate adaptive feedback mechanisms that enable evidence-based policy refinement and learning.

7.6 Theoretical Integration and Conceptual Model

The proposed Integrated Health–Labor–Fiscal Framework (IHLF) combines insights from Health Capital Theory (health as a productive asset), Learning Health System Theory (iterative improvement), Welfare Economics (intergenerational equity and efficiency), and Systems Theory of Policy Integration (interconnectedness across health, labor, and fiscal systems). It emphasizes optimizing health, labor participation, and fiscal adaptability for sustainable aging, supported by transparent governance and social inclusiveness. Figure 6 shows how the framework ties health system sustainability, labor participation, and fiscal governance, highlighting their mutual dependence. Improvements in health boost workability; greater labor participation increases fiscal revenues; sound fiscal governance sustains health systems. Governance reinforces institutional coordination, data-driven policymaking, and adaptive practices. The IHLF operationalizes these concepts, framing healthy aging as both a social goal and an economic necessity for 21st-century policy systems.

Figure 6. Integrated Health–Labor–Fiscal Framework (IHLF) Model

Source: Author's elaboration based on the Global Reports.

8. POLICY RECOMMENDATIONS AND CONCLUSION

The global challenge of aging populations requires more than fragmented policy responses; it demands a systemic, integrated policy paradigm that unites health, labor, fiscal, and social systems into a coherent framework. This section provides evidence-based, actionable recommendations derived from global best practices and empirical insights. It builds on the Integrated Health–Labor–Fiscal Framework (IHLF) to operationalize sustainable and equitable aging workforce systems.

8.1 Policy Recommendations

8.1.1 Strengthen Governance and Multi-Actor Collaboration

Effective governance is essential for coordinating policies that link health, labor, and social protection systems. A multi-actor, multi-level approach engaging public institutions, private enterprises, and community stakeholders enhances accountability, coherence, and innovation in aging workforce strategies. Evidence from the European Innovation Partnership on Active and Healthy Ageing (EIP on AHA) demonstrates that inclusive collaboration fosters system resilience and accelerates policy integration (Illario et al., 2019). Governments should establish National Councils on Sustainable Aging and Workforce Development and institutionalize participatory consultation frameworks involving employers, labor unions, caregivers, and advocacy groups to ensure cohesive, transparent, and adaptive policy implementation.

8.1.2 Embed Fiscal Sustainability through Adaptive Policy Instruments

Fiscal sustainability must remain the foundation of all health and labor market policies. Governments should adopt adaptive fiscal systems that link health investments to productivity outcomes, ensuring resilience through efficient taxation, strategic public investment, and sustainable long-term care financing. It is recommended that systems should enhance fiscal stability while supporting inclusive growth (Secretariat, 2023). Policy actions include establishing aging sustainability funds combining health insurance and labor revenues, developing dynamic fiscal models to project aging-related expenditures over 20–30 years, and incentivizing public–private partnerships for health infrastructure, telehealth, and eldercare innovation.

8.1.3 Foster Workforce Sustainability and Health System Resilience

The sustainability of aging societies hinges on developing a resilient and adaptable workforce across both the health sector and the broader economy. Evidence from the Partnership for Health System Sustainability and Resilience (PHSSR-PT) highlights the importance of participatory policymaking and cross-sectoral integration in establishing resilient systems (Oliveira et al., 2025). Policy priorities should focus on strengthening workforce training and digital competencies, adopting flexible retirement and re-engagement incentives for older workers, and integrating occupational health promotion into labor market strategies to enhance productivity, reduce absenteeism, and ensure the long-term vitality of both health and economic systems.

8.1.4 Integrate Long-Term Care (LTC) into Universal Health Coverage (UHC)

Ensuring the financial and organizational sustainability of long-term care (LTC) systems is essential for managing demographic aging and safeguarding fiscal stability. Evidence from EU and Asian experiences underscores the importance of balancing public and private financing, promoting innovation, and enhancing informal and community-based care networks (Dąbrowska et al., 2025; Pariso et al., 2025). Integrating LTC within Universal Health Coverage (UHC) frameworks can promote equitable access, while comprehensive LTC insurance models, such as China's pilot schemes, enhance financial protection. Additionally, adopting technology-enabled home and community care systems can reduce institutional costs and support independent, dignified aging.

8.1.5 Promote Healthy Aging and Social Equity

Healthy aging transcends biomedical dimensions and represents a crucial imperative for socioeconomic and environmental equity. Achieving the UN Sustainable Development Goals (SDGs) requires an integrated approach linking health, sustainability, and social justice (Mavrodaris et al., 2022). Policies should adopt life-course-based prevention strategies targeting chronic diseases, dementia, and functional decline, while fostering age-friendly environments that promote mobility, mental well-being, and community participation. Aligning environmental, urban, and aging policies can enhance both equity and resilience, ensuring that longevity translates into inclusive, sustainable well-being across all population groups and reinforcing the broader objective of economically and socially sustainable aging systems.

8.1.6 Strengthen Global and Regional Cooperation

Global and regional cooperation is essential for managing demographic transitions and promoting sustainable aging. International collaboration fosters innovation, knowledge exchange, and the mobilization of shared resources across diverse economic contexts. The WHO European Healthy Aging Framework underscores the importance of cross-border coordination to achieve equitable financing, integrated long-term care, and age-friendly environments. Policy priorities should include establishing global platforms for policy innovation, harmonizing cross-national health and labor data systems, and promoting North–South partnerships that adapt OECD best practices to the institutional and fiscal realities of emerging economies, thereby advancing inclusive and resilient aging systems.

8.2 Theoretical and Strategic Integration

These recommendations are grounded in key theoretical constructs: Health Capital Theory linking health investments to labor productivity and economic growth, Systems Theory viewing health, labor, and fiscal systems as interdependent subsystems, Welfare Economics and Intergenerational Equity ensuring fair resource distribution between age cohorts, and Resilience and Sustainability Theory emphasizing adaptive capacity and institutional robustness in policy systems (Ballout, 2025).

8.3 Conclusion

The intersection of health system sustainability and labor market participation in an aging workforce represents one of the most critical policy frontiers of the twenty-first century. As demonstrated throughout this chapter, population aging is not solely a fiscal challenge but a potential catalyst for economic renewal when addressed through integration, innovation, and inclusivity. The proposed Integrated Health–Labor–Fiscal Framework (IHLF) provides a strategic foundation for aligning health investment, workforce participation, and fiscal stability. By extending healthy working lives, enhancing preventive health systems, and optimizing resource allocation, societies can preserve productivity while maintaining fiscal and social balance.

Sustaining economic and health resilience in aging societies will require evidence-based governance, adaptive fiscal policies, and strong community engagement, all of which are supported by international cooperation. Above all, it demands a paradigm shift that recognizes health as an essential form of human and economic capital rather than a public expenditure liability. Building sustainable aging workforces, therefore, calls for coordinated, whole-of-government and whole-of-society approaches that are theory-informed, data-driven, and ethically grounded in equity, dignity, and intergenerational justice. Through such integration, longevity can be transformed from a source of fiscal pressure into a foundation for sustainable prosperity and social cohesion.

Conflict of Interest Declaration:

The authors declare that they have no conflicts of interest regarding the publication of this chapter.

AI Use Declaration:

The authors acknowledge that artificial intelligence tools were used solely to improve language clarity and readability. The authors reviewed and approved all content and are fully responsible for the final version of this chapter.

Funding:

This research received no external funding. All analyses and interpretations are the sole responsibility of the authors.

REFERENCES

Abdulwahab, L. O., & Azam, H. (2026). Platform Work in Europe's Green and Care Economies: Regulatory Pathways for Sustainability, Social Protection, and Fair Work. In *Regulating the Gig Economy in the European Union: Challenges, Innovations, and Global Impacts* (pp. 99–124). IGI Global Scientific Publishing. https://www.igi-global.com/chapter/platform-work-in-europes-green-and-care-economies/395612

Abdulwahab, L. O., Daniel, O., Gul, A., & Bubari, H. U. (2026). The Economic Impact of Digital Health Innovations on Disease Prevention: Cost-Effectiveness, ROI, and Policy Implications. In *Reshaping Health Promotion and Disease Prevention Through Digital Innovation* (pp. 29–56). IGI Global Scientific Publishing. DOI: 10.4018/979-8-3373-3531-5.ch002

Abio, G., Patxot, C., Souto, G., & Istenič, T. (2021). The role of gender, education and family in the welfare organization: Disaggregating National Transfer Accounts. *The Journal of the Economics of Ageing*, *20*, 100348. Advance online publication. DOI: 10.1016/j.jeoa.2021.100348

Abrha, T., & Weldeyohans, B. (2025). The Role of Human Capital in Economic Development: A Theoretical Analysis. *Journal of Human Resource Management*. DOI: 10.11648/j.jhrm.20251302.11

Ademi, Z., Ackerman, I., Zomer, E., & Liew, D. (2021). Productivity-Adjusted Life-Years: A New Metric for Quantifying Disease Burden. *PharmacoEconomics*, *39*(3), 271–273. DOI: 10.1007/s40273-020-00999-z PMID: 33428173

Alavi, K., Sutan, R., Shahar, S., Manaf, M. R. A., Jaafar, M. H., Maulud, K. A. A., Embong, Z., Keliwon, K., & Markom, R. (2022). Connecting the Dots between Social Care and Healthcare for the Sustainability Development of Older Adult in Asia: A Scoping Review. *Sustainability (Basel)*, *14*(5), 2573. Advance online publication. DOI: 10.3390/su14052573

Alsaeed, T., Washington, T., & Xia, B. (2025). Comprehensive analysis of Australia's aged care system to inform policies for a sustainable future. *Frontiers in Public Health*, *13*, 1525988. Advance online publication. DOI: 10.3389/fpubh.2025.1525988 PMID: 40290496

Ambrosini, M. (2018). Rowing upstream: The resilience of immigrants in the long Italian recession. *Sociologia del Lavoro*, (149), 201–214. DOI: 10.3280/SL2018-149S14

Azadehyaei, H., Zhang, Y., Song, Y., Gottschalk, T., & Anderson, G. S. (2025). Economic Evaluation of Proactive PTSI Mitigation Programs for Public Safety Personnel and Frontline Healthcare Professionals: A Systematic Review and Meta-Analysis. *International Journal of Environmental Research and Public Health, 22*(5), 809. Advance online publication. DOI: 10.3390/ijerph22050809 PMID: 40427922

Azhar, N., & Omar, A. (2025). AGING WORKFORCE IN MALAYSIA: NAVIGATING CHALLENGES AND SHAPING POLICIES. *Quantum Journal of Social Sciences and Humanities*. DOI: 10.55197/qjssh.v6i2.615

Ballout, S. (2025). Trauma, Mental Health Workforce Shortages, and Health Equity: A Crisis in Public Health. *International Journal of Environmental Research and Public Health, 22*(4), 620. Advance online publication. DOI: 10.3390/ijerph22040620 PMID: 40283844

Becker, G. S. (1975). Introduction to the Second Edition, Human Capital: A Theoretical and Empirical Analysis, with Special Reference to Education. In *Human Capital: A Theoretical and Empirical Analysis, with Special Reference to Education, Second Edition* (pp. 1–8). NBER. https://www.nber.org/books-and-chapters/human-capital-theoretical-and-empirical-analysis-special-reference-education-second-edition/introduction-second-edition-human-capital-theoretical-and-empirical-analysis-special-reference

Bettin, G., & Sacchi, A. (2020). Health spending in Italy: The impact of immigrants. *European Journal of Political Economy, 65*, 101932. Advance online publication. DOI: 10.1016/j.ejpoleco.2020.101932

Bloom, D. E., Cafiero, E., Jané-Llopis, E., Abrahams-Gessel, S., Bloom, L. R., Fathima, S., Feigl, A. B., Gaziano, T., Hamandi, A., & Mowafi, M. (2012). *The global economic burden of noncommunicable diseases*. Program on the Global Demography of Aging. https://ideas.repec.org/p/gdm/wpaper/8712.html?utm_medium=email&utm_source=transaction

Bloom, D. E., & Canning, D. (2000). The Health and Wealth of Nations. *Science, 287*(5456), 1207–1209. DOI: 10.1126/science.287.5456.1207 PMID: 10712155

Boado-Penas, M. del C., Naka, P., & Settergren, O. (2020). Last lessons learned from the Swedish public pension system. In M. Peris-Ortiz, J. álvarez-García, I. Domínguez-Fabián, & P. Devolder (Eds.), *Economic Challenges of Pension Systems: A Sustainability and International Management Perspective* (pp. 235–254). Springer International Publishing. DOI: 10.1007/978-3-030-37912-4_11

Boodoo, C., & Hosein, P. (2024). Global Decline in Fertility Rates: Trends, Influencing Factors, and Future Projections. *IEEE Int. Conf. Technol. Manag., Oper. Decis., ICTMOD*. 2024 IEEE International Conference on Technology Management, Operations and Decisions, ICTMOD 2024. DOI: 10.1109/ICTMOD63116.2024.10878235

Bravo, J. M., Ayuso, M., Holzmann, R., & Palmer, E. (2023). Intergenerational actuarial fairness when longevity increases: Amending the retirement age. *Insurance, Mathematics & Economics, 113*, 161–184. DOI: 10.1016/j.insmatheco.2023.08.007

Buti, M., Cabezas, J., Domínguez-Hernández, R., Cantero, H., & Casado, M. Á. (2025). Socioeconomic impact of chronic delta hepatitis in Spain: Indirect costs of work absenteeism, presenteeism, and premature mortality. *PLoS One*, *20*(6), e0324834. Advance online publication. DOI: 10.1371/journal.pone.0324834 PMID: 40540477

Caoyan, Q. I., Ziyi, C. H. E. N., Qiankui, Z. H. A. O., Yuan, S. U. N., Qiang, H. O. U., Guodong, L. U., & Wuzhong, L. I. U. (2024). Research on aging population of working age in North America: Current situation and policies. *Huanjing Yu Zhiye Yixue*, *41*(9), 971–976. DOI: 10.11836/JEOM24171

Chavez, H., & Vizuete-Sandoval, D. (2025). Widening the divide, reloading dependency: The political economy of data and AI capability building in Latin America. *Globalizations*, 1–23. Advance online publication. DOI: 10.1080/14747731.2024.2441625

Chiang, H.-Y., Cheng, Y., Hasselhorn, H. M., Hsu, C.-C., Yang, Y.-C., & Cheng, W.-J. (2025). Influence of pension availability on the association between work conditions and labor market exit for health reasons: Evidence from a Taiwanese older adults cohort. *BMC Public Health*, *25*(1), 1022. Advance online publication. DOI: 10.1186/s12889-025-22215-3 PMID: 40097978

Chłoń-Domińczak, A. (2021). Population ageing and financing consumption of the older generation in the european union. In Fischer, G., & Strauss, R. (Eds.), *Europe's Income, Wealth, Consumption, and Inequality* (pp. 395–427). Oxford University Press., DOI: 10.1093/oso/9780197545706.003.0011

Chodavadia, P., Teo, I., Poremski, D., Fung, D. S. S., & Finkelstein, E. A. (2023). Prevalence and economic burden of depression and anxiety symptoms among Singaporean adults: Results from a 2022 web panel. *BMC Psychiatry*, *23*(1), 104. DOI: 10.1186/s12888-023-04581-7 PMID: 36782116

Chybalski, F. (2018). Intergenerational fairness from an economic perspective: Overview of some theoretical and methodological issues. *Business and Economic Horizons*, *14*(2), 268–281. DOI: 10.15208/beh.2018.21

Clarke, D., Doerr, S., Hunter, M., Schmets, G., Soucat, A., & Paviza, A. (2019). The private sector and universal health coverage. *Bulletin of the World Health Organization*, *97*(6), 434–435. DOI: 10.2471/BLT.18.225540 PMID: 31210681

Cordeiro, R., Fischer, F., & Shinjo, S. (2022). Systemic autoimmune diseases and work outcomes in Brazil: A scoping review. *Revista de Saude Publica*, *56*, 24. Advance online publication. DOI: 10.11606/s1518-8787.2022056003918 PMID: 35476102

Costa-Black, K. M., & Arteberry, C. (2020). The social value of Participatory Ergonomics from a practitioner's perspective. *Proceedings of the Human Factors and Ergonomics Society Annual Meeting*, *64*(1), 919–923. DOI: 10.1177/1071181320641219

Crawshaw, P., Gray, J., Haighton, C., & Lloyd, S. (2024). Health inequalities and health-related economic inactivity: Why good work needs good health. *Public Health in Practice (Oxford, England)*, *8*, 100555. Advance online publication. DOI: 10.1016/j.puhip.2024.100555 PMID: 39559489

Cristea, M., Noja, G., tefea, P., & Sala, A. L. (2020). The Impact of Population Aging and Public Health Support on EU Labor Markets. *International Journal of Environmental Research and Public Health*, *17*(4), 1439. Advance online publication. DOI: 10.3390/ijerph17041439 PMID: 32102277

Crossdale, R., & Penning, N. (2024). THE ROLE OF HEALTH IN RETIREMENT PLANNING TOWARDS EXTENDED WORKING LIVES. *Innovation in Aging*, *8*(Supplement_1), 1219–1219. DOI: 10.1093/geroni/igae098.3903

Dąbrowska, A., Fandrejewska, A., Stańczyk, E., & Szalonka, K. (2025). *Consumer and Innovations in e-Health Services: Examples of European Countries*. Taylor and Francis., DOI: 10.4324/9781003507307

Damasceno, J. O., Batista, C. P., & Oliveira, A. M. C. (2021). Labor reform and its implications for workers' health. *Revista de Direito Sanitario*, *21*. Advance online publication. DOI: 10.11606/issn.2316-9044.rdisan.2021.156343

de Castro, G. M. C., & Toneto, R. (2019). Infraestrutura publica e crescimento dos municipios brasileiros: Analise espacial entre 1970 e 2010. *Economia Aplicada*, *23*(2), 5–32. DOI: 10.11606/1980-5330/ea115755

Demirtas, E. D., & Flahault, A. (2025). A Scoping Review on the Economic Impacts of Healthy Ageing Promotion and Disease Prevention in OECD Member Countries. *International Journal of Environmental Research and Public Health*, *22*(8), 1161. Advance online publication. DOI: 10.3390/ijerph22081161 PMID: 40869748

Doling, J., Finer, C. J., & Maltby, T. (2018). *Ageing Matters: European Policy Lessons from the East*. Taylor and Francis., DOI: 10.4324/9781351163248

Duque, M., & Otaegui, A. (2023). Digital Dependency as a Burden: Impact of Active Aging for Technology Adoption in Brazil and Chile. *Anthropology and Aging*, *44*(2), 28–44. DOI: 10.5195/aa.2023.422

Eriksson, A., & Dellve, L. (2020). Learning Processes as Key for Success in Workplace Health Promotion Interventions in Health Care. *Frontiers in Public Health*, *8*, 576693. Advance online publication. DOI: 10.3389/fpubh.2020.576693 PMID: 33304874

Ginting, M. L., Sum, G., Wang, S. Z., Ding, Y. Y., & Tay, L. (2025). Integrated frailty and intrinsic capacity care model for community-dwelling older adults in Singapore: A rapid qualitative study of anticipated implementation barriers and enablers using the Consolidated Framework for Implementation Research and its Outcomes Addendum. *Frontiers in Health Services*, *5*, 1563686. Advance online publication. DOI: 10.3389/frhs.2025.1563686 PMID: 40343232

Grenčíková, A., Španková, J., Rigó, R., & Gullerová, M. (2023). Population aging in terms of generational cohorts in the context of labor productivity in the Slovak Republic. *Problems and Perspectives in Management*, *21*(4), 577–590. Advance online publication. DOI: 10.21511/ppm.21(4).2023.43

Greve, B. (2018). At the heart of the Nordic occupational welfare model: Occupational welfare trajectories in Sweden and Denmark. *Social Policy and Administration*, *52*(2), 508–518. DOI: 10.1111/spol.12380

Grimm, S. E., van Mastrigt, G., & Hiligsmann, M. (2025). Advancing the economics of prevention: Emerging methods and approaches. *Expert Review of Pharmacoeconomics & Outcomes Research*, *25*(9), 1255–1262. DOI: 10.1080/14737167.2025.2570689 PMID: 41048050

Grossman, M. (1972). *The Demand for Health: A Theoretical and Empirical Investigation*. NBER. https://www.nber.org/books-and-chapters/demand-health-theoretical-and-empirical-investigation

Guerbaai, R. A., DeGeest, S., Popejoy, L. L., Simon, M., Wellens, N. I. H., Denhaerynck, K., & Zúñiga, F. (2023). Evaluating the implementation fidelity to a successful nurse-led model (INTERCARE) which reduced nursing home unplanned hospitalisations. *BMC Health Services Research*, *23*(1), 138. Advance online publication. DOI: 10.1186/s12913-023-09146-8 PMID: 36759902

Gullslett, M. K., Ronchi, E., Lundberg, L., Larbi, D., Lind, K. F., Tayefi, M., Ngo, P. D., Sy, T. R., Adib, K., & Hamilton, C. (2024). Telehealth development in the WHO European region: Results from a quantitative survey and insights from Norway. *International Journal of Medical Informatics*, *191*, 105558. Advance online publication. DOI: 10.1016/j.ijmedinf.2024.105558 PMID: 39084085

Gunarsa, S. (2020). *Fiscal Policy, Public Debt and Economic Performance in Developing Countries: An Empirical Analysis*. DOI: 10.25904/1912/1900

Hallett, N., Rees, H., Hannah, F., Hollowood, L., & Bradbury-Jones, C. (2024). Workplace interventions to prevent suicide: A scoping review. *PLoS One*, *19*(5), e0301453. Advance online publication. DOI: 10.1371/journal.pone.0301453 PMID: 38696511

Huang, G., Wu, W., Wen, Q., Lu, L., & Pan, J. (2025). Building an integrated healthcare system of China: An assessment of coupling coordination between disease prevention, medical services, and healthcare financing from 2012 to 2021. *Health Economics Review*, *15*(1), 30. Advance online publication. DOI: 10.1186/s13561-025-00616-9 PMID: 40186730

Huffstetler, A. N., Phillips, R. L., Leyns, C. C., Willis, J. S., & Canchihuaman, F. A. (2023). People-centered health services. In Mezzich, J. E., Appleyard, W. J., Glare, P., Snaedal, J., & Wilson, C. R. (Eds.), *Person Centered Medicine* (pp. 135–150). Springer International Publishing., DOI: 10.1007/978-3-031-17650-0_8

Illario, M., Coscioni, E., Luca, V. D., Cataldi, M., Postiglione, A., & Iaccarino, G. (2019). Editorial: Multi-Actor Collaboration in Healthcare to Address the Emerging Health Needs of an Aging Population. *Translational Medicine @ UniSa, 19*, 1–4. DOI: 10.14273/unisa-2731

Inukai, S. (2025). The impacts of raising the public pension eligibility age on time allocation of elderly people: Evidence from Japan. *Journal of Economic Behavior & Organization*, *233*, 106984. Advance online publication. DOI: 10.1016/j.jebo.2025.106984

Jarmain, S., Elliot, J., Meyer, M., Williams, C., Alpaugh-Bishop, A., Smith, A., & Moore, L. (2025). Value-creating Learning Health Systems – an Organizing Framework for the Journey to Integrated Care. *International Journal of Integrated Care*, *25*, 643. Advance online publication. DOI: 10.5334/ijic.ICIC24603

Keramat, S. A., Comans, T., Pearce, A., Basri, R., Hashmi, R., & Dissanayaka, N. N. (2025). Psychological distress and productivity loss: A longitudinal analysis of Australian working adults. *The European Journal of Health Economics*, *26*(8), 1503–1524. DOI: 10.1007/s10198-025-01764-9 PMID: 40304834

Kosunen, M., Ruotsalainen, J., Kallio, A., Metsä, R., Raittinen, P., Lehmus, L., Korhonen, M. J., & Purmonen, T. (2025). Healthcare Resource Utilization and Associated Costs During the First 5 Years After Diagnosis and at the End of Life: A Nationwide Cohort Study of Patients with Multiple Myeloma in Finland. *PharmacoEconomics Open*, *9*(1), 57–68. DOI: 10.1007/s41669-024-00524-4 PMID: 39240292

Lanza Queiroz, B., & Lobo Alves Ferreira, M. (2021). The evolution of labor force participation and the expected length of retirement in Brazil. *The Journal of the Economics of Ageing*, *18*, 100304. Advance online publication. DOI: 10.1016/j.jeoa.2020.100304

Lassila, J., & Valkonen, T. (2019). *Alternative Demography-based Projection Approaches for Public Health and Long-term Care Expenditure*. https://consensus.app/papers/alternative-demographybased-projection-approaches-for-lassila-valkonen/aa05600c19785c3785b3c5882f842287/

Lawal, C. I., Friday, S. C., Ayodeji, D. C., & Sobowale, A. (2024). Strategic Framework for Transparent, Data-Driven Financial Decision-Making in Achieving Sustainable National Development Goals. *International Journal of Advanced Multidisciplinary Research and Studies*. DOI: 10.62225/2583049X.2024.4.6.4098

Lee, J.-W. (2025). Comment on "Japan's Aging Workforce: Determinants and Outlook.". *Asian Economic Policy Review*, *20*(2), 263–264. Advance online publication. DOI: 10.1111/aepr.12507

Lee, R. (2025). Population Aging and Public Policy. In An, C.-B. (Ed.), *Evidence-Based Policy Analysis: Lessons Learned* (pp. 197–224). Oxford University Press., DOI: 10.1093/oso/9780197801826.003.0010

Li, Y., Cui, M., Pang, Y., Zhan, B., Li, X., Wang, Q., Chen, F., Zhou, Z., & Yang, Q. (2024). Association of physical activity with socio-economic status and chronic disease in older adults in China: Cross-sectional findings from the survey of CLASS 2020 after the outbreak of COVID-19. *BMC Public Health*, *24*(1), 37. Advance online publication. DOI: 10.1186/s12889-023-17492-9 PMID: 38166980

Liu, Y.-T., Zhou, Y.-D., & Cai, J.-L. (2023). Effects of Health Status on the Labor Supply of Older Adults with Different Socioeconomic Status. *Sustainability (Basel)*, *15*(2), 1511. Advance online publication. DOI: 10.3390/su15021511

Liu, Z., Shi, R., Jiang, L., Tang, F., Qiu, Z., & Yao, L. (2025). Impact of Long-Term Care Insurance on health out-of-pocket expenditure ratios for older adults. *Frontiers in Public Health*, *13*, 1616761. Advance online publication. DOI: 10.3389/fpubh.2025.1616761 PMID: 40735199

Lu, Y., Karanikas, N., & Carroll, J.-A. (2025). Identification of needs of integrated approaches of occupational health and safety and health promotion. *Health Promotion Perspectives*, *15*(2), 153–164. DOI: 10.34172/hpp.025.44202 PMID: 40988950

Lunenfeld, B., Mskhalaya, G., Zitzmann, M., Corona, G., Arver, S., Kalinchenko, S., Tishova, Y., & Morgentaler, A. (2021). Recommendations on the diagnosis, treatment and monitoring of testosterone deficiency in men. *The Aging Male*, *24*(1), 119–138. DOI: 10.1080/13685538.2021.1962840 PMID: 34396893

Lussi, C., Bickenbach, J., Halvorsen, R., & Sabariego, C. (2024). Trends over the past 15 years in long-term care in Switzerland: A comparison with Germany, Italy, Norway, and the United Kingdom. *BMC Geriatrics*, *24*(1), 627. Advance online publication. DOI: 10.1186/s12877-024-05195-8 PMID: 39044146

Malik, M., Singh, S., & Pattanaik, F. (2022). Economics of Healthy Aging in India: A Multidimensional Perspective. *IZA Journal of Labor Policy*, *12*(1), 20220004. Advance online publication. DOI: 10.2478/izajolp-2022-0004

Mansouri, M., Bouhjar, A., Cadimi, I., Haisoufi, D., Fares, R., & Malainine, C. (2025). Study of the Impact of Economic Factors and Healthcare System Capacity on the Elderly Population in Morocco: A Health Economics Perspective. *The Open Public Health Journal*, *18*(1), e18749445421746. Advance online publication. DOI: 10.2174/0118749445421746250826065105

Mansyur, M. (2021). Occupational Health, Productivity and Evidence-Based Workplace Health Intervention. *Acta Medica Philippina*, *55*(6). Advance online publication. DOI: 10.47895/amp.v55i6.4273

Mavrodaris, A., Lafortune, L., & Brayne, C. (2022). The future longevity: Designing a synergistic approach for healthy ageing, sustainability, and equity. *The Lancet. Healthy Longevity*, *3*(9), 584–586. DOI: 10.1016/S2666-7568(22)00145-3 PMID: 35935473

Mehboob, K. (2025). Cost-Benefit Analysis of Preventive Healthcare Programs. *Pakistan Journal of Health Sciences*. DOI: 10.54393/pjhs.v6i4.3068

Meka'a, C. B., & Moneboulou, M. M. A. (2024). Analysis of the accounting effect of the demographic dividend in Cameroon. *Journal of Social and Economic Development*. Advance online publication. DOI: 10.1007/s40847-024-00375-z

Michaeli, D. T., Michaeli, J. C., Albers, S., & Michaeli, T. (2024). The Healthcare Workforce Shortage of Nurses and Physicians: Practice, Theory, Evidence, and Ways Forward. *Policy, Politics & Nursing Practice*, *25*(4), 216–227. DOI: 10.1177/15271544241286083 PMID: 39396540

Mihajlović, V., & Miladinov, G. (2024). Impact of Population Ageing on Economic Growth in Emerging EU Countries. *Ekonomicky Casopis*, *72*(1–2), 50–71. DOI: 10.31577/ekoncas.2024.01-02.03

Nagarajan, N., & Sixsmith, A. (2021). Policy Initiatives to Address the Challenges of an Older Population in the Workforce. *Ageing International*, *48*(1), 41–77. DOI: 10.1007/s12126-021-09442-w PMID: 34465930

Nagarajan, N., Wada, M., Fang, M., & Sixsmith, A. (2019). Defining organizational contributions to sustaining an ageing workforce: A bibliometric review. *European Journal of Ageing*, *16*(3), 337–361. DOI: 10.1007/s10433-019-00499-w PMID: 31543728

Nair, P. S. (2014). Population aging in sub-Saharan Africa: Present and prospects. *Gerontech.*, *13*(2), 266. DOI: 10.4017/gt.2014.13.02.429.00

Nikolov, P., & Adelman, A. (2018). Short-Run Health Consequences of Retirement and Pension Benefits: Evidence from China. *Forum for Health Economics & Policy*, *21*(2), 20170031. Advance online publication. DOI: 10.1515/fhep-2017-0031 PMID: 30964747

Noone, J., Knox, A., O'Loughlin, K., McNamara, M., Bohle, P., & Mackey, M. (2018). An analysis of factors associated with older workers' employment participation and preferences in Australia. *Frontiers in Psychology*, *9*(DEC), 2524. Advance online publication. DOI: 10.3389/fpsyg.2018.02524 PMID: 30618949

OECD. (2023). Pensions at a Glance 2023: OECD and G20 Indicators. *OECD Pensions at a Glance*, *2023*. Advance online publication. DOI: 10.1787/678055dd-en

Oka, Y., Wachi, M., & Kida, N. (2024). Physical Therapist-Led Initiatives for the Prevention and Improvement of Chronic Pain Among Workers: A Case Study of Hosting Workshops Based on Survey Results in a Corporate Setting. *International Journal of Environmental Research and Public Health*, *21*(12), 1709. Advance online publication. DOI: 10.3390/ijerph21121709 PMID: 39767548

Oliveira, M. D., Tavares, A. I., Miranda, R., Trindade, R., & Vieira, A. C. L. (2025). A novel policy dialogue to build sustainable and resilient health systems: Findings from PHSSR Portugal. *Health Research Policy and Systems*, *23*(1), 58. Advance online publication. DOI: 10.1186/s12961-025-01329-5 PMID: 40390059

Pariso, P., Picariello, M., & Marino, A. (2025). Driving Technological Efficiency in European Healthcare: The Role of Digital Innovation Across EU. *International Journal of Energy Economics and Policy*, *15*(4), 490–498. DOI: 10.32479/ijeep.17898

Péntek, M., Beretzky, Z., Brodszky, V., Szabó, J., Kovács, L., Kincses, Ã., Baji, P., Zrubka, Z., Rencz, F., & Gulácsi, L. (2020). Health-related productivity of the Hungarian population. A cross-sectional survey. *Orvosi Hetilap*, *161*(36), 1522–1533. DOI: 10.1556/650.2020.31798 PMID: 32886627

Piłat, A., Gałaś, A., Wilga, M., Cabello, M., Koskinen, S., Haro, J., Leonardi, M., & Tobiasz–Adamczyk, B. (2020). Gender perspective in the analysis of the relationship between health and work cessation, and how to deal with it. *International Journal of Occupational Medicine and Environmental Health*, *33*(3), 365–384. Advance online publication. DOI: 10.13075/ijomeh.1896.01351 PMID: 32329474

Profeta, P. (2023). Population Ageing and Gender Gaps: Labor Market, Family Relationships, and Public Policy. In Bloom, D. E., Sousa-Poza, A., & Sunde, U. (Eds.), *The Routledge Handbook of the Economics of Ageing* (pp. 437–451). Taylor and Francis., DOI: 10.4324/9781003150398-28

Qiao, X., Wang, B., & Guo, H. (2021). Chronic Diseases and Labor Force Participation Among Presenile and Senile Chinese. *Frontiers in Public Health*, *9*, 675927. Advance online publication. DOI: 10.3389/fpubh.2021.675927 PMID: 34604151

Rahimi, Z., Ghorbani-Shahna, F., & Bahrami, A. (2021). Design, Implementation, and Evaluation of Industrial Ventilation Systems and Filtration for Silica Dust Emissions from a Mineral Processing Company. *Indian Journal of Occupational and Environmental Medicine*, *25*(4), 192–197. DOI: 10.4103/ijoem.IJOEM_55_19 PMID: 35197669

Ramos-Herrera, M. C., & Sosvilla-Rivero, S. (2020). Fiscal Sustainability in Aging Societies: Evidence from Euro Area Countries. *Sustainability (Basel)*, *12*(24), 10276. Advance online publication. DOI: 10.3390/su122410276

Ranganathan, N. M. (2017). Universal social pension for elderly individuals in India Public expenditure requirements and fiscal sustainability. *Indian Growth and Development Review*, *10*(2), 89–116. DOI: 10.1108/IGDR-07-2017-0047

Rinaldi, C., Bortoluzzi, S., Airoldi, C., Leigheb, F., Nicolini, D., Russotto, S., Vanhaecht, K., & Panella, M. (2021). The Early Detection of Osteoporosis in a Cohort of Healthcare Workers: Is There Room for a Screening Program? *International Journal of Environmental Research and Public Health*, *18*(3), 1368. Advance online publication. DOI: 10.3390/ijerph18031368 PMID: 33540940

Rouzet, D., Sánchez, A. C., Renault, T., & Roehn, O. (2019). *Fiscal challenges and inclusive growth in ageing societies*. OECD Economic Policy Papers., DOI: 10.1787/c553d8d2-

Rozman, M., & Cančer, V. (2021). The Appropriate Work Environment for Older Employees: The Case of Slovenia. *Business Systems Research, 12*(2), 172–186. DOI: 10.2478/bsrj-2021-0026

Secretariat, C. (2023). *Fiscal Policy Options for Resilient and Sustainable Development*. DOI: 10.14217/comsec.1106

Selekler, H. M., Gökmen, G., Alvur, T. M., & Steiner, T. J. (2015). Productivity losses attributable to headache, and their attempted recovery, in a heavy-manufacturing workforce in Turkey: Implications for employers and politicians. *The Journal of Headache and Pain, 16*(1), 1–8. DOI: 10.1186/s10194-015-0579-4 PMID: 26573819

Serra, C., Soler-Font, M., García, A. M. M., Peña, P., Vargas-Prada, S., & Ramada, J. (2019). Prevention and management of musculoskeletal pain in nursing staff by a multifaceted intervention in the workplace: Design of a cluster randomized controlled trial with effectiveness, process and economic evaluation (INTEVAL_Spain). *BMC Public Health, 19*(1), 348. Advance online publication. DOI: 10.1186/s12889-019-6683-7 PMID: 30922285

Silvaggi, F., Eigenmann, M., Scaratti, C., Guastafierro, E., Toppo, C., Lindstrom, J., Rantala, E., Imaz-Iglesia, I., Barnfield, A., Maassen, A., & Leonardi, M. (2020). Employment and Chronic Diseases: Suggested Actions for The Implementation of Inclusive Policies for The Participation of People with Chronic Diseases in the Labour Market. *International Journal of Environmental Research and Public Health, 17*(3), 820. Advance online publication. DOI: 10.3390/ijerph17030820 PMID: 32013004

Sisubalan, N., Vijay, N., Kesika, P., Newbegin, M., Shalini, R., Sivamaruthi, B. S., & Chaiysut, C. (2025). The Contribution of Wearable Devices and Artificial Intelligence to Promoting Healthy Aging. *Current Pharmaceutical Biotechnology, 27*. Advance online publication. DOI: 10.2174/011389201039050025091110423 1 PMID: 41031500

Stepanova, O. (2019). Fiscal sustainability under the conditions of emerging longevity economy. *Ekonomìka ì Prognozuvannâ*. DOI: 10.15407/econforecast2019.01.031

Suhrcke, M., Sauto Arce, R., McKee, M., & Rocco, L. (2008). *The economic costs of ill health in the European Region: Background document*. World Health Organization. Regional Office for Europe. https://iris.who.int/handle/10665/350693

Tang, B., & Li, Z. (2021). A Country-Level Empirical Study on the Fiscal Effect of Elderly Population Health: The Mediating Role of Healthcare Resources. *Health Care, 10*(1), 30. Advance online publication. DOI: 10.3390/healthcare10010030 PMID: 35052194

Tao, W., Zeng, Z., Dang, H., Li, P., Chuong, L., Yue, D., Wen, J., Zhao, R., Li, W., & Kominski, G. (2020). Towards universal health coverage: Achievements and challenges of 10 years of healthcare reform in China. *BMJ Global Health, 5*(3), e002087. Advance online publication. DOI: 10.1136/bmjgh-2019-002087 PMID: 32257401

Temsumrit, N. (2023). Can aging population affect economic growth through the channel of government spending? *Heliyon, 9*(9), e19521. Advance online publication. DOI: 10.1016/j.heliyon.2023.e19521 PMID: 37809751

Tsuji, I. (2020). Current status and issues concerning Health Japan 21 (second term). *Nutrition Reviews, 78*(Supplement_3), 14–17. DOI: 10.1093/nutrit/nuaa079 PMID: 33259610

Uchida, Y., & Ono, T. (2024). Generational Distribution of Fiscal Burdens: A Positive Analysis. *International Economic Review, 65*(1), 393–430. DOI: 10.1111/iere.12654

Uścińska, G. (2023). Women on the labour market and in old-age pension insurance. In M. Duszczyk & J. Mecina (Eds.), *[PRACA, BEZROBOCIE, ZATRUDNIENIE: Wartości i działania w rozwoju polityki rynku pracy. Ksiega jubileuszowa profesor Małgorzaty Szylko-Skoczny]: Work, Unemployment, Employment: Values and Actions in The Development of Labour Market Policy. A Jubilee Book Dedicated to Professor Malgorzata Szylko-Skoczny* (pp. 119–134). Wydawnictwa Uniwersytetu Warszaskiego. DOI: 10.31338/uw.9788323563846.pp.119-134

van de Poll, M. K., Bergström, G., Jensen, I., Nybergh, L., Kwak, L., Lornudd, C., & Lohela-Karlsson, M. (2020). Cost-Effectiveness of a Problem-Solving Intervention Aimed to Prevent Sickness Absence among Employees with Common Mental Disorders or Occupational Stress. *International Journal of Environmental Research and Public Health, 17*(14), 5234. Advance online publication. DOI: 10.3390/ijerph17145234 PMID: 32698470

van Dongen, J. V., & van der Beek, A. J. (2022). Economic evaluations in occupational health: What brings the best bang for the buck? *Scandinavian Journal of Work, Environment & Health, 48*(4), 249–252. DOI: 10.5271/sjweh.4026 PMID: 35380166

Vučković, V., & Banović, R. Š. (2021). Who and what holds back reforms in croatia? – The political economy perspective. *Drustvena Istrazivanja (Zagreb), 30*(4), 675–698. DOI: 10.5559/di.30.4.02

Wu, C., Cao, Y., & Xu, H. (2025). How Population Aging Drives Labor Productivity: Evidence from China. *Sustainability (Basel), 17*(11), 5046. Advance online publication. DOI: 10.3390/su17115046

Yamamura, E. (2025). Grandchildren and Views about Consumption Tax. *Review of Behavioral Economics*, *12*(1), 97–127. DOI: 10.1561/105.00000205

Yaqoob, M., Bani, Y., Ishak, S., & Rosland, A. (2024). Impact of Demographic Dividend on Economic Growth in Developing Countries. *Thailand and the World Economy*, *42*(3), 236–252.

Yolusever, A. (2025). *Economics of Longevity and Aging Populations*. İktisat İşletme ve Uluslararası İlişkiler Dergisi., DOI: 10.58654/jebi.1627286

Yuan, S., Jia, M., & Wang, F. (2022). Implementation of Integrated Care for the Aged Population in Anhui and Fujian Province of China: A Qualitative Study. *International Journal of Integrated Care*, *22*(0), 20. Advance online publication. DOI: 10.5334/ijic.6419 PMID: 35756341

Zhou, Y., Pan, Y., & Ma, L. (2023). Research progress on intrinsic capacity in older adults. *Chinese Journal of Geriatrics*, *42*(1), 108–112. DOI: 10.3760/cma.j.issn.0254-9026.2023.01.021

Chapter 8 Social Determinants of Health in an Older Population: A Bibliometric Review of Scientific Literature

Amiya Abdul Khadar
http://orcid.org/0009-0002-0861-8115
Lovely Professional University, India

Pooja Kansra
http://orcid.org/0000-0003-2229-0662
Lovely Professional University, India

ABSTRACT

The main objective of this study is to conduct a comprehensive review of the various studies related to population ageing and its impact on health with a specific focus on the social determinants that influence the same. The present study aims to not only shed light on the evolution and advancement in this research domain but also help to identify key areas for future research exploration. The study used the scientometrics review methodology, which relies on the bibliometric analysis. he R-based bibliometric and visualization of similarities (VOS) viewer open-source software were used to conduct the analysis. The study has found that the most relevant themes identified by the authors in population ageing and social determinants of health are education, affordable healthcare, elderly health, social support and physical activity. The finding of the chosen studies offers a distinctive and valuable

DOI: 10.4018/979-8-3373-7483-3.ch008

contribution to the field of health and demographics as it is one of the first known studies to systematically review population ageing and its connection to social determinants of health.

1. INTRODUCTION

Elderly health refers to the overall welfare of older individuals, encompassing their physical mental and social aspects of life (Naz et al., 2021). As people become aged, their bodies undergo numerous changes, they become more susceptible to health problems and diseases (Evashwick et al., 1984). The focus of elderly health is to prioritize and increase the health and emotional welfare of elderly population with the goal of preserving and enhancing their overall health and quality of life so that they can live longer, healthier and more active life (Naz et al. 2021; Stone, 2009). This includes preventing and managing age-related conditions such as arthritis, osteoporosis, heart disease, dementia and other chronic illness (Schnitzer et al., 2020). Elderly health also involves addressing mental health issues, including anxiety and depression, and promoting social engagement and connectedness which can help prevent loneliness and isolation (Radford et al., 2019; A. Goyal & Kajal, 2014; Hamano et al., 2011). Given the increasing global population of older adults, the well-being of older people is a crucial component of overall societal health. (WHO, 2022). As a result, population ageing has become a global phenomenon that policymakers, researchers and stakeholders are discussing and debating in the twenty-first century (Banerjee, 2021; Verma et al., 2013).

In the past few years, many researchers and scholars have made efforts to study the standard of living and well-being of elderly people (Hamiduzzaman et al., 2021; Maheshwari et al., 2021; Schenker & Costa, 2019; Pasqualini et al., 2017; Yunus et al., 2017; Iliffe et al., 2010; Hellström & Hallberg, 2001). Numerous researchers have studied and written extensively about the physical and emotional welfare of elderly people. These studies have helped in shedding light on several dimensions of elderly health and have helped in improving the overall standard of living of elderly people. The research work in elderly health and ageing is extensive and varied and covers many different areas thus conducting a broad bibliometric analysis is required to find out the different factors that influence elderly well-being. Based on our current understanding, there have been limited bibliometric studies conducted from the specific perspective of how factors such as physical activity, nutrition, depression and anxiety and socio-economic and environmental factors are impacting population ageing and well-being.

In light of this an attempt has been made by the present study to fill a vacuum in the existing research on population ageing and social determinants of health by undertaking bibliometric analysis in an organised and straightforward way, while always attempting to answer the following research questions:

RQ1. How literature on population ageing has developed over the past decade and find the most cited research studies?
RQ2. What are some of the significant articles, authors, journals, countries and affiliations that have made substantial contributions to the advancement of this research field?
RQ3. What are the emerging themes in the research field of elderly healthcare and ageing and how do they influence the progress of further studies?

2. REVIEW OF LITERATURE

2.1 Factors affecting the health of older people and their well-being

Ageing is an inevitable process and with age comes several physical, emotional and social challenges which can impact the physical and mental welfare of the older generation (Banerjee, 2021). Several studies have been done regarding how these factors influence the everyday living of older people . As people become aged their physical health declines which can lead to several chronic diseases like arthritis, hypertension, diabetes and cardiovascular diseases (Verma et al., 2020; Radford et al., 2019; Sanjel et al., 2012). Numerous studies have reached the consensus that engaging in consistent physical activity can assist in preserving physical abilities and averting age-related health deterioration (Sahoo et al., 2021; Radford et al., 2019; Kabayama et al., 2017; Pasqualini et al., 2017). As the population ages, the physical health of individuals declines, leading to many chronic diseases like arthritis, hypertension, diabetes and cardiovascular diseases. Another dimension of research of elderly studies was the role of nutrition in older people health and well-being (Wilson et al., 2020; Nawaz et al., 2012; Gonzlez-Gonzlez et al., 2011). The scientific research has provided the evidence that adopting a well-balanced and nutritious diet can contribute to sustaining optimal health and reducing chronic ailments risks (Majumder et al., 2017; Nawaz et al., 2012). Furthermore, certain nutrients such as vitamin D and calcium have been shown to be particularly important for maintaining bone health in elderly people (Verma et al., 2020; Feng et al., 2019; Graue et al., 2013). Mental health was also a subject of significance in the research field of elderly health (Maheshwari et al., 2021; Kabayama et al., 2017; A. Goyal & Kajal, 2014; Hamano et al., 2011). Depression and anxiety can be observed frequently among the older adults and can significantly impact their quality of life (Maheshwari et al.,

2021; Feng et al., 2019; Niederstrasser et al., 2019; Radford et al., 2019; Verma et al., 2019). The researchers have identified various factors which can contribute to mental health issues in older adults, including social isolation, chronic illness, and cognitive decline. Effective interventions such as counselling and medication can help to improve mental health outcomes for elderly people (Kabayama et al., 2017; A. Goyal & Kajal, 2014; Iliffe et al., 2010; Fernández-Olano et al., 2006). Finally, researchers have also analysed the impact of social and environmental aspects on older people health (Courtney et al., 2022; Pasqualini et al., 2017; Nawaz et al., 2012; Iliffe et al., 2010; Pyle & Stoller, 2003). Instances of social isolation have been correlated with heightened vulnerability to depression, cognitive impairment and physical deterioration. Environmental factors such as air pollution and access to green spaces have also been shown to have an impact on older people health (Vaishnav et al., 2022).

2.2 What Is Bibliometric Analysis?

Bibliometric analysis is a quantitative approach used to study and evaluate scientific publications and their impact (Bhat et al., 2023; Mishra et al., 2022; Donthu et al., 2021). It involves analysing bibliographic data, such as citations, authorship, and publication patterns, to understand trends and patterns in the literature. This widely used and effective approach helps the exploration and analysis of extensive quantities of data (Donthu et al., 2021). Bibliometric analysis can be used to evaluate individual researchers, research groups or entire fields of study. It is used to identify key researchers, journals or institutions in a particular field and helps identify emerging research areas (Bhat et al., 2023; Mishra et al., 2022; Cobo et al., 2011; Kessler, 1963). Commonly used bibliometric indicators depict the number of publications, h-index, g-index, citation counts and journal impact factor (Aria & Cuccurullo, 2017). The bibliometric analysis is also often used to evaluate academic performance, inform research funding decisions, and identify potential collaborators. Another major use of bibliometric analysis is finding research gaps and areas of potential collaboration between researchers and institutions (Gálvez-Sánchez et al., 2021; Cash-Gibson et al., 2018). Sciento metric mapping using bibliometric analysis is a research technique that examines how different areas of study are connected by analysing their intellectual exchanges and structural linkages. To achieve this, various methods such as citation analysis, co-citation analysis, thematic clustering, co-authorship analysis and co-keyword analysis are used (Mishra et al., 2022; Donthu et al., 2021; Biancone et al., 2020;van Eck & Waltman, 2010).

3. RESEARCH METHODOLOGY

The bibliometric study is a subfield of scientometrics, which involves using quantitative techniques to analyse various types of publications, such as articles and papers, which is further used to identify the trends and patterns within a particular field of study (Mishra et al., 2022; Donthu et al., 2021; Hood & Wilson, 2001; Groos & Pritchard, 1969). The present research utilized the Scopus database to retrieve articles using specific search keywords such as "Population Ageing", "Social determinants of health" or "SDH", and "Elderly". The search was further refined by applying the filter for the English Language. This study specifically focused on analysing articles and reviews published in journals, while excluding book chapters and conference papers from the analysis (Mishra et al., 2022; P. Goyal et al., 2013). The study exclusively fixated on papers published in English, considering the writer's proficiency in the language. English is widely utilized in scientific publications, and a substantial number of top-tier bibliometrics papers adhere to this language pattern. (Cash-Gibson et al., 2018; Cobo et al., 2011; van Eck & Waltman, 2010). For this study, 164 documents published between 2010 and 2022 were collected. While both Scopus and Web of Science are widely recognized bibliometric databases, the study solely relied on data sourced from Scopus. This choice was motivated by Scopus's broader array of sources, including a comprehensive database of citations and abstracts, particularly in terms of coverage of multiple journals. R-based bibliometrix tool along with VOSviewer was used to conduct the bibliometric study. These two software tools are commonly used for analysing research trends via citation analysis, keyword analysis and collaboration analysis etc which enables researchers to delve into various aspects of scholarly literature and explore patterns and trends within the research landscape. They are preferred over the other programs because R-biblometrix is reliable for statistical analysis and VOSviewer is effective in creating clear and visually appealing graphics. Both programs work directly with files imported from Scopus (Mishra et al., 2022; Donthu et al., 2021; van Eck & Waltman, 2010).

4. STUDY RESULTS

4.1 A global overview on Population Ageing and SDH

The search using relevant keywords yielded a total of 164 articles from 64 different journals, which were retrieved from the database as shown in Table 1. The chosen keywords included "Population Ageing", "Social determinants of health" or "SDH" and "Elderly" to capture a comprehensive insight into the research area while also ensuring that the credibility of sources or journals used is maintained.

Table 1. Search syntax and general information

Search Syntax	TITLE-ABS-KEY ("Social determinants of health" OR "SDH" AND "Elderly" OR "Population Ageing") AND (LIMIT-TO (DOCTYPE, "ar") OR LIMIT-TO (DOCTYPE, "re")) and (LIMIT TO (LANGUAGE, "English"))
Criteria Quantity Articles 164 Journals 64 Authors 961 Institutions 308 Countries 36 Cited references 8,110	

Figure 1 shows the overall number of publications associated with population ageing SDH from 2010 to 2022. The data shows that only 2 publication was available online in 2010 which later increased to 19 in 2022. The number of publications began to rise significantly from the year 2017 and reached its peak in 2019. The emergence of Covid 19 was the major reason for the spike in numbers in 2019 and 2020 (Wilson et al., 2020). It is anticipated that this figure will experience further growth in the upcoming years.

Figure 1. Number of Publication from 2010 to 2022

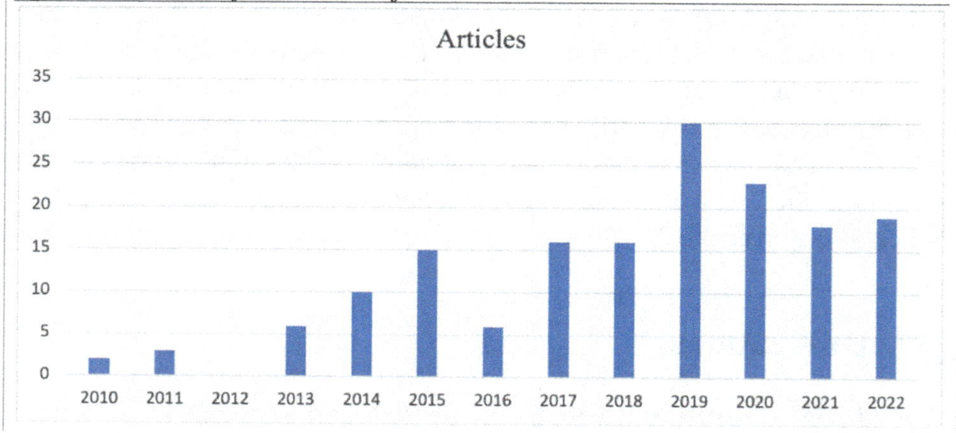

Table 2. Most Influential Journals

Sources	Articles
PLOS ONE	33
Social Science And Medicine	22
Journal Of Aging And Health	10
Archives Of Gerontology And Geriatrics	8
Journals Of Gerontology - Series B Psychological Sciences And Social Sciences	6
Ssm - Population Health	5
Journal Of Alzheimer's Disease	4
Scientific Reports	4
Geriatrics And Gerontology International	3
Journal Of Affective Disorders	3

Table 2 shows the publication journals which was most influential in the last decade. *PLOS ONE* tops the list with a total of 33 publications followed by *Social Science and Medicine* with 22 research papers and articles published and *Journal of Aging and Health* with 10 publications.

Figure 2. Source growth of the relevant Journal

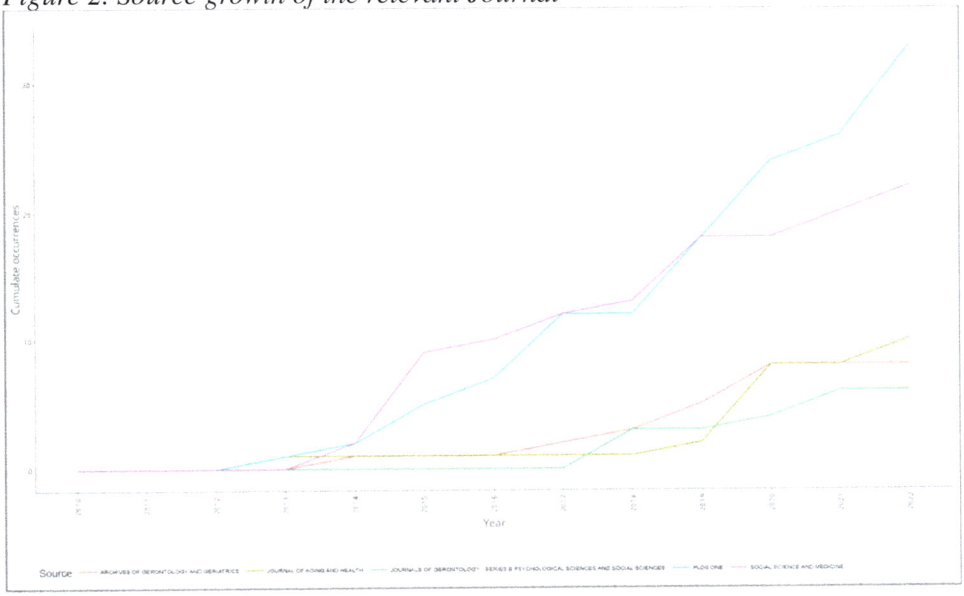

Figure 2 depicts the source growth of the relevant journal from 2010 to 2022, There has been a notable improvement in the number of publications. The graph also depicts the gap in publishing time such as Journals Of Gerontology - Series B Psychological Sciences and Social Sciences had zero publication on the topic from 2013 to 2017. The authors who hold the most influence in this field are presented in Table 3. By examining the h-index and publication count, it was determined that Wu Y and Zhang Y hold the highest position, having an h-index of 3 and a cumulative publication count of 3 articles. Other influential authors include Glymour Mm, Gustafsson Pe, Hayward Md, Huang Y, Jasilionis D, Jones K and Lee J.

Table 3. Most Influential Authors

Authors	*Articles*	*h-index*
Wu Y	3	3
Zhang Y	3	3
Glymour Mm	3	2
Gustafsson Pe	2	2
Hayward Md	2	2
Huang Y	2	2
Jasilionis D	2	2
Jones K	2	2
Lee J	2	2

According to Table 4, the University of California emerged as the most prolific institution with respect to the overall sum of published works among the influential affiliations. They published 19 articles, followed by Hospital Universitari Germans Trias I Pujol and Padova University Hospital, each with 11 published articles.

Table 4. Most Influential Affiliations

Affiliation	*Articles*
University Of California	19
Hospital Universitari Germans Trias I Pujol	11
Padova University Hospital	11
Umeå University	9
University Of Maryland School Of Medicine	9
University Of Waikato	9

continued on following page

Table 4. Continued

Affiliation	*Articles*
Emory University	7
Federal University Of Sergipe	7
University Of Alabama At Birmingham	7
University Of Michigan	7

Table 5 presents the list of the ten most frequently referenced articles. Tile of the paper, the author's name, the year it was published and the total citation per year are given in the table (Table 5). (Hayward et al., 2015) attained the highest citation per year at 16.33, securing the top position on the list. (Haslam et al., 2014) and (Alang et al., 2020) followed the list with citations per year of 14.00 and 12.50 respectively. It can be observed that the citation per year for this field of study has been increasing over the years. Among the top 10 most cited articles, three were published in *Social Science and Medicine* which was also the 2nd highest in the most influential journals list (Table 2), Two were published in PloS ONE. According to Figure 2, both Social Science and Medicine and PloS ONE experienced the most significant growth in the number of published articles.

Table 5. Top 10 most cited articles

Author	*Title*	*SO*	*TC per year*
Hayward et al., 2015	Trends and group differences in the association between educational attainment and U.S. adult mortality: Implications for understanding education's causal influence.	*Social Science and Medicine*	16.33
Haslam et al., 2014	"The we's have it": Evidence for the distinctive benefits of group engagement in enhancing cognitive health in ageing.	*Social Science and Medicine*	14.00
Alang et al., 2020	Police Brutality and Mistrust in Medical Institutions.	*Journal of Racial and Ethnic Health Disparities*	12.50
Jamei et al., 2017	Predicting all-cause risk of 30-day hospital readmission using artificial neural networks.	*PLoS ONE*	10.26
Domènech-Abella et al., 2018	The association between socioeconomic status and depression among older adults in Finland, Poland and Spain: A comparative cross-sectional study of distinct measures and pathways.	*Journal of Affective Disorders*	8.67
Finlay, 2018	'Walk like a penguin': Older Minnesotans' experiences of (non)therapeutic white space.	*Social Science and Medicine*	8.17

continued on following page

Table 5. Continued

Author	*Title*	*SO*	*TC per year*
Koehn et al., 2013	Revealing the shape of knowledge using an intersectionality lens: Results of a scoping review on the health and health care of ethnocultural minority older adults.	*Ageing and Society*	5.64
Saito et al., 2014	Relative deprivation, poverty, and subjective health: JAGES cross-sectional study	*PLoS ONE*	5.00
Lundell et al., 2013	Public views about health causation, attributions of responsibility, and inequality	*Journal of Health Communication*	4.91
Abdou & Fingerhut, 2014	Stereotype threat among black and white women in health care settings.	*Cultural Diversity and Ethnic Minority Psychology*	4.90

TC: Total Citation

Numerous studies have examined the relationships between the socio-economic, psychological, and institutional aspects, and how these elements interrelate to impact the health of a given population and their experience with health services. An example showing the importance of education even decades later, and as a result, in determining the long term health of an individual is Hayward et al. (2015), where he explains how educational output can account for different levels of mortalities in adults in the U.S. Similarly, Haslam et al. (2014) show that the mental health of the elderly is better when they participate in social groups, which is a social phenomenon where social identity and group participation play a great role in improving health. Negative health effects of social violence and police brutality as a form of social violence and injustice are also documented in the study of Alang et al. (2020), where he shows that police brutality undermined the trust of the health system among the marginalized social groups and communities, and they became less motivated to seek medical care. In their study, Jamei et al. (2017) showed that artificial neural networks can be used to predict health care outcomes, which is a study on the use of advanced technologies in the health care field, and to in the case of predict hospital readmissions. In social determinants of mental health, Finlay (2018) and Abella et al. (2018) show the impact of social factors on the depression of elderly people in a number of European nations. Koehn et al. (2013) highlight intersectional identities and environmental context and how they influence health experiences of older adults, especially among ethnocultural minorities. Moreover, Saito et al. (2014) show that relative deprivation and poverty tend to make one's health subjectively worse. Public views on health inequality, and most precisely, Lundell et al. (2013) demonstrate that health responsibility beliefs shape one's views on health inequality, and thus, are of substantial relevance to health inequality. Furthermore, Abdou and Fingerhut (2014) show how the threat of stereotyping in health care settings can worsen the experience of Black and White women, thus highlighting the impact of psychosocial interstress in health care settings. These studies portray the impact of social positions, socioeconomic factors, social identity, trust in institutions, and societal framework on health and healthcare inequities and outcomes.

Figure 3 shows the keyword trend and from 2016 to 2018 a dynamic phase characterized by the emergence of various trending topics with a high frequency of discussion was observed in the literature. Some of these topics include SDH, ageing, gender, and so on. The figure shows that SDH and ageing have most frequented trending topic from 2016 to 2020.

Figure 3. Trend Topic in Population Ageing and Social Determinants of Health

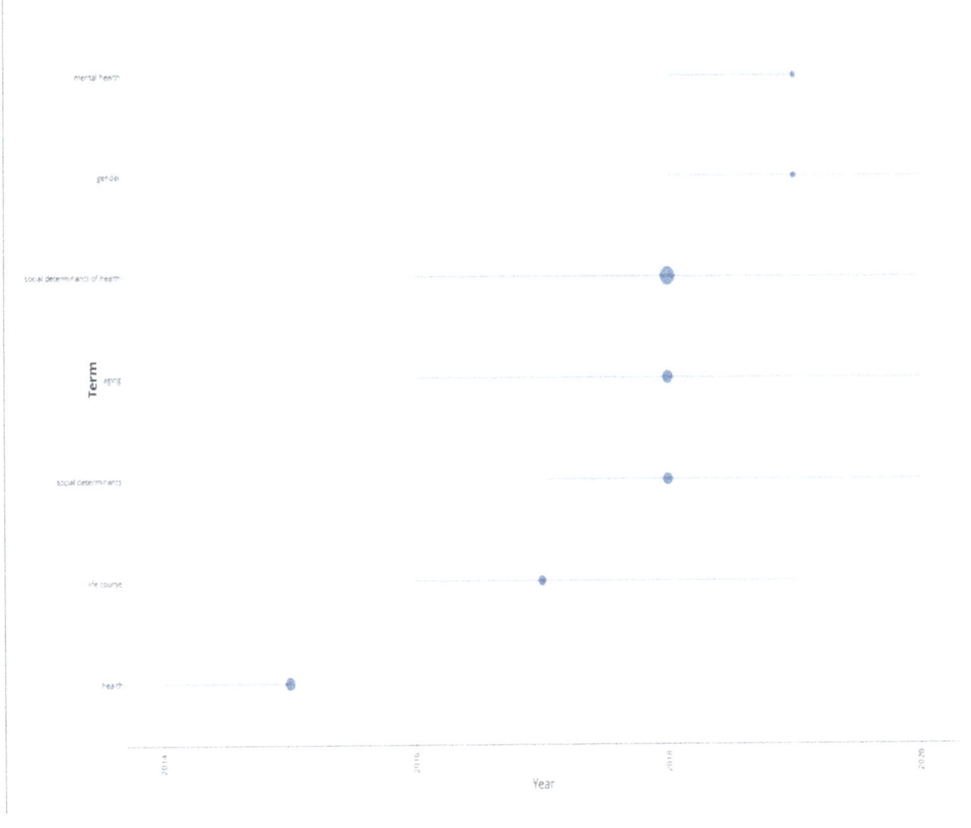

The authors' keywords, given by the authors themselves during the publication process, are visually depicted in Figure 4 in a thematic clustering. This figure presents a representation of the grouping or organization of these keywords based on their related themes. Through the utilization of a clustering algorithm, these keywords are organized into distinct themes or groups. We can interpret the different clusters based on two variables: centrality which depicts the relevance degree and density which depicts the development degree. This allows us to understand the characteristics of each cluster in terms of how central the keywords are to the cluster and how dense the keyword connections are within each cluster. Centrality and density are commonly used measures in clustering algorithms to understand the characteristics of clusters (Cobo et al., 2011).

Figure 4. Thematic Map

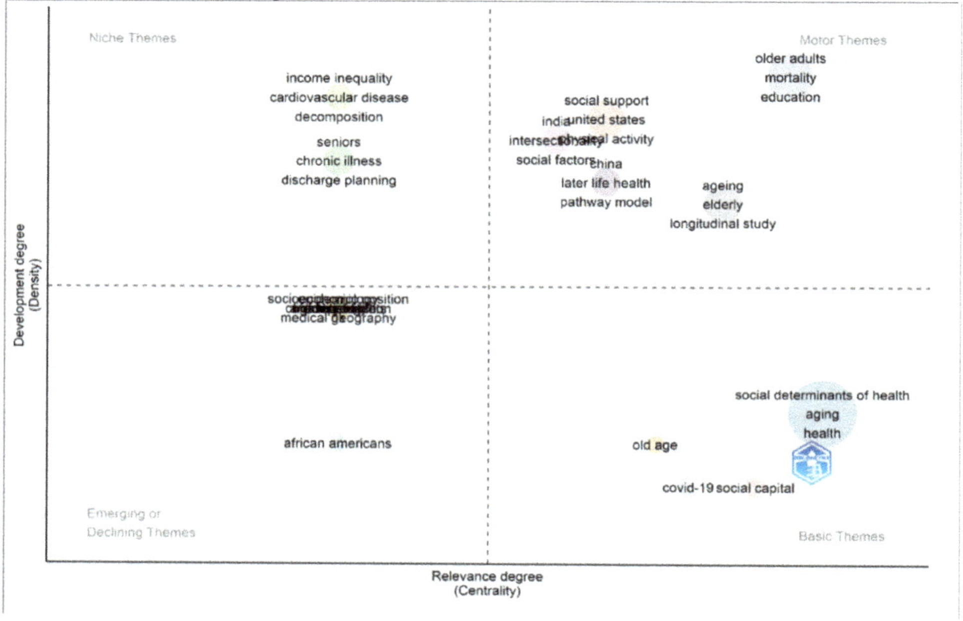

The quadrant on the upper right, which depicts high density and high centrality, represents keywords highly significant to the main theme (Figure 4). The keyword that falls in this category plays a significant role in the study theme and is called motor themes. "Older adults", "Mortality", "Education", "Ageing", "Elderly", "Social Support", "Physical activity", "United States", "India" etc all fall under this quadrant. These keywords are significant for the current research theme. Within the upper left quadrant, there are themes that exhibit a high density of keywords but possess low centrality, indicating their limited relevance to the research area. They are called niche themes "Income Inequality", "Cardiovascular diseases", "decomposition", "Older" and "Chronic illness" etc fall under this category. The lower left quadrant indicates themes with both low centrality and low density, suggesting that these themes are either emerging or declining in relevance within the research area.

"Socioeconomic status", "Medical geography", "African Americans" etc fall under this category. The final quadrant on the lower right represents the themes that are considered basic and recurring within the research area. These themes have a stable presence and are frequently addressed in various studies. "Social determinants of health", "Aging", "Health", "Old Age", "Covid 19" and "Social Capital" etc fall under this category.

Figure 5. Country's Collaboration Map

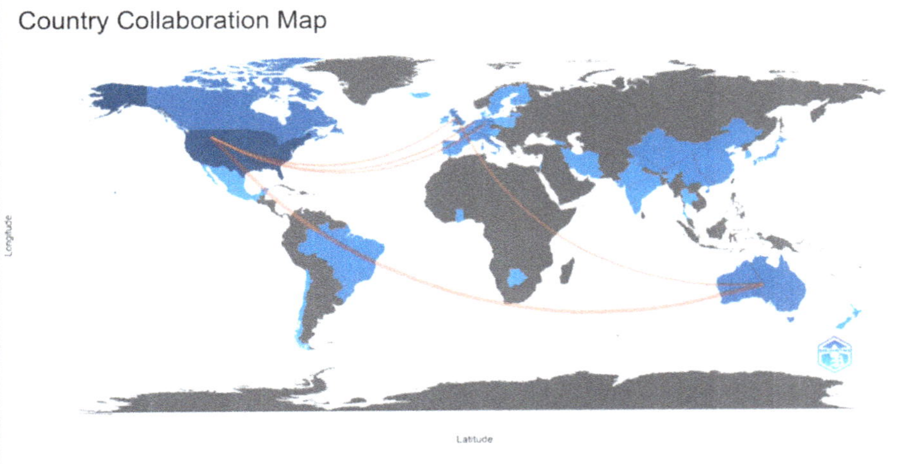

Figure 5 depicts the map of country collaborations in the research field. "USA," "Australia," and "UK" have established the most extensive network of collaborations in the field of population ageing and SDH. These countries surpass others in terms of their collaborative output and productivity.

Table 6. Country output in terms of the production of articles

Country Output	*Country*	*Output*
USA 56	AUSTRALIA	3
CANADA 10	CHINA	3
UNITED KINGDOM 10	INDIA	3
SWITZERLAND 6	SWEDEN	3
BRAZIL 5	BELGIUM	2
SPAIN 5	FRANCE	2

continued on following page

Table 6. Continued

Country Output	*Country*	*Output*
ITALY 4	GERMANY	2
JAPAN 4	IRAN	2
NETHERLANDS 4	SINGAPORE	2

Figure 6 depicts the primary countries in terms of the publication count within the relevant research field. The USA holds the top position with 56 publications, followed by Canada, the United Kingdom, and Switzerland with 10, 10, and 6 publications respectively. India ranks 11th in terms of article production. Additional details can be found in Table 6.

4.2 Intellectual Structure

The co-citation analysis and visual depictions are used to conduct the intellectual structure analysis of the bibliometrics study.

4.2.1 Co-citation analysis. To examine the connection between scientific publications by assessing how frequently they are cited together in other scholarly works co-citation analysis is used. It is a way to identify the intellectual connections between authors, papers, and fields of research. Additionally, co-citation analysis is utilized to find out papers, authors, and journals which are the most influential within a specific field. It also helps to uncover the intellectual associations that prevail between diverse subfields of study. (Mishra et al., 2022; Donthu et al., 2021; Aria & Cuccurullo, 2017). Co-citation analysis can be used to create maps of scientific research that indicate how different fields of study and their subfields are related to each other (Donthu et al., 2021). These maps can be useful in identifying emerging trends in research, finding potential collaborators in the field, and identifying research gaps in the literature that can help with new research Fields(De Castro & Frazzon, 2017).

By examining 164 publications, a comprehensive analysis revealed a total of 961 authors. Through the utilization of co-citation analysis, the authors who were frequently co-cited were identified, represented by the nodes in Figure 6. The figure also illustrates the formation of five clusters, representing the network of co-cited authors in the field of population ageing and SDH. Every cluster in the visualization represents a group of authors who are frequently referenced together within this specific research field.

The first cluster consists of 6 authors, Berkman I.F, Kawachi I, Krieger N, Seeman T, Seeman T.E and Subramanian S.V. The second cluster consists of 5 authors, Hayward M.D, House J.S, Hummer R.A, Ross C.E and William D.R. The third cluster consists of 5 authors, Kivimaki M, Mackenbach J.P, Marmot M, Marmot

M.G and Steptoe A. Cluster 4 consist of 3 authors, Glymour M.M, Kuh D, Langa K.M and the cluster 5 consist of 2 authors, Rockwood K and Wilson R.S (Figure 6).

Figure 6. Co-citation of Authors

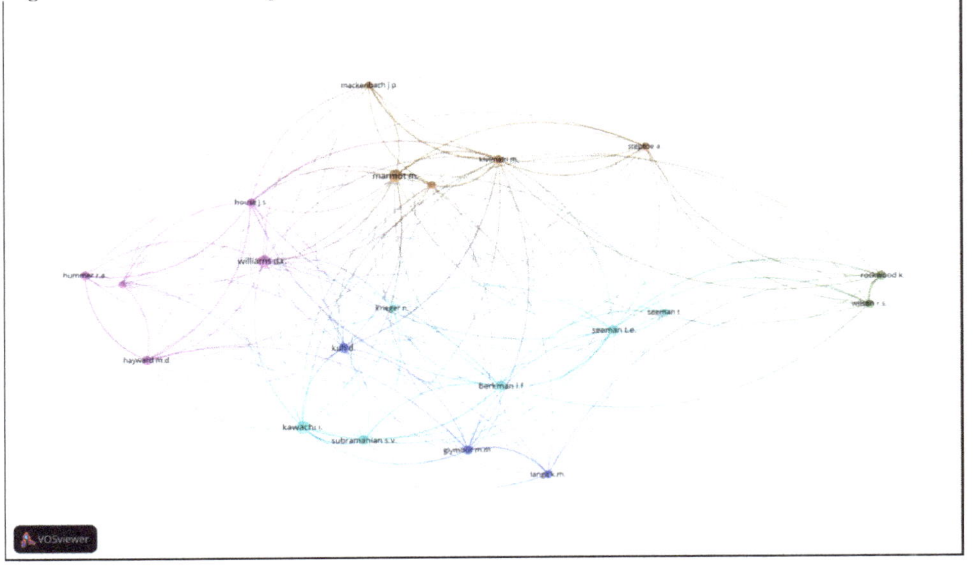

4.2.2 Co-occurrence of keywords. The most frequently used keywords in this field of research can be observed through this study (Figure 7). Keywords can be located below the abstract, it helps in highlighting the key details of the research paper.

Figure 7. Relevant Keywords

Figure 6, Figure 7 and Figure 8 visualise the relationships and connections between different keywords based on their frequent appearance together within the publication. The result shows that keywords such as "social determinants of health", "ageing", "older adults", and "depression" are among the most often used terms in existing publications on this research field. Other keywords which have the prospective to impact this field of research are "socio-economic status", "mental health", "mortality" and 'self-related health". The literature on population ageing has heavily depended on these concepts over time, and understanding them will aid authors and academics in comprehending this body of work (Figure 8).

Figure 8. Co-occurrence of Keywords

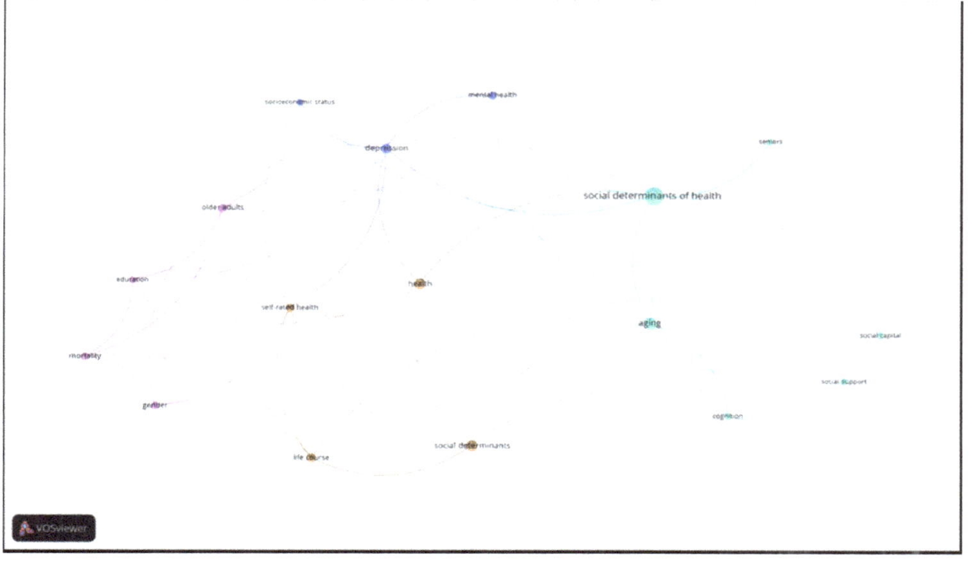

4.3 Developing Trends in the Literature of Population Ageing

The following themes were observed as the most prominent themes in the literature on population ageing.

4.3.1 SDH and Population Ageing. SDH encompass a range of social and non-medical elements that can impact an individual's well-being. These factors include social, economic, environmental, and political reasons that can influence an individual's physical and mental wellness (Hamiduzzaman et al., 2021; Schnitzer et al., 2020). The concept of SDH highlights the idea that health consequences are not solely determined by individuals' biology or lifestyle but are also affected by broader societal factors. The SDH can substantially impact the health and overall welfare of older individuals. Elderly people with low socioeconomic status may have limited access to healthcare services, poor nutrition, and inadequate housing, leading to poor health outcomes such as several non-communicable diseases, disability and loneliness(Schnitzer et al., 2020; Radford et al., 2019; Domènech-Abella et al., 2018). Addressing the social determinants of health by providing proper healthcare facilities and services and promoting healthy ageing can help to reduce the negative effect of population ageing on world health.

4.3.2 Mental Health and Depression on Population Ageing. As individuals age, they become more susceptible to several mental health issues including depression, anxiety and cognitive decline (Tan et al., 2022; Verma et al., 2019; Feng et al., 2019). Depression and loneliness are common mental health issues that can be observed in older people. Depression and loneliness can lead to several issues for older people such as feeling irritable, restlessness and loss of interest in activities, and difficulties in concentrating and making decisions (Domènech-Abella et al., 2018; A. Goyal & Kajal, 2014).

4.3.3 Social Support and Population Ageing. Social support is an important aspect of elderly well-being, especially for older people who may be more exposed to social isolation and solitude as they age. Social support can take many forms such as emotional support, practical assistance and social involvement (Hamiduzzaman et al., 2021; Sanjel et al., 2012; Hamano et al., 2011). Several pieces of literature have discussed the positive impact of social support on elderly people and their well-being, social support can provide a sense of belonging, reduce the negative feeling and improve mental health and anxiety(Maheshwari et al., 2021; Kendig et al., 2017; Fernández-Olano et al., 2006).

5. DISCUSSIONS AND IMPLICATIONS

The present study was broadly based on population ageing and its influence on health, analysing research from the previous 13 years. The present research delved into the social factors contributing to an ageing population's health outcomes. Population ageing refers to the problem of a growing proportion of older people in a population over time (Banerjee, 2021). SDH refers to the circumstances in which individuals are born, reside, work, and grow older, and these factors profoundly influence their health results (Hamiduzzaman et al., 2021; Saito et al., 2014). As the population ages discussing and analysing these social determinants becomes increasingly important in promoting and ensuring healthy ageing and well-being of elderly people. The present study has used the conceptual and intellectual framework for the bibliometric study which makes it different from previous ageing-related bibliometric research. The present study has contributed to advancing the theoretical progress of the research field being studied through two main approaches. Firstly, it has provided a thorough overview of the study area by summarising and examining key citations, thematic mapping, co-citation and co-occurrence of keywords etc. This synthesis of information will provide a valuable resource for academics and researchers by offering them a guiding framework for future research works. Secondly, it has undertaken the task of identifying and visualizing the predominant motifs that showcase the evolving nature of the subject. These motifs were carefully selected and plotted to illustrate this research field's ongoing trends and development. Doing this allows us to capture the dynamic nature of the subject and provides valuable insight into its progression over time. The bibliometrics study showed that population ageing is significantly impacted by social determinants of health, especially socioeconomic factors. The economic implication of population ageing includes the cost of providing the social support. The growing population of elderly people places a strain on healthcare systems and social security programs (Nawaz et al., 2012; Hamano et al., 2011). This research will assist the government and policymakers to understand the concept and the intricacies and complexities associated with the idea. This study will help gain a deep understanding of the concept, which can further lead to strategic interventions. Moreover, this research will provide managers and future researchers in this field with valuable assistance in identifying sources that can offer practical insights related to this concept which can help them make informed decisions regarding this research field. Our study also assesses the impact and influence of research publications, authors and affiliations of authors in the field of population ageing thus showcasing the visibility and significance of research outputs. By analysing publication patterns, researchers can gain insight into the emerging research topics and trends within this field of study as well as reveal the interconnections and collaborations within the research community. Further research in this field can primarily study the following themes: longevity and healthy ageing, social and economic implications, healthcare and long-term care of elderly people, psychological and cognitive well-being, intergenerational relationships and social participation, ageing and technology and global perspective on population ageing. Policymakers and healthcare practitioners may acquire knowledge about the variables impacting the health of older people by doing a bibliometric evaluation of the scientific literature on socioeconomic determinants of health in an ageing population. A thorough grasp of the social, economic, and environmental factors that affect the ageing population's well-being may be obtained from this examination. The results of this study may be used by legislators and healthcare professionals to create interventions and health policies that are specifically tailored to the demands of the ageing population. Comprehending the societal factors involved facilitates the creation of focused approaches intended to encourage age-appropriate living, avert chronic illnesses, and enhance the general well-being of elderly people. By integrating pertinent results into their curriculum, educational institutions and training programmes in the healthcare industry might reap benefits from this bibliometric research. In light of an ageing population, this study provides a road map for developing instructional materials and training programmes that highlight the socioeconomic determinants of health. This may improve the expertise and abilities of medical personnel, equipping them to provide elder patients with more efficient and comprehensive treatment. Future studies on ageing and health may be guided by the conclusions drawn from this bibliometric review. Researchers and academics may utilise this data to highlight topics for more research, find gaps in the existing literature, and advance the field's continuing body of knowledge. Researcher collaboration may promote a more cohesive and productive research community when it involves scholars with similar interests, as revealed by bibliometric trends. A comprehensive knowledge of the socioeconomic variables influencing the health of the ageing population may also be beneficial to local communities and public health programmes. The findings of this study have the potential to impact community-based initiatives and programmes that support social inclusion, healthy ageing, and healthcare service accessibility. Stakeholders may collaborate to create age-friendly settings that promote older persons' well-being by incorporating these results into community planning.

The role of social inequalities in shaping health outcomes among older adults

The cumulative impact of social inequalities over a lifetime significantly affect the health outcomes of older adults. Aging and health concerns cannot be reduced to purely biological processes or to the availability of health care. The health of older people is determined by their position within social structures. The absence of social status, education, social inclusiveness, and the absence of trust in social institutions all determine the health of older people. Additionally, society provides more equitable health sustainment opportunities, and these factors frequently create inequitable distributions of health and health care, both in quantity and quality. Among the older populations, the health impact of social inequalities is greatest in the area of economic status. The economic level of a person and the slimness of their financial resources present the most hurdles to obtaining the most basic health-sustaining and health-promoting social resources, including health care, food, housing, and any other resource that is a social determinant of health. Especially serious is the economic disadvantage that results from postponing the obtaining of health services, from not utilizing, and from informal, and often, inadequate, caregiving. The accumulation of these disadvantages is a common health outcome that is chronic disease, and poor quality of life in old age. Educational attainment significantly impacts health outcomes. More education usually means that one has better health literacy which aids in comprehending health information and navigating healthcare systems. Educated people are more likely to engage in preventative health behaviors and to follow advice from health professionals. Educated people are also more likely to access the needed health care services. On the other hand, older adults with less education often have a harder time understanding the instructions that health professionals give, and self-managing chronic health conditions. The also have problems taking advantage of the health services that are available. Consequently, the inequalities in education that we see in the older population have a direct impact on health and longevity. Health inequalities are compounded by social exclusion and isolation of older adults. Post-retirement, many elderly people lose their social networks, especially after losing family members or as a result of personal mobility limitations. Social isolation is a major risk factor for depression and an accelerant of cognitive decline. Social isolation also impacts physical health negatively. health. Older people in marginalized groups, such as ethnic minorities, people from low socioeconomic status, and those living in rural areas are more likely to experience social isolation. These older adults also encounter additional challenges to accessing health care and social services, which contribute to the above psychological stress. Excluded elderly people are more health problems and have less opportunities for healthy ageing. How much people trust institutions affects how much the use the healthcare available to them. Older adults may avoid seeking medical attention or following treatment plans when trust in healthcare systems and public institutions is absent. Historical discrimination and inequitable distribution of resources, negative contacts with public institutions, and inequitable health care provision create an environment of mistrust, which is most pronounced in marginalized groups. Such mistrust lessens the impact of healthcare interventions and exacerbates existing health inequities.

6. CONCLUSION AND LIMITATION OF THE STUDY

This research paper aimed to investigate the past literature on population ageing and social determinants of health for the last 13 years. To assess the progress of the field a comprehensive bibliometric analysis of 164 research articles from 64 journals published between 2010 and 2022 was conducted. The study utilized several bibliometric methods to address the predetermined research objectives. To answer the first two objectives of the study citation analysis was used, the study result showed that a consistent increase can be observed in the number of publications in this field of research over the past couple of years. There was a significant rise in the number of journals published in this research field over the year, reaching its peak in 2019. This indicates an increase in research interest in his area. The h-index and number of publications were observed during this time period and Wu Y AND Zhang Y have been the most influential authors in this field. The publication journal that was the most influential in this research field for the last decade was PLOS ONE with 33 publications. With respect to affiliations that were most influential, the University of California tops the list of the most influential affiliation with a total of 19 publications so far. Finally, the United States of America was the most impactful country regarding the overall production of publications. These findings are consistent with (Mahmood & Dhakal, 2022) they acknowledged the contribution of developed economies in producing ageing population and society-related studies and (Gu et al., 2019). The study shows that the number of publications in the population ageing field is increasing but still scattered. Population ageing is a multifaceted and complex phenomenon that requires proactive and comprehensive responses from researchers, government and society as a whole. By embracing the opportunities and addressing the challenges associated with an ageing population, we can create an inclusive and sustainable society that can be beneficial to people of all ages. Thus, it is crucial to acknowledge and value the contributions of elderly people while striving for better policies and practices that can promote elderly health, well-being and active participation in all aspects of life. In spite of the fact that this study is of high quality, that it is quite relevant, and that it covers a wide scope, some limitations must be noted. The most notable limitation of the research is that it only makes use of a single database for the collection and compilation of data. Excluding additional databases leads to the removal of potentially significant articles that could be very helpful to the field of population ageing. This is true despite the fact that the majority of bibliometric studies in the published literature use a single database for analysis in order to avoid duplicating findings. Because of this, the fact that the research only referred to a single database is a major limitation. Another one of this study's shortcomings is that it does not adequately take into account the contextualization of the citation structure of the articles. Even if the kind of citation structure used in the research on population ageing is presented in this study in a manner that is crystal obvious, the context and goal of using such a structure cannot be deduced from the findings of this research.

ACKNOWLEDGMENT

The study is supported by the Indian Council of Social Science Research (ICSSR) under the Doctoral Fellowship program.

REFERENCES

Alang, S., McAlpine, D. D., & Hardeman, R. (2020). Police Brutality and Mistrust in Medical Institutions. *Journal of Racial and Ethnic Health Disparities*, *7*(4), 760–768. DOI: 10.1007/s40615-020-00706-w PMID: 31989532

Aria, M., & Cuccurullo, C. (2017). bibliometrix: An R-tool for comprehensive science mapping analysis. *Journal of Informetrics*, *11*(4), 959–975. DOI: 10.1016/j.joi.2017.08.007

Banerjee, S. (2021). Determinants of rural-urban differential in healthcare utilization among older people population in India. *BMC Public Health*, *21*(1), 1–18. DOI: 10.1186/s12889-021-10773-1 PMID: 33388037

Bhat, A. A., Rashid, I., Hassan, S. U., & Kansra, P. (2023). Social determinants of health and health outcomes: a bibliographic review of the scientific literature from 2000 to 2021. *Global Knowledge, Memory and Communication*.

Biancone, P., Saiti, B., Petricean, D., & Chmet, F. (2020). The bibliometric analysis of Islamic banking and finance. *Journal of Islamic Accounting and Business Research*, *11*(9), 2069–2086. DOI: 10.1108/JIABR-08-2020-0235

Cash-Gibson, L., Rojas-Gualdrón, D. F., Pericàs, J. M., & Benach, J. (2018). Inequalities in global health inequalities research: A 50-year bibliometric analysis (1966-2015). *PLoS One*, *13*(1), 1–22. DOI: 10.1371/journal.pone.0191901 PMID: 29385197

Cobo, M. J., López-Herrera, A. G., Herrera-Viedma, E., & Herrera, F. (2011). An approach for detecting, quantifying, and visualizing the evolution of a research field: A practical application to the Fuzzy Sets Theory field. *Journal of Informetrics*, *5*(1), 146–166. DOI: 10.1016/j.joi.2010.10.002

Courtney, M. G., Roberts, J., & Godde, K. (2022). How social/environmental determinants and inflammation affect salivary telomere length among middle-older adults in the health and retirement study. *Scientific Reports*, *12*(1), 1–12. DOI: 10.1038/s41598-022-12742-z PMID: 34992227

De Castro, V. F., & Frazzon, E. M. (2017). Benchmarking of best practices: An overview of the academic literature. *Benchmarking, 24*(3), 750–774. DOI: 10.1108/BIJ-03-2016-0031

Domènech-Abella, J., Mundó, J., Leonardi, M., Chatterji, S., Tobiasz-Adamczyk, B., Koskinen, S., Ayuso-Mateos, J. L., & Haro, J. M. (2018). The association between socioeconomic status and depression among older adults in Finland, Poland and Spain: A comparative cross-sectional study of distinct measures and pathways. *Journal of Affective Disorders, 241*, 311–318. DOI: 10.1016/j.jad.2018.08.077 PMID: 30142590

Donthu, N., Kumar, S., Mukherjee, D., Pandey, N., & Lim, W. M. (2021). How to conduct a bibliometric analysis: An overview and guidelines. *Journal of Business Research, 133*, 285–296. DOI: 10.1016/j.jbusres.2021.04.070

Evashwick, C., Rowe, G., Diehr, P., & Branch, L. (1984). Factors explaining the use of health care services by older people. *Health Services Research, 19*(3), 357–382. http://www.ncbi.nlm.nih.gov/pubmed/6746297%0Ahttp://www.pubmedcentral.nih.gov/articlerender.fcgi?artid=PMC1068819 PMID: 6746297

Feng, Z., Jones, K., & Phillips, D. R. (2019). Social exclusion, self-rated health and depression among older people in China: Evidence from a national survey of older persons. *Archives of Gerontology and Geriatrics, 82*, 238–244. DOI: 10.1016/j.archger.2019.02.016 PMID: 30875525

Fernández-Olano, C., Hidalgo, J. D. L. T., Cerdá-Díaz, R., Requena-Gallego, M., Sánchez-Castaño, C., Urbistondo-Cascales, L., & Otero-Puime, A. (2006). Factors associated with health care utilization by older people in a public health care system. *Health Policy (Amsterdam), 75*(2), 131–139. DOI: 10.1016/j.healthpol.2005.02.005 PMID: 15961181

Gálvez-Sánchez, F. J., Lara-Rubio, J., Verdú-Jóver, A. J., & Meseguer-Sánchez, V. (2021). Research advances on financial inclusion: A bibliometric analysis. *Sustainability (Basel), 13*(6), 1–19. DOI: 10.3390/su13063156

Gonzlez-Gonzlez, C., Snchez-García, S., Jurez-Cedillo, T., Rosas-Carrasco, O., Gutiérrez-Robledo, L. M., & García-P a, C. (2011). Health care utilization in older people Mexican population: Expenditures and determinants. *BMC Public Health, 11*(1), 192. Advance online publication. DOI: 10.1186/1471-2458-11-192

Goyal, A., & Kajal, K. (2014). Prevalence of depression in elderly population in the southern part of Punjab. *Journal of Family Medicine and Primary Care, 3*(4), 359. DOI: 10.4103/2249-4863.148109 PMID: 25657943

Goyal, P., Rahman, Z., & Kazmi, A. A. (2013). Corporate sustainability performance and firm performance research: Literature review and future research agenda. *Management Decision*, *51*(2), 361–379. DOI: 10.1108/00251741311301867

Graue, M., Dunning, T., Hausken, M. F., & Rokne, B. (2013). Challenges in managing elderly people with diabetes in primary care settings in Norway. *Scandinavian Journal of Primary Health Care*, *31*(4), 241–247. DOI: 10.3109/02813432.2013.854445 PMID: 24205973

Groos, O. V., & Pritchard, A. (1969). Documentation notes. *The Journal of Documentation*, *25*(4), 344–349. DOI: 10.1108/eb026482

Gu, Y. H., Bai, J. B., Chen, X. L., Wu, W. W., Liu, X. X., & Tan, X. D. (2019). Healthy aging: A bibliometric analysis of the literature. *Experimental Gerontology*, *116*(115), 93–105. DOI: 10.1016/j.exger.2018.11.014 PMID: 30590123

Hamano, T., Yamasaki, M., Fujisawa, Y., Ito, K., Nabika, T., & Shiwaku, K. (2011). Social capital and psychological distress of elderly in Japanese rural communities. *Stress and Health*, *27*(2), 163–169. DOI: 10.1002/smi.1324 PMID: 27486618

Hamiduzzaman, M., De Bellis, A., Abigail, W., Kalaitzidis, E., & Harrington, A. (2021). The World Is Not Mine – Barriers to Healthcare Access for Bangladeshi Rural Elderly Women. *Journal of Cross-Cultural Gerontology*, *36*(1), 69–89. DOI: 10.1007/s10823-020-09420-w PMID: 33449242

Haslam, C., Cruwys, T., & Haslam, S. A. (2014). "The we's have it": Evidence for the distinctive benefits of group engagement in enhancing cognitive health in aging. *Social Science & Medicine*, *120*, 57–66. DOI: 10.1016/j.socscimed.2014.08.037 PMID: 25222136

Hayward, M. D., Hummer, R. A., & Sasson, I. (2015). Trends and group differences in the association between educational attainment and U.S. adult mortality: Implications for understanding education's causal influence. *Social Science & Medicine*, *127*, 8–18. DOI: 10.1016/j.socscimed.2014.11.024 PMID: 25440841

Hellström, Y., & Hallberg, I. R. (2001). Perspectives of elderly people receiving home help on health, care and quality of life. *Health & Social Care in the Community*, *9*(2), 61–71. DOI: 10.1046/j.1365-2524.2001.00282.x PMID: 11560722

Hood, W. W., & Wilson, C. S. (2001). The literature of bibliometrics, scientometrics, and informetrics. *Scientometrics*, *52*(2), 291–314. DOI: 10.1023/A:1017919924342

Iliffe, S., Kharicha, K., Harari, D., Swift, C., Goodman, C., & Manthorpe, J. (2010). User involvement in the development of a health promotion technology for older people: Findings from the SWISH project. *Health & Social Care in the Community, 18*(2), 147–159. DOI: 10.1111/j.1365-2524.2009.00882.x PMID: 19708867

Kabayama, M., Watanabe, C., Ryuno, H., & Kamide, K. (2017). Positive and negative associations of individual social capital factors with health among community-dwelling older people. *Geriatrics & Gerontology International, 17*(12), 2427–2434. DOI: 10.1111/ggi.13094 PMID: 28643419

Kendig, H., Gong, C. H., Yiengprugsawan, V., Silverstein, M., & Nazroo, J. (2017). Life course influences on later life health in China: Childhood health exposure and socioeconomic mediators during adulthood. *SSM - Population Health, 3*, 795–802. DOI: 10.1016/j.ssmph.2017.10.001 PMID: 29349264

Kessler, M. M. (1963). Bibliographic Coupling Between Scientific Papers Received. *Journal of the Association for Information Science and Technology, 14*(1), 10–25.

Maheshwari, S. K., Chaturvedi, R., & Sharma, P. (2021). Effectiveness of psycho-educational intervention on psychological distress and self-esteem among resident elderly: A study from old age homes of Punjab, India. *Clinical Epidemiology and Global Health, 11*, 100733. DOI: 10.1016/j.cegh.2021.100733

Mahmood, M. N., & Dhakal, S. P. (2022). Ageing population and society: A scientometric analysis. *Quality & Quantity*, (August). Advance online publication. DOI: 10.1007/s11135-022-01509-3 PMID: 36039154

Majumder, S., Aghayi, E., Noferesti, M., Memarzadeh-Tehran, H., Mondal, T., Pang, Z., & Deen, M. J. (2017). Smart homes for elderly healthcare—Recent advances and research challenges. *Sensors (Basel), 17*(11), 2496. Advance online publication. DOI: 10.3390/s17112496 PMID: 29088123

Mishra, H. G., Pandita, S., Bhat, A. A., Mishra, R. K., & Sharma, S. (2022). Tourism and carbon emissions: a bibliometric review of the last three decades: 1990–2021. *Tourism Review, 77*(2), 636–658. DOI: 10.1108/TR-07-2021-0310

Nawaz, N., Maann, A. A., Akhter, S., & Ashraf, I. (2012). Health status of elderly women in socio-economic and cultural context in Punjab, Pakistan. *Sarhad Journal of Agriculture, 28*(2), 373–378. http://www.aup.edu.pk/sj_pdf/HEALTH STATUS OF ELDERLY WOMEN -254-2011.pdf

Naz, L., Ghimire, U., & Zainab, A. (2021). Behavioral factors associated with utilization of healthcare services among elderly in Pakistan: Evidence from a nationally representative survey. *BMC Geriatrics*, *21*(1), 1–11. DOI: 10.1186/s12877-021-02005-3 PMID: 33435874

Niederstrasser, N. G., Rogers, N. T., & Bandelow, S. (2019). Determinants of frailty development and progression using a multidimensional frailty index: Evidence from the english longitudinal study of ageing. *PLoS One*, *14*(10), 1–16. DOI: 10.1371/journal.pone.0223799 PMID: 31665163

Pasqualini, M., Lanari, D., Minelli, L., Pieroni, L., & Salmasi, L. (2017). Health and income inequalities in Europe: What is the role of circumstances? *Economics and Human Biology*, *26*, 164–173. DOI: 10.1016/j.ehb.2017.04.002 PMID: 28445843

Pyle, M. A., & Stoller, E. P. (2003). Oral Health Disparities Among older people: Interdisciplinary Challenges for the Future. *Journal of Dental Education*, *67*(12), 1327–1336. DOI: 10.1002/j.0022-0337.2003.67.12.tb03726.x PMID: 14733265

Radford, K., Lavrencic, L. M., Delbaere, K., Draper, B., Cumming, R., Daylight, G., Mack, H. A., Chalkley, S., Bennett, H., Garvey, G., Hill, T. Y., Lasschuit, D., & Broe, G. A. (2019). Factors Associated with the High Prevalence of Dementia in Older Aboriginal Australians. *Journal of Alzheimer's Disease*, *70*(1), S75–S85. DOI: 10.3233/JAD-180573 PMID: 30507573

Sahoo, H., Govil, D., James, K. S., & Prasad, R. D. (2021). Health issues, health care utilization and health care expenditure among elderly in India: Thematic review of literature. *Aging and Health Research*, *1*(2), 100012. DOI: 10.1016/j.ahr.2021.100012

Saito, M., Kondo, K., Kondo, N., Abe, A., Ojima, T., & Suzuki, K. (2014). Relative deprivation, poverty, and subjective health: JAGES cross-sectional study. *PLoS One*, *9*(10), e111169. Advance online publication. DOI: 10.1371/journal.pone.0111169 PMID: 25350284

Sanjel, S., Mudbhari, N., Risal, A., & Khanal, K. (2012). The utilization of health care services and their determinants among older people population of Dhulikhel Municipality". *Kathmandu University Medical Journal*, *10*(37), 34–39. DOI: 10.3126/kumj.v10i1.6911 PMID: 22971859

Schenker, M., & Da Costa, D. H. (2019). Advances and challenges of health care of older people population with chronic diseases in primary health care. *Ciencia & Saude Coletiva*, *24*(4), 1369–1380. DOI: 10.1590/1413-81232018244.01222019 PMID: 31066839

Schnitzer, S., Blüher, S., Teti, A., Schaeffner, E., Ebert, N., Martus, P., Suhr, R., & Kuhlmey, A. (2020). Risk Profiles for Care Dependency: Cross-Sectional Findings of a Population-Based Cohort Study in Germany. *Journal of Aging and Health*, *32*(5), 352–360. DOI: 10.1177/0898264318822364 PMID: 30658538

Tan, V., Chen, C., & Merchant, R. A. (2022). "Association of social determinants of health with frailty, cognitive impairment, and self-rated health among older adults". *PLoS ONE*, Vol.*17*, pp. 1–18. Available at: DOI: 10.1371/journal.pone.0277290

Vaishnav, L. M., Joshi, S. H., Joshi, A. U., & Mehendale, A. M. (2022). The National Programme for Health Care of older people: A Review of its Achievements and Challenges in India. *Annals of Geriatric Medicine and Research*, *26*(3), 183–195. DOI: 10.4235/agmr.22.0062 PMID: 36039665

van Eck, N. J., & Waltman, L. (2010). Software survey: VOSviewer, a computer program for bibliometric mapping. *Scientometrics*, *84*(2), 523–538. DOI: 10.1007/s11192-009-0146-3 PMID: 20585380

Verma, M., Grover, S., Singh, T., Dahiya, N., & Nehra, R. (2020). Screening for cognitive impairment among older people attending the noncommunicable diseases clinics in a rural area of Punjab, North India". *Asian Journal of Psychiatry*, *50*, 102001. DOI: 10.1016/j.ajp.2020.102001 PMID: 32248085

Verma, M., Grover, S., Tripathy, J. P., Singh, T., Nagaraja, S. B., Kathirvel, S., Singh, G., & Nehra, R. (2019). Co-existing non-communicable diseases and mental illnesses amongst older people in Punjab, India. *European Endocrinology*, *15*(2), 106–112. DOI: 10.17925/EE.2019.15.2.106 PMID: 31616502

Wilson, T. L., Scala-Foley, M., Kunkel, S. R., & Brewster, A. L. (2020). Fast-track Innovation: Area Agencies on Aging Respond to the COVID-19 Pandemic". *Journal of Aging & Social Policy*, *32*(4), 432–438. DOI: 10.1080/08959420.2020.1774313 PMID: 32515297

Yunus, N. M., Abd Manaf, N. H., Omar, A., Juhdi, N., Omar, M. A., & Salleh, M. (2017). "Determinants of healthcare utilisation among older people in Malaysia". In *Institutions and Economies*, Vol. 9, No. 3, pp. 117–142).

KEY TERMS AND DEFINITIONS

Bibliometric Analysis: Bibliometric analysis involves looking at quantifiable aspects of a field of research, such as scientific publications, and attempting to measure these aspects to make inferences about, and understand, the structural and developmental aspects of a research domain

Co-citation Analysis: Co-citation analysis identifies perceived intellectual relationships and dominant research clusters within a discipline by measuring how frequently two documents, authors, or journals are cited together.

Healthy Ageing: Healthy ageing is the ability to continue and sustain functional capability, good physical health, sound mental health, and social engagement to help individuals to live longer, healthier and more active lives.

Population Ageing: Population ageing refers to the increasing proportion of older people within a population over time due to declining fertility and increasing life expectancy.

Social Inequality in Health: Social inequality in health refers to the systematic variation in health status and health care accessibility across different social groups.

Social Support: Social support identifies the emotional, informational, and practical aid assistance from family, friends, and community networks that help individuals cope with stress and enhance mental and physical health, especially among the elderly.

Socio Determinants of Health (SDH): It is the social, economic, environmental and political conditions in which an individual is born, lives, works, and ages. It influences the health outcome and access to care.

Socio-economic Status: An individual's socioeconomic status (SES) is their social and economic standing, and is most often assessed by one's income, level of education, and type of occupation.

Compilation of References

Abdulwahab, L. O., & Azam, H. (2026). Platform Work in Europe's Green and Care Economies: Regulatory Pathways for Sustainability, Social Protection, and Fair Work. In *Regulating the Gig Economy in the European Union: Challenges, Innovations, and Global Impacts* (pp. 99–124). IGI Global Scientific Publishing. https://www.igi-global.com/chapter/platform-work-in-europes-green-and-care-economies/395612

Abdulwahab, L. O., Daniel, O., Gul, A., & Bubari, H. U. (2026). The Economic Impact of Digital Health Innovations on Disease Prevention: Cost-Effectiveness, ROI, and Policy Implications. In *Reshaping Health Promotion and Disease Prevention Through Digital Innovation* (pp. 29–56). IGI Global Scientific Publishing. DOI: 10.4018/979-8-3373-3531-5.ch002

Abio, G., Patxot, C., Souto, G., & Istenič, T. (2021). The role of gender, education and family in the welfare organization: Disaggregating National Transfer Accounts. *The Journal of the Economics of Ageing*, *20*, 100348. Advance online publication. DOI: 10.1016/j.jeoa.2021.100348

Abrha, T., & Weldeyohans, B. (2025). The Role of Human Capital in Economic Development: A Theoretical Analysis. *Journal of Human Resource Management*. DOI: 10.11648/j.jhrm.20251302.11

Acar, E. Ö. (2016). Türkiye'de Yapısal Dönüşüm ve İşgücü Piyasaları Üzerine Bir İnceleme. *Pamukkale Üniversitesi Sosyal Bilimler Enstitüsü Dergisi*, *25*, 53–72.

Acemoglu, D., & Restrepo, P. (2017). Secular stagnation? The effect of aging on economic growth in the age of automation. *The American Economic Review*, *107*(5), 174–179. DOI: 10.1257/aer.p20171101

Adair, P., AlAzzawi, S., & Hlasny, V. (2024). Fostering decent jobs, formalising informal employment and spurring job mobility in MENA countries. *Economic Notes*, *53*(2), e12240. DOI: 10.1111/ecno.12240

Ademi, Z., Ackerman, I., Zomer, E., & Liew, D. (2021). Productivity-Adjusted Life-Years: A New Metric for Quantifying Disease Burden. *PharmacoEconomics*, *39*(3), 271–273. DOI: 10.1007/s40273-020-00999-z PMID: 33428173

Ahmad, M., Peng, T., Awan, A., & Ahmed, Z. (2023). Policy framework considering resource curse, renewable energy transition, and institutional issues: Fostering sustainable development and sustainable natural resource consumption practices. *Resources Policy*, *86*, 104173. DOI: 10.1016/j.resourpol.2023.104173

Ahmed, M., & Ahmed, M. J. (2026). Sustainable Industrial Operations Through IoT-Generated Big Data Insights. In *Sustainable Operations in the Age of AI and Big Data* (pp. 37–82). DOI: 10.4018/979-8-2600-0216-2.ch002

Ahmed, M., Al Amareen, O. S., & Arafat, Y. (2026). Harnessing Big Data for Reverse Logistics and Waste Management: Pathways to Sustainable Supply Chains. In *Enhancing Sustainability in Global Supply Chains With Big Data Analytics* (pp. 175–210). IGI Global Scientific Publishing. DOI: 10.4018/979-8-3373-6896-2.ch006

Ahmed, F., Kousar, S., Pervaiz, A., Trinidad-Segovia, J. E., del Pilar Casado-Belmonte, M., & Ahmed, W. (2022). Role of green innovation, trade and energy to promote green economic growth: A case of South Asian Nations. *Environmental Science and Pollution Research International*, *29*(5), 6871–6885. DOI: 10.1007/s11356-021-15881-4 PMID: 34462851

Akaike, H. (2003). A new look at the statistical model identification. *IEEE Transactions on Automatic Control*, *19*(6), 716–723. DOI: 10.1109/TAC.1974.1100705

Akkermans, J., de Lange, A. H., van der Heijden, B. I., Kooij, D. T., Jansen, P. G., & Dikkers, J. S. (2016). What about time? Examining chronological and subjective age and their relation to work motivation. *Career Development International*, *21*(4), 419–439. DOI: 10.1108/CDI-04-2016-0063

Alang, S., McAlpine, D. D., & Hardeman, R. (2020). Police Brutality and Mistrust in Medical Institutions. *Journal of Racial and Ethnic Health Disparities*, *7*(4), 760–768. DOI: 10.1007/s40615-020-00706-w PMID: 31989532

Alavi, K., Sutan, R., Shahar, S., Manaf, M. R. A., Jaafar, M. H., Maulud, K. A. A., Embong, Z., Keliwon, K., & Markom, R. (2022). Connecting the Dots between Social Care and Healthcare for the Sustainability Development of Older Adult in Asia: A Scoping Review. *Sustainability (Basel)*, *14*(5), 2573. Advance online publication. DOI: 10.3390/su14052573

Ali, S. B., & Frank, H. A. (2018). Retirement Planning Decisions: Choices Between Defined Benefit and Defined Contribution Plans. *American Review of Public Administration*, *49*(2), 218–235. DOI: 10.1177/0275074018765809

Alsaeed, T., Washington, T., & Xia, B. (2025). Comprehensive analysis of Australia's aged care system to inform policies for a sustainable future. *Frontiers in Public Health*, *13*, 1525988. Advance online publication. DOI: 10.3389/fpubh.2025.1525988 PMID: 40290496

Amani, J., & Fussy, D. S. (2022). Retirement planning mistakes undermining the post-retirement adjustment and well-being. *Educational Gerontology*, *49*(2), 158–173. DOI: 10.1080/03601277.2022.2096306

Ambrosini, M. (2018). Rowing upstream: The resilience of immigrants in the long Italian recession. *Sociologia del Lavoro*, (149), 201–214. DOI: 10.3280/SL2018-149S14

Amorim, S. M., & França, L. H. (2019). Reasons for Retirement and Retirement Satisfaction. Psicologia: Teoria E Pesquisa, 35. https://doi.org/DOI: 10.1590/0102.3772e3558

Andabayeva, G., Movchun, V., Dubovik, M., Kurpebayeva, G., & Cai, X. (2024). Labor market dynamics in developing countries: Analysis of employment transformation at the macro-level. *Journal of Innovation and Entrepreneurship*, *13*(1), 65. DOI: 10.1186/s13731-024-00417-0

André, C., Gal, P., & Schief, M. (2024). Enhancing productivity and growth in an ageing society: Key mechanisms and policy options (OECD Economics Department Working Papers No. 1807). OECD Publishing. DOI: 10.1787/18151973

Aria, M., & Cuccurullo, C. (2017). bibliometrix: An R-tool for comprehensive science mapping analysis. *Journal of Informetrics*, *11*(4), 959–975. DOI: 10.1016/j.joi.2017.08.007

Arnberg, K., Larsen, E., & Östman, A.-C. (2022). Gender and economic history in the Nordic countries. *The Scandinavian Economic History Review*, *70*(2), 113–122. DOI: 10.1080/03585522.2022.2078403

Atta, N., & Sharifi, A. (2024). A systematic literature review of the relationship between the rule of law and environmental sustainability. *Sustainable Development (Bradford)*, *32*(6), 7051–7068. DOI: 10.1002/sd.3087

Auerbach, A., & Kotlikoff, L. (1987). *Dynamic fiscal policy*. Cambridge University Press.

Austen, S., & Giles, M. (2003). The Likely Effects of Ageing on Women's Involvement in the Paid Workforce. *Australian Bulletin of Labour, 29*(3), 257–278.

Awan, U., Sroufe, R., & Shahbaz, M. (2021). Industry 4.0 and the circular economy: A literature review and recommendations for future research. *Business Strategy and the Environment*, *30*(4), 2038–2060. DOI: 10.1002/bse.2731

Ayerbe, E., Berecibar, M., Clark, S., Franco, A. A., & Ruhland, J. (2022). Digitalization of Battery Manufacturing: Current Status, Challenges, and Opportunities. *Advanced Energy Materials*, *12*(17), 2102696. Advance online publication. DOI: 10.1002/aenm.202102696

Ayub Khan, A., Ali Laghari, A., Rashid, M., Li, H., Rehman Javed, A., & Reddy Gadekallu, T. (2023). Artificial intelligence and blockchain technology for secure smart grid and power distribution Automation: A State-of-the-Art Review. *Sustainable Energy Technologies and Assessments*, *57*, 103282. DOI: 10.1016/j.seta.2023.103282

Azadehyaei, H., Zhang, Y., Song, Y., Gottschalk, T., & Anderson, G. S. (2025). Economic Evaluation of Proactive PTSI Mitigation Programs for Public Safety Personnel and Frontline Healthcare Professionals: A Systematic Review and Meta-Analysis. *International Journal of Environmental Research and Public Health*, *22*(5), 809. Advance online publication. DOI: 10.3390/ijerph22050809 PMID: 40427922

Azhar, N., & Omar, A. (2025). AGING WORKFORCE IN MALAYSIA: NAVIGATING CHALLENGES AND SHAPING POLICIES. *Quantum Journal of Social Sciences and Humanities*. DOI: 10.55197/qjssh.v6i2.615

Baharin, R., & Saad, S. (2018). Ageing population and health care expenditure: Evidence using time series analysis. *Geografia, 14*(4).

Bahrami, B. (2001). Factors affecting faculty retirement decisions. *The Social Science Journal, 38*(2), 297–305. DOI: 10.1016/S0362-3319(01)00114-8

Baker, M., Gruber, J., & Milligan, K. (2010). The Interaction of Youth and Elderly Labor Markets in Canada. In Gruber, J., & Wise, D. A. (Eds.), *Social Security Programs and Retirement around the World: The Relationship to Youth Employment* (pp. 77–97). University of Chicago Press., https://www.nber.org/system/files/chapters/c8252/c8252.pdf DOI: 10.7208/chicago/9780226309507.003.0003

Ballout, S. (2025). Trauma, Mental Health Workforce Shortages, and Health Equity: A Crisis in Public Health. *International Journal of Environmental Research and Public Health*, *22*(4), 620. Advance online publication. DOI: 10.3390/ijerph22040620 PMID: 40283844

Banerjee, S. (2021). Determinants of rural-urban differential in healthcare utilization among older people population in India. *BMC Public Health*, *21*(1), 1–18. DOI: 10.1186/s12889-021-10773-1 PMID: 33388037

Baruch, Y., Sayce, S., & Gregoriou, A. (2014). Retirement in a global labour market: A call for abolishing the fixed retirement age. *Personnel Review*, *43*(3), 464–482. DOI: 10.1108/PR-04-2013-0059

Baybora, D. (2010). Çalışma Yaşamında Yaş Ayrımcılığı ve Amerika Birleşik Devletleri'nde Yaş Ayrımcılığı Düzenlemesi Üzerine. *Çalışma ve Toplum*, 1(24), 1-30.

Bayl-Smith, P. H., & Griffin, B. (2014). Age discrimination in the workplace: Identifying as a late-career worker and its relationship with engagement and intended retirement age. *Journal of Applied Social Psychology*, *44*(9), 588–599. DOI: 10.1111/jasp.12251

Bazzana, D. (2020). Ageing population and pension system sustainability: Reforms and redistributive implications. *Economia Politica (Bologna)*, *37*(3), 971–992. DOI: 10.1007/s40888-020-00183-8

Becker, G. S. (1975). Introduction to the Second Edition, Human Capital: A Theoretical and Empirical Analysis, with Special Reference to Education. In *Human Capital: A Theoretical and Empirical Analysis, with Special Reference to Education, Second Edition* (pp. 1–8). NBER. https://www.nber.org/books-and-chapters/human-capital-theoretical-and-empirical-analysis-special-reference-education-second-edition/introduction-second-edition-human-capital-theoretical-and-empirical-analysis-special-reference

Beier, M., & Kanfer, R. (2009). *Motivation in Training and Development*. Taylor & Francis.

Belgacem, A., & Vacher, J. (2023). *Why is Tunisia's unemployment so high? Evidence from policy factors* (IMF Working Paper No. 2023/219). International Monetary Fund. DOI: 10.5089/9798400257025.001

Betancourt Morales, C. M., & Zartha Sossa, J. W. (2020). Circular economy in Latin America: A systematic literature review. *Business Strategy and the Environment*, *29*(6), 2479–2497. DOI: 10.1002/bse.2515

Bettin, G., & Sacchi, A. (2020). Health spending in Italy: The impact of immigrants. *European Journal of Political Economy*, *65*, 101932. Advance online publication. DOI: 10.1016/j.ejpoleco.2020.101932

Bhat, A. A., Rashid, I., Hassan, S. U., & Kansra, P. (2023). Social determinants of health and health outcomes: a bibliographic review of the scientific literature from 2000 to 2021. *Global Knowledge, Memory and Communication.*

Biancone, P., Saiti, B., Petricean, D., & Chmet, F. (2020). The bibliometric analysis of Islamic banking and finance. *Journal of Islamic Accounting and Business Research, 11*(9), 2069–2086. DOI: 10.1108/JIABR-08-2020-0235

Bloom, D. E., & Finlay, J. E. (2008). Demographic Change and Economic Growth in Asia. *PGDA Working Paper No. 41* (p. 1-31). https://www.hsph.harvard.edu/wp-content/uploads/sites/1288/2013/10/PGDA_WP_41.pdf

Bloom, D. E., & Sousa-Poza, A. (2013). *Ageing and productivity* (No. 63-2012). FZID Discussion Paper. https://www.econstor.eu/bitstream/10419/68601/1/735218625.pdf

Bloom, D. E., Boersch-Supan, A., McGee, P., & Seike, A. (2011). Population aging: facts, challenges, and responses. *Benefits and compensation International, 41*(1), 22.

Bloom, D. E., Cafiero, E., Jané-Llopis, E., Abrahams-Gessel, S., Bloom, L. R., Fathima, S., Feigl, A. B., Gaziano, T., Hamandi, A., & Mowafi, M. (2012). *The global economic burden of noncommunicable diseases*. Program on the Global Demography of Aging. https://ideas.repec.org/p/gdm/wpaper/8712.html?utm_medium=email&utm_source=transaction

Bloom, D. E., Canning, D., & Fink, G. (2011). Implications of Population Aging for Economic Growth. *National Bureau of Economic Research Working Paper Series, No:16705* (p. 1-38). https://www.nber.org/system/files/working_papers/w16705/w16705.pdf

Bloom, D. E., & Canning, D. (2000). The Health and Wealth of Nations. *Science, 287*(5456), 1207–1209. DOI: 10.1126/science.287.5456.1207 PMID: 10712155

Bloom, D. E., Canning, D., & Fink, G. (2010). Implications of population ageing for economic growth. *Oxford Review of Economic Policy, 26*(4), 583–612. DOI: 10.1093/oxrep/grq038

Bloom, D. E., Canning, D., Fink, G., & Finlay, J. E. (2007). Fertility, Female Labor Force Participation, and the Demographic Dividend. *Working Paper Series (National Bureau of Economic Research), 13583*, 1–43. https://www.nber.org/system/files/working_papers/w13583/w13583.pdf. DOI: 10.3386/w13583

Bloom, D. E., & Williamson, J. G. (1998). Demographic transitions and economic miracles in emerging Asia. *The World Bank Economic Review, 12*(3), 419–455. DOI: 10.1093/wber/12.3.419

Bloom, D., Canning, D., & Sevilla, J. (2003). *The demographic dividend: A new perspective on the economic consequences of population change*. Rand Corporation. DOI: 10.7249/MR1274

Boado-Penas, M. del C., Naka, P., & Settergren, O. (2020). Last lessons learned from the Swedish public pension system. In M. Peris-Ortiz, J. álvarez-García, I. Domínguez-Fabián, & P. Devolder (Eds.), *Economic Challenges of Pension Systems: A Sustainability and International Management Perspective* (pp. 235–254). Springer International Publishing. DOI: 10.1007/978-3-030-37912-4_11

Boodoo, C., & Hosein, P. (2024). Global Decline in Fertility Rates: Trends, Influencing Factors, and Future Projections. *IEEE Int. Conf. Technol. Manag., Oper. Decis., ICTMOD*. 2024 IEEE International Conference on Technology Management, Operations and Decisions, ICTMOD 2024. DOI: 10.1109/ICTMOD63116.2024.10878235

Börsch-Supan, A., Ludwig, A., & Winter, J. (2006). Aging, pension reform and capital flows: A multi-country simulation model. *Economica*, *73*, 625–658.

Bossé, R., Aldwin, C. M., Levenson, M. R., & Ekerdt, D. J. (1987). Mental health differences among retirees and workers: Findings from the normative aging study. *Psychology and Aging*, *2*(4), 383–389. DOI: 10.1037/0882-7974.2.4.383 PMID: 3268232

Box, G. E. P., Jenkins, G. M., Reinsel, G. C., & Ljung, G. M. (2015). *Time series analysis: Forecasting and control* (5th ed.). Wiley.

Bravo, J. M., Ayuso, M., Holzmann, R., & Palmer, E. (2023). Intergenerational actuarial fairness when longevity increases: Amending the retirement age. *Insurance, Mathematics & Economics*, *113*, 161–184. DOI: 10.1016/j.insmatheco.2023.08.007

Broer, P., & Westerhout, E. (1997). Pension policies and lifetime uncertainty in an applied general equilibrium model. In Broer, P., & Lassila, J. (Eds.), *Pension policies and public debt in dynamic CGE models* (pp. 110–138). Physica-Verlag.

Brown, A., & Guttmann, R. (2017). Ageing and Labour Supply in Advanced Economies. *Reserve Bank of Australia, Bulletin*, December Quarter, 37-46. https://www.rba.gov.au/publications/bulletin/2017/dec/pdf/bu-1217-5-ageing-and-labour-supply-in-advanced-economies.pdf

Brown, J. R. (2007). *Rational and behavioral perspectives on the role of annuities in retirement planning* (NBER Working Paper No. 13537). National Bureau of Economic Research.

Brown, R. L., Durbin, J., & Evans, J. M. (1975). Techniques for Testing the Constancy of Regression Relationships over Time. *Journal of the Royal Statistical Society. Series B, Statistical Methodology*, *37*(2), 149–192. DOI: 10.1111/j.2517-6161.1975.tb01532.x

Buti, M., Cabezas, J., Domínguez-Hernández, R., Cantero, H., & Casado, M. Á. (2025). Socioeconomic impact of chronic delta hepatitis in Spain: Indirect costs of work absenteeism, presenteeism, and premature mortality. *PLoS One*, *20*(6), e0324834. Advance online publication. DOI: 10.1371/journal.pone.0324834 PMID: 40540477

Cahill, M., Galvin, R., & Pettigrew, J. (2021). The retirement experiences of women academics: A qualitative, descriptive study. *Educational Gerontology*, *47*(7), 297–311. DOI: 10.1080/03601277.2021.1929266

Caldwell, J. C., & Caldwell, B. K. (1997). Asia's demographic transition. *Asian Development Review*, *15*(1), 52–87. DOI: 10.1142/S0116110597000031

Campiglio, L., & Lorenzetti, L. A. (2022). *Generational Economics*., DOI: 10.1007/978-3-031-14541-4_8

Caoyan, Q. I., Ziyi, C. H. E. N., Qiankui, Z. H. A. O., Yuan, S. U. N., Qiang, H. O. U., Guodong, L. U., & Wuzhong, L. I. U. (2024). Research on aging population of working age in North America: Current situation and policies. *Huanjing Yu Zhiye Yixue*, *41*(9), 971–976. DOI: 10.11836/JEOM24171

Carmel, S., & Tur-Sinai, A. (2021). Cognitive decline among European retirees: Impact of early retirement, nation-related and personal characteristics. *Ageing and Society*, *42*(10), 2343–2369. DOI: 10.1017/S0144686X21000064

Carone, G. (2005). Long-term Labour Force Projections for the 25 EU Member States: A Set of Data for Assessing the Economic Impact of Ageing. *European Economy. European Commiission Economic Papers Number 235*. November 2005, ISBN: 92-894-8874-3. https://ec.europa.eu/economy_finance/publications/pages/publication576_en.pdf

Cash-Gibson, L., Rojas-Gualdrón, D. F., Pericàs, J. M., & Benach, J. (2018). Inequalities in global health inequalities research: A 50-year bibliometric analysis (1966-2015). *PLoS One*, *13*(1), 1–22. DOI: 10.1371/journal.pone.0191901 PMID: 29385197

Challoumis, C. (2025). Economocracy: Global Economic Governance. *Economies*, *13*(8), 230. DOI: 10.3390/economies13080230

Chang, D. F., & Lai, K. L. (2019). Trajectory of the population dependency index by using ARIMA models. *ICIC Express Letters. Part B, Applications*, *10*(3), 195–202.

Chateau, J. (2003). *Demographic and economic uncertainties in a large scale computable OLG model* (Working Paper No. 187). University of Washington.

Chavez, H., & Vizuete-Sandoval, D. (2025). Widening the divide, reloading dependency: The political economy of data and AI capability building in Latin America. *Globalizations*, 1–23. Advance online publication. DOI: 10.1080/14747731.2024.2441625

Chen, T., & Guestrin, C. (2016). XGBoost: A scalable tree boosting system. In *Proceedings of the 22nd ACM SIGKDD International Conference on Knowledge Discovery and Data Mining* (pp. 785–794).

Chevalier, A., & Viitanen, T. K. (2002). The Causality between Female Labour Force Participation and The Availability of Childcare. *Applied Economics Letters*, *9*(14), 915–918. DOI: 10.1080/13504850210138469

Chiang, H.-Y., Cheng, Y., Hasselhorn, H. M., Hsu, C.-C., Yang, Y.-C., & Cheng, W.-J. (2025). Influence of pension availability on the association between work conditions and labor market exit for health reasons: Evidence from a Taiwanese older adults cohort. *BMC Public Health*, *25*(1), 1022. Advance online publication. DOI: 10.1186/s12889-025-22215-3 PMID: 40097978

Chichilnisky, G., Hammond, P. J., & Stern, N. (2020). Fundamental utilitarianism and intergenerational equity with extinction discounting. *Social Choice and Welfare*, *54*(2–3), 397–427. DOI: 10.1007/s00355-019-01236-z

Chłoń-Domińczak, A. (2021). Population ageing and financing consumption of the older generation in the european union. In Fischer, G., & Strauss, R. (Eds.), *Europe's Income, Wealth, Consumption, and Inequality* (pp. 395–427). Oxford University Press., DOI: 10.1093/oso/9780197545706.003.0011

Chodavadia, P., Teo, I., Poremski, D., Fung, D. S. S., & Finkelstein, E. A. (2023). Prevalence and economic burden of depression and anxiety symptoms among Singaporean adults: Results from a 2022 web panel. *BMC Psychiatry*, *23*(1), 104. DOI: 10.1186/s12888-023-04581-7 PMID: 36782116

Chybalski, F. (2018). Intergenerational fairness from an economic perspective: Overview of some theoretical and methodological issues. *Business and Economic Horizons*, *14*(2), 268–281. DOI: 10.15208/beh.2018.21

Clarke, D., Doerr, S., Hunter, M., Schmets, G., Soucat, A., & Paviza, A. (2019). The private sector and universal health coverage. *Bulletin of the World Health Organization*, *97*(6), 434–435. DOI: 10.2471/BLT.18.225540 PMID: 31210681

Cobo, M. J., López-Herrera, A. G., Herrera-Viedma, E., & Herrera, F. (2011). An approach for detecting, quantifying, and visualizing the evolution of a research field: A practical application to the Fuzzy Sets Theory field. *Journal of Informetrics*, *5*(1), 146–166. DOI: 10.1016/j.joi.2010.10.002

Comolli, C. L., Neyer, G., Andersson, G., Dommermuth, L., Fallesen, P., Jalovaara, M., Jónsson, A. K., Kolk, M., & Lappegård, T. (2021). Beyond the Economic Gaze: Childbearing During and After Recessions in the Nordic Countries. *European Journal of Population = Revue Européenne de Démographie*, *37*(2), 473–520. DOI: 10.1007/s10680-020-09570-0 PMID: 33230356

Coppola, M., & Wilke, C. B. (2010). How Sensitive are Subjective Retirement Expectations to Increases in the Statutory Retirement Age? The German Case. SSRN Electronic Journal. DOI: 10.2139/ssrn.1701630

Coppola, M., & Wilke, C. B. (2014). At What Age Do You Expect to Retire? Retirement Expectations and Increases in the Statutory Retirement Age. *Fiscal Studies*, *35*(2), 165–188. DOI: 10.1111/j.1475-5890.2014.12027.x

Corak, M. (2020). Intergenerational Mobility: What Do We Care About? What Should We Care About? *The Australian Economic Review*, *53*(2), 230–240. DOI: 10.1111/1467-8462.12372

Cordeiro, R., Fischer, F., & Shinjo, S. (2022). Systemic autoimmune diseases and work outcomes in Brazil: A scoping review. *Revista de Saude Publica*, *56*, 24. Advance online publication. DOI: 10.11606/s1518-8787.2022056003918 PMID: 35476102

Corlet Walker, C., Druckman, A., & Jackson, T. (2021). Welfare systems without economic growth: A review of the challenges and next steps for the field. *Ecological Economics*, *186*, 107066. DOI: 10.1016/j.ecolecon.2021.107066

Costa-Black, K. M., & Arteberry, C. (2020). The social value of Participatory Ergonomics from a practitioner's perspective. *Proceedings of the Human Factors and Ergonomics Society Annual Meeting*, *64*(1), 919–923. DOI: 10.1177/1071181320641219

Courtney, M. G., Roberts, J., & Godde, K. (2022). How social/environmental determinants and inflammation affect salivary telomere length among middle-older adults in the health and retirement study. *Scientific Reports*, *12*(1), 1–12. DOI: 10.1038/s41598-022-12742-z PMID: 34992227

Crawshaw, P., Gray, J., Haighton, C., & Lloyd, S. (2024). Health inequalities and health-related economic inactivity: Why good work needs good health. *Public Health in Practice (Oxford, England)*, *8*, 100555. Advance online publication. DOI: 10.1016/j.puhip.2024.100555 PMID: 39559489

Cremer, H., & Pestieau, P. (2010). Longevity and annuities: An introduction. *Journal of Public Economic Theory*, *12*(1), 1–5.

Cristea, M., Noja, G. G., Stefea, P., & Sala, A. L. (2020). The Impact of Population Aging and Public Health Support on EU Labor Markets. *International Journal of Environmental Research and Public Health*, *17*(4), 1439. DOI: 10.3390/ijerph17041439 PMID: 32102277

Crossdale, R., & Penning, N. (2024). THE ROLE OF HEALTH IN RETIREMENT PLANNING TOWARDS EXTENDED WORKING LIVES. *Innovation in Aging*, *8*(Supplement_1), 1219–1219. DOI: 10.1093/geroni/igae098.3903

Cupák, A., Kolev, G. I., & Brokešová, Z. (2019). Financial literacy and voluntary savings for retirement: Novel causal evidence. *European Journal of Finance*, *25*(16), 1606–1625. DOI: 10.1080/1351847X.2019.1641123

Dąbrowska, A., Fandrejewska, A., Stańczyk, E., & Szalonka, K. (2025). *Consumer and Innovations in e-Health Services: Examples of European Countries*. Taylor and Francis., DOI: 10.4324/9781003507307

Damasceno, J. O., Batista, C. P., & Oliveira, A. M. C. (2021). Labor reform and its implications for workers' health. *Revista de Direito Sanitario*, *21*. Advance online publication. DOI: 10.11606/issn.2316-9044.rdisan.2021.156343

Danladi, S., Prasad, M. S. V., Modibbo, U. M., Ahmadi, S. A., & Ghasemi, P. (2023). Attaining Sustainable Development Goals through Financial Inclusion: Exploring Collaborative Approaches to Fintech Adoption in Developing Economies. *Sustainability (Basel)*, *15*(17), 13039. DOI: 10.3390/su151713039

Das, S., Mourmouras, A., & Rangazas, P. (2024). *Overlapping-Generations Model of Economic Growth*., DOI: 10.1007/978-3-031-59728-2_2

Dave, D., Rashad, I., & Spasojevic, J. (2008). The Effects of Retirement on Physical and Mental Health Outcomes. *Southern Economic Journal*, *75*(2), 497–523. DOI: 10.1002/j.2325-8012.2008.tb00916.x

Daviaud, E., Kelly, G., Cornell, J., Geffen, L., & Solanki, G. (2019). Population ageing in South Africa: Trends, impact, and challenges for the health sector. *South African Health Review*, *2019*(1), 175–182. PMID: 34671174

Dax, T., & Copus, A. (2022). European Rural Demographic Strategies: Foreshadowing Post-Lisbon Rural Development Policy? *WORLD (Oakland, Calif.)*, *3*(4), 938–956. DOI: 10.3390/world3040053 de Castro, G. M. C., & Toneto, R. (2019). Infraestrutura publica e crescimento dos municipios brasileiros: Analise espacial entre 1970 e 2010. *Economia Aplicada, 23*(2), 5–32. DOI: 10.11606/1980-5330/ea115755

De Castro, V. F., & Frazzon, E. M. (2017). Benchmarking of best practices: An overview of the academic literature. *Benchmarking, 24*(3), 750–774. DOI: 10.1108/BIJ-03-2016-0031

Deeti, A. (2023). *The conundrum of the pension system in India: A comprehensive study in the context of India's growth story.*

Demirtas, E. D., & Flahault, A. (2025). A Scoping Review on the Economic Impacts of Healthy Ageing Promotion and Disease Prevention in OECD Member Countries. *International Journal of Environmental Research and Public Health, 22*(8), 1161. Advance online publication. DOI: 10.3390/ijerph22081161 PMID: 40869748

Department of Labor Sri Lanka. (2023). Minimum Retirement Age of Workers Act, No. 28 Of 2021. https://labourdept.gov.lk/images/PDF_upload/NewAmendments/28-2021_e.pdf

Dickey, D. A., & Fuller, W. A. (1979). Distribution of the estimators for autoregressive time series with a unit root. *Journal of the American Statistical Association, 74*(366), 427–431. DOI: 10.2307/2286348

Didžgalvytė, M., & Lukšaitė, I. (2014). Demografinio Senėjimo Itaka Ekonominiams Rodikliams. *Taikomoji Ekonomika: Sisteminiai Tyrimai,* 65-81. https://portalcris.vdu.lt/server/api/core/bitstreams/9844c052-3a67-4ccb-87d5-574574517df6/content

Dixon, S. (2003). Implications of Population Ageing for the Labour Market. In Flowers, A. (Ed.), *Labour Market Trends, Organisation for Economic Co-operation and Development* (pp. 67–76). Special Feature., http://www.re-integrate.eu/resources/webre--implications-of-population-ageing-for-the-labour-market.pdf

do Nascimento, L. G. (2020). Population trends in BRICS: Developments and projections. *BRICS Journal of Economics, 1*(4), 82–94. DOI: 10.38050/2712-7508-2020-1-4-8

Docquier, F., Liégeois, P., Loupias, C., & Crettez, B. (2002). Vieillissement et inégalités intergénérationnelles en France: Une approche par l'équilibre général. *Revue Économique, 53*(4), 767–786.

Doling, J., Finer, C. J., & Maltby, T. (2018). *Ageing Matters: European Policy Lessons from the East.* Taylor and Francis., DOI: 10.4324/9781351163248

Domènech-Abella, J., Mundó, J., Leonardi, M., Chatterji, S., Tobiasz-Adamczyk, B., Koskinen, S., Ayuso-Mateos, J. L., & Haro, J. M. (2018). The association between socioeconomic status and depression among older adults in Finland, Poland and Spain: A comparative cross-sectional study of distinct measures and pathways. *Journal of Affective Disorders*, *241*, 311–318. DOI: 10.1016/j.jad.2018.08.077 PMID: 30142590

Donovan, K., & Schoellman, T. (2023). The role of labor market frictions in structural transformation*. *Oxford Development Studies*, *51*(4), 362–374. DOI: 10.1080/13600818.2023.2276702

Donthu, N., Kumar, S., Mukherjee, D., Pandey, N., & Lim, W. M. (2021). How to conduct a bibliometric analysis: An overview and guidelines. *Journal of Business Research*, *133*, 285–296. DOI: 10.1016/j.jbusres.2021.04.070

Drentea, P. (2002). Retirement and Mental Health. *Journal of Aging and Health*, *14*(2), 167–194. DOI: 10.1177/089826430201400201 PMID: 11995739

Duque, M., & Otaegui, A. (2023). Digital Dependency as a Burden: Impact of Active Aging for Technology Adoption in Brazil and Chile. *Anthropology and Aging*, *44*(2), 28–44. DOI: 10.5195/aa.2023.422

Elgar, F. J., Stefaniak, A., & Wohl, M. J. A. (2020). The trouble with trust: Time-series analysis of social capital, income inequality, and COVID-19 deaths in 84 countries. *Social Science & Medicine*, *263*, 113365. DOI: 10.1016/j.socscimed.2020.113365 PMID: 32981770

Emon, M. M. H. (2025a). Circularity Meets AI: Revolutionizing Consumer Engagement Through Green Marketing. In *Transforming Business Practices With AI-Powered Green Marketing* (pp. 169–208). IGI Global Scientific Publishing. DOI: 10.4018/979-8-3373-3017-4.ch007

Emon, M. M. H. (2025b). Cybersecurity in the Smart City Era: Overcoming Challenges With Modern Cryptographic Solutions. In *Securing Smart Cities Through Modern Cryptography Technologies* (pp. 43–74). IGI Global Scientific Publishing. DOI: 10.4018/979-8-3373-3326-7.ch002

Emon, M. M. H. (2025d). Ethical Intelligence in Motion: Leveraging AI for Responsible Sourcing in Supply Chain and Logistics. In *Navigating Responsible Business Practices Through Ethical AI* (pp. 207–240). DOI: 10.4018/979-8-3373-3104-1.ch008

Emon, M. M. H. (2025f). Navigating the Digital Labyrinth: Personal Data Privacy and Security at Individual and Organizational Levels. In *User-Centric Cybersecurity Implications for Sustainable Digital Transformation* (pp. 257–288). IGI Global Scientific Publishing. DOI: 10.4018/979-8-3373-3171-3.ch008

Emon, M. M. H. (2025g). Overcoming Hurdles: Navigating Challenges in the Adoption of Smart Logistics. In *Emerging Trends in Smart Logistics Technologies* (A. Hlali, pp. 197–228). IGI Global Scientific Publishing. DOI: 10.4018/979-8-3373-2434-0.ch007

Emon, M. M. H. (2025h). Purpose-Driven Intelligence in Green Marketing: Leveraging AI for CSR-Centric and Sustainable Brand Positioning. In *Transforming Business Practices With AI-Powered Green Marketing* (pp. 89–122). IGI Global Scientific Publishing. DOI: 10.4018/979-8-3373-3017-4.ch004

Emon, M. M. H., & Chowdhury, M. S. A. (2025a). AI and IoT-Powered Smart Logistics: Transforming Supply Chains for Efficiency and Sustainability. In *Emerging Trends in Smart Logistics Technologies* (A. Hlali, pp. 45–72). IGI Global Scientific Publishing. DOI: 10.4018/979-8-3373-2434-0.ch002

Emon, M. M. H., & Chowdhury, M. S. A. (2025b). Safeguarding Student Data: Privacy and Security Challenges in AI-Powered Education Tools. In *Enhancing Student Support and Learning Through Conversational AI* (pp. 191–228). IGI Global Scientific Publishing. DOI: 10.4018/979-8-3373-3316-8.ch008

Emon, M. M. H., & Khan, T. (2026). Decoding Visual Brand Identity Through Computer Vision: AI-Driven Insights for Modern Branding. In *AI, Machine Learning, and Image Processing in Market Research and Branding* (pp. 33–66). IGI Global Scientific Publishing. DOI: 10.4018/979-8-3373-4506-2.ch002

Emon, M. M. H., & Mazid-Ul-Haque, M. (2025). Balancing Usability and Security: Enhancing User Experience Without Compromising Privacy. In *User-Centric Cybersecurity Implications for Sustainable Digital Transformation* (pp. 309–342). IGI Global Scientific Publishing. DOI: 10.4018/979-8-3373-3171-3.ch010

Emon, M. M. H., Rahman, K. M., Nath, A., Mahsin-Ul-Islam, M., Rifat, H. H., & Kutub, J. (2025). Exploring Drivers of Sustainable E-Commerce Adoption among SMEs in Bangladesh: A TOE Framework Approach for Industry 5.0 Transformation. *2025 IEEE 7th International Conference on Sustainable Technologies For Industry 5.0 (STI)*, 1–6. DOI: 10.1109/STI69347.2025.11367600

Emon, M. M. H. (2023). A Systematic Review of the Causes and Consequences of Price Hikes in Bangladesh. *Review of Business and Economics Studies*, *11*(2), 49–58. DOI: 10.26794/2308-944X-2023-11-2-49-58

Emon, M. M. H. (2025c). Digital transformation in emerging markets: Adoption dynamics of AI image generation in marketing practices. *Telematics and Informatics Reports*, *20*, 100267. DOI: 10.1016/j.teler.2025.100267

Emon, M. M. H. (2025e). Leveraging AI on Social Media & Digital Platforms to Enhance English Language Teaching and Learning. In *AI-Powered English Teaching* (pp. 211–238). IGI Global Scientific Publishing., DOI: 10.4018/979-8-3373-1952-0.ch007

Emon, M. M. H. (2025i). The Mediating Role of Supply Chain Responsiveness in the Relationship Between Key Supply Chain Drivers and Performance: Evidence from the FMCG Industry. *Brazilian Journal of Operations & Production Management*, *22*(1), 2580. DOI: 10.14488/BJOPM.2580.2025

Emon, M. M. H., & Ahmed, M. (2025). Technological adoption in green practices as a mediator between green supply chain practices and operational performance: Evidence from the agro-processing and food industry. *Brazilian Journal of Operations & Production Management*, *22*(4), 2695. DOI: 10.14488/BJOPM.2695.2025

Emon, M. M. H., Chowdhury, M. S. A., Islam, M. S., & Nath, A. (2026). Value Perception, Digital Ownership, and Scarcity in Consumer-Brand Interactions Within Digital Payment Ecosystems. In *Impacts of Digital Payment Systems on Marketing* (pp. 231–270). IGI Global Scientific Publishing., DOI: 10.4018/979-8-3373-4526-0.ch008

Emon, M. M. H., & Khan, T. (2024a). A Systematic Literature Review on Sustainability Integration and Marketing Intelligence in the Era of Artificial Intelligence. *Review of Business and Economics Studies*, *12*(4), 6–28. DOI: 10.26794/2308-944X-2024-12-4-6-28

Emon, M. M. H., & Khan, T. (2024b). Unlocking Sustainability through Supply Chain Visibility: Insights from the Manufacturing Sector of Bangladesh. *Brazilian Journal of Operations & Production Management*, *21*(4), 2194. DOI: 10.14488/BJOPM.2194.2024

Emon, M. M. H., & Khan, T. (2025a). Corporate Social Responsibility for Sustainable Development: A Systematic Review of Business Contributions to Address Global Challenges. *Review of Business and Economics Studies*, *13*(2), 6–39. DOI: 10.26794/2308-944X-2025-13-2-6-39

Emon, M. M. H., & Khan, T. (2025b). The Rise of Circular Supply Chains: Recycling and Closed-Loop Systems Could Mitigate Inflationary Pressures. In *Supply Chain Disruptions and Impact on Global Inflation* (pp. 195–226). IGI Global., DOI: 10.4018/979-8-3373-1982-7.ch008

Emon, M. M. H., & Khan, T. (2025c). The Role of Traditional Media in Crisis Amplification: How Mainstream Media Magnifies Fake News and Ethical Dilemmas in Supply Chain Crises. In *Mass Media and Impact of Fake News on Supply Chains* (pp. 59–90). IGI Global., DOI: 10.4018/979-8-3373-2175-2.ch003

Emon, M. M. H., Nath, A., & Nipa, M. N. (2025). *AI for a Greener Tomorrow: Harnessing Artificial Intelligence for Environmental Sustainability*. IGI Global Scientific Publishing., DOI: 10.4018/979-8-3373-2387-9.ch010

EPF. (2023). *Annual report. 2020*. Retrieved from https://epf.lk/wp-content/uploads/2023/03/annualreport_2020_english.pdf

Eriksson, A., & Dellve, L. (2020). Learning Processes as Key for Success in Workplace Health Promotion Interventions in Health Care. *Frontiers in Public Health*, *8*, 576693. Advance online publication. DOI: 10.3389/fpubh.2020.576693 PMID: 33304874

Erol, M. T. (2012). Avrupa Birliği'nde Nüfusun Yaşlanması ve Sağlık Harcamalarına Etkisi. *Sosyal Güvence*, *0*(1), 54–81.

Evashwick, C., Rowe, G., Diehr, P., & Branch, L. (1984). Factors explaining the use of health care services by older people. *Health Services Research*, *19*(3), 357–382. http://www.ncbi.nlm.nih.gov/pubmed/6746297%0Ahttp://www.pubmedcentral.nih.gov/articlerender.fcgi?artid=PMC1068819 PMID: 6746297

Faruqee, H. (2002). Population Aging and Its Macroeconomic Implications: A Framework for Analysis. *IMF Working Paper*, *02/16*(16), 1–32. DOI: 10.5089/9781451843415.001

Fawagreh, K., Gaber, M. M., & Elyan, E. (2014). Random forests: From early developments to recent advancements. *Systems Science & Control Engineering*, *2*(1), 602–609. DOI: 10.1080/21642583.2014.956265

Fehr, H., Jokisch, S., Kallweit, M., Kindermann, F., & Kotlikoff, L. (2013). Generational policy in closed and open dynamic general equilibrium models. In Dixon, P., & Jorgenson, D. (Eds.), *Handbook of computable general equilibrium modeling* (Vol. 1, pp. 1719–1800). Elsevier.

Fehr, H., Kallweit, M., & Kindermann, F. (2017). Families and social security. *European Economic Review*, *91*, 30–56.

Feng, Z., Jones, K., & Phillips, D. R. (2019). Social exclusion, self-rated health and depression among older people in China: Evidence from a national survey of older persons. *Archives of Gerontology and Geriatrics*, *82*, 238–244. DOI: 10.1016/j.archger.2019.02.016 PMID: 30875525

Fernández-Olano, C., Hidalgo, J. D. L. T., Cerdá-Díaz, R., Requena-Gallego, M., Sánchez-Castaño, C., Urbistondo-Cascales, L., & Otero-Puime, A. (2006). Factors associated with health care utilization by older people in a public health care system. *Health Policy (Amsterdam)*, *75*(2), 131–139. DOI: 10.1016/j.healthpol.2005.02.005 PMID: 15961181

Ferraz, D., Falguera, F. P. S., Mariano, E. B., & Hartmann, D. (2021). Linking Economic Complexity, Diversification, and Industrial Policy with Sustainable Development: A Structured Literature Review. *Sustainability (Basel)*, *13*(3), 1265. DOI: 10.3390/su13031265

Ferreira, F. H. G., Moramarco, D., & Peragine, V. (2026). Economic development and inequality of opportunity: Kuznets meets the Great Gatsby? *Structural Change and Economic Dynamics*, *76*, 94–114. DOI: 10.1016/j.strueco.2025.11.006

Feyrer, J. (2007). Demographics and productivity. *The Review of Economics and Statistics*, *89*(1), 100–109. DOI: 10.1162/rest.89.1.100

Finkelstein, A., & Poterba, J. (2002). Selection effects in the United Kingdom individual annuities market. *Economic Journal (London)*, *112*(476), 28–50.

Fisher, I. (1930). *The theory of interest: As determined by impatience to spend income and opportunity to invest it.* The Macmillan Company.

Gálvez-Sánchez, F. J., Lara-Rubio, J., Verdú-Jóver, A. J., & Meseguer-Sánchez, V. (2021). Research advances on financial inclusion: A bibliometric analysis. *Sustainability (Basel)*, *13*(6), 1–19. DOI: 10.3390/su13063156

Gavrilov, L. A., & Heuveline, P. (2003). Aging of Population. In Demeny, P., & McNicoll, G. (Eds.), *The Encyclopedia of Population* (pp. 32–37). Macmillan Reference USA.

Georges, P., & Seçkin, A. (2016). From pro-natalist rhetoric to population policies in Turkey? An OLG general equilibrium analysis. *Economic Modelling*, *56*, 79–93.

Georges, P., & Seçkin, A. (2017). *The role of life annuities in assessing the economic impact of demographic changes – An OLG general equilibrium investigation* [Manuscript]. University of Ottawa.

Gerhardinger, L. C., de Andrade, M. M., Corrêa, M. R., & Turra, A. (2020). Crafting a sustainability transition experiment for the brazilian blue economy. *Marine Policy*, *120*, 104157. DOI: 10.1016/j.marpol.2020.104157

Geza, W., Ngidi, M. S. C., Slotow, R., & Mabhaudhi, T. (2022). The Dynamics of Youth Employment and Empowerment in Agriculture and Rural Development in South Africa: A Scoping Review. *Sustainability*, *14*(9), 5041. DOI: 10.3390/su14095041 PMID: 37691717

Ghosheh, N. S.Jr, Lee, S., & McCann, D. (2006). Conditions of Work and Employment for Older Workers in Industrialized Countries: Understanding the Issues. *SSRN*, (15), 1–60. DOI: 10.2139/ssrn.2932201

Ginting, M. L., Sum, G., Wang, S. Z., Ding, Y. Y., & Tay, L. (2025). Integrated frailty and intrinsic capacity care model for community-dwelling older adults in Singapore: A rapid qualitative study of anticipated implementation barriers and enablers using the Consolidated Framework for Implementation Research and its Outcomes Addendum. *Frontiers in Health Services*, *5*, 1563686. Advance online publication. DOI: 10.3389/frhs.2025.1563686 PMID: 40343232

Gölçek, A. G. (2024). The Economics of Aging: Global Trends and Perspectives. In *Perspectives on the Economics of Aging* (pp. 1–20). IGI Global Scientific Publishing., DOI: 10.4018/979-8-3693-7753-6.ch001

Goli, S., Reddy, A. B., James, K. S., & Srinivasan, V. (2019). Economic independence and social security among India's elderly. *Economic and Political Weekly*, *54*(39), 32–41.

Gonzlez-Gonzlez, C., Snchez-García, S., Jurez-Cedillo, T., Rosas-Carrasco, O., Gutiérrez-Robledo, L. M., & García-P a, C. (2011). Health care utilization in older people Mexican population: Expenditures and determinants. *BMC Public Health*, *11*(1), 192. Advance online publication. DOI: 10.1186/1471-2458-11-192

Goyal, A., & Kajal, K. (2014). Prevalence of depression in elderly population in the southern part of Punjab. *Journal of Family Medicine and Primary Care*, *3*(4), 359. DOI: 10.4103/2249-4863.148109 PMID: 25657943

Goyal, K., & Kumar, S. (2021). Financial literacy: A systematic review and bibliometric analysis. *International Journal of Consumer Studies*, *45*(1), 80–105. DOI: 10.1111/ijcs.12605

Goyal, P., Rahman, Z., & Kazmi, A. A. (2013). Corporate sustainability performance and firm performance research: Literature review and future research agenda. *Management Decision*, *51*(2), 361–379. DOI: 10.1108/00251741311301867

Graue, M., Dunning, T., Hausken, M. F., & Rokne, B. (2013). Challenges in managing elderly people with diabetes in primary care settings in Norway. *Scandinavian Journal of Primary Health Care, 31*(4), 241–247. DOI: 10.3109/02813432.2013.854445 PMID: 24205973

Grenčíková, A., Španková, J., Rigó, R., & Gullerová, M. (2023). Population aging in terms of generational cohorts in the context of labor productivity in the Slovak Republic. *Problems and Perspectives in Management, 21*(4), 577–590. Advance online publication. DOI: 10.21511/ppm.21(4).2023.43

Greve, B. (2018). At the heart of the Nordic occupational welfare model: Occupational welfare trajectories in Sweden and Denmark. *Social Policy and Administration, 52*(2), 508–518. DOI: 10.1111/spol.12380

Grimm, S. E., van Mastrigt, G., & Hiligsmann, M. (2025). Advancing the economics of prevention: Emerging methods and approaches. *Expert Review of Pharmacoeconomics & Outcomes Research, 25*(9), 1255–1262. DOI: 10.1080/14737167.2025.2570689 PMID: 41048050

Grimshaw, D. (2014). At Work But Earning Less: Trends in Decent Pay and Minimum Wages For Young People. *Employment Working Paper No. 162* (p. 1-69.)

Grinin, L., Grinin, A., & Korotayev, A. (2023). Global Aging and our Futures. *World Futures*, •••, 1–21. DOI: 10.1080/02604027.2023.2204791

Groos, O. V., & Pritchard, A. (1969). Documentation notes. *The Journal of Documentation, 25*(4), 344–349. DOI: 10.1108/eb026482

Grossman, M. (1972). *The Demand for Health: A Theoretical and Empirical Investigation*. NBER. https://www.nber.org/books-and-chapters/demand-health-theoretical-and-empirical-investigation

Gruber, J., & Wise, D. A. (2010). *Social Security Programs and Retirement Around the World: The Relationship to Youth Employment.* Chicago University Press, Chicago, National Bureau of Economic Research Conference Report. DOI: 10.7208/chicago/9780226309507.001.0001

Gruss, B., & Noureldin, D. (2025). Sustaining growth in an aging world. *Finance & Development, 62*(2). International Monetary Fund. https://www.imf.org/en/publications/fandd/issues/2025/06/sustaining-growth-in-an-aging-world-bertrand-gruss

Guerbaai, R. A., DeGeest, S., Popejoy, L. L., Simon, M., Wellens, N. I. H., Denhaerynck, K., & Zúñiga, F. (2023). Evaluating the implementation fidelity to a successful nurse-led model (INTERCARE) which reduced nursing home unplanned hospitalisations. *BMC Health Services Research*, *23*(1), 138. Advance online publication. DOI: 10.1186/s12913-023-09146-8 PMID: 36759902

Gullslett, M. K., Ronchi, E., Lundberg, L., Larbi, D., Lind, K. F., Tayefi, M., Ngo, P. D., Sy, T. R., Adib, K., & Hamilton, C. (2024). Telehealth development in the WHO European region: Results from a quantitative survey and insights from Norway. *International Journal of Medical Informatics*, *191*, 105558. Advance online publication. DOI: 10.1016/j.ijmedinf.2024.105558 PMID: 39084085

Gunarsa, S. (2020). *Fiscal Policy, Public Debt and Economic Performance in Developing Countries: An Empirical Analysis.* DOI: 10.25904/1912/1900

Gu, Y. H., Bai, J. B., Chen, X. L., Wu, W. W., Liu, X. X., & Tan, X. D. (2019). Healthy aging: A bibliometric analysis of the literature. *Experimental Gerontology*, *116*(115), 93–105. DOI: 10.1016/j.exger.2018.11.014 PMID: 30590123

Guzmán, P. C., Coelli, F., & Nilsson, E. (2025). Raising Employment among Women and Older Workers: A policy Lever for Ageing Economies. *The Centre for Economic Policy Research (CEPR).* https://cepr.org/voxeu/columns/raising-employment-among-women-and-older-workers-policy-lever-ageing-economies

Hair Jr, J. F., Sarstedt, M., Ringle, C. M., & Gudergan, S. P. (2017). Advanced issues in partial least squares structural equation modeling. saGe publications.

Hallett, N., Rees, H., Hannah, F., Hollowood, L., & Bradbury-Jones, C. (2024). Workplace interventions to prevent suicide: A scoping review. *PLoS One*, *19*(5), e0301453. Advance online publication. DOI: 10.1371/journal.pone.0301453 PMID: 38696511

Hamano, T., Yamasaki, M., Fujisawa, Y., Ito, K., Nabika, T., & Shiwaku, K. (2011). Social capital and psychological distress of elderly in Japanese rural communities. *Stress and Health*, *27*(2), 163–169. DOI: 10.1002/smi.1324 PMID: 27486618

Hamiduzzaman, M., De Bellis, A., Abigail, W., Kalaitzidis, E., & Harrington, A. (2021). The World Is Not Mine – Barriers to Healthcare Access for Bangladeshi Rural Elderly Women. *Journal of Cross-Cultural Gerontology*, *36*(1), 69–89. DOI: 10.1007/s10823-020-09420-w PMID: 33449242

Handing, E. P., Strobl, C., Jiao, Y., Feliciano, L., & Aichele, S. (2022). Predictors of depression among middle-aged and older men and women in Europe: A machine learning approach. *The Lancet Regional Health. Europe*, *18*, 18. DOI: 10.1016/j.lanepe.2022.100391 PMID: 35519235

Hantrais, L., Brannen, J., & Bennett, F. (2020). Family change, intergenerational relations and policy implications. *Contemporary Social Science*, *15*(3), 275–290. DOI: 10.1080/21582041.2018.1519195

Harasty, C., & Ostermeier, M. (2020). *Population ageing: Alternative measures of dependency and implications for the future of work.*

Hasan Emon, M. M., Mustafizur Rahman, K., Ahmed, M., Ara Chowdhury, M. S., Ferdous Emee, A., & Kutub, J. (2026). AI Enabled Industry 4.0 Practices for Enhancing Sustainability Performance: Evidence from Manufacturing Firms in an Emerging Economy. *2026 5th International Conference on Electrical, Computer & Telecommunication Engineering (ICECTE)*, 1–6. DOI: 10.1109/ICECTE69292.2026.11429215

Hasan Emon, M. M., Rahman, K. M., Ahmed, M., Islam, M. R., Kabir, S. M. I., & Emee, A. F. (2026). Understanding Employees' Behavioral Intentions Toward Cybersecurity Adoption in Banks: Evidence from an Emerging Economy. *2026 5th International Conference on Electrical, Computer & Telecommunication Engineering (ICECTE)*, 1–6. DOI: 10.1109/ICECTE69292.2026.11429312

Hasan, M. K., Emon, M. M. H., Hlali, A., & Khan, T. (2026). *Sustainable Operations in the Age of AI and Big Data* (Hasan, M. K., Emon, M. M. H., Hlali, A., & Khan, T., Eds.). IGI Global Scientific Publishing., DOI: 10.4018/979-8-2600-0216-2

Hasan, M. K., Khan, T., Hlali, A., & Emon, M. M. H. (2026). *Enhancing Sustainability in Global Supply Chains With Big Data Analytics* (Hasan, M. K., Khan, T., Hlali, A., & Emon, M. M. H., Eds.). IGI Global Scientific Publishing., DOI: 10.4018/979-8-3373-6896-2

Haslam, C., Cruwys, T., & Haslam, S. A. (2014). "The we's have it": Evidence for the distinctive benefits of group engagement in enhancing cognitive health in aging. *Social Science & Medicine*, *120*, 57–66. DOI: 10.1016/j.socscimed.2014.08.037 PMID: 25222136

Hayward, M. D., Hummer, R. A., & Sasson, I. (2015). Trends and group differences in the association between educational attainment and U.S. adult mortality: Implications for understanding education's causal influence. *Social Science & Medicine*, *127*, 8–18. DOI: 10.1016/j.socscimed.2014.11.024 PMID: 25440841

Hellström, Y., & Hallberg, I. R. (2001). Perspectives of elderly people receiving home help on health, care and quality of life. *Health & Social Care in the Community*, *9*(2), 61–71. DOI: 10.1046/j.1365-2524.2001.00282.x PMID: 11560722

Henkens, K., Remery, C., & Schippers, J. (2008). Shortages in an ageing labour market: An analysis of employers' behaviour. *International Journal of Human Resource Management*, *19*(7), 1314–1329. https://data.worldbank.org/indicator/SP.POP.0014.TO?end=2024&locations=TR&start=1966. DOI: 10.1080/09585190802110117

Hill, P. L., & Weston, S. J. (2017). Evaluating eight-year trajectories for sense of purpose in the health and retirement study. *Aging & Mental Health*, *23*(2), 233–237. DOI: 10.1080/13607863.2017.1399344 PMID: 29212348

Hinton, P. R., McMurray, I., & Brownlow, C. (2014). *SPSS explained*. Routledge. DOI: 10.4324/9781315797298

Hood, W. W., & Wilson, C. S. (2001). The literature of bibliometrics, scientometrics, and informetrics. *Scientometrics*, *52*(2), 291–314. DOI: 10.1023/A:1017919924342

Hu, W.-Y., & Scott, J. S. (2007). *Behavioral obstacles to the annuity market* [SSRN Working Paper]. March.

Hu, Y. (2024). A Study on the Correlation Between Women's ReEmployment Problems and Economic Growth in Japan in The Context of Population Aging. In P. Dou and K. Zhang (Eds.), *Proceedings of the 2023 International Conference on Economic Management, Financial Innovation and Public Service (EMFIPS 2023)* (p. 692-701), Advances in Economics, Business and Management Research 287. https://www.atlantis-press.com/proceedings/emfips-23/126000880

Huang, G., Wu, W., Wen, Q., Lu, L., & Pan, J. (2025). Building an integrated healthcare system of China: An assessment of coupling coordination between disease prevention, medical services, and healthcare financing from 2012 to 2021. *Health Economics Review*, *15*(1), 30. Advance online publication. DOI: 10.1186/s13561-025-00616-9 PMID: 40186730

Huffstetler, A. N., Phillips, R. L., Leyns, C. C., Willis, J. S., & Canchihuaman, F. A. (2023). People-centered health services. In Mezzich, J. E., Appleyard, W. J., Glare, P., Snaedal, J., & Wilson, C. R. (Eds.), *Person Centered Medicine* (pp. 135–150). Springer International Publishing., DOI: 10.1007/978-3-031-17650-0_8

Hyndman, R. J., & Koehler, A. B. (2006). Another look at measures of forecast accuracy. *International Journal of Forecasting*, *22*(4), 679–688. DOI: 10.1016/j.ijforecast.2006.03.001

Hyndman, R. J., Zeng, Y., & Shang, H. L. (2021). Forecasting the old-age dependency ratio to determine a sustainable pension age. *Australian & New Zealand Journal of Statistics*, *63*(2), 241–256. DOI: 10.1111/anzs.12330

Iliffe, S., Kharicha, K., Harari, D., Swift, C., Goodman, C., & Manthorpe, J. (2010). User involvement in the development of a health promotion technology for older people: Findings from the SWISH project. *Health & Social Care in the Community*, *18*(2), 147–159. DOI: 10.1111/j.1365-2524.2009.00882.x PMID: 19708867

Illario, M., Coscioni, E., Luca, V. D., Cataldi, M., Postiglione, A., & Iaccarino, G. (2019). Editorial: Multi-Actor Collaboration in Healthcare to Address the Emerging Health Needs of an Aging Population. *Translational Medicine @ UniSa, 19*, 1–4. DOI: 10.14273/unisa-2731

Imrohoroglu, S. (2025). Aging, population projections, and public pensions (CIGS Working Paper Series 25-018E). The Canon Institute for Global Studies. https://cigs.canon/en/uploads/2025/07/WP25-018E_250717_selahattin02.pdf

Imrohoroglu, S. (1998). A quantitative analysis of capital income taxation. *International Economic Review*, *39*(2), 307–328.

Institut National de la Statistique (INS). (2025). Recensement Général de la Population et de l'Habitat 2024: Bilan Démographique. https://www.ins.tn/sites/default/files-ftp3/files/2025-05/Bilan_D%C3%A9mographique.pdf

Insurance Association of Turkey. (2018). *Life insurance review and research committee position paper*. https://www.tsb.org.tr/images/Documents/Teknik/Hayat%20Sigortas%C4%B1%20Pozisyon%20Belgesi%20-%20Ocak%202018-%C4%B0ngilizce.pdf

International Labour Organization (ILO). (2024). *ILOSTAT database: Labour force participation rate – Tunisia*. https://ilostat.ilo.org/data/

Inukai, S. (2025). The impacts of raising the public pension eligibility age on time allocation of elderly people: Evidence from Japan. *Journal of Economic Behavior & Organization*, *233*, 106984. Advance online publication. DOI: 10.1016/j.jebo.2025.106984

Irmen, A., & Litina, A. (2022). The Implications of Population Aging for Immigrant- and Gender-Related Attitudes. In Bloom, D. E., Sousa-Poza, A., & Sunde, U. (Eds.), *The Routledge Handbook of the Economics of Ageing* (pp. 1009–1032). Routledge Taylor & Francis Group.

Islam, M. T., & Hossen, M. B. (2025). *Latin American Countries (LAC): An Economic Overview* (pp. 45–73). DOI: 10.1007/978-3-031-81362-7_3

Ivanova, A., Zemlyanova, E., Sabgayda, T., Semyonova, V., Zubko, A., & Kryukova, I. (2023). Demographic ageing, health status and life quality of the elderly in Russia. *China Population and Development Studies*, *7*(2), 130–159. DOI: 10.1007/s42379-023-00133-4

Jackson, D., & Tomlinson, M. (2020). Investigating the relationship between career planning, proactivity and employability perceptions among higher education students in uncertain labour market conditions. *Higher Education*, *80*(3), 435–455. DOI: 10.1007/s10734-019-00490-5

Jafino, B. A., Kwakkel, J. H., & Taebi, B. (2021). Enabling assessment of distributive justice through models for climate change planning: A review of recent advances and a research agenda. *Wiley Interdisciplinary Reviews: Climate Change*, *12*(4), e721. Advance online publication. DOI: 10.1002/wcc.721

Jakštienė, S., Purvinis, O., & Narbutas, V. (2014). Assessment of the Impact of Competencies for the Employment of Pre- retirement age people in Lithuania (applying the method of fuzzy logics). https://www.semanticscholar.org/paper/Assessment-of-the-Impact-of-Competencies-for-the-of-Jak%C5%A1tien%C4%97-Purvinis/7fca494639d42793e9683472d2f548b40b3126ed

Jarmain, S., Elliot, J., Meyer, M., Williams, C., Alpaugh-Bishop, A., Smith, A., & Moore, L. (2025). Value-creating Learning Health Systems – an Organizing Framework for the Journey to Integrated Care. *International Journal of Integrated Care*, *25*, 643. Advance online publication. DOI: 10.5334/ijic.ICIC24603

Johnston, D. W., & Lee, W. S. (2009). Retiring to the good life? The short-term effects of retirement on health. *Economics Letters*, *103*(1), 8–11. DOI: 10.1016/j.econlet.2009.01.015

Johnston, L. A. (2024). The BRICS are "getting old before getting rich": Trends and prospects. In *Complexity thinking and China's demography within and beyond mainland China: A geopolitical overview* (pp. 215–248). Springer. DOI: 10.1007/978-981-97-0172-8_9

Kabayama, M., Watanabe, C., Ryuno, H., & Kamide, K. (2017). Positive and negative associations of individual social capital factors with health among community-dwelling older people. *Geriatrics & Gerontology International*, *17*(12), 2427–2434. DOI: 10.1111/ggi.13094 PMID: 28643419

Kalwij, A., Kapteyn, A., & de Vos, K. (2010). Retirement of older workers and employment of the young. *De Economist*, *158*(4), 341–359. https://d-nb.info/119241893X/34. DOI: 10.1007/s10645-010-9148-z

Kamran, M., Rafique, M. Z., Nadeem, A. M., & Anwar, S. (2023). Does Inclusive Growth Contribute Towards Sustainable Development? Evidence from Selected Developing Countries. *Social Indicators Research, 165*(2), 409–429. DOI: 10.1007/s11205-022-03020-6

Karabıyık, İ. (2012). Türkiye'de Çalışma Hayatında Kadın İstihdamı. *Marmara Üniversitesi İ.İ.B.F. Dergisi, XXXII*(I), 231–260.

Karakaş, Ö. (2020). Dijitalleşme ve Kadın Emeği. *Terrabayt*, Nisan 30, 2020. https://terrabayt.com/yasam/dijitallesme-ve-kadin-emegi/

Kasnauskienė, G., & Andriuškaitė, M. (2017). Economic Implications of Ageing Lithuanian Population. *Organizations and Markets in Emerging Economies, 8*(1), 44–62. https://www.journals.vu.lt/omee/article/view/14196/13091. DOI: 10.15388/omee.2017.8.1.14196

Kaygusuz, E. D., Filiztekin, A., & Göker, Z. G. (2024). Türkiye'de Kadınların İşgücüne Katılımı: Genel Eğilimler, Bölgesel ve Demografik Farklar, Tutumlar. *TÜBİTAK Projesi Aralık 2024,* 1-46. https://kagider.s3.eu-central-1.amazonaws.com/uploads/projectPictures/cc50b333-266d-4198-bf95-ab0d383a8440.pdf

Kenc, T., & Sayan, S. (2001). Demographic shock transmission from large to small countries: An overlapping generations CGE analysis. *Journal of Policy Modeling, 23*, 677–702.

Kendig, H., Gong, C. H., Yiengprugsawan, V., Silverstein, M., & Nazroo, J. (2017). Life course influences on later life health in China: Childhood health exposure and socioeconomic mediators during adulthood. *SSM - Population Health, 3*, 795–802. DOI: 10.1016/j.ssmph.2017.10.001 PMID: 29349264

Keramat, S. A., Comans, T., Pearce, A., Basri, R., Hashmi, R., & Dissanayaka, N. N. (2025). Psychological distress and productivity loss: A longitudinal analysis of Australian working adults. *The European Journal of Health Economics, 26*(8), 1503–1524. DOI: 10.1007/s10198-025-01764-9 PMID: 40304834

Kessler, M. M. (1963). Bibliographic Coupling Between Scientific Papers Received. *Journal of the Association for Information Science and Technology, 14*(1), 10–25.

Keyes, K. M., & Platt, J. M. (2024). Annual Research Review: Sex, gender, and internalizing conditions among adolescents in the 21st century – trends, causes, consequences. *Journal of Child Psychology and Psychiatry, and Allied Disciplines, 65*(4), 384–407. DOI: 10.1111/jcpp.13864 PMID: 37458091

Khan, T., & Emon, M. M. H. (2025a). Preparing for the Next Disruption: Lessons Learned From Past Crises and Building a Playbook for Future Supply Chain Shocks. In *Supply Chain Disruptions and Impact on Global Inflation* (pp. 253–286). IGI Global Scientific Publishing. DOI: 10.4018/979-8-3373-1982-7.ch010

Khan, T., & Emon, M. M. H. (2025b). Resilient Supply Chains: Lessons From Past Crisis Strategies Companies Can Adopt to Create More Resilient Supply Chains. In *Mass Media and Impact of Fake News on Supply Chains* (pp. 285–318). IGI Global. DOI: 10.4018/979-8-3373-2175-2.ch011

Khan, T., & Hasan Emon, M. M. (2024). Determinants of AI Image Generator Adoption Among Marketing Agencies: The Mediating Effects of Perceived Usefulness. *2024 IEEE 3rd International Conference on Robotics, Automation, Artificial-Intelligence and Internet-of-Things (RAAICON)*, 177–182. DOI: 10.1109/RAAICON64172.2024.10928548

Khan, T., & Hasan Emon, M. M. (2025). AI-Generated Content and Its Influence on Consumer Trust and Purchase Behaviour: Evidence from Bangladesh's E-Commerce Industry. *2025 IEEE 2nd International Conference on Computing, Applications and Systems (COMPAS)*, 1–6. DOI: 10.1109/COMPAS67506.2025.11381790

Khan, T., Emon, M. M. H., & Nath, A. (2024). Quantifying the Effects of AI-Driven Inventory Management on Operational Efficiency in Online Retail. *2024 27th International Conference on Computer and Information Technology (ICCIT)*, 2092–2097. DOI: 10.1109/ICCIT64611.2024.11021996

Khan, T., Emon, M. M. H., & Rahman, S. (2024). Marketing Strategy Innovation via AI Adoption: A Study on Bangladeshi SMEs in the Context of Industry 5.0. *2024 6th International Conference on Sustainable Technologies for Industry 5.0 (STI)*, 1–6. DOI: 10.1109/STI64222.2024.10951050

Khan, T., & Emon, M. M. H. (2024). Exploring the Potential of the Blue Economy: A Systematic Review of Strategies for Enhancing International Business in Bangladesh in the context of Indo-Pacific Region. *Review of Business and Economics Studies*, *12*(2), 55–73. DOI: 10.26794/2308-944X-2024-12-2-55-73

Khan, T., & Emon, M. M. H. (2025c). The role of digital supply chain practices in enhancing firm performance: Insights from the manufacturing sector of Bangladesh. *Brazilian Journal of Operations & Production Management*, *22*(2), 2493. DOI: 10.14488/BJOPM.2493.2025

Khan, T., Emon, M. M. H., Rahman, K. M., Nipa, M. N., & Fuad, M. N. (2025). The Role of AI in Driving Customer Engagement Through Technological, Organizational and Environmental Enablers in E-Commerce. *2025 International Conference on Quantum Photonics, Artificial Intelligence, and Networking (QPAIN)*, 1–6. DOI: 10.1109/QPAIN66474.2025.11171949

Kinoshita, Y., & Kochhar¸, K. (2016). Women can help offset the problems of an aging population and a shrinking workforce. *Finance & Development*, *53*(1), 1–3. https://www.imf.org/external/pubs/ft/fandd/2016/03/kinoshita.htm

Klasen, S., Le, T. T. N., Pieters, J., & Santos Silva, M. (2021). What Drives Female Labour Force Participation? Comparable Micro-level Evidence from Eight Developing and Emerging Economies. *The Journal of Development Studies*, *57*(3), 417–442. DOI: 10.1080/00220388.2020.1790533

Klasen, S., & Pieters, J. (2015). What explains the stagnation of female labor force participation in urban India? *The World Bank Economic Review*, *29*(3), 449–478. DOI: 10.1093/wber/lhv003

Klos, J., Krieger, T., & Stöwhase, S. (2022). Measuring intra-generational redistribution in PAYG pension schemes. *Public Choice*, *190*(1–2), 53–73. DOI: 10.1007/s11127-021-00914-w

Kolodziej, I. W., & García-Gómez, P. (2019). Saved by retirement: Beyond the mean effect on mental health. *Social Science & Medicine*, *225*, 85–97. DOI: 10.1016/j.socscimed.2019.02.003 PMID: 30822608

Kondo, A. (2016). Effects of Increased Elderly Employment on Other Workers' Employment and Elderly's Earnings in Japan. *IZA Journal of Labor Policy*, *5*(2), 1–23. https://www.researchgate.net/publication/292187914_Effects_of_increased_elderly_employment_on_other_workers'_employment_and_elderly's_earnings_in_Japan. DOI: 10.1186/s40173-016-0063-z

Kosine, N. R., & Lewis, M. V. (2008). Growth and Exploration: Career Development Theory and Programs of Study. *Career and Technical Education Research*, *33*(3), 227–243. DOI: 10.5328/CTER33.3.227

Kosunen, M., Ruotsalainen, J., Kallio, A., Metsä, R., Raittinen, P., Lehmus, L., Korhonen, M. J., & Purmonen, T. (2025). Healthcare Resource Utilization and Associated Costs During the First 5 Years After Diagnosis and at the End of Life: A Nationwide Cohort Study of Patients with Multiple Myeloma in Finland. *PharmacoEconomics Open*, *9*(1), 57–68. DOI: 10.1007/s41669-024-00524-4 PMID: 39240292

Kotlikoff, L. J., Smetters, K. A., & Walliser, J. (2007). Mitigating America's demographic dilemma by pre-funding social security. *Journal of Monetary Economics*, *54*, 247–266.

Krapp, A. (2005). Basic needs and the development of interest and intrinsic motivational orientations. *Learning and Instruction*, *15*(5), 381–395. DOI: 10.1016/j.learninstruc.2005.07.007

Krejcie, R. V., & Morgan, D. W. (1970). Determining Sample Size for Research Activities. *Educational and Psychological Measurement*, *30*(3), 607–610. DOI: 10.1177/001316447003000308

Krueger, D., & Ludwig, A. (2007). On the consequences of demographic change for rates of return to capital, and the distribution of wealth and welfare. *Journal of Monetary Economics*, *54*(1), 48–87.

Kuiate, C., & Noland, T. R. (2019). Attracting and retaining core competency: A focus on cost stickiness. *Journal of Accounting & Organizational Change*, *15*(4), 678–700. DOI: 10.1108/JAOC-04-2018-0038

Lal, B. (2023). The BRICS countries: Trends of demographic and economic development. *International Journal of Scientific Research*, *12*(4), 702–708.

Lanza Queiroz, B., & Lobo Alves Ferreira, M. (2021). The evolution of labor force participation and the expected length of retirement in Brazil. *The Journal of the Economics of Ageing*, *18*, 100304. Advance online publication. DOI: 10.1016/j.jeoa.2020.100304

Lassila, J., & Valkonen, T. (2019). *Alternative Demography-based Projection Approaches for Public Health and Long-term Care Expenditure*. https://consensus.app/papers/alternative-demographybased-projection-approaches-for-lassila-valkonen/aa05600c19785c3785b3c5882f842287/

Lawal, C. I., Friday, S. C., Ayodeji, D. C., & Sobowale, A. (2024). Strategic Framework for Transparent, Data-Driven Financial Decision-Making in Achieving Sustainable National Development Goals. *International Journal of Advanced Multidisciplinary Research and Studies*. DOI: 10.62225/2583049X.2024.4.6.4098

Lee, J.-W. (2025). Comment on "Japan's Aging Workforce: Determinants and Outlook.". *Asian Economic Policy Review*, *20*(2), 263–264. Advance online publication. DOI: 10.1111/aepr.12507

Lee, R. (2020). Population aging and the historical development of intergenerational transfer systems. *Genus*, *76*(1), 31. DOI: 10.1186/s41118-020-00100-8

Lee, R. (2025). Population Aging and Public Policy. In An, C.-B. (Ed.), *Evidence-Based Policy Analysis: Lessons Learned* (pp. 197–224). Oxford University Press., DOI: 10.1093/oso/9780197801826.003.0010

Lee, R., & Mason, A. (2011). *Population aging and the generational economy: A global perspective*. Edward Elgar Publishing. DOI: 10.4337/9780857930583

Lee, R., & Mason, A. (2011). *Population aging and the generational economy—A global perspective*. Edward Elgar Publishing.

Lee, Z. (2023). The Skill-Specific Automatability of Aging Workers and Its Impact on Retirement Decisions. *Work, Aging and Retirement*. Advance online publication. DOI: 10.1093/workar/waad008

Li, H., Zeng, Y., Gan, L., Tuersun, Y., Yang, J., Liu, J., & Chen, J. (2022). Urban–rural disparities in the healthy ageing trajectory in China: A population-based study. *BMC Public Health*, *22*(1), 1406. DOI: 10.1186/s12889-022-13757-x PMID: 35870914

Li, M., & Ao, Y. (2026). Equity in public decision-making: A dynamic comparative study of urban–rural elderly care institution resource allocation in China. In *Institutional elderly care in China: Resource allocation and spatial optimization* (pp. 81–112). Springer. DOI: 10.1007/978-981-95-5092-0_4

Lindwall, M., Berg, A. I., Bjälkebring, P., Buratti, S., Hansson, I., Hassing, L., Henning, G., Kivi, M., König, S., Thorvaldsson, V., & Johansson, B. (2017). Psychological Health in the Retirement Transition: Rationale and First Findings in the HEalth, Ageing and Retirement Transitions in Sweden (HEARTS) Study. *Frontiers in Psychology*, *8*, 1634. Advance online publication. DOI: 10.3389/fpsyg.2017.01634 PMID: 29018374

Lisenkova, K., McGregor, P. G., Pappas, N., Swales, J. K., Turner, K., & Wright, R. E. (2010). Scotland the Grey: A Linked Demographic-Computable General Equilibrium (CGE) Analysis of the Impact of Population Ageing and Decline. Regional Studies. *Regional Studies*, *44*(10), 1351–1368. DOI: 10.1080/00343400701654228

Liu, D., & Zhao, R. (2024). The Impact of Population Aging on Employment. *Journal of Education. Humanities and Social Sciences*, *36*, 65–70.

Liu, Y.-T., Zhou, Y.-D., & Cai, J.-L. (2023). Effects of Health Status on the Labor Supply of Older Adults with Different Socioeconomic Status. *Sustainability (Basel)*, *15*(2), 1511. Advance online publication. DOI: 10.3390/su15021511

Liu, Z., Shi, R., Jiang, L., Tang, F., Qiu, Z., & Yao, L. (2025). Impact of Long-Term Care Insurance on health out-of-pocket expenditure ratios for older adults. *Frontiers in Public Health, 13*, 1616761. Advance online publication. DOI: 10.3389/fpubh.2025.1616761 PMID: 40735199

Li, Y., Cui, M., Pang, Y., Zhan, B., Li, X., Wang, Q., Chen, F., Zhou, Z., & Yang, Q. (2024). Association of physical activity with socio-economic status and chronic disease in older adults in China: Cross-sectional findings from the survey of CLASS 2020 after the outbreak of COVID-19. *BMC Public Health, 24*(1), 37. Advance online publication. DOI: 10.1186/s12889-023-17492-9 PMID: 38166980

Ljung, G. M., & Box, G. E. P. (1978). On a measure of lack of fit in time series models. *Biometrika, 65*(2), 297–303. DOI: 10.1093/biomet/65.2.297

Lopez-Acevedo, G., Ranzani, M., Sinha, N., & Elsheikhi, A. (2023). *Informality and inclusive growth in the Middle East and North Africa*. World Bank Group. DOI: 10.1596/978-1-4648-1988-9

Lundberg, S. M., & Lee, S. I. (2017). A unified approach to interpreting model predictions. In *Advances in Neural Information Processing Systems* (Vol. 30).

Lundberg, J. (2024). Intergenerational redistribution in a pay-as-you-go pension system. *The Journal of the Economics of Ageing, 29*, 100534. DOI: 10.1016/j.jeoa.2024.100534

Lunenfeld, B., Mskhalaya, G., Zitzmann, M., Corona, G., Arver, S., Kalinchenko, S., Tishova, Y., & Morgentaler, A. (2021). Recommendations on the diagnosis, treatment and monitoring of testosterone deficiency in men. *The Aging Male, 24*(1), 119–138. DOI: 10.1080/13685538.2021.1962840 PMID: 34396893

Luo, S. (2017). *Aging, dissaving, and the role of life annuities* [M.A. major paper]. Department of Economics, University of Ottawa.

Luo, W. (2023). *Inequality, Demography and Fiscal Policy*. Springer Nature Singapore., DOI: 10.1007/978-981-99-0518-8

Lussi, C., Bickenbach, J., Halvorsen, R., & Sabariego, C. (2024). Trends over the past 15 years in long-term care in Switzerland: A comparison with Germany, Italy, Norway, and the United Kingdom. *BMC Geriatrics, 24*(1), 627. Advance online publication. DOI: 10.1186/s12877-024-05195-8 PMID: 39044146

Lütkepohl, H. (2013). *Introduction to multiple time series analysis*. Springer.

Lu, Y., Karanikas, N., & Carroll, J.-A. (2025). Identification of needs of integrated approaches of occupational health and safety and health promotion. *Health Promotion Perspectives*, *15*(2), 153–164. DOI: 10.34172/hpp.025.44202 PMID: 40988950

Lu, Z., Mahalik, M. K., Padhan, H., Gupta, M., & Gozgor, G. (2021). Effects of age dependency and urbanization on energy demand in BRICS: Evidence from the machine learning estimator. *Frontiers in Energy Research*, *9*, 749065. DOI: 10.3389/fenrg.2021.749065

Ly, A. M., & Cope, M. R. (2023). New Conceptual Model of Social Sustainability: Review from Past Concepts and Ideas. *International Journal of Environmental Research and Public Health*, *20*(7), 5350. DOI: 10.3390/ijerph20075350 PMID: 37047965

Lytle, M. C., Foley, P. F., & Cotter, E. W. (2015). Career and Retirement Theories. *Journal of Career Development*, *42*(3), 185–198. DOI: 10.1177/0894845314547638 PMID: 26101455

MacKinnon, J. G. (1996). Numerical distribution functions for unit root and cointegration tests. *Journal of Applied Econometrics*, *11*(6), 601–618. DOI: 10.1002/(SICI)1099-1255(199611)11:6<601::AID-JAE417>3.0.CO;2-T

MacLennan, M., Osório, R. G., & de Arruda, P. L. (2014). *Youth and employment among the BRICS* (Issue 28).

Maestas, N., Mullen, K. J., & Powell, D. (2016). The Effect of Population Aging on Economic Growth, Whe Labor Force and Productivity. *RAND Working Paper* (p. 1-55). https://papers.ssrn.com/sol3/papers.cfm?abstract_id=2533260

Maestas, N., Mullen, K., & Powell, D. (2014). *The Effect of Population Aging on Economic Growth* (No. 14-012). Stanford Institute for Economic Policy Research.

Magammulla, C. C., Fernando, M. A. C. S. S., & Silva, C. W. C. (2023). Factors Affecting The Perception Towards The Retirement Age: A Case Of Public Sector Employees In Western Province, Sri Lanka. 1st International Conference On Social Sciences And Languages (Icssl - 2023) Sri Lanka, Sabaragamuwa University (2023-01-12) http://repo.lib.sab.ac.lk:8080/xmlui/handle/susl/3219

Maheshwari, S. K., Chaturvedi, R., & Sharma, P. (2021). Effectiveness of psycho-educational intervention on psychological distress and self-esteem among resident elderly: A study from old age homes of Punjab, India. *Clinical Epidemiology and Global Health*, *11*, 100733. DOI: 10.1016/j.cegh.2021.100733

Mahmood, M. N., & Dhakal, S. P. (2022). Ageing population and society: A scientometric analysis. *Quality & Quantity*, (August). Advance online publication. DOI: 10.1007/s11135-022-01509-3 PMID: 36039154

Maimaris, W., Hogan, H., & Lock, K. (2010). The Impact of Working Beyond Traditional Retirement Ages on Mental Health: Implications for Public Health and Welfare Policy. *Public Health Reviews*, *32*(2), 532–548. DOI: 10.1007/BF03391615

Majumder, S., Aghayi, E., Noferesti, M., Memarzadeh-Tehran, H., Mondal, T., Pang, Z., & Deen, M. J. (2017). Smart homes for elderly healthcare—Recent advances and research challenges. *Sensors (Basel)*, *17*(11), 2496. Advance online publication. DOI: 10.3390/s17112496 PMID: 29088123

Malik, M., Singh, S., & Pattanaik, F. (2022). Economics of Healthy Aging in India: A Multidimensional Perspective. *IZA Journal of Labor Policy*, *12*(1), 20220004. Advance online publication. DOI: 10.2478/izajolp-2022-0004

Malla, M. H., & Pathranarakul, P. (2022). Fiscal Policy and Income Inequality: The Critical Role of Institutional Capacity. *Economies*, *10*(5), 115. DOI: 10.3390/economies10050115

Mansouri, M., Bouhjar, A., Cadimi, I., Haisoufi, D., Fares, R., & Malainine, C. (2025). Study of the Impact of Economic Factors and Healthcare System Capacity on the Elderly Population in Morocco: A Health Economics Perspective. *The Open Public Health Journal*, *18*(1), e18749445421746. Advance online publication. DOI: 10.2174/0118749445421746250826065105

Mansyur, M. (2021). Occupational Health, Productivity and Evidence-Based Workplace Health Intervention. *Acta Medica Philippina*, *55*(6). Advance online publication. DOI: 10.47895/amp.v55i6.4273

Mavrodaris, A., Lafortune, L., & Brayne, C. (2022). The future longevity: Designing a synergistic approach for healthy ageing, sustainability, and equity. *The Lancet. Healthy Longevity*, *3*(9), 584–586. DOI: 10.1016/S2666-7568(22)00145-3 PMID: 35935473

Meçik, O., & Afşar, M. (2014). Türkiye Ekonomisinde Yapısal Dönüşümler ve İşgücü Piyasasındaki Gelişmeler. *Optimum Ekonomi ve Yönetim Bilimleri Dergisi*, *1*(2), 1–23.

Megeri, M. N., & Bheemanna, B. (2023). Forecasting population and economic characteristics with ARIMA models in India. *International Journal of Agricultural and Statistics Sciences*, *19*(2), 513-526. DOI: 10.59467/IJASS.2023.19.513

Mehboob, K. (2025). Cost-Benefit Analysis of Preventive Healthcare Programs. *Pakistan Journal of Health Sciences*. DOI: 10.54393/pjhs.v6i4.3068

Meinhold, R., Wagner, C., & Dhar, B. K. (2025). Digital sustainability and eco-environmental sustainability: A review of emerging technologies, resource challenges, and policy implications. *Sustainable Development (Bradford), 33*(2), 2323–2338. DOI: 10.1002/sd.3240

Meka'a, C. B., & Moneboulou, M. M. A. (2024). Analysis of the accounting effect of the demographic dividend in Cameroon. *Journal of Social and Economic Development*. Advance online publication. DOI: 10.1007/s40847-024-00375-z

Michaeli, D. T., Michaeli, J. C., Albers, S., & Michaeli, T. (2024). The Healthcare Workforce Shortage of Nurses and Physicians: Practice, Theory, Evidence, and Ways Forward. *Policy, Politics & Nursing Practice, 25*(4), 216–227. DOI: 10.1177/15271544241286083 PMID: 39396540

Mi, H., Fan, X., Lu, B., Cai, L., & Piggott, J. (2020). Preparing for population ageing: Estimating the cost of formal aged care in China. *The Journal of the Economics of Ageing, 17*, 100183. DOI: 10.1016/j.jeoa.2018.12.002

Mihajlović, V., & Miladinov, G. (2024). Impact of Population Ageing on Economic Growth in Emerging EU Countries. *Ekonomicky Casopis, 72*(1–2), 50–71. DOI: 10.31577/ekoncas.2024.01-02.03

Mihajlović, V., & Miladinov, G. (2024). Impact of population ageing on economic growth in emerging EU countries. *Ekonomický časopis. Journal of Economics, 72*(1-2), 50–71.

Mihajlović, V., & Miladinov, G. (2024). Population ageing and economic growth: Evidence from advanced and emerging economies. *Economic Modelling, 125*, 106286. DOI: 10.1016/j.econmod.2023.106286

Minami, U., Nishi, M., Fukaya, T., Hasebe, M., Nonaka, K., Koike, T., Suzuki, H., Murayama, Y., Uchida, H., & Fujiwara, Y. (2015). Effects of the Change in Working Status on the Health of Older People in Japan. *PLoS One, 10*(12), e0144069. DOI: 10.1371/journal.pone.0144069 PMID: 26633033

Ministry of Development of the Republic of Türkiye. (2018). *On Birinci Kalkınma Planı (2019-2023), Sosyal Güvenlik Sisteminin Sürdürülebilirliği*. Özel İhtisas Komisyonu Raporu, Ankara 2018. https://www.sbb.gov.tr/wp-content/uploads/2020/04/SosyalGuvenlikSistemininSurdurulebilirligiOzelIhtisasKomisyonuRaporu.pdf

Mishra, H. G., Pandita, S., Bhat, A. A., Mishra, R. K., & Sharma, S. (2022). Tourism and carbon emissions: a bibliometric review of the last three decades: 1990–2021. *Tourism Review*, *77*(2), 636–658. DOI: 10.1108/TR-07-2021-0310

Mizuochi, M. (2021). Effect of Retirement Timing on Health. In *Exploring the Effect of Retirement on Health in Japan. SpringerBriefs in Population Studies*. Springer., DOI: 10.1007/978-981-16-2638-8_4

Modigliani, F., & Brumberg, R. (2013). Utility Analysis and the Consumption Function: An Interpretation of Cross-Section Data 1. In *Post-keynesian economics* (pp. 388-436). Routledge.

Mosca, I., & Barrett, A. M. (2014). The Impact of Voluntary and Involuntary Retirement on Mental Health: Evidence from Older Irish Adults. SSRN Electronic Journal. DOI: 10.2139/ssrn.2543918

Mounsey, S., Veerman, L., Jan, S., & Thow, A. M. (2020). The macroeconomic impacts of diet-related fiscal policy for NCD prevention: A systematic review. *Economics and Human Biology*, *37*, 100854. DOI: 10.1016/j.ehb.2020.100854 PMID: 32062400

Mourtzis, D., Angelopoulos, J., & Panopoulos, N. (2022). A Literature Review of the Challenges and Opportunities of the Transition from Industry 4.0 to Society 5.0. *Energies*, *15*(17), 6276. DOI: 10.3390/en15176276

Munim, Z. H., Dushenko, M., Jimenez, V. J., Shakil, M. H., & Imset, M. (2020). Big data and artificial intelligence in the maritime industry: A bibliometric review and future research directions. *Maritime Policy & Management*, *47*(5), 577–597. DOI: 10.1080/03088839.2020.1788731

Munnel, A. H., & Wu, A. Y. (2012). Will Delayed Retirement by the Baby Boomers Lead to Higher Unemployment Among Younger Workers? *Center for Retirement Research at Boston College Working Paper No: 2012-22* (p. 1-54). https://papers .ssrn.com/sol3/papers.cfm?abstract_id=2162093

Muszyńska, M. M., & Rau, R. (2012). The old-age healthy dependency ratio in Europe. *Journal of Population Ageing*, *5*(3), 151–162. DOI: 10.1007/s12062-012-9068-6 PMID: 22924086

Nagarajan, N., & Sixsmith, A. (2021). Policy Initiatives to Address the Challenges of an Older Population in the Workforce. *Ageing International*, *48*(1), 41–77. DOI: 10.1007/s12126-021-09442-w PMID: 34465930

Nagarajan, N., Wada, M., Fang, M., & Sixsmith, A. (2019). Defining organizational contributions to sustaining an ageing workforce: A bibliometric review. *European Journal of Ageing*, *16*(3), 337–361. DOI: 10.1007/s10433-019-00499-w PMID: 31543728

Nagy, N., Rudolph, C. W., & Zacher, H. (2022). Reciprocal relationships between subjective age and retirement intentions. *European Journal of Work and Organizational Psychology*, *31*(4), 583–595. DOI: 10.1080/1359432X.2021.2016700

Nair, P. S. (2014). Population aging in sub-Saharan Africa: Present and prospects. *Gerontech.*, *13*(2), 266. DOI: 10.4017/gt.2014.13.02.429.00

Narayan, P. K., & Narayan, S. (2004). Estimating Income and Price Elasticities of Imports for Fiji in a Cointegration Framework. *Economic Modelling*, *22*(3), 423–438. DOI: 10.1016/j.econmod.2004.06.004

Nawaz, N., Maann, A. A., Akhter, S., & Ashraf, I. (2012). Health status of elderly women in socio-economic and cultural context in Punjab, Pakistan. *Sarhad Journal of Agriculture*, *28*(2), 373–378. http://www.aup.edu.pk/sj_pdf/HEALTH STATUS OF ELDERLY WOMEN -254-2011.pdf

Naz, L., Ghimire, U., & Zainab, A. (2021). Behavioral factors associated with utilization of healthcare services among elderly in Pakistan: Evidence from a nationally representative survey. *BMC Geriatrics*, *21*(1), 1–11. DOI: 10.1186/s12877-021-02005-3 PMID: 33435874

Negrini, A., Panari, C., Simbula, S., & Alcover, C. M. (2013). The push and pull factors related to early retirees' mental health status: A comparative study between Italy and Spain. *Journal of Work and Organizational Psychology*, *29*(2), 51–58. DOI: 10.5093/tr2013a8

Nelischer, C., & Loukaitou-Sideris, A. (2023). Intergenerational Public Space Design and Policy: A Review of the Literature. *Journal of Planning Literature*, *38*(1), 19–32. DOI: 10.1177/08854122221092175

Ngcamu, B. S. (2023). Climate change effects on vulnerable populations in the Global South: A systematic review. *Natural Hazards*, *118*(2), 977–991. DOI: 10.1007/s11069-023-06070-2

Niederstrasser, N. G., Rogers, N. T., & Bandelow, S. (2019). Determinants of frailty development and progression using a multidimensional frailty index: Evidence from the english longitudinal study of ageing. *PLoS One*, *14*(10), 1–16. DOI: 10.1371/journal.pone.0223799 PMID: 31665163

Nikolov, P., & Adelman, A. (2018). Short-Run Health Consequences of Retirement and Pension Benefits: Evidence from China. *Forum for Health Economics & Policy, 21*(2), 20170031. Advance online publication. DOI: 10.1515/fhep-2017-0031 PMID: 30964747

Noh, B., Youm, C., Goh, E., Lee, M., Park, H., Jeon, H., & Kim, O. Y. (2021). XGBoost-based machine learning approach to predict the risk of falls in older adults using gait outcomes. *Scientific Reports, 11*(1), 12183. DOI: 10.1038/s41598-021-91797-w PMID: 34108595

Noone, J., Knox, A., O'Loughlin, K., McNamara, M., Bohle, P., & Mackey, M. (2018). An analysis of factors associated with older workers' employment participation and preferences in Australia. *Frontiers in Psychology, 9*(DEC), 2524. Advance online publication. DOI: 10.3389/fpsyg.2018.02524 PMID: 30618949

Nordin, N., Nordin, N. N., & Ahmad, N. A. (2015). The Effects of the Ageing Population on Healthcare Expenditure: A Comparative Study of China and India. *First International Conference on Economics and Banking (ICEB-15)*, 297-310. https://www.researchgate.net/publication/299963935_The_Effects_of_the_Ageing_Population_on_Healthcare_Expenditure_A_Comparative_Study_of_China_and_India

Notestein, F. W. (1945). Population-The long view. *Food for the World.*, 36-57.

O'Loughlin, K., Hussain, R., & Kendig, H. (2021). Attitudes towards Australia's baby boomers and intergenerational equity. *The Sociological Review, 69*(4), 792–811. DOI: 10.1177/0038026120963367

OECD. (2019). *Working Better with Age*. OECD Publishing. https://www.oecd.org/content/dam/oecd/en/publications/reports/2019/08/working-better-with-age_e6265636/c4d4f66a-en.pdf

OECD. (2023). Pensions at a Glance 2023: OECD and G20 Indicators. *OECD Pensions at a Glance, 2023*. Advance online publication. DOI: 10.1787/678055dd-en

OECD. (2024). *Life Expectancy at 65 (indicator)* [Data set]. https://data.oecd.org/healthstat/life-expectancy-at-65.htm

OECD. (2025). *OECD Employment Outlook 2025: Can We Get Through the Demographic Crunch?* OECD Publishing., DOI: 10.1787/194a947b-

OECD. (2025a). *Elderly population (indicator)* [Data set]. https://data-explorer.oecd.org/vis?lc=en&pg=0&snb=1&vw=tb&df[ds]=dsDisseminateFinalDMZ&df[id]=DSD_POPULATION%40DF_POP_HIST&df[ag]=OECD.ELS.SAE&df[vs]=&pd=1988%2C2024&dq=TUR.POP.PT_POP._T.Y_LT15%2BY15T24%2BY15T64%2BY_GE65.&ly[rw]=AGE&ly[cl]=TIME_PERIOD&to[TIME_PERIOD]=false

OECD. (2025b). *Population Projections* [Data set]. https://data-explorer.oecd.org/vis?df[ds]=DisseminateFinalDMZ&df[id]=DSD_POPULATION%40DF_POP_PROJ&df[ag]=OECD.ELS.SAE&dq=TUR.POP.PT_POP.M%2BF%2B_T.Y_GE65.&pd=2024%2C2070&to[TIME_PERIOD]=false&vw=tb

OECD. (2025c). *Historical Population Data* [Data set]. https://data-explorer.oecd.org/vis?lc=en&pg=0&snb=1&vw=tb&df[ds]=dsDisseminateFinalDMZ&df[id]=DSD_POPULATION%40DF_POP_HIST&df[ag]=OECD.ELS.SAE&df[vs]=&pd=1960%2C2025&dq=TUR.POP.PT_POP%2BPS.F%2BM%2B_T.Y_LT15%2BY15T24%2BY15T64%2BY_GE65.&ly[rw]=AGE&ly[cl]=TIME_PERIOD&to[TIME_PERIOD]=false

OECD. (2025d). *Labour Force Participation Rate, Employment and Unemployment by five-year age group and sex – indicators* [Data set]. https://data-explorer.oecd.org/vis?df[ds]=DisseminateFinalDMZ&df[id]=DSD_LFS%40DF_LFS_INDIC&df[ag]=OECD.ELS.SAE&dq=TUR.UNE_RATE%2BLF_RATE%2BEMP_RATIO.PT_POP_SUB%2BPT_LF_SUB.F%2BM%2B_T.Y15T24%2BY25T54%2BY55T64%2BY_GE65.LF%2BEMP%2BUNE&pd=1960%2C2024&to[TIME_PERIOD]=false&vw=tb

Öğütoğulları, E., & Kılıç, C. (2016). Türkiye İşgücü Piyasasında Yeni Bir Problem Alanı: 40 Yaş ve Üstü İşsizler. *Çalışma İlişkileri Dergisi*, 7(1), 85-97.

Oka, Y., Wachi, M., & Kida, N. (2024). Physical Therapist-Led Initiatives for the Prevention and Improvement of Chronic Pain Among Workers: A Case Study of Hosting Workshops Based on Survey Results in a Corporate Setting. *International Journal of Environmental Research and Public Health*, *21*(12), 1709. Advance online publication. DOI: 10.3390/ijerph21121709 PMID: 39767548

Oliveira, B. L. C. A., & Pinheiro, A. K. B. (2023). Changes in health behaviors in elderly Brazilians: Data from the 2013 and 2019 National Health Surveys. *Ciencia & Saude Coletiva*, *28*, 3111–3122. DOI: 10.1590/1413-812320232811.16702022 PMID: 37970996

Oliveira, M. D., Tavares, A. I., Miranda, R., Trindade, R., & Vieira, A. C. L. (2025). A novel policy dialogue to build sustainable and resilient health systems: Findings from PHSSR Portugal. *Health Research Policy and Systems*, *23*(1), 58. Advance online publication. DOI: 10.1186/s12961-025-01329-5 PMID: 40390059

Olmsted, J. C. (2024). Care labor, intergenerational equity, and (social) sustainability. *Review of Social Economy*, *82*(1), 51–75. DOI: 10.1080/00346764.2021.1964586

Önder, N. (2013). Türkiye'de Kadın İşgücünün Görünümü. *Çalışma ve Sosyal Güvenlik Bakanlığı Çalışma Dünyası Dergisi*, 1(1), p. 35-61.

Opatha, H. H. D. N. P. (2022). The Retirement Age: An Informative Analysis. *Sri Lankan Journal of Human Resource Management*, *12*(1), 39. Advance online publication. DOI: 10.4038/sljhrm.v12i1.5679

Organisation for Economic Co-operation and Development (OECD). (2023). *Pensions at a Glance: Dependency ratios and population ageing*. OECD Publishing. https://www.oecd.org/en/publications/pensions-at-a-glance-2023_678055dd-en.html

Padhi, B., & Triveni, T. (2025). The Indian Labor Market and Elderly: Acclimatizing to an Aging Population in the Workplace. İn S. Irudaya Rajan (Ed.), *Handbook of Aging, Health and Public Policy* (p. 2013–2034). Springer Nature. https://link.springer.com/rwe/10.1007/978-981-99-7842-7_26

Paiva, L. H., & Ansiliero, G. (2025). The Brazilian Old-Age Social Protection System. In *Handbook of Aging, Health and Public Policy: Perspectives from Asia* (pp. 1471–1485). Springer Nature Singapore. DOI: 10.1007/978-981-99-7842-7_18

Pariso, P., Picariello, M., & Marino, A. (2025). Driving Technological Efficiency in European Healthcare: The Role of Digital Innovation Across EU. *International Journal of Energy Economics and Policy*, *15*(4), 490–498. DOI: 10.32479/ijeep.17898

Pasqualini, M., Lanari, D., Minelli, L., Pieroni, L., & Salmasi, L. (2017). Health and income inequalities in Europe: What is the role of circumstances? *Economics and Human Biology*, *26*, 164–173. DOI: 10.1016/j.ehb.2017.04.002 PMID: 28445843

Patterson, I., & Balderas, A. (2020). Continuing and Emerging Trends of Senior Tourism: A Review of the Literature. *Journal of Population Ageing*, *13*(3), 385–399. DOI: 10.1007/s12062-018-9228-4

Péntek, M., Beretzky, Z., Brodszky, V., Szabó, J., Kovács, L., Kincses, Ã., Baji, P., Zrubka, Z., Rencz, F., & Gulácsi, L. (2020). Health-related productivity of the Hungarian population. A cross-sectional survey. *Orvosi Hetilap*, *161*(36), 1522–1533. DOI: 10.1556/650.2020.31798 PMID: 32886627

Perez-Arce, F., & Prados, M. J. (2021). THE DECLINE IN THE U.S. LABOR FORCE PARTICIPATION RATE: A LITERATURE REVIEW. *Journal of Economic Surveys*, *35*(2), 615–652. DOI: 10.1111/joes.12402

Pesaran, M. H., Shin, Y., & Smith, R. J. (2001). Bounds Testing Approaches to the Analysis of Level Relationships. *Journal of Applied Econometrics*, *16*(3), 289–326. DOI: 10.1002/jae.616

Petmesidou, M., & Guillén, A. M. (2022). Europe's green, digital and demographic transition: A social policy research perspective. *Transfer: European Review of Labour and Research*, *28*(3), 317–332. DOI: 10.1177/10242589221107498

Picchio, M., & Ours, J. C. V. (2020). Mental health effects of retirement. *De Economist*, *168*(3), 419–452. DOI: 10.1007/s10645-020-09369-8

Piłat, A., Gałaś, A., Wilga, M., Cabello, M., Koskinen, S., Haro, J., Leonardi, M., & Tobiasz–Adamczyk, B. (2020). Gender perspective in the analysis of the relationship between health and work cessation, and how to deal with it. *International Journal of Occupational Medicine and Environmental Health*, *33*(3), 365–384. Advance online publication. DOI: 10.13075/ijomeh.1896.01351 PMID: 32329474

Presidency of the Republic of Türkiye, Strategy and Budget Presidency (2026a). *1924-2017 Sektörel Büyüme Hızları ve GSYH Deflatörü* [Data set]. tab1-10

Presidency of the Republic of Türkiye, Strategy and Budget Presidency (2026b). *GSYH ve Alt Bileşenlerinin Ortalama Büyüme Hızı, Temel Ekonomik Göstergeler Veritabanı* [Data set]. https://www.sbb.gov.tr/temel-ekonomik-gostergeler-veritabani/

Prskawetz, A., Fent, T., Barthel, W., Crespo-Cuaresma, J., Lindh, T., Malmberg, B., & Halvarsson, M. (2007). The relationship between demographic change and economic growth in the EU. *Report for Tender VT/2005/035*.

Pyle, M. A., & Stoller, E. P. (2003). Oral Health Disparities Among older people: Interdisciplinary Challenges for the Future. *Journal of Dental Education*, *67*(12), 1327–1336. DOI: 10.1002/j.0022-0337.2003.67.12.tb03726.x PMID: 14733265

Qiao, X., Wang, B., & Guo, H. (2021). Chronic Diseases and Labor Force Participation Among Presenile and Senile Chinese. *Frontiers in Public Health*, *9*, 675927. Advance online publication. DOI: 10.3389/fpubh.2021.675927 PMID: 34604151

Radford, K., Lavrencic, L. M., Delbaere, K., Draper, B., Cumming, R., Daylight, G., Mack, H. A., Chalkley, S., Bennett, H., Garvey, G., Hill, T. Y., Lasschuit, D., & Broe, G. A. (2019). Factors Associated with the High Prevalence of Dementia in Older Aboriginal Australians. *Journal of Alzheimer's Disease*, *70*(1), S75–S85. DOI: 10.3233/JAD-180573 PMID: 30507573

Rahimi, Z., Ghorbani-Shahna, F., & Bahrami, A. (2021). Design, Implementation, and Evaluation of Industrial Ventilation Systems and Filtration for Silica Dust Emissions from a Mineral Processing Company. *Indian Journal of Occupational and Environmental Medicine*, *25*(4), 192–197. DOI: 10.4103/ijoem.IJOEM_55_19 PMID: 35197669

Rai, R., Jongenelis, M. I., Jackson, B., Newton, R. U., & Pettigrew, S. (2020). Retirement and Physical Activity: The Opportunity of a Lifetime or the Beginning of the End? *Journal of Aging and Physical Activity*, *28*(3), 365–375. DOI: 10.1123/japa.2019-0023 PMID: 31743090

Ramos-Herrera, M. C., & Sosvilla-Rivero, S. (2020). Fiscal Sustainability in Aging Societies: Evidence from Euro Area Countries. *Sustainability (Basel)*, *12*(24), 10276. Advance online publication. DOI: 10.3390/su122410276

Ranganathan, N. M. (2017). Universal social pension for elderly individuals in India Public expenditure requirements and fiscal sustainability. *Indian Growth and Development Review*, *10*(2), 89–116. DOI: 10.1108/IGDR-07-2017-0047

Rentz, J. O., & Reynolds, F. D. (1991). Forecasting the effects of an aging population on product consumption: An age–period–cohort framework. *JMR, Journal of Marketing Research*, *28*(3), 355–360. DOI: 10.1177/002224379102800310

Republic of Türkiye Ministry of Family and Social Policies. General Directorate of Women's Status (2014). Türkiye'de Kadın İşgücü Profili İstatistiklerinin Analizi. Duygu Matbaacılık, 1-192. https://www.aile.gov.tr/uploads/ksgm/uploads/pages/dagitimda-olan-yayinlar/turkiye-de-kadin-isgucu-profili-ve-istatistiklerinin-analizi-nihai-rapor.pdf

Rinaldi, C., Bortoluzzi, S., Airoldi, C., Leigheb, F., Nicolini, D., Russotto, S., Vanhaecht, K., & Panella, M. (2021). The Early Detection of Osteoporosis in a Cohort of Healthcare Workers: Is There Room for a Screening Program? *International Journal of Environmental Research and Public Health*, *18*(3), 1368. Advance online publication. DOI: 10.3390/ijerph18031368 PMID: 33540940

Rios-Rull, J. (2001). Population changes and capital accumulation: The aging of the baby boom. *Advances in Macroeconomics, 1*(1), Article 7.

Rios-Rull, J. (1996). Life-cycle economies and aggregate fluctuations. *The Review of Economic Studies*, *63*, 465–489.

Romaioli, D., & Contarello, A. (2019). "I'm Too Old for …" Looking into a Self-Sabotage Rhetoric and its Counter-narratives in an Italian Setting. *Journal of Aging Studies*, *48*, 25–32. DOI: 10.1016/j.jaging.2018.12.001 PMID: 30832927

Rosen, B., & Jerdee, T. H. (1989). Retirement policies: Evidence of the need for change. *Human Resource Management, 28*(1), 87–103. DOI: 10.1002/hrm.3930280106

Rouzet, D., Sánchez, A. C., Renault, T., & Roehn, O. (2019). *Fiscal challenges and inclusive growth in ageing societies*. OECD Economic Policy Papers., DOI: 10.1787/c553d8d2-

Rozman, M., & Cančer, V. (2021). The Appropriate Work Environment for Older Employees: The Case of Slovenia. *Business Systems Research, 12*(2), 172–186. DOI: 10.2478/bsrj-2021-0026

Rusconi, R. (2008). *National annuity markets: Features and implications* (OECD Working Papers on Insurance and Private Pensions No. 24). OECD Publishing.

Saba, T., & Guerin, G. (2005). Extending Employment beyond Retirement Age: The Case of Health Care Managers in Quebec. *Public Personnel Management, 34*(2), 195–214. DOI: 10.1177/009102600503400205

Şahin, L., & Yıldırım, K. (2015). On Dokuzuncu Yüzyıldan Günümüze Türkiye'de İşsizlikle Mücadele Politikaları. *Çalışma ve Toplum*, 2015/2, 111-152.

Sahoo, H., Govil, D., James, K. S., & Prasad, R. D. (2021). Health issues, health care utilization and health care expenditure among elderly in India: Thematic review of literature. *Aging and Health Research, 1*(2), 100012. DOI: 10.1016/j.ahr.2021.100012

Saito, M., Kondo, K., Kondo, N., Abe, A., Ojima, T., & Suzuki, K. (2014). Relative deprivation, poverty, and subjective health: JAGES cross-sectional study. *PLoS One, 9*(10), e111169. Advance online publication. DOI: 10.1371/journal.pone.0111169 PMID: 25350284

Saleem, H., Shabbir, M. S., & Bilal khan, M. (2020). The short-run and long-run dynamics among FDI, trade openness and economic growth: Using a bootstrap ARDL test for co-integration in selected South Asian countries. *South Asian Journal of Business Studies, 9*(2), 279–295. DOI: 10.1108/SAJBS-07-2019-0124

Salem, M. B., Blanchet, D., Bozio, A., & Roger, M. (2008). Labor Force Participation by the Elderly and Employment of the Young: The Case of France. *Paris School of Economics Working Paper No: 2008–57* (p. 1-40). https://halshs.archives-ouvertes.fr/halshs-00586064/document

Salokangas, R. K., & Joukamaa, M. (1991). Physical and Mental Health Changes in Retirement Age. *Psychotherapy and Psychosomatics, 55*(2–4), 100–107. DOI: 10.1159/000288415 PMID: 1891555

Samorodov, A. (1999). Ageing and Labour Markets for Older Workers. *Employment and Training Papers 33* (p. 1-38). https://www.ilo.org/sites/default/files/wcmsp5/groups/public/%40ed_emp/documents/publication/wcms_120333.pdf

Sanjel, S., Mudbhari, N., Risal, A., & Khanal, K. (2012). The utilization of health care services and their determinants among older people population of Dhulikhel Municipality". *Kathmandu University Medical Journal, 10*(37), 34–39. DOI: 10.3126/kumj.v10i1.6911 PMID: 22971859

Satı, Z. E., & Yılmaz, B. O. (2020). Endüstri 4.0 Ortamında Değişen İş ve Mesleklerin Türkiye'de Kadın İstihdamına Etkileri. *Strategic Public Management Journal,* 6(11), 54-76. https://dergipark.org.tr/tr/download/article-file/1129246

Schenker, M., & Da Costa, D. H. (2019). Advances and challenges of health care of older people population with chronic diseases in primary health care. *Ciencia & Saude Coletiva, 24*(4), 1369–1380. DOI: 10.1590/1413-81232018244.01222019 PMID: 31066839

Schnitzer, S., Blüher, S., Teti, A., Schaeffner, E., Ebert, N., Martus, P., Suhr, R., & Kuhlmey, A. (2020). Risk Profiles for Care Dependency: Cross-Sectional Findings of a Population-Based Cohort Study in Germany. *Journal of Aging and Health, 32*(5), 352–360. DOI: 10.1177/0898264318822364 PMID: 30658538

Schoneveld, G. C. (2020). Sustainable business models for inclusive growth: Towards a conceptual foundation of inclusive business. *Journal of Cleaner Production, 277,* 124062. DOI: 10.1016/j.jclepro.2020.124062

Seçkin, A., Georges, P., & Sahanoğulları, N. (2014). *National transfer accounts for Turkey* [Manuscript]. University of Ottawa & Istanbul Bilgi University.

Secretariat, C. (2023). *Fiscal Policy Options for Resilient and Sustainable Development.* DOI: 10.14217/comsec.1106

Selekler, H. M., Gökmen, G., Alvur, T. M., & Steiner, T. J. (2015). Productivity losses attributable to headache, and their attempted recovery, in a heavy-manufacturing workforce in Turkey: Implications for employers and politicians. *The Journal of Headache and Pain, 16*(1), 1–8. DOI: 10.1186/s10194-015-0579-4 PMID: 26573819

Şen, M. (2018). Geçmişten Günümüze Türkiye'de İşsizliğin Seyri: İşsizlikle Mücadelede Türkiye İş Kurumu (İşkur). *2 nd International Symposium Humanities and Social Sciences 04-07 August 2018 / COMRAT* (p. 96-116)

Serban, A. C. (2012). Aging Population and Effects on Labour Market. *Procedia Economics and Finance. International Conference on Applied Economics (ICOAE),* 1, 356-364.

Serel, H., & Özdemir, B. S. (2017). Türkiye'de Kadın İstihdamı ve Ekonomik Büyüme İlişkisi. *Yönetim ve Ekonomi Araştırmaları Dergisi / Journal of Management and Economics Research,* 15(3), p. 132-148

Serra, C., Soler-Font, M., García, A. M. M., Peña, P., Vargas-Prada, S., & Ramada, J. (2019). Prevention and management of musculoskeletal pain in nursing staff by a multifaceted intervention in the workplace: Design of a cluster randomized controlled trial with effectiveness, process and economic evaluation (INTEVAL_Spain). *BMC Public Health*, *19*(1), 348. Advance online publication. DOI: 10.1186/s12889-019-6683-7 PMID: 30922285

Sewdas, R., de Wind, A., van der Zwaan, L. G., van der Borg, W. E., Steenbeek, R., van der Beek, A. J., & Boot, C. R. (2017). Why older workers work beyond the retirement age: A qualitative study. *BMC Public Health*, *17*(1), 672. Advance online publication. DOI: 10.1186/s12889-017-4675-z PMID: 28830399

Shahjahan, R. A., Estera, A. L., Surla, K. L., & Edwards, K. T. (2022). "Decolonizing" Curriculum and Pedagogy: A Comparative Review Across Disciplines and Global Higher Education Contexts. *Review of Educational Research*, *92*(1), 73–113. DOI: 10.3102/00346543211042423

Sharma, H. B., Vanapalli, K. R., Cheela, V. S., Ranjan, V. P., Jaglan, A. K., Dubey, B., Goel, S., & Bhattacharya, J. (2020). Challenges, opportunities, and innovations for effective solid waste management during and post COVID-19 pandemic. *Resources, Conservation and Recycling*, *162*, 105052. DOI: 10.1016/j.resconrec.2020.105052 PMID: 32834486

Shcherbakova, E. M. (2022). Population dynamics in Russia in the context of global trends. *Studies on Russian Economic Development*, *33*(4), 409–421. DOI: 10.1134/S1075700722040098 PMID: 35911060

Shen, X., Yin, F., & Jiao, C. (2023). Predictive models of life satisfaction in older people: A machine learning approach. *International Journal of Environmental Research and Public Health*, *20*(3), 2445. DOI: 10.3390/ijerph20032445 PMID: 36767810

Shultz, K. S., & Wang, M. (2007). The Influence of Specific Physical Health Conditions on Retirement Decisions. *International Journal of Aging & Human Development*, *65*(2), 149–161. DOI: 10.2190/AG.65.2.c PMID: 17957985

Silvaggi, F., Eigenmann, M., Scaratti, C., Guastafierro, E., Toppo, C., Lindstrom, J., Rantala, E., Imaz-Iglesia, I., Barnfield, A., Maassen, A., & Leonardi, M. (2020). Employment and Chronic Diseases: Suggested Actions for The Implementation of Inclusive Policies for The Participation of People with Chronic Diseases in the Labour Market. *International Journal of Environmental Research and Public Health*, *17*(3), 820. Advance online publication. DOI: 10.3390/ijerph17030820 PMID: 32013004

Sinclair, S. H., & Smetters, K. A. (2004). *Health shocks and the demand for annuities* (Technical Paper Series No. 2004-09). Congressional Budget Office.

Sisubalan, N., Vijay, N., Kesika, P., Newbegin, M., Shalini, R., Sivamaruthi, B. S., & Chaiysut, C. (2025). The Contribution of Wearable Devices and Artificial Intelligence to Promoting Healthy Aging. *Current Pharmaceutical Biotechnology*, *27*. Advance online publication. DOI: 10.2174/0113892010390500250911104231 PMID: 41031500

Slaveva, K. (2023). Study on the changes in the age dependency ratio and their effects on the economy. *Population (Naselenie)*, *41*(2), 83–105.

Souza, J. S., Reis, E. A., Godman, B., Campbell, S. M., Meyer, J. C., Sena, L. W., & Godói, I. P. (2024). Users' perceptions of access to and quality of Unified Health System services in Brazil: Implications for healthcare management. *International Journal of Environmental Research and Public Health*, *21*(6), 721. DOI: 10.3390/ijerph21060721 PMID: 38928967

Spear, S. E., & Young, W. (2023). OLG – The Next Generations, 1960–1970. In *Overlapping Generations: Methods, Models and Morphology* (pp. 19–41). Emerald Publishing Limited. DOI: 10.1108/S1571-038620230000032006

Stepanova, O. (2019). Fiscal sustainability under the conditions of emerging longevity economy. *Ekonomìka ì Prognozuvannâ*. DOI: 10.15407/econforecast2019.01.031

Suhrcke, M., Sauto Arce, R., McKee, M., & Rocco, L. (2008). *The economic costs of ill health in the European Region: Background document*. World Health Organization. Regional Office for Europe. https://iris.who.int/handle/10665/350693

Suresh, K. G., Thomas, J., Menon, V. A., & TK, S. K. (n.d.). Exploring the socioeconomic determinants of population and economic indicators using machine learning and time series analysis.

Swanepoel, D. (2023). An Intergenerational Justice Approach to Technological Unemployment. *Asian Journal of Business Ethics*, *12*(2), 239–256. DOI: 10.1007/s13520-023-00172-7

Szabó, G., Allen, J., Stephens, C., & Alpass, F. (2018). Is retirement associated with physical health benefits? A longitudinal investigation with older New Zealanders. *Age and Ageing*, *48*(2), 267–272. DOI: 10.1093/ageing/afy176 PMID: 30379990

Tan, V., Chen, C., & Merchant, R. A. (2022). "Association of social determinants of health with frailty, cognitive impairment, and self-rated health among older adults". *PLoS ONE*, Vol.*17*, pp. 1–18. Available at: DOI: 10.1371/journal.pone.0277290

Tang, B., & Li, Z. (2021). A Country-Level Empirical Study on the Fiscal Effect of Elderly Population Health: The Mediating Role of Healthcare Resources. *Health Care*, *10*(1), 30. Advance online publication. DOI: 10.3390/healthcare10010030 PMID: 35052194

Tang, F., Choi, E., & Goode, R. (2013). Older Americans Employment and Retirement. *Ageing International*, *38*(1), 82–94. DOI: 10.1007/s12126-012-9162-3

Tang, L., Sun, S., & Yang, W. (2021). Does government education expenditure boost intergenerational mobility? Evidence from China. *International Review of Economics & Finance*, *74*, 13–22. DOI: 10.1016/j.iref.2021.02.001

Tao, W., Zeng, Z., Dang, H., Li, P., Chuong, L., Yue, D., Wen, J., Zhao, R., Li, W., & Kominski, G. (2020). Towards universal health coverage: Achievements and challenges of 10 years of healthcare reform in China. *BMJ Global Health*, *5*(3), e002087. Advance online publication. DOI: 10.1136/bmjgh-2019-002087 PMID: 32257401

Temsumrit, N. (2023). Can aging population affect economic growth through the channel of government spending? *Heliyon*, *9*(9), e19521. Advance online publication. DOI: 10.1016/j.heliyon.2023.e19521 PMID: 37809751

Thanh Trong, L., Nguyen, C. V., & Pham, T. H. (2024). Demographic ageing and economic growth: New evidence from emerging economies. *Journal of Asian Economics*, *88*, 101646. DOI: 10.1016/j.asieco.2023.101646

Thanh Trong, N., Thi Dong, N., & Thi Ly, P. (2024). Population aging and economic growth: Evidence from ASEAN countries. *Cogent Business &amp. Cogent Business & Management*, *11*(1), 2298055. Advance online publication. DOI: 10.1080/23311975.2023.2298055

The V-Dem Institute. (2023). *V-Dem (Varieties of Democracy) (Global Standards Local knoeledge)* [Data set]. https://www.v-dem.net/data/the-v-dem-dataset/

Thieme, P., Brusch, M., & Büsch, V. (2015). The role of continuing training motivation for work ability and the desire to work past retirement age. European journal for Research on the Education and Learning of Adults, 6(1), 25-38. https://opus4.kobv.de/opus4-srh/frontdoor/index/index/docId/768

Thießen, U. (2007). *Aging and Structural Change. DIW Discussion Papers, No. 742*. German Institute for Economic Research., https://www.econstor.eu/bitstream/10419/27266/1/550070923.PDF

Tian, Y., & Shi, Z. (2022). Effects of physical activity on daily physical function in Chinese middle-aged and older adults: A longitudinal study from CHARLES. *Journal of Clinical Medicine*, *11*(21), 6514. DOI: 10.3390/jcm11216514 PMID: 36362742

Tibber, M. S., Walji, F., Kirkbride, J. B., & Huddy, V. (2022). The association between income inequality and adult mental health at the subnational level—A systematic review. *Social Psychiatry and Psychiatric Epidemiology*, *57*(1), 1–24. DOI: 10.1007/s00127-021-02159-w PMID: 34386869

Tsuji, I. (2020). Current status and issues concerning Health Japan 21 (second term). *Nutrition Reviews*, *78*(Supplement_3), 14–17. DOI: 10.1093/nutrit/nuaa079 PMID: 33259610

TÜİK. (2025). *Nüfus Projeksiyonları, 2018-2080* [Data set]. https://data.tuik.gov.tr/Bulten/Index?p=Nufus-Projeksiyonlari2018-2080-30567

TURKSTAT. (2023). *Sektöre göre İstihdam Edilenler, İşgücü İstatistikleri* [Data set]. https://data.tuik.gov.tr/Bulten/Index?p=Isgucu-Istatistikleri-2022-49390, TURKSTAT (2025). *Ekonomik Faaliyete Göre İstihdam Edilenler. İşgücü İstatistikleri* [Data set]. https://veriportali.tuik.gov.tr/tr/press/49390 *Erişim tarihi: 30.07.2023.*

Turra, C. M., & Mitchell, O. S. (2005). *The impact of health status and out-of-pocket medical expenditures on annuity valuation* (Research Brief No. RB 2005-079). University of Michigan Retirement Research Center.

Uchida, Y., & Ono, T. (2024). Generational Distribution of Fiscal Burdens: A Positive Analysis. *International Economic Review*, *65*(1), 393–430. DOI: 10.1111/iere.12654

Uğur, S. (2002). Sosyal Güvenliğimizdeki Son Değişikliklerin Değerlendirilmesi. *Dokuz Eylül Üniversitesi Sosyal Bilimler Enstitüsü Dergisi*, *4*(2), 131–146.

Ullman, A. N., & Kittner, N. (2024). Are global efforts coordinated for a Just Transition? A review of civil society, financial, government, and academic Just Transition frameworks. *Energy Research & Social Science*, *108*, 103371. DOI: 10.1016/j.erss.2023.103371

Uścińska, G. (2023). Women on the labour market and in old-age pension insurance. In M. Duszczyk & J. Mecina (Eds.), *[PRACA, BEZROBOCIE, ZATRUDNIENIE: Wartości i działania w rozwoju polityki rynku pracy. Ksiega jubileuszowa profesor Małgorzaty Szylko-Skoczny]: Work, Unemployment, Employment: Values and Actions in The Development of Labour Market Policy. A Jubilee Book Dedicated to Professor Malgorzata Szylko-Skoczny* (pp. 119–134). Wydawnictwa Uniwersytetu Warszaskiego. DOI: 10.31338/uw.9788323563846.pp.119-134

Uyanık, Y., & Başyiğit, R. (2018). Demografik Yapı İçinde Yaşlı Nüfusun Görünümü ve Aktif Yaşlanma Yaklaşımı Perspektifinde Politika Örnekleri. *İş ve Hayat,* 4(8), 273-310.

Vahidi Monfared, H., & Moini, A. (2019). A system dynamics model to forecast population ageing in Iran. *Kybernetes, 48*(6), 1216–1241. DOI: 10.1108/K-04-2018-0166

Vaishnav, L. M., Joshi, S. H., Joshi, A. U., & Mehendale, A. M. (2022). The National Programme for Health Care of the Elderly: Achievements and challenges in India. *Annals of Geriatric Medicine and Research, 26*(3), 183–189. DOI: 10.4235/agmr.22.0062 PMID: 36039665

Valls Martínez, M., Santos-Jaén, J. M., Amin, F., & Martín-Cervantes, P. A. (2021). Pensions, Ageing and Social Security Research: Literature Review and Global Trends. *Mathematics, 9*(24), 3258. DOI: 10.3390/math9243258

van Bilsen, S., Mehlkopf, R. J., & van Stalborch, S. (2022). Intergenerational Transfers in the New Dutch Pension Contract. *De Economist, 170*(1), 37–67. DOI: 10.1007/s10645-022-09399-4

van de Poll, M. K., Bergström, G., Jensen, I., Nybergh, L., Kwak, L., Lornudd, C., & Lohela-Karlsson, M. (2020). Cost-Effectiveness of a Problem-Solving Intervention Aimed to Prevent Sickness Absence among Employees with Common Mental Disorders or Occupational Stress. *International Journal of Environmental Research and Public Health, 17*(14), 5234. Advance online publication. DOI: 10.3390/ijerph17145234 PMID: 32698470

van Dongen, J. V., & van der Beek, A. J. (2022). Economic evaluations in occupational health: What brings the best bang for the buck? *Scandinavian Journal of Work, Environment & Health, 48*(4), 249–252. DOI: 10.5271/sjweh.4026 PMID: 35380166

van Eck, N. J., & Waltman, L. (2010). Software survey: VOSviewer, a computer program for bibliometric mapping. *Scientometrics, 84*(2), 523–538. DOI: 10.1007/s11192-009-0146-3 PMID: 20585380 van Rensburg, M. Domican, S., & Kennedy, A. (2021). *The Economic Impacts of an Ageing Population in New Zealand, Background Paper for the 2021 Statement on the Long-term Fiscal Position.* New Zealand Treasury, 1-73. https://www.treasury.govt.nz/sites/default/files/2021-09/ltfs21-bp-economic-impact-ageing-population-nz.pdf

Verma, M., Grover, S., Singh, T., Dahiya, N., & Nehra, R. (2020). Screening for cognitive impairment among older people attending the noncommunicable diseases clinics in a rural area of Punjab, North India". *Asian Journal of Psychiatry, 50*, 102001. DOI: 10.1016/j.ajp.2020.102001 PMID: 32248085

Verma, M., Grover, S., Tripathy, J. P., Singh, T., Nagaraja, S. B., Kathirvel, S., Singh, G., & Nehra, R. (2019). Co-existing non-communicable diseases and mental illnesses amongst older people in Punjab, India. *European Endocrinology, 15*(2), 106–112. DOI: 10.17925/EE.2019.15.2.106 PMID: 31616502

Vermeer, N. (2016). Age Anchors and the Expected Retirement Age: An Experimental Study. *De Economist, 164*(3), 255–279. DOI: 10.1007/s10645-016-9276-1

Vickerstaff, S., & Van der Horst, M. (2021). The Impact of Age Stereotypes and Age Norms on Employees' Retirement Choices: A Neglected Aspect of Research on Extended Working Lives. *Frontiers in Sociology, 6*, 686645. DOI: 10.3389/fsoc.2021.686645 PMID: 34141736

Vo, K., Forder, P. M., Tavener, M., Rodgers, B., Banks, E., Bauman, A., & Byles, J. E. (2014). Retirement, age, gender and mental health: Findings from the 45 and Up Study. *Aging & Mental Health, 19*(7), 647–657. DOI: 10.1080/13607863.2014.962002 PMID: 25271125

Voyvoda, E., & Yeldan, E. (2005). Managing Turkish debt: An OLG investigation of the IMF's fiscal programming model for Turkey. *Journal of Policy Modeling, 27*(6), 743–765.

Vučković, V., & Banović, R. Š. (2021). Who and what holds back reforms in croatia? – The political economy perspective. *Drustvena Istrazivanja (Zagreb), 30*(4), 675–698. DOI: 10.5559/di.30.4.02

Wang, S. (2020). Spatial patterns and social-economic influential factors of population aging: A global assessment from 1990 to 2010. *Social Science & Medicine, 253*, 112963. DOI: 10.1016/j.socscimed.2020.112963 PMID: 32289647

Wang, X., & Squires, G. (2024). Intergenerational transfer, parental support and housing: A literature review. *Property Management, 42*(2), 192–234. DOI: 10.1108/PM-04-2023-0037

WAPES. (World Association of Public Employment Services) (2023). Impact of Global Population Ageing on Employment and the Labour Market. *STUDIES & SURVEYS*, 1-10. https://wapes.org/wp-content/uploads/2023/02/Impact-of-global-population-ageing.pdf

Werners, S. E., Wise, R. M., Butler, J. R. A., Totin, E., & Vincent, K. (2021). Adaptation pathways: A review of approaches and a learning framework. *Environmental Science & Policy*, *116*, 266–275. DOI: 10.1016/j.envsci.2020.11.003

Wicaksono, G., & Mansury, Y. (2020). An Agent-Based Model of Wealth Inequality with Overlapping Generations, Local Interactions, and Intergenerational Transfers. In *Innovations in Urban and Regional Systems* (pp. 213–239). Springer International Publishing., DOI: 10.1007/978-3-030-43694-0_10

Wietzke, F. (2020). Poverty, Inequality, and Fertility: The Contribution of Demographic Change to Global Poverty Reduction. *Population and Development Review*, *46*(1), 65–99. DOI: 10.1111/padr.12317

Wiktorowicz, J. (2017). Extending Working Life: Which Competencies are Crucial in Near-Retirement Age? *Journal of Adult Development*, *25*(1), 48–60. DOI: 10.1007/s10804-017-9274-9 PMID: 29527111

Wilson, T. L., Scala-Foley, M., Kunkel, S. R., & Brewster, A. L. (2020). Fast-track Innovation: Area Agencies on Aging Respond to the COVID-19 Pandemic". *Journal of Aging & Social Policy*, *32*(4), 432–438. DOI: 10.1080/08959420.2020.1774313 PMID: 32515297

Woodman, D. (2022). Generational change and intergenerational relationships in the context of the asset economy. *Distinktion : Scandinavian Journal of Social Theory*, *23*(1), 55–69. DOI: 10.1080/1600910X.2020.1752275

World Bank. (2014). The unfinished revolution: Bringing opportunity, good jobs and greater wealth to all Tunisians. World Bank Group. https://www.worldbank.org/content/dam/Worldbank/document/MNA/tunisia_report/tunisia_report_the_unfinished_revolution_eng_synthesis.pdf

World Bank. (2024). *Fertility rate, total (births per woman) – Tunisia*. World Development Indicators. https://data.worldbank.org/indicator/SP.DYN.TFRT.IN?locations=TN

World Bank. (2024). *Life expectancy at birth, total (years) – Tunisia*. World Development Indicators. https://data.worldbank.org/indicator/SP.DYN.LE00.IN?locations=TN

World Bank. (2024). *Population ages 65 and above (% of total population) – Tunisia*. World Development Indicators. https://data.worldbank.org/indicator/SP.POP.65UP.TO.ZS?locations=TN

World Bank. (2024). Tunisia economic monitor, Fall 2024. World Bank Group. https://www.worldbank.org/en/country/tunisia/overview

World Bank. (2024). *Unemployment, total (% of total labor force) – Tunisia*. World Development Indicators. https://data.worldbank.org/indicator/SL.UEM.TOTL.ZS?locations=TN

World Bank. (2025a). *World Development Indicators, Birth Rate, crude (per 1,000 people)* [Data set]. https://data.worldbank.org/indicator/SP.POP.0014.TO?end=2024&locations=TR&start=1966

World Bank. (2025b). *World Development Indicators, Death Rate, crude (per 1,000 people)* [Data set]. https://data.worldbank.org/indicator/SP.DYN.CDRT.IN?locations=TR

World Bank. (2025c). *World Development Indicators, Population Ages 0-14 (% of total Population)* [Data set]. https://data.worldbank.org/indicator/SP.POP.0014.TO.ZS?locations=TR

World Bank. (2025d). *World Development Indicators, Population Ages 65+ ((% of total Population)* [Data set]. https://data.worldbank.org/indicator/SP.POP.0014.TO.ZS?locations=TR

Wu, C., Cao, Y., & Xu, H. (2025). How Population Aging Drives Labor Productivity: Evidence from China. *Sustainability (Basel)*, *17*(11), 5046. Advance online publication. DOI: 10.3390/su17115046

Wu, C., Odden, M. C., Fisher, G. G., & Stawski, R. S. (2016). Association of retirement age with mortality: A population-based longitudinal study among older adults in the USA. *Journal of Epidemiology and Community Health*, *70*(9), 917–923. DOI: 10.1136/jech-2015-207097 PMID: 27001669

Xie, Z., Chen, S., He, C., Cao, Y., Du, Y., Yi, L., & Wang, P. (2024). Trends and age–period–cohort effects on the incidence of falls from 1990 to 2019 in BRICS countries. *Heliyon*, *10*(5), e26771. DOI: 10.1016/j.heliyon.2024.e26771

Yaari, M. E. (1965). Uncertain lifetime, life insurance, and the theory of the consumer. *The Review of Economic Studies*, *32*(2), 137–150.

Yamamura, E. (2025). Grandchildren and Views about Consumption Tax. *Review of Behavioral Economics*, *12*(1), 97–127. DOI: 10.1561/105.00000205

Yaqoob, M., Bani, Y., Ishak, S., & Rosland, A. (2024). Impact of Demographic Dividend on Economic Growth in Developing Countries. *Thailand and the World Economy*, *42*(3), 236–252.

Yeh, M.-J. (2022). Intergenerational contract in Ageing Democracies: Sustainable Welfare Systems and the interests of future generations. *Medicine, Health Care, and Philosophy*, *25*(3), 531–539. DOI: 10.1007/s11019-022-10098-9 PMID: 35697971

Yolusever, A. (2025). *Economics of Longevity and Aging Populations*. İktisat İşletme ve Uluslararası İlişkiler Dergisi., DOI: 10.58654/jebi.1627286

Yuan, S., Jia, M., & Wang, F. (2022). Implementation of Integrated Care for the Aged Population in Anhui and Fujian Province of China: A Qualitative Study. *International Journal of Integrated Care*, *22*(0), 20. Advance online publication. DOI: 10.5334/ijic.6419 PMID: 35756341

Yunus, N. M., Abd Manaf, N. H., Omar, A., Juhdi, N., Omar, M. A., & Salleh, M. (2017). "Determinants of healthcare utilisation among older people in Malaysia". In *Institutions and Economies*, Vol. 9, No. 3, pp. 117–142).

Zhang, C. (2012). The Relationship between Elderly Employment and Youth Employment: Evidence from China. *MPRA Paper No.37221* (p. 1-25). https://mpra.ub.uni-muenchen.de/37221/1/MPRA_paper_37221.pdf

Zhang, D., Wang, Y., & Jiao, Y. (2022). The Impact of Social Pension Schemes on the Mental Health of the Chinese Elderly: A Mediating Effect Perspective of Two-Way Intergenerational Support. *International Journal of Environmental Research and Public Health*, *19*(14), 8721. DOI: 10.3390/ijerph19148721 PMID: 35886572

Zhang, H., Ke, L., & Ding, D. (2021). The Effect of Chinese Population Aging on Income Inequality: Based on a Micro-Macro Multiregional Dynamic CGE Modelling Analysis. *Emerging Markets Finance & Trade*, *57*(5), 1399–1419. DOI: 10.1080/1540496X.2019.1623781

Zhou, Y., Pan, Y., & Ma, L. (2023). Research progress on intrinsic capacity in older adults. *Chinese Journal of Geriatrics*, *42*(1), 108–112. DOI: 10.3760/cma.j.issn.0254-9026.2023.01.021

Zhuang, J., Khaskheli, M. B., Shen, C., Jafri, M. A. H., & Shamsi, I. H. (2025). A comparative study of economic activity and sustainable development in China and Three South Asian Countries. *Discover Sustainability*, *6*(1), 170. DOI: 10.1007/s43621-025-00885-8

Žnidaršič, J., & Dimovski, V. (2010). Reluctance Towards Older Workers in Slovenia. *The International Business & Economics Research Journal*, *9*(2), 83–100. DOI: 10.19030/iber.v9i2.525

Zuo, X., Chen, G., & Sun, X. (2017). Population Aging and Its Impact on Employment. In Tian, X. (Ed.), *China's Population Aging and the Risk of 'Middle-income Trap', Research Series on the Chinese Dream and China's Development Path* (pp. 107–123). Springer., DOI: 10.1007/978-981-10-4941-5_4

Zweifel, P., & Ferrari, M. (1992). Is There a Sisyphus Syndrome in Health Care. *Developments in Health Economics and Public Policy*, *1*, 311–330. DOI: 10.1007/978-94-011-2392-1_15 PMID: 10172497

About the Contributors

Oytun Meçik is a Professor in the Department of Economics at Eskişehir Osmangazi University. He completed his undergraduate studies at Eskişehir Osmangazi University in 2008, earned his master's degree from Uşak University in 2010, and received his Ph.D. in Economics from Anadolu University in 2014. He was awarded the title of Associate Professor in Macroeconomics in 2017 and was promoted to full Professor in 2023. Prof. Dr. Meçik's research primarily focuses on labor markets, social and economic networks, and contemporary issues in applied economics. His recent work centers on social capital, education–employment mismatch, the economic implications of digital transformation, and innovation economics. In addition to his academic contributions, Prof. Dr. Meçik actively serves as an editor and editorial board member for several national and international journals and publishing houses. He is a member of the Turkish Economic Association and the Regional Science Turkish National Committee. In 2024, he was awarded the title of Social Mediator.

***

Lawal Abdulwahab Olamilekan has a PhD in Economics from the Universiti Brunei Darussalam, School of Business and Economics (AACSB-accredited). He holds a master's degree in health economics and a bachelor's in economics education from Taraba State University, Nigeria. His research interests encompass natural resource economics, health economics, development, and macroeconomics, with a particular focus on Africa and emerging economies. With over seven years of academic experience, he has taught and supervised students across Nigeria, Somalia, Somaliland, and Brunei, demonstrating a solid foundation in higher education. His teaching expertise covers economics, management, and public health, while his research contributions include conference papers, journal articles, and book chapters. Lawal's proficiency in quantitative and qualitative methodologies, coupled with his advanced skills in econometric modeling and the use of software such as Stata, SPSS, and EViews, instills confidence in his technical abilities. He is a member of the World Economics Association and the Institute of Chartered Economists of Nigeria. He continues to engage in collaborative research that bridges health policy, governance, and economic development, providing evidence-based insights for sustainable growth and development.

Zyed Achour is a Senior Lecturer at the National Institute of Labor and Social Studies, University of Carthage. He holds a Master's degree in Management Sciences from the University of Bordeaux (France) and a Ph.D. in Management Sciences from the University of Tunis (Tunisia). His research focuses on corporate social responsibility, sustainable development, labor studies, trade unionism, gender diversity, and strategic human resource management. He has edited academic books, coordinated interdisciplinary volumes, and published extensively in peer-reviewed journals. In 2025, he authored Integrating Governance and Corporate Social Responsibility in Employee Share Ownership (IGI Global), which received an Honorable Mention for the Joyce Rothschild Award in 2026, underscoring the impact and quality of his scholarly contributions.

Mohd Adil is currently working as a Senior Research Fellow (SRF) in the Department of Economics at Jamia Millia Islamia (JMI), New Delhi, India. His research interests are mainly centered around the field of international trade with special reference to the trade dynamics of India with its major trade partners in the chemical sector. His research has also been emphasizing the integration of advanced econometric tools with machine learning approaches for carrying out the analysis and forecasting. His research has also been exploring the application of such approaches for carrying out research in the domain of demography with special reference to forecasting the trends of population ageing and dependency ratios for the emerging economies of the world.

Md Mahdi Hasan Ahid is a research practitioner in the field of business and management, with a strong focus on key areas such as supply chain management, strategic innovation, marketing, enterprise efficiency, and management information systems. His research explores how emerging technologies and data-driven approaches can optimize organizational processes, enhance marketing effectiveness, and support sustainable growth across business ecosystems. By aligning innovation with practical business needs, he addresses real-world challenges through applied and impactful research. Ahid's work bridges academic theory and professional practice, making significant contributions to the evolving landscape of business, management, and digital transformation.

Patrick Georges has a Ph.D. in Economics (Ottawa), a graduate degree in international relations and comparative politics (Louvain-la-Neuve, Belgium), and a degree in applied economics (Fucam, Mons, Belgique). Before joining the University of Ottawa, he taught at the University of British Columbia and worked as a senior economist for the federal government, including for the Department of Finance and the Department of Human Resources and Skills Development. His research concerns international trade and finance, population ageing, fiscal policy, and public debt management. He uses general equilibrium modeling and other simulation models as tools to improve understanding of the economic impacts of alternative public policies.

Saba Ismail is currently working as a Professor in the Department of Economics at Jamia Millia Islamia (JMI), New Delhi, India. She has completed her Ph.D. in Economics with specialization in growth economics. Her research interests include growth and development, international economics, econometrics, and time series analysis. Her research has been quite prolific with the publication of numerous research articles and books in the domain of economics. Her research has been published in the form of research articles in various national and international research journals with high impact factor and also in the form of books. Her research has been quite diverse and has included topics such as international trade, economic growth, and the application of advanced econometric tools for carrying out the analysis.

Sharmin Jahan, an Assistant Professor at Daffodil International University in Bangladesh, with having a strong research background including 15 years of teaching experiences. She holds a BBA and an MBA in Marketing from the University of Dhaka in Bangladesh, where she achieved outstanding academic results & Currently pursuing her PhD in Marketing at the same institution.

Pooja Kansra is Head of the Department at Mittal School of Business, Lovely Professional University, Punjab, India. Her areas of interest include econometric methods, microeconomics, macroeconomics, managerial economics, quantitative techniques, and the economics of health and education. She holds a Master's in Economics from Guru Nanak Dev University, Amritsar, and a Doctorate degree from Punjab Technical University, Jalandhar. She is a member of the Indian Economic Association. Her research interests include health economics, insurance, and service operation management. She is an avid researcher and has presented papers at various national and international conferences. She has numerous research papers published in refereed national and international journals of repute.

Amiya Abdul Khadar is a Ph.D. scholar at Mittal School of Business, Lovely Professional University, Jalandhar. Her areas of interest include health economics, consumer behaviour, and development economics. She has published research papers in refereed national and international journals of repute. She has also presented several research papers at institutes of national repute.

Javed Mahmud is an Assistant Professor of Business Administration with a distinguished career in both academia and industry. He holds a Doctorate of Business Administration from the University of Dhaka and an MBA from Victoria University, Australia as well as an MBA from the most prestigious business school in Bangladesh, the IBA of the University of Dhaka. An expert in marketing and management, Dr. Mahmud has taught at numerous universities and has published research on consumer behavior and business management. He is also the Founder President of the Doctor of Business Administration Forum of Bangladesh.

Soeb Md. Shoayeb Noman is an Associate Professor in the Department of Business Administration at Uttara University, Bangladesh, with over 14 years of experience in teaching, research, and academic leadership. He currently serves as Director of the BBA Program and Additional Director (Excellence in Teaching–Learning) at the Institutional Quality Assurance Cell (IQAC). Dr. Noman holds a PhD in Economics from Jahangirnagar University, an MBA in Finance & Banking from IBA-JU, and a MSc & a BSc (Hons.) in Economics from the same institution. He has research interests in health economics, agricultural economics, financial inclusion, public finance, fiscal policy, monetary policy, economic growth, and macroeconomic performance in South Asia. He has published extensively in national and international journals, contributed to numerous development research projects, and is actively involved as a reviewer and editorial board member for several academic journals.

Md. Adnan Rahman is an Associate Professor of Digital Marketing and MIS at Uttara University, Dhaka, Bangladesh. Additionally, he is the Director of the Office of Brand & Communication and Public Relations of this university. Dr. Adnan is a postdoctoral researcher at Infrastructure University Kuala Lumpur (IUKL), Malaysia. Dr. Adnan holds a PhD in Marketing from Putra Business School (AACSB-Accredited), UPM, Malaysia; an MSc in MIS; and an MA in IHRM from the University of Bedfordshire, United Kingdom.

Sevilay Sarıca graduated from Hacettepe University, Faculty of Economics and Administrative Sciences, Department of Economics in 1993. She received her master's and doctoral degrees in economics from Hacettepe University. She started working at the Department of Economics, Faculty of Economics and Administrative

Sciences, Çankırı Karatekin University in 2007 and continues to work as a faculty member at the same University. Their areas of expertise include Macroeconomics, Growth, Employment, Unemployment, Economic Policies, Population Aging and Inflation.

Aylin Seçkin Georges has a Ph.D. in Economics (Carleton), an MA degree in European Economics (Universite Libre de Bruxelles), an undergraduate BA degree in Economics (Bogazici). Before joining the University of Ottawa, she taught at Bilgi University. Her research concerns population ageing, art and cultural economics. She is also DBA Thesis supervisor at the Business School of Lausanne. She has published in various leading academic journals on population aging, on art and cultural economics such as Economics Bulletin, Economic Modelling, Applied Financial Economics, Canadian Public Policy, Empirical Economics, Journal of Cultural Economics, Acta Oeconomica. She has also published a book entitled Sanatın Ekonomisi (The Economics of Art), by Hayalperest Publishing House, 2021. She has also a video series called The Economics of Everything on FluTV. https://www.youtube.com/@flu.She is the Co-Founder of Forsico.io, AI-based project management tool.

Zerin Tasnim is an Assistant Professor of Supply Chain Management at North South University, Dhaka, Bangladesh, where she also serves as the Course Coordinator for the MBA program. She holds a PhD in Management from Putra Business School, Universiti Putra Malaysia (UPM), and a BSc in Mechanical Engineering from Bangladesh University of Engineering and Technology (BUET). Dr. Tasnim brings an interdisciplinary academic background and a global research perspective to her work, with research interests spanning digital supply chains, healthcare logistics, and sustainable and green operations.

Index

A

B

C

D

E

F

I

L

M

O

P

R

S

T

W

X

www.ingramcontent.com/pod-product-compliance
Lightning Source LLC
LaVergne TN
LVHW081538300926
849161LV00006B/1476